Praise for Business unIntelligence

"Barry connects the burgeoning yet Byzantine world of 1s and 0s to the real world with an example-laden tour of where we've come from and how we've got here. The book is as entertaining as it is informative and will provide a valuable foundation for CIOs planning their next steps after analytics and big data." — Doug Laney, VP Research, Information Innovation & Business Analytics, Gartner

"Barry's predictions, in this book, about the future of data and its management, will certainly not all be borne out by the course of events. On the other hand, I am convinced that many of them will. But what's important about this book is that Barry is thinking the big thoughts about the big trends in data and information management. He shows us that there is more to managing data than finding new uses for new technologies, and that by thinking about how society generates and uses massive new volumes of data, we may yet be able to manage this tsunami of Big Data rather than merely reacting to it." — Dr. Tom Johnston, Chief Scientist at Asserted Versioning, LLC

"This important book succeeds in finding the common ground between rationality and intuition, intelligence and insight, stability and innovation, business and IT. From rightful criticism of today's data-centric BI, you are taken into broader contexts, such as working with information rather than data and coping with both big data and the insides of people's heads. The target is the 'biz-tech ecosystem', not just EDW/BI. We, the information-driven, move up to the enterprise level. Full of good recaps of history and technology the end-result is a direction-setting, holistic architecture on two levels—indeed an impressive tour de force!" — Thomas Frisendal, author of Design Thinking Business Analysis

"Business Intelligence is entering a period of profound change and Business Unintelligence is destined to become an important work in understanding why. Dr. Devlin exposes how BI remains resolutely disconnected from the business processes and people it is supposed to support and how it is simply not keeping pace with new forms of data afforded by mobile, social and the internet of things. It is rigorous examination, not just of what is missing, but what is needed to support the emerging and agile business of tomorrow." — Dale Roberts, VP Professional Services, Artesian Solutions

"Business Unintelligence is a practical guide to the industry. Barry draws on his 30+ years of experience, delivering a balance of technology and real world insights to take the reader from the early days of business intelligence through today and into the future. All BI professionals will benefit from the comprehensive and actionable content in the book." — Shawn Rogers, Vice President Research, Enterprise Manag...

BUSINESS UNINTELLIGENCE

INSIGHT AND INNOVATION
BEYOND ANALYTICS AND BIG DATA

DR. BARRY DEVLIN

Technics Publications, LLC
New Jersey

Published by:
Technics Publications, LLC
2 Lindsley Road
Basking Ridge, NJ 07920 U.S.A.
www.technicspub.com

Edited by Carol Lehn
Cover design by Mark Brye

This book is printed on acid-free paper.

ISBN, print ed.   978-1-935504-56-6
ISBN, Kindle ed.   978-1-935504-57-3
ISBN, ePub ed.   978-1-935504-58-0

First Printing 2013

Library of Congress Control Number: 2013948310

ATTENTION SCHOOLS AND BUSINESSES: Technics Publications books are available at quantity discounts with bulk purchase for educational, business, or sales promotional use. For information, please email Steve Hoberman, President of Technics Publications, at me@stevehoberman.com.

FOR INGS
MY MUSE AND MENTOR
LOVE AND LIGHT
OF MY LATER LIFE

"The right way to wholeness is made up of fateful detours and wrong turnings." C.G. Jung

TABLE OF CONTENTS

> *"It is by going down into the abyss that we recover the treasures of life. Where you stumble, there lies your treasure."* — Joseph Campbell

> *"Not everything that can be counted counts and not everything that counts can be counted."* — William Bruce Cameron[1]

Sometimes—in truth, always—one has to trust life in the process of living itself. The unfolding of what needs to be, at precisely the right time and place. And so it was with this book. It has been over four years in gestation, more than twice as long as the pregnancy of an elephant. And also a period during which the yellow, Hadoop specimen has been trampling the world of information.

The outline of my story has been clear from the moment of conception, in a white paper I published in 2009. The detailed plot and exposition have evolved as the world of information technology (IT) and, particularly, business intelligence (BI) has been transformed since then. The title, too, has been transfigured.

On what I mean by Business unIntelligence

The term *business intelligence* has long struck me as something of an oxymoron. Much of the business behavior I've encountered has been far from intelligent. Perhaps I'm a little cynical, but *business dysfunction* often seems the appropriate term. Furthermore, intelligence is surely setting the bar far too low today, in the second decade of the 21st century; BI, in practice, too often means little more than the generation of reports filled with backward-looking data.

---

[1] This quote is often attributed to Albert Einstein. Quote Investigator disagrees (http://quoteinvestigator.com/2010/05/26/everything-counts-einstein/). He provides a context for Cameron's use that I could not resist:

"It would be nice if all of the data which sociologists require could be enumerated because then we could run them through IBM machines and draw charts as the economists do. However, not everything that can be counted counts, and not everything that counts can be counted" (Cameron, 1967).

Can't business do better? What about intuition, insight or inspiration? Should we not also consider social aspects, given that business is largely a collective, collaborative venture?

I played with many of these positive terms in search of a title. But none have the breadth of vision I desire; many have already been appropriated by marketing. In the interim, technologies have evolved and business priorities have shifted. It became clear that the book must begin from what is wrong in how business *is* today and how to fix it. *Business unIntelligence.*

Slowly, gradually, it also became clear that this, too, is precisely what business today needs. Rationality of thought and far beyond it. Logic of process, predefined and emergent. The confluence of reason and inspiration, emotion and intention, collaboration and competition—all that comprises the human and social milieu that is business. Not business intelligence. Business unIntelligence.

For whom the book flows

I believe that business and IT people should be talking. And more importantly, listening—a conversation. I would like to initiate an ongoing exchange of ideas, from business to IT and IT to business.

Business success in the first decades of the new millennium will be hewn from the bedrock of technology. Built on the innovation of business vision. Circumscribed by the possibilities and limitations of technology. Defined by the people and organizations that craft and consume it. My aim in this writing is to bridge the gap that has too long separated business and IT.

This book is for the CIO and the COO. For the technology-savvy business executive and the business-aware IT manager. Business strategist and IT architect. For the business visionaries who see tomorrow's needs and the technical gurus who envisage their solutions. There are surely sections too technical for the business person, or too general for the technologist. I invite you to dip in or dive out as you see fit, following always that golden thread of collaboration between business and IT.

For me, this book succeeds only where it forges new relationships between the realm of business and the kingdom of IT.

To those who made this book possible

Ethologist and diver Hans Hass, who died as this book was being finalized, declared that *"everything responsible for our 'human existence' is due to an anonymous multitude of others who have lived before us, whose achievements have been bestowed upon us as gifts."*

So, too, have dozens of friends and colleagues across the IT industry and, in particular, the BI community bestowed the gifts of their knowledge upon me over three decades of diving in data and swimming in seas of information. There are far too many to mention all of you individually. To each of you unsung heroes, thank you for your precious pearls of wisdom.

This book is deliberately eclectic; I believe it is only by trawling wide that we can discover the answers to the particularly pressing issues of our times. My inspiration ranges from astrology to zoology, Imago to IT, and everything in between. I extend my gratitude to each of my mentors, whether personal or through their writings, for introducing me to their fascinating worlds.

Much of my knowledge and experience of IT and business intelligence was gained during nearly 25 years with IBM as architect, consultant, manager and Distinguished Engineer. To all my past colleagues there, especially those in IISL and the IBM Academy of Technology, thank you for your support and guidance.

As an independent analyst and consultant, I am indebted to those clients who sponsored my white papers and other activities—Attivio, B-Eye-Network, Composite Software, Denodo, EMA, IBM, IRM UK, Lyzasoft, MongoDB, NeutrinoBI, ParAccel, TDWI, Teradata and Wherescape—supporting me in the innovative and autonomous thinking from which this book emerged.

Special thanks to Scott Davis, Bill O'Connell, Henry Cook, Bob Eve, Claudia Imhoff, Dan Graham, Gary Baverstock, Michael Whitehead, Bill Hoggarth, Mark Madsen, Chris Winter, Tom Fastner, Martyn Irons, John O'Brien and Jeff Jonas—and my reviewers listed below—for inspiring and energizing discussions on many of the topics covered here. To those I've omitted, please excuse my faulty memory.

The book is set in Lato Light, a member of a sanserif typeface family designed in the Summer 2010 by Warsaw-based designer Łukasz Dziedzic (*lato* is Polish for *summer*) and published under the Open Font License (www.latofonts.com). Thanks, Łukasz. Headings are set in Google Marcellus SC, also under Open Font License.

I am profoundly grateful to Steve Hoberman, my publisher, for all his support and infinite patience from the time we first discussed this project in 2010 to its much postponed delivery. My thanks also to Carol Lehn for her careful editing and Erin Elizabeth for detailed proofreading of the manuscript. To the reviewers who took time from their busy schedules to read the draft, I deeply appreciate your energy and enthusiasm, especially those of you who endorsed the work in such positive terms—Wayne Eckerson, Thomas Frisendal, Doug Laney, Tom Johnston, Dale Roberts and Shawn Rogers. Thanks also to those of you who offered to do so, but ran out of runway. And to my daughter, Katherine—thank you for reading the book from cover to cover, and especially for the yellow, origami elephant in Figure 6-3!

Last, and most, to my wife of five years. Anybody who has written a book knows just how an author disappears for months on end in the writing process, especially as the final countdown nears. Thank you, Ings, for all your love and unending support for me throughout the process. You made it all possible. And worthwhile.

So now, I lift my weary fingers from the keyboard and gaze from my office window across Table Mountain National Park and the Twelve Apostles. You have been my constant companions in wind and sun, and, today, in winter rain. Thank you for calming me when words failed me and inspiring me to greater heights with your ever-changing moods.

Cape Town,
September 1st, 2013

Roadmap

→ *Business unIntelligence:* More than BI and different to BI, moving to a more realistic way of thinking about decision making in business

→ *Information, process and people:* Introducing the three components of a new architecture

→ *Biz-tech ecosystem:* The emerging business model, where business and IT contribute equally

→ *IDEAL:* A conceptual enterprise architecture that is the basis for conversation between business and IT

→ *REAL:* A logical architecture enabling implementation of the biz-tech ecosystem

CHAPTER 1

A MODERN TRINITY

As a species, we are counters of things. Namers and classifiers of parts and subparts. Sorters and arrangers of what is. Analyzers of what was or might have been. Organizers of what should be. Adders to and subtracters from the meaning of life and the value of our activities. Nowhere is this characteristic more obvious than in the context of modern business. We tell ourselves repeatedly: *"You can't manage what you can't measure."*[1]

Perhaps it was always so. The Lebombo bone, a baboon's fibula, was excavated from the Border Cave in Swaziland in 1973. Possibly a counting or tally stick, the 29 distinct notches suggest counting the days of a lunar or menstrual calendar. It has been dated to about 35,000 years ago (Bogoshi, et al., 1987). Another baboon's fibula, the Ishango bone, shown in Figure 1-1, was found in the Congo in 1960 (de Heinzelin, 1962). Perhaps 15,000 years younger than Lebombo, it shows a complex pattern of markings, the meaning of which is unclear, although several mathematical theories have been advanced. Since the birth of civilization, as we grandiosely name it, we have been calculating and recording. Writing, we were told, emerged from Sumerian accounting practices in 3,200 BC (Schmandt-Besserat, 1996) to

Figure 1-1:
Ishango bone, c.
20,000 years old,
Royal Belgian Institute
of Natural Sciences,
Brussels

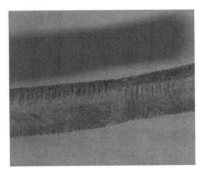

---
[1] Versions of this phrase have been attributed to a long list of experts. Ironically, for a book on information, the original source is unknown.

record ancient business contracts. The poet in me despairs. Later research suggests writing may have emerged with the cave paintings of Chauvet, Lascaux and elsewhere 20,000 years earlier (Ferraro, 2010). My inner bard rejoices.

Science is the great counter, labeler and classifier of today's world. Carl Linnaeus set forth his grand taxonomy of living things in *Systema Naturæ* as far back as 1735. Lord Kelvin informed us in the late 19th century that *"when you cannot express it in numbers, your knowledge is of a meagre and unsatisfactory kind; it may be the beginning of knowledge, but you have scarcely, in your thoughts, advanced to the stage of Science, whatever the matter may be."* Today, ontologies, taxonomies and classification systems attempt to define and describe every aspect of existence. Computers, with their scything logic of *either-or* and *both-and*, have allowed us to count and sort, arrange and organize, analyze and judge with a rational ruthlessness and a previously unknown efficiency.

Now, in the birthing decades of a new millennium, we have become—it seems to me—obsessive-compulsive in our pursuit of measurements and rush to judgments. The size of this, the quantity of that, the quality of the other. And nowhere has this become more obvious than in business, government and the social enterprises that dominate life in the "developed" world. This is the well-worked and manure-heavy soil from which this book springs.

The remainder of this chapter introduces some key thoughts and concepts, and serves as a roadmap to the rest of the book.

1.1   WHY NOW? WHY BUSINESS UNINTELLIGENCE?

Many have already said it: change is most definitely a time we're living through. The quote about uncertainty at the top of this chapter (Drucker, 1992), written some twenty years ago by Peter Drucker, a business thinker and management consultant, emphasizes this. And reminds us that the perception is far from new. There is no doubt that uncertainty has increased dramatically since then. The social and economic fabric of our world is being torn apart and remade anew in constant and repeated seismic events. Sovereign debt ratings of formerly unassailable

AAA countries have been downgraded with monotonous regularity. Previously blue chip businesses in every industry have fallen as new kids on the block arise. Product development life cycles and even product lives themselves have contracted to the point where consumers behave like battle-weary troops. Business people live on constant high alert—with predictable health impacts—for the next competitor or product that may derail their best-laid plans.

The dominant scientific paradigm through which modern humanity understands the world has also taken on an air of uncertainty. Physics was first on that path with quantum mechanics. Other disciplines—from biology to sociology, chemistry to psychology—have followed. As Nancy Cartwright remarked so eloquently in *The Dappled World: A Study of the Boundaries of Science, "The laws that describe this world are a patchwork, not a pyramid. They do not take after the simple, elegant and abstract structure of a system of axioms and theorems"* (Cartwright, 1999).

Figure 1-2:
A century of phone evolution

Within this reality, technology—particularly information technology (IT)—is seen both as villain and potential savior. Advances in technology allow the wheels of industry and the hoops of commerce to spin ever faster. In 2009/10, Spread Networks considered it financially justified to invest perhaps $300 million in cutting and drilling its way from Chicago to New York to lay the shortest possible fiber optic cable and shave three milliseconds off the journey time for stock trades between the two cities (Steiner, 2010). Faster action leads to faster tracking and the demand for ever more immediate decision making. Always-on communications and real-time information become mandatory. The result is an ever-closer symbiosis between business and technology—what I call the *biz-tech ecosystem*—that includes all aspects of technology. However, it is in IT that the emergence of this ecosystem is most evident. Until recently, the relationship between business and IT was probably best described as that of master and servant. The role of the IT department was to listen to and understand the needs of the business, to interpret them in light of what was possible with existing (and, preferably, already purchased) technology, and to deliver the best and most cost-effective solution. However, as IT becomes ever more core to the business, as it becomes a necessary foundation of so much business functionality, and as it becomes ever more complex, IT must step up to a new role. IT must learn to become the advocate for what technology can do for the business. No longer master and servant, but equal partners in an utterly changed game.

This change of role started to first become evident in business intelligence (BI) in the 1990s, as the new analysis and control functionality of data warehousing and data mining began to offer the possibility of re-architecting key business processes. In Walmart, for example, BI technology allowed a complete reengineering of the supply chain, enabled only through cooperative effort by IT and business to use new technology to create completely novel solutions. This trend has spread far beyond the confines of BI, with mobile technology, remote sensing, the Internet and the Cloud, as well as a multitude of hardware and software advances, all potentially changing business in the most fundamental ways. I explore the biz-tech ecosystem in Chapter 2, which provides a political and organizational foundation for the remainder of the book.

And introducing... Business unIntelligence

Within this new environment, traditional BI feels old-fashioned. Decision making has changed utterly. Verbose reports and tardy queries miss the needs of business that demands just-in-time delivery and real-time offers to Web customers. Decision making—no longer the preserve of middle managers or business analysts[2]— occurs throughout the business, from boardroom to front office. Big data streaming from external sources in enormous volumes demands a different approach to management and use. The market has responded with a plethora of new terminology: operational analytics, decision management, business discovery, predictive analytics, and more. But, major challenges remain unaddressed.

The old IT boundaries between operational, informational and collaborative systems have broken down in the biz-tech ecosystem. We need a holistic view of all the IT support systems. Although BI

---

[2] As is common throughout BI, I use the name *business analysts* to refer to business users who are skilled in analysis of data in support of decision making.

may have driven that much of this change, it is no longer in charge of its destiny. The future is bigger than BI, bigger, indeed, than any subset of IT. Yet, BI and data warehousing—in their concepts and history—provide for me the clearest path to the bright new future. Given my history in these topics, you might expect me to say that, but the evidence emerges throughout these pages. The knowledge and skills of BI practitioners will be the catalyst for the change required across the entire business and IT environment because it is these selfsame BI practitioners who have principally struggled with the changes outlined here. But, they will need to step boldly beyond the old boundaries. It is to them that the phrase *Business unIntelligence* must appeal. The dissonance must provoke new thinking. What is lacking in today's BI? How can the lessons of nearly three decades of BI support a business world where basic intelligence about the market, performance and so on is now the table stakes to play? Beyond intelligence, how can insight and innovation be nurtured and operationalized? How would a post-BI business work?

For now, I leave the phrase to percolate in your mind as you consider the biz-tech ecosystem and the modern trinity of people, process and information. I return to it in closing to challenge you to apply it in your wisdom to your business, whatever each may be.

1.2   WHAT'S IT ALL ABOUT, TRINITY?[3]

If you are, as I am, someone who has long focused on data or information (we'll come to the distinction between the two later) usage in business, I imagine that in the following sections, you'll see sufficient evidence to conclude that information is a foundational topic of this book. And you would be justified in that.

Information—explicit and recorded—is widely recognized as being at the core of the modern world. Civilization, as we understand it, emerged only with the ability to make permanent records of transactions made and deals agreed; or, to be more precise, what we had perceived to have occurred. Yes, accountants are credited with founding civilization. Without information, civilized society is im-

---

[3] *Alfie*, the Burt Bacharach and Hal David (1965) theme song for the movie of the same name about a man who has to rethink his life purpose.

Figure 1-3:
Globular envelope and accounting tokens in clay. Uruk period, *Louvre, Paris.*

possible. Information, whether as simple as the sealed clay envelope of tokens shown in Figure 1-3, or as complex as a spinning disk of magnetically encoded bits, is an absolute necessity if you are to know I've promised you five of next spring's lambs in exchange for the 15 sacks of corn that kept my children alive over the winter.

Another type of explicit, but softer, information lies in the stories we tell ourselves and others about the world. Whether in memorized myth or digitized document, it is how one person passes her skills and knowledge to another, handing on the learning of one generation to the next. Moreover, it points to the tacit knowledge that is who we feel ourselves to be, how we share our dreams, and the subtleties of spirit that make us human. Transactions and stories, these two delicately different types of information are now central to our lives. We live in the so-called *Information Age.* In business, information is cited as the latest asset to be managed, protected and sweated. Socially, we connect in a web of shared information that increasingly defines and delimits our lives through Facebook and more.

However, there is more to it. As a child, I was an eager data gatherer and maker of lists and catalogues. I transcribed information about the stars in the local library, amassed automobile registrations, collected stamps. But, by the age of fourteen, it had become reasonably clear that my use for much of that information was... nil. What was the value of it? Perhaps this is why trainspotting[4] never appealed to me. In business, for sure, information without a purpose is like shooting practice without a target. Purpose spawns action, and action implies a *process* that runs from observation of the real world to decision making and on to the implementation of change as needed. And there's also the often laborious process involved in gathering the information and structuring it into something that can be seen, analyzed, and, hopefully, used. My parents would surely have confirmed this view as I built my underused,

---

[4] A particularly English and solitary hobby of collecting locomotive numbers of passing trains. Not to be confused here with the 1996 movie of the same name where "trainspotting" is urban slang for shooting up heroin or similar drugs!

paper-based databases of automobile registrations. So, process is vital to information, as both precursor and successor. Without process, we have neither information nor a way to put it to use.

There's a third element in the picture; if you see only information and process, you need a break from the screen! Look in a mirror, if nothing else. The third, implied element is *people*. Only people can assign meaning and value to information—or anything else. Information is gathered by and for people. Only people can define purpose. Process exists to meet the needs of people. And, dare I say it? Business exists, not to make money, but for and because of peoples' needs to interact and trade the fruits of their labors.

You have now been introduced to the three elements of the modern trinity for which this chapter is named. We shall encounter them again and again throughout the remainder of this book. Business can exist only when all three elements are present. Over history, we see that one may have been emphasized over the others at different times or in different circumstances. In the Industrial Revolution, whether in Europe of the 18th and 19th centuries or in modern-day China, people are the starting point. Process is largely implied; information needs are minimal. Gradually, the emphasis moves to process as labor becomes more expensive and a process focus drives efficiency and quality. Information grows in importance, until we reach the Information Age, where the focus moves there entirely.

But, it's important to understand that the biz-tech ecosystem can only function properly with a proper balance of all three elements. When we design a marketing campaign, we must consider people creating and using information in the context of a process. Designing and building our products, no matter how automated and/or outsourced the manufacture, is an information-producing and consuming process bounded by people. We—people—sell to and support our customers—more people—through processes that are founded on information about them, their needs and behaviors.

Let us now look at these three components—information, people and process—in a little more detail, pointing out the structure and contents of the remaining chapters of the book as we go.

1.3   PANDORA'S BOX OF INFORMATION

S o, let's talk a bit more about *information*. Any such discussion is certain to open the Pandora's Box of data vs. information, both explicit and tacit, not to mention knowledge and wisdom. Out of the box will also leap the once trendy knowledge management and the now fashionable Enterprise 2.0, ancient data warehousing and today's big data, content management and business intelligence. In Hesiod's ancient tale, all the evils of the world escaped when poor Pandora, overcome with curiosity, opened the lid but could not close it, leaving only Hope remaining. Sometimes, delving too deep into information can feel that way!

However, a practical—as opposed to theoretical— exploration of information, its representation and usage, is a vital foundation for building the biz-tech ecosystem. As I explore different characteristics of information in Chapters 3-6 and 8, I also describe the early evolution of information stored in computers and constrained by early approaches to application development and data storage. The simplicity (in retrospect) of thinking and the limitations of technology at the beginning of the computer age created a deep divide between business needs and our ability to use data to solve them. They continue to influence our beliefs about it today. In short, we need to bridge the historical chasm between people and information.

Figure 1-4:
Pandora's Box,
based on a painting
by F.S. Church.

Now, as we slip into the teens of the 21st century, *big data* has become flavor *du jour*. We Tweet our thoughts and Facebook our opinions; books are digitized and conversations texted; we record and share our lives on Flickr and YouTube. Such information is growing exponentially, and has become the largest volume of information stored or used by many businesses. Meanwhile, we have begun to incorporate a multitude of electronic sensors in everything from cell phones to jet engines. RFID tags are ubiquitous. The resulting flow of measurements constitutes a whole new class of data, the Internet of Things, with message volumes orders of magnitude larger than the transactions we've handled prior to now. This information explosion, still in its early stages, is driving the emergence of new industries and changing how many existing enterprises do business. It is both driving and being driven by emerging technologies. Its importance rivals the growth of the Internet in the 1990s. I'll munge[5] this information deluge in Chapter 6.

The singular form of the noun *information* is unfortunate, leading to unconscious assumptions about the uniqueness or singularity of our information resources. Before personal computers and, in particular, before the widespread digitization of printed and other information, it was relatively easy to ascertain its provenance and manage its distribution and replication. With highly centralized and controlled mainframe computing, electronic information creation was limited, and copies kept to a minimum; management was relatively straightforward. Similarly, physical content such as books, magazines, music and movies were produced with expensive equipment and were difficult to copy. Centralized management and control was the norm. By the 1980s, this model of information management was beginning to change. As business users began to use PCs, they began to create new information and make copies of existing information at an increasing rate. Word processors began to churn out text. Spreadsheets ingested numbers, combined and created them anew. This was only the beginning of the information deluge. But already, questions were beginning to arise about how to manage information, how to identify an original or reliable copy, how to tell the difference between public and personal information, and how to control its dissemination. Many of these questions remain unanswered as the problem has reached epic proportions, with the vast expanse of information distributed on the Internet, and the ongoing digitization of almost every form of content. I'll explore the issues of information distribution, privacy, security, copyright, ownership—information governance in its broadest sense—in Chapters 4 and 8.

---

[5] Munge: To transform data in an undefined or unexplained manner. http://en.wiktionary.org/wiki/munge

1.4   PROCESS, PROCESS EVERY WHERE[6]

Figure 1-5:
The Rime of the Ancient Mariner, Samuel Coleridge.

The following thought *process* is unlikely to be universally true. However, in my career, I have observed that there are "process people" and "information people" and that these two types of people seldom, if ever get one another. In IT organizations, the information people huddle together in the BI team room, discussing data models, information quality and similar esoteric topics. They regard the process people—the developers responsible for the transaction systems of the business—with some distrust and incomprehension. The feelings are reciprocated. In business, the situation is repeated. The vast majority of business people are focused on doing: making this, selling that, managing the other. They are the action takers, following the steps of a process to get the job done. And somewhere, probably in a backroom, is a small cadre of business analysts, whose focus is information. The atmosphere when they meet at the water cooler is strained; they speak different languages.

For the benefit of both process and information people alike, let me paraphrase Coleridge's ancient mariner:

> *"Process, process every where,*
> *Nor information linked"*

The poem itself, together with Coleridge's unusual glosses, seems to challenge us to consider what we can know with certainty from the information we imbibe and the means by which such information comes to us. The former is considered in Chapter 4; the latter brings us back directly to the question of process.

Focusing once more on business intelligence, information-centric people—whether builders or users of BI tools—have found it easy to imagine that process is either nonexistent or unimportant. Vendors, for the most part, seem comfortable to confine their products to the aspects of decision making that focus on data provision and

---

[6] *"Water, water every where / Nor any drop to drink"*, from *The Rime of the Ancient Mariner* by Samuel Taylor Coleridge, 1798.

analysis. It's what they understand and where they make their money. For users, I believe this assumption is based on a misunderstanding and, perhaps, a touch of arrogance. Decisions, and the circumstances in which they are taken, are indeed unpredictable and highly variable. The misunderstanding is that such variability precludes a process; the arrogance comes from equating process with the highly predetermined and mechanistic automation found on production lines. Similarly, according to Arthur T. Evans: *"Doctors think it's mundane to follow guidelines. It's much more gratifying to come up with a decision on your own. Anyone can follow an algorithm. There is a tendency to say, 'I can do better... otherwise, why are they paying me so much money?'"* (Gladwell, 2005)

Neither party is correct. Process plays a significant role; however, it is a qualitatively different type of process to that seen in the production or operational environment. The decision-making process is highly adaptive, social in nature, and spans the breadth of the organization and beyond. A far cry from the production line, with its predetermined actions and the severely limited responsibilities assigned to its workers. Of course, there is a role for algorithms and checklists synthesized from the best available prior work, especially where speed of deciding or volume of decisions are an issue.

However, we can envisage a process that focuses more on supporting decision makers with suggestions for relevant information and potentially knowledgeable contacts. That monitors and remembers novel actions that might come in handy in a subsequent decision. That underpins the highly social environment in which most corporate decisions are taken. And that enables and drives innovation—the Holy Grail of many businesses today. These are the topics of Chapters 7 and 9.

1.5   There's nowt so queer as folk[7]

IT geeks are often accused of considering *people* to be somehow strange—difficult to understand and satisfy. Coming from the world of strict if-then-else application programming or formal semantic information modeling, the almost infinite variability of

---

[7] A North of England colloquialism meaning "people are strange!"

people, their needs and beliefs, and their approaches to life—and business—is indeed a challenge to IT. And yet it is this very variability that allows businesses to handle change, to react to it in novel ways, and to create original solutions to challenging circumstances. Through the decisions they make and the actions they take, people are ultimately and fully responsible for every new idea and practical innovation ever introduced in response to a changing world.

However, it is, without doubt, people who make the business what it is. What is a business, at its simplest, other than the coming together of a number of people with the intention of pursuing a set of broadly related goals? Thus, we can include both profit-making and nonprofit enterprises, governmental and nongovernmental concerns, as well as more loosely defined associations of people with a purpose. We include the people who are formally engaged, such as owners, employees, partners and contractors, and those with looser associations, such as customers, clients, and even prospects. Moreover, we can immediately see the importance of people and their social interactions in the processes of running a business and, further, decision making as the linchpin of these processes.

The computerization of social interaction has arguably been one of the most important developments over the past five years in society at large and, more recently and to a lesser extent, in business. In the outer world, this trend is known as Web 2.0, which emerged from the zeitgeist of the new millennium. Web 2.0, in its current sense, was born in 2004 at a conference organized by O'Reilly Media and MediaLive. Tim O'Reilly's definition, *"Web 2.0 is the business revolution in the computer industry caused by the move to the internet as platform..."* (O'Reilly, 2006) is widely quoted but rather obscure. Perhaps the best way to define Web 2.0 is in comparison to what went before. Web "1.0" introduced computer communication via the Internet; Web 2.0 enables people to converse and collaborate with one another there. Web 2.0 represents an evolving democratization of the Internet, not a statement about tools and technologies. Creativity has been open sourced. Content and applications are developed and distributed because people want to. Centralized control has given way to dispersed cooperation. Wikipedia, written and reviewed by the self-appointed masses, has displaced *Encyclopædia Britannica*, controlled and produced by anointed experts.

Social media, from Twitter to Facebook, from Flickr to YouTube, as well as widespread blogging, has created an environment where people are free to openly share their observations and opinions, and to receive feedback and reaction.

How to unleash such creativity and collaboration within the business environment? Not only is it desirable, it is essential. The current generation of people entering the workforce expects nothing less. From a corporate viewpoint, however, the question arises of how to align that creativity and collaboration with business goals and control it sufficiently to conform to corporate norms and legal limitations. These are the aims of Enterprise 2.0, the business flavor of Web 2.0 (McAfee, 2009). In the context of running and managing a business, Enterprise 2.0 opens up enormous opportunities as well as posing significant challenges. It promises to unleash the creativity of decision makers who gain access to an information base far wider than previously envisaged. It offers collaboration in real time with both peers and superiors that can drive innovation and speed decision making. And it presents the opportunity for the business to directly harvest and benefit from the wisdom and experience of *edge workers*—the people who work intimately with customers and prospects, products and partners, and thus have direct access to what's going on in the real, outside world—for the first time.

I describe in Chapters 8 and 9 how people—their drives, roles and interactions—must move to center stage if we are to successfully reinvent how we manage and run our business in the 21st century. That this movement has already begun is undeniable. We must now accelerate and steer it towards completion.

1.6 ARCHITECTING THE BIZ-TECH ECOSYSTEM

The preceding sections have cast a very wide net. The biz-tech ecosystem drives new ways of doing business and demands novel approaches to IT. The trinity of information, process and people includes literally every aspect of the business. We can and will explore them all in depth, but how can we make sense of this big picture, bring order to the chaos? Enterprise architecture (EA) is the discipline by which we design the business we desire: its structures and organization, how it operates, and how it uses information technology. EA has, at its foundation, people, process and information—the who, how and what of the Zachman framework (Zachman, 1987), (Zachman, 2011). Loosely following the same framework, I will use two levels of detail throughout the book—conceptual and logical architectures—to provide structures within which we can consider the overall shape of the new biz-tech ecosystem. In Chapter 10, I will briefly return to these architecture types and discuss implementation considerations that arise.

The IDEAL conceptual architecture

The purpose of the conceptual architecture is to provide a complete, balanced overview of the trinity of people, process and information. One possible representation could be an equilateral triangle with the three components at the angles. It's a useful picture to remind us of the required balance; in many areas of business, the role of information is underappreciated, while IT often underestimates the human aspect. In IT, either process or information is emphasized, one over the other, depending on where in the IT organization we look. However, a layered conceptual architecture, as shown in Figure 1-6, is more appropriate, emphasizing the relationships between the three components. This diagram places information at the foundation and process as a mediating layer between information and the people who first create or capture it and, later, make use of it. This conceptual architecture, however obvious or simple it may seem, allows us to envisage how BI and, indeed, the entire IT environment, will need to change in order to fully support the needs of the modern business world. I introduce this new architectural thinking in stages throughout the book.

This conceptual level of architecture defines and is driven by nine highly desirable char-

Figure 1-6:
IDEAL conceptual architecture for the biz-tech ecosystem

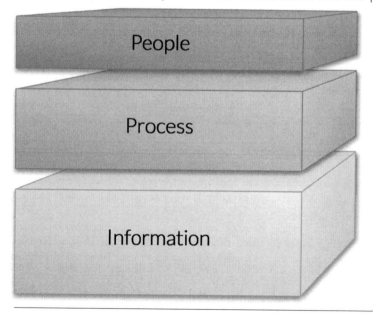

acteristics that apply in varying degrees to each layer detailed in Chapter 10. In the interests of providing a memorable name for this level of the architecture, I have chosen a subset of these to create the acronym IDEAL—integrated, distributed, emergent, adaptive and latent. The last characteristic is worth mentioning here. Being latent, or hidden, the conceptual architecture is not in a form that can be directly implemented. Process cannot be completely separate from information in the real world. People typically resist being either architected or implemented. This leads to the need for a logical level architecture, which bridges from desirable characteristics at a conceptual level to various possible physical implementations that interest vendors and IT departments.

REAL, *the logical architecture*

As will become clear throughout the book, the characteristics of the information layer of the IDEAL architecture are more important than those of the other layers in defining what is desirable and possible in the real world implementation of the biz-tech eco-system. As a result, the logical architecture takes a view that places information front and center. A realistic, extensible, actionable and labile (REAL) platform for information and the processes through which it is created and used, shown in Figure 1-7, is the heart of the structure proposed. This architecture is radically different from the prior layered data warehouse architecture.

The figure depicts three pillars of information with different usage characteristics, with con-text-setting information (the component previously known as metadata) spanning the three pillars. These pillars—defined in Chapter 6—are, from

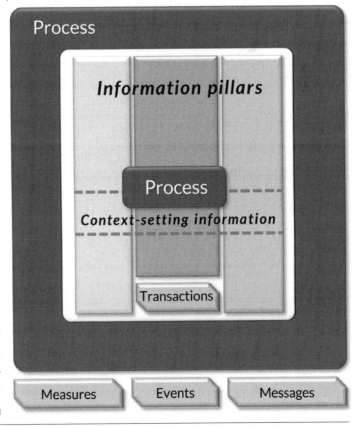

Figure 1-7:
The REAL logical
architecture

left to right: (i) machine-generated data, (ii) process-mediated data and (iii) human-sourced information. Process surrounds and is embedded in this information, providing support for applications and workflows, and the infrastructure to collect, integrate, manage and access information. The individual components of this process layer will be detailed in later chapters. Three key sources of information for use within the enterprise—measures, events and messages—are identified, as well as the more traditional transactions used within all business processes. Conceptually, these four sources, too, are information, but at the REAL, logical level it is important to understand how information actually ends up as part of the resources of an enterprise. People are, of course, implicit in all of this, running and managing the business via the processes and information depicted here. As with the conceptual architecture, this picture is developed in stages throughout the book.

1.7   CONCLUSIONS

You have now accompanied me on a whistle-stop tour of the land of information, the ocean of process, and the kingdom of people. It's a journey that spans over 35,000 years of human development, but less than seventy years of IT evolution. To reach our destination in the coming pages, we will need to understand how technology has changed and will continue to transform our lives and businesses. We will explore information from its smallest speck to its largest conglomeration. This will take much of the book to do. We will also play with people to see what makes them tick. And diving into the deep seas of process, we will appreciate how peoples' desires and needs translate to action, and are recorded in information.

Our destination is the definition of new concepts and high-level conceptual and physical architectures describing how business and IT must work together in the emergent biz-tech ecosystem. We will focus on decision making and how decisions translate to action; in particular, we will explore the foundational role that information plays in all of this. We will look briefly to the new types of tools and techniques that will be needed in a context dominated in the past by traditional BI thinking and products. And we'll give some thought as to how we will need to drive and manage the necessary social and organizational change that this approach demands.

This book is the thinking manager's overview, the executive's handbook to the biz-tech ecosystem for the coming decades. It is the IT architect's roadmap to the same destination. Although we give some brief consideration to implementation concerns, further extensive exploration is required to delve deeper into the physical architecture level of technology choices, platforms and networks, and the extensive organizational challenges that will surely arise.

I look forward to accompanying you on this path.

Roadmap

→ *Mind the Gap:* The chasm between business and IT dates to the earliest days of computers; it is simply a legacy of the technical complexity of the earliest systems

→ *Business-IT convergence:* Beginning it the 1990s, first, BI and, then, the Web have demonstrated the real value that can be achieved when business takes technology on board and IT is intimately involved

→ *Biz-tech ecosystem characteristics:*
(i)   Reintegration of technologies and organizations
(ii) Interdependence of business and IT innovation
(iii) Cross-over of skills between business and IT
(iv) Cooperation between businesses
(v) Trust replaces competitive and adversarial behavior

→ *Organizational implications:* IT moves to a partnership role with the business, and business and IT develop strategies and plan implementations together

| *"The roots of great innovation are never just in the technology itself. They are always in the wider historical context."* | David Brooks |

| *"All change is not growth, as all movement is not forward."* | Ellen Glasgow |

Why do we choose to do things the way we do them? Because they work? Or because they worked once and we haven't checked recently if there might be a better way? On a personal level, many of us resist change. Often we have assumptions so old, so deeply embedded that we don't even give them a thought. In the business environment, change is even more difficult because what works at one time is often baked into the structures and process definitions of the enterprise.

But, change we must. It is the imperative of every living organism. Without change, life ceases. Without change, businesses also die. The latest change that the business world is experiencing is the emergence of the biz-tech ecosystem—a confluence of business needs and technology trends that overturn the fundamentals of many long-established practices in both business and IT.

But, change—in its form and direction—is seldom clear-cut. Even as we explore today's world and tomorrow's possibilities, it's vital to also visit yesterday's realities to understand their limitations (and strengths) and how they influence our thinking today. To unravel the three strands of information, process and people introduced in Chapter 1, we must first follow the threads back into the early history of computing to see how particular beliefs around IT and its relationship to business have emerged. We start way back in the early 1960s and in the following decades.

We then introduce the key characteristics of the biz-tech ecosystem, beginning with three wide-ranging examples from the past twenty years, where recognition of information as an asset is a central tenet. The initial technological signs can be seen as far back as the 1990s. The difference now, almost 25 years later, is that these seeds have matured and grown into a highly diverse and interdependent technology jungle that today's business users dare to enter in significant numbers. And they are ready and able to do so; having grown up with computing and communications technology that, three decades ago, would have been seen as magic by the majority of business people.

Of course, all is not sweetness and light. No change is only for the better. And so it is with the biz-tech ecosystem. This new way of doing business—of being a business or a person—in the new interconnected world presents its own unique and complex challenges. The biz-tech ecosystem poses significant questions about information ownership, privacy and the continued existence of certain types of business activity. In practice, business and IT need to start planning for a new way of working together.

2.1   THE BIRTH OF THE BEAST

Before anyone could discuss data, information, and even knowledge; before debates on how business users might like to see sales figures and their trends depicted; before architectural diatribes and marketing dissimulation about the benefits of dimensional modeling, columnar databases, or massively parallel processing, someone had to build the Beast—the basic hardware, software and tools needed to automate the running and managing of a business.

Figure 2-1:
IBM System/360
used by NASA in
the late 1960s

While primitive forms of electronic computers have existed since the 1940s, most historians mark the mid-1960s as a key inflection point. In 1964, IBM announced the first general-purpose computer, the IBM System/360, the first computer to distinguish between architecture and implementation, assuring upward scalability (the ability to move to a larger machine with the same architecture) and backward compatibility (programs developed on older models can run on newer ones). Developers could now place greater focus on the structure of their own applications and data, rather than on the challenges of the underlying technology. While highly complex to run and manage by today's standards, this machine was a huge leap forward in usability for application programmers. As a result, the System/360 and follow-on hardware and software largely dominated commercial computing for more than two decades. And as you can see from Figure 2-1, the System/360 also physically dominated those who used it. The picture graphically suggests that human thought and behavior must become subservient to the technology in order to get the machine to do what was required. People needed to think like machines rather than having computers think like humans. This philosophy still lives on in some areas of IT, most clearly perhaps in the area of data and information.

Long before the term *information technology* was widely used, data processing (DP) was all the rage. That phrase, and even the word

Figure 2-2:
Univac magnetic tape drives at Lawrence Livermore National Laboratory in the mid-1950s

computer itself, provides an insight into what people perceived these machines to be doing: performing calculations on numbers—processing data. In the 1960s, even after the introduction of the System/360, a primary focus in application development was on the technical details of how to store and manipulate *data*. In this context, data consists of facts—measurements, statistics, the output of physical sensors—largely numeric in form, and used as the foundation for calculation or simple reasoning. Computers have always excelled at these functions, but in the early years, space to store the data to be manipulated was at a premium. Memory was of the order of tens or maybe hundreds of kilobytes; fitting the code, never mind the data, in memory was a challenge.

Sequential, or serial, access to data was the norm throughout the early years of computing. For large volumes of data (and a megabyte was a large volume back then) and fast access, magnetic tape reigned supreme from the 1950s on. Flat files, or sets of identical records, were written and read in sequence from beginning to end of the set. Altering one record required the entire file to be rewritten. For smaller volumes and much lower access speeds, punched cards sufficed—but individual records could be re-punched, at least! Although disk storage, with its characteristic random access technology, had also been around since the middle of the same decade, its physical size, weight, technical complexity and cost limited its widespread adoption for data storage.

With such limitations in technology, it makes sense that beyond coding applications (often in machine code or assembler) the full focus of computing well into the 1960s was on data—the smallest, simplest representation of the facts and figures required to do the calculation, well-structured in a manner such that it could be created and used in the same sequence, and specifically designed for the needs of the application in hand. Memory sizes gradually increased, disk drives were introduced, and processing power grew throughout the 1950s and 1960s. But, the mindset of programmers and users alike remained almost entirely oriented to individually designed and managed data files, even as Charles Bachman crafted his integrated data store (IDS) in 1961 (Hayes, 2002)—the first database, a topic we explore in Chapter 3.

First steps

By the early 1970s, disk storage had become mainstream. The IBM 3340 direct access storage device (DASD), for example, introduced in 1973, had two 30MB spindles. It was nicknamed the "30-30" after a famous Winchester rifle, and the disks were thus known as Winchesters. With sealed, removable and relatively portable disk assemblies, reduced complexity and costs, this technology allowed widespread random access to data. Winchesters were the "serial killers" of their time, a key transition point when disks displaced sequential devices such as tape drives as the primary store for data. The ability and, indeed, the need to write, find, read and rewrite individual data items rather than entire files represented a fundamental change in thinking about data. The speed and flexibility of

Figure 2-3:
CDC disk farm at
Lawrence Livermore
circa 1970. Each unit
stored approximately
100 megabytes.

access allowed the beginnings of the move from *batch* applications that churned through the data overnight to *online* applications that interacted with people in real time. Among the earliest of such systems was the computer-based airline ticket reservations system, SABRE, introduced by American Airlines in 1964 (Copeland, et al., 1995). Another significant advance was the concept of integrated data processing—consolidation of the data requirements of multiple applications onto a shared data source.

Such *mainframe* computing represents the genesis of business use of computers and saw its heyday in the 1970s and 1980s, before the upsurge in minicomputers and, especially, personal computing, a menagerie of mini-beasts to which we'll return in Chapter 4. Despite many predictions of its death, mainframe computing continues to occupy a significant role in computing today. More importantly, the scale and complexity of the technology drove thinking on how computing should be managed and supported in business. This thinking has changed little since then; it's to this topic we next turn.

Care and feeding of the Beast

The earliest uses of computers in business could be best described as experimental, the reserve of technicians who understood intimately the needs and habits of the Beast. Getting it to perform anything was an art; getting it to perform well was akin to magic. In the earliest days, a vast console of switches and lights had to be set and monitored for every task. Even into the 1970s, a missing or

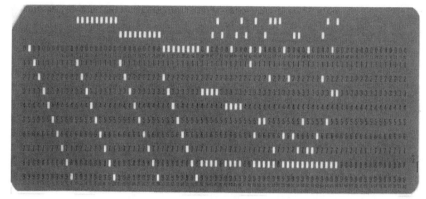

Figure 2-4:
An 80-column punched card with the 1964 EBCDIC character set

misplaced comma in job control language (JCL) on a punched card was sufficient to waste an entire night's computing work. Small wonder that, for many years, computer vendors offered a free systems engineer with every large computer purchased. Businesses had no choice but to create an entire organization dedicated to the care and feeding of the Beast: systems and application programmers to speak its arcane language, data and database administrators to feed it, data entry clerks to prepare its food on punched cards (Figure 2-4) and more. The Data Processing department was born. As DP evolved, it took on four distinct, interrelated roles in roughly the order shown:

1. *Technology expertise:* Acquiring, managing and troubleshooting the computer hardware and software infrastructure

2. *Application development:* Translation of business procedures into programs and code that could be run on computers

3. *Data management:* Design and development of procedures to ensure data preservation, quality and consistency, especially as programs began to share common data resources

4. *Architecture and standards:* Definition and creation of a well-structured environment for all computing activities

The link between business and the DP department was tenuous in the extreme and almost exclusively through the application development role—business analysts were charged with understanding and interpreting business needs such that programmers could code the applications to automate administrative procedures—an iterative process that was both slow and error-prone. The subservient position of DP as an interpreter and implementer of known and defined business needs was thus created. In modern parlance, a service organization, a cost center. Somewhere along the way, DP renamed itself IT, the much more impressive information technology department. It didn't help; IT became renowned as an organization that, as often as not, got in the way of the business when significant changes were required. Both indispensable and resented, the IT department was increasingly isolated from the mainstream of the business.

Data entry clerks and their punched cards are long gone, as business people now do all their own data entry. Indeed, even secretarial work has given way to executives typing—with two fingers. Now, the thought resonates that if only the business people could find a way to translate their needs into computer speak, IT could be binned. Outsourcing of IT and computers is but another twist of the same screw. But it misses a key point—business is not only dependent on the Beast; the Beast has become the business in many cases. The financial industry's instruments and derivatives, not to mention money, exist only within the bowels of computers. Manufacturing and distribution is similarly beholden. Movies are built on computer-generated imagery (CGI). So where, other than IT, can business find the skill, knowledge and expertise to apply computer technology creatively to identify new business opportunities, to enhance existing processes as new technology emerges?

We've lingered long in these old computer rooms to understand their legacy, one that lives on in how IT perceives its role and how business looks at IT. Both must change, and change dramatically, in order to grow. That change has already begun. But now it is accelerating beyond anything we've already seen.

ThoughtPoint

It's time IT grew up! Being a cost center is rather childlike—tell us what to do and we'll be good little boys and girls. Unfortunately, in hard times, kicking the teenagers out becomes the only option. Information technology is no longer so arcane. It's also a core component of every business. Today's IT departments have the opportunity to become contributors to the business if they are willing to become technology innovators rather than technical geeks.

2.2   BEAUTY AND THE BEAST—THE BIZ-TECH ECOSYSTEM

Figure 2-5:
Beauty and the Beast,
Anne Anderson,
1902

So, if the Beast is the computer, it makes sense that business is Beauty, right? In the fairytale, the Beast gives the young woman many gifts of wealth and knowledge, and she comes to value him as a friend, although he begs daily for her hand in marriage. Beauty only comes to truly love the Beast when she believes he's dying. Her tears fall on his face, freeing him from the wicked fairy's spell and transforming him into the handsome prince, whom she, of course, marries and they live happily ever after…

There is hardly a business today that could survive without the computer. So much of the administrative drudgery of payroll, billing, supply chain management, and more has been computerized that the Beast has become indispensable. And yet, many CEOs hardly see him even as a friend, and surely a friend without benefits! This low regard is illustrated clearly in the drive over the past decade to outsource IT and computing, placing it at the same level of intrinsic importance as office cleaning, building maintenance, and security—far from the core competencies of the business. On the other hand, far from being appreciated only on his deathbed, the Beast has also ingratiated himself in increasingly novel ways over the past two decades in certain industries. Forward-looking businesses have found numerous opportunities to use computing to reinvent various aspects of their fundamental business processes.

In 2006, Profs. Andrew McAfee and Erik Brynjolfsson recognized that an approximate doubling in IT spending in US businesses in the decade beginning 1995 corresponded to a similar increase in productivity. Interested in the link between IT spending and competitiveness, they undertook a two-year study comparing relative increases in IT spending to three quantifiable indicators of competitiveness (McAfee & Brynjolfsson, 2008). Industries with the highest IT spending showed distinct signs of hyper-competition: increasing market concentration around a small number of players, extreme turbulence in market leadership, and wider spreads in gross profit margins between leaders and laggards. The authors concluded that the leading companies were leveraging IT to change and improve their operations in fundamental ways. It is just such ongoing change and improvement as business and IT cooperate that characterizes the biz-tech ecosystem. As the authors note, *"deploying IT serves two distinct roles—as a catalyst for innovative ideas and as an engine for delivering them"*, emphasizing how business processes can be quickly and consistently reinvented across the business when IT is fully engaged. They place less emphasis on the role of information as a catalyst for change. Arguably, it is only since 2008 that this has become obvious, although some examples date back much further.

Reconstructing business with IT

Three examples show how IT deployment—when combined with real business vision—facilitates innovation and delivers value. In them, we can also see the full extent of the emerging ecosystem. Beauty is clearly growing to love the Beast.

Business intelligence reinvents retail

In the early 1990s, most companies dabbling in the nascent data warehousing / business intelligence environment were doing just that—dabbling. Even some more advanced companies were looking to answer simple questions like "How many life insurance policies did we sell last week?" Retailers, ever driven by tight margins, were more specific in their needs. Understanding past performance in sales was all very well, but what they really needed were tools to drive down inventory costs, thereby increasing margins. The emergence of data warehousing in parallel with advances in point-of-sale and other technological advances led to a data-driven approach that changed the industry forever. Walmart is the poster child of this revolution in retailing and has certainly been uniquely successful, but other retailers around the world were and still are doing much the same thing. The secret was in the cash registers, or to be precise, the data they gathered. By the late 1980s, cash registers had become increasingly automated, computerized and, in many cases, connected to central computers. Barcode scanners were replacing manual price entry, allowing the recording of the actual items passing through the checkout. Items purchased together in a single transaction at a particular time of day could be identified.

Figure 2-6:
Hungarian three-column full-keyboard cash register, 1902

With the increased use of credit cards and loyalty programs, transactions could be related to specific customers. From a BI viewpoint, such information can, of course, be analyzed to track trends in sales, store performance, customer preferences, and so on.

However, of far more interest to retailers was the possibility of using this data operationally to drive efficiency in inventory management, staffing and product promotion. Transaction data from the registers was sent directly into the inventory management and stock reordering systems to minimize or eliminate stock outages or oversupply. A detailed knowledge of sales trends was used in negotiations with suppliers to drive down costs. Items purchased together allowed decisions about stock placement or promotions. Correlating purchases with weather conditions or unusual events enabled predictions to be made about what to stock up on when similar conditions arose in the future. Today, from a distance of some 20 years, none of the above is particularly surprising. In fact, it is an everyday reality for every retailer, both online and off. However, back then, it revolutionized retail and, arguably, enabled the meteoric rise of the company that most successfully adopted these techniques, namely Walmart. This use of sales and related information in a deliberate and integrated fashion across the entire retail value chain is an early and persuasive example of the biz-tech ecosystem and its power to change an entire industry.

A key aspect to note here is how automation and extensive data recording in different parts of the business, often for differing primary objectives, can become a powerful change agent when a tipping point is reached. Cash registers, as the name implies, were introduced to record and secure cash takings. Barcode scanners were attached in the early 1980s in increasing numbers to reduce data entry errors and speed checkout throughput. With barcodes, the financial interest in cash sales was linked to inventory management. The computer networks that had been installed to aggregate and report daily sales numbers from stores to headquarters now began to carry information about the products that were being sold and, by implication, needed to be reordered. Stocktaking became an automated and ongoing process, from point-of-sale back to shelf stocking, and all the way to goods received at central warehouses. Electronic links back to suppliers completed the supply chain, driving new procedures for just-in-time ordering and receiving of the required stock.

Fundamental to all of this change was close, ongoing two-way co-operation between business and IT. Unlike the situation in the prior master/servant relationship between business and IT, this new way of doing business can only emerge in a partnership of equals in the biz-tech ecosystem. Another key aspect, which will be apparent mostly to BI practitioners, is that this approach blurs an ancient distinction in computer usage between *operational* and *informational* use of data. We'll deal with this important topic in Chapter 5.

The Web recreates the library

It is a common misconception among IT and, in particular, BI professionals that by far the most important role for computers in business is computational. The name *computer* itself confirms the impression. Computation, by definition, is centered on numerical data; text and other types of information are ancillary to the computation, stored and presented only for the benefit of human interpretation and understanding of the calculated results. Fortunately, there is more to life! The business Beauty is inspired by more than numbers; the Beast can do more than add and subtract. This second example of the biz-tech ecosystem ventures into these softer landscapes.

Figure 2-7:
The Great Library of Alexandria, 19th century engraving, Otto Von Corven.

These landscapes are populated by books, documents, and textual and graphical information of many sorts. Such information forms the foundation for a range of activities in business, as well as in general life, that might be called *recording and researching reality*—perhaps a more literally correct homage to the Victorian 3 Rs of reading, writing and arithmetic. Today, computers and digital devices are at the heart of these new 3 Rs. In personal life, what was once letter writing and diary keeping have moved to email and blogging. Writing has become typing into a word processor, soon to be replaced by speaking to voice recognition software. The vast majority of information created or captured today is digital. Older books, papers and paintings are being scanned and digitized.

Similarly, research has moved from physical libraries to digital archives, most notably the Web. To *google* has been recognized by the Oxford English dictionary as a common verb since 2006, meaning, obviously, to search on the Internet. Wikipedia, as of December, 2012, contains nearly twenty million articles in over 270 languages. Computers and, in particular, the Internet have become the largest library of information ever assembled by humankind. And while far from perfect, our ability to reliably and rapidly find information on almost any topic is orders of magnitude greater than it has ever been. The explosion of recorded information and our increasing ability to research it is another example of the biz-tech ecosystem in operation. Computers and digital technology have expanded and enhanced our ability to record our reality for posterity. As technology has improved, we've found new ways to capture our experiences and thoughts. And, as we demand new ways to express ourselves, technology pushes the boundaries further. Our research is no longer limited to the nearest physical library; the virtual Web library is ours for the taking—and the making. Gradually, with the emergence of Web 2.0 techniques, information flow is becoming bidirectional. In the past, largely centralized and powerful authorities wrote and published; the masses purchased and consumed the media thus produced, from books to music to movies and TV.

Once again, we see the hallmarks of the biz-tech ecosystem, taking business in its widest meaning. There is the interconnected development of the business need and the technical solution, as well as the cross-fertilization of business and IT skills. Also, the collapsing of boundaries and barriers between information silos. The ongoing digitization of such information has significant implications for traditional BI and IT, in general. It also poses major challenges for our traditional concepts of authorship and intellectual property (IP). We explore these topics further in Chapters 6 and 8.

Big data redefines automobile insurance

Just as BI set the scope for many of the advances in information usage in the 1990s and the Web in the 2000s, big data looks set to dominate information thinking in the 2010s. The term *big data*, as we shall see in Chapter 6, covers a multitude of sins. But for this final example of the biz-tech ecosystem, we focus on one subset of the field: sensor-generated data and, specifically, vehicle telematics. Telematics is, broadly speaking, the process of transmitting and receiving of computer-generated data. When applied to vehicles, it has a more specific meaning: the transmission of data—on-board diagnostics (OBD)—derived from electronic sensors, through an on-board controller/computer, and the use of this data to remotely monitor a range of conditions and events occurring in the vehicle.

Electronic environmental sensors are becoming ever cheaper and increasingly ubiquitous. These sensors are used to measure specific aspects of the environment or the behavior of a machine or device. Many of us are already familiar with sensors in cell/mobile phones, digital cameras, and tablets that detect the device's location (GPS sensor), orientation, movement, and so on. Similar devices have long been fitted to expensive machines, such as aircraft engines, to record many operational characteristics, such as fuel consumption, rotation speeds, acceleration, and so on. All of these measurements are passed to an on-board computer and recorded in the aircraft's black box. Furthermore, airplane manufacturers have enabled the continuous transmission of key data from the aircraft to the manufacturer's service center to allow ongoing quality monitoring and preventative maintenance. As the technology has dropped in price and cell phone communications have become pervasive, automobile manufacturers have begun to fit such systems, particularly on high-end or fleet models, for similar purposes.

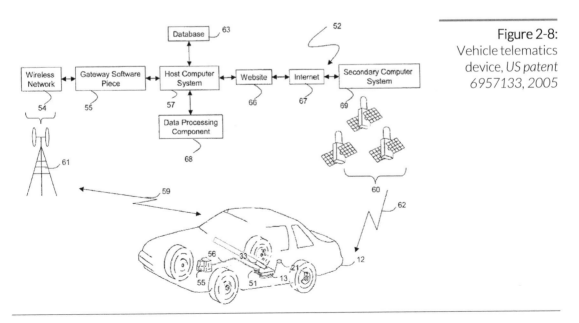

Figure 2-8:
Vehicle telematics
device, *US patent
6957133, 2005*

In the mid-2000s, automobile insurers began to trial the use of this data to monitor driving behavior with a view to "pay-as-you-drive" (PAYD) insurance policies. Full-fledged systems have since been rolled out in various countries. Typical data gathered includes time of use, mileage driven, speed, sudden accelerations and braking, as well as accidents. Based on driving behavior, premiums are adjusted up or down or discounts offered, often with near-immediate effect—an entirely new business model for automobile insurance.

From the point of view of the biz-tech ecosystem, we see a familiar pattern emerging. PAYD insurance products can only be offered using technology previously beyond this industry. Data collected for one purpose is sequestered for another to support an innovative and process-changing idea. Business and IT must cooperate closely to understand how a new set of technologies can be used to change existing business processes and how such changes can be incorporated into existing IT systems.

Sweating the information asset

Living in the Information Age, information is regularly cited by executives as the latest and greatest business asset. And yet, accountants steadfastly resist the rather obvious step of including the value of information on the balance sheet as a form of intangible asset, although the cost of collecting, storing and managing it is clearly there. One immediate and evident result is IT's longstanding difficulty in justifying enterprise information management projects. The financials of businesses that focus largely on information reflect poorly, if at all, the true value of the business. The difference between the approx. $100B market value of Facebook at its IPO in May, 2012 and its $7B book value points to the value of the information it stores about its users. And all ironically *"generated by nearly a billion unassuming, unpaid information workers"* (Laney, 2012).

Information, as the essence of the Information Age and the foundation layer of the IDEAL conceptual architecture, is clearly in need of a better approach to its valuation. Information economics, or *infonomics*, forms the basis of this effort to treat information as one would other intangible assets. Laney offers a list of reasons: influencing company valuation; contractual risk assessment; borrowing, bartering and selling information; as well as calculating true return on investment (ROI) of information projects—collection, management, security, use and disposal. Furthermore, treating information as a true asset leads to new insights about its value in a business on the leading edge of the biz-tech ecosystem. For example, it is often suggested that information has value only when used in some business process. This view fails to appreciate the probable future economic benefit that normal accounting practice would assign to assets, and which

> **Biz-tech ecosystem**
>
> *The evolving environment where business is fully or heavily dependent on information technology for all activities.*
>
> *IT adopts the role of partner and co-creator in business innovation.*
>
> *Business completely values and engages the full potential of IT.*

therefore undervalues such information and overestimates the cost of keeping it. Such information may well have longer term competitive value, as seen in the phenomenal success of information-based businesses such as Google and Facebook. If they had been driven solely by pure accounting measures, they would never have retained much of their petabyte-sized data stores.

Much of the sweating of information assets of businesses to date has been driven by visionary business and IT leaders who identified novel and game-changing opportunities. As the biz-tech ecosystem is more widely adopted, the opportunities will become less novel and offer lower returns. Nonetheless, there will continue to be gains and losses to be made. A realistic, quantified accounting of the value of information as an actual asset, with both realized and potential value, must become a core feature of the calculation of return on investment on biz-tech ecosystem development projects.

2.3   KEY FEATURES OF THE BIZ-TECH ECOSYSTEM

The biz-tech ecosystem is revolutionary in the longer term. It has started small and grown imperceptibly over much of the past twenty years. The pace is accelerating. The following points characterize the concept. The earlier ones are already solidifying; those further down the list are only emerging.

1. *Reintegration:* As business and IT have become increasingly interdependent, the silos within and across both organizations have grown increasingly difficult to maintain; they deliver inef-

ficiencies, miscommunications and errors. The cracks can no longer be hidden from Web-savvy customers. Coherence has already become mandatory; reintegration of the technology and the organizations across the entire business is underway.

2. *Interdependence:* Business and technology are each driven, one by the other, in a tight loop. New technology enables new business possibilities; new business opportunities drive advances in technology. This is a classic positive feedback loop that leads from a slow start to exponential growth rates. This is visible today in the Web denizens such as Google, Facebook and Twitter, where the business knows it *is* the technology and *vice versa*. Interdependence Day is within reach of many more businesses that are becoming information-driven.

3. *Cross-over:* Business people need the skill to understand sufficient technology to envision how new advances could be used to recreate the business. Similarly, IT people need the business acumen to see how business needs can be satisfied in new ways by emerging technology. The old division of skills no longer works. Fortunately, most of today's younger business people grew up with computer technology and networked living; they get IT in a way prior generations of managers didn't. But, IT people still need to learn to look beyond the technology. And beyond the specific problem at hand; they need to anticipate business needs.

4. *Cooperation:* The old boundaries between the business, its suppliers and customers, and governmental agencies are beginning to dissolve as information refuses to be confined to old channels and stores. With time of the essence, delays and misunderstandings must be eliminated. Free flow of information becomes the norm.

5. *Trust:* Competitive and adversarial relationships become counterproductive and are replaced by trust and cooperation. This is the coming tipping point. The old eat-or-be-eaten model that underpins modern capitalism must fade away; the alternative is a runaway hypercompetitive environment that devours itself in ever-decreasing circles.

In many ways, these earlier characteristics are anathema to business and IT as they have operated for five decades already. Many beliefs and assumptions spring from the way computing evolved and was delivered; despite some progress, they continue to limit thinking today. The latter two characteristics will prove challenging for some. They challenge the economic model of Western society. Unfortunately, without some fundamental change in our thinking about business and people, the Beast is capable of wreaking destruction beyond our wildest nightmares.

2.4   Tyranny of the Beast

The evolution of the biz-tech ecosystem is proceeding apace. From a traditional commercial viewpoint, technology offers better intelligence about the market, faster reactions and turnaround, higher productivity, lower costs, and bigger profits. From the point of view of the technologists and technology vendors, the ecosystem promises to align their interests ever more closely with that of the business, increasing their influence and making them indispensable. So far, so good. But, is it all sweetness and light? The three examples described above illustrate the sweetness of commercial success, the light of expanded and freer use of information. But, each also has its dark side. Hints that we must carefully consider unintended or unexpected consequences of the onward march of technology.

Figure 2-9:
Frankenstein by Mary Shelley, frontispiece to the 1831 edition, Theodore Von Holst

The information-driven reengineering of the retail supply chain (and associated efforts) at Walmart alone is credited with contributing 12% of the productivity gains in the US economy in the second half of the 1990s (Fishman, 2003). However, the information stored (together with the enormous size of the retailer) has fundamentally changed the relationship between the company and its suppliers, enabling Walmart to make ever more arduous demands for lower prices from suppliers, probably far beyond their ability to reduce their costs. This clearly drives manufacturing to ever lower cost economies and forces local manufacturers out of business, with consequent social, financial and environmental impacts. Unemployed customers are even more price conscious—if they can afford to shop at all—and a vicious cycle of cost-driven actions ensues: the classic race to the bottom.

Similarly, the extensive democratization of information on the Web reduces the perceived value of content creation and makes it increasingly difficult for authors, artists, film makers and other content creators to finance their time and benefit from their creativity. The trend towards ebooks, for example, enables an entirely new way in which readers and authors can interact and co-create content far beyond the knowledge of a single author. However, the current business model, where ebooks sell for approximately the same price as a paperback version of the same book, poses some interesting questions: who benefits from the savings in paper, printing, warehousing and distribution costs inherent in the ebook product? Will authors and readers together begin to disempower the publishing industry as it currently exists? If so, what new business model will then emerge? More worryingly for society in general is the devaluation of information. The rush to report first displaces reasoned consideration of both nuances and consequences. The fact that everyone can publish an opinion on Twitter or Facebook about anything devalues authoritative judgment; all positions across the bell curve of opinion from one extreme to the other achieve some measure of equal standing. In *Too Big to Know*, David Weinberger quotes Senator Daniel Patrick Moynihan's *"Everyone is entitled to his own opinions, but not to his own facts"*, to illustrate that the difference between opinion and fact has become infinitely blurred in a networked world where everybody and nobody is an expert on any topic. And there is the irony that a brief search of Wikipedia will show that even the existence of Moynihan's quote may or may not be a fact (Weinberger, 2012).

PAYD automobile insurance provides another example of an industry redefining the fundamental core of its business with an apparent disregard for the longer-term consequences. The original purpose of insurance is to spread the risk of unanticipated costs over a large number of people who pay a regular premium in case they have an accident, but who are aware that, statistically, they have a relatively small chance of recovering their investment. From the earliest days of the industry, of course, insurance companies have profited from actuarially estimating the risk they carry and avoiding or loading the highest risk clients. BI and data mining have allowed extensive, flexible and reactive segmentation of the risk base and allowed insurance companies to sell cheaper premiums to lower risk customers—and devalued the concept of spreading risk across a large customer base. PAYD finally turns the concept on its head by monitoring behavior for risk and offering willing participants lower premium costs. The longer-term consequences for spreading risk are not yet clear. However, it would appear that there is an ever-growing segment of the population for whom insurance may be priced beyond their reach. Is this still insurance? Or is it an attempt to manage behavior?

This example, in particular, provokes us to ask how technology may change business. At a lower level, it poses questions about how valid it may be to apply data collected for one purpose to another. Are measurements of speed, acceleration, braking, etc. valid proxies for driver behavior? Are there privacy issues? What about data ownership? Are processes defined for traditional business suitable and robust enough for the purpose of managing behavior rather than estimating risk? More broadly, it suggests that, given enough data and sufficiently powerful technology, companies can reinvent the goals and basis of their business using customer data, without informing them of the broader and longer-term consequences of their actions. We are led to significant questions about how business and society will interact. How will people's needs and expectations fit within this new model? What are the consequences for those drivers who do not wish to be continuously monitored? What is the outlook for traditional insurance and the concept of spreading the financial impact of unforeseeable events? Furthermore, both this and the retail example flag significant concerns about privacy, which we'll address in Chapter 8.

Technologists too often take the view that their inventions are inherently neutral in societal effect—that it's up to somebody else to make the call if it is to be used for good or ill. The biz-tech ecosystem is not amenable to such thinking. Vendors, analysts and implementers alike have a key role to play in deciding how and when a particular innovation should be applied beyond sole consideration of their company's bottom line.

ThoughtPoint

2.5   IN PRACTICE—ALL CHANGE IN THE ORGANIZATION

With the snowballing commoditization of technology, and the increasing attractiveness of Cloud and utility models for IT provision, the pressure to outsource the IT organization has grown rapidly in recent years. The drivers include lowering costs, unavailability of skilled people, and a focus on core business competencies. While the first two of these drivers continue to have some weight, the biz-tech ecosystem mandates that IT is a core competency. Any organization that wants to drive business faster, broaden its reach, improve its efficiency, and increase innovation must recognize that information technology in general, and the Web, in particular, are central to achieving these aims. As a result, businesses that plan to participate fully in the biz-tech ecosystem should look to near term procedural and organizational changes:

✓ Review existing and planned IT outsourcing decisions to evaluate likely impacts on business innovation in the use of new and evolving technologies.

✓ Evaluate all external Cloud initiatives for possible limitations on advanced technology use in areas of likely business process innovation. Investigate impact of lock-in to technologies offered by vendors as well as restrictions in data use, limitations on moving systems back on premises and other forms of lock-in.

✓ Assess high-level IT skill levels of business managers and executives, as well as business knowledge of IT staff, from designers and architects up. Provide suitable cross-training and/or experience programs to ensure excellence in communication and ability to engage creatively between business and IT personnel.

✓ Involve suitably skilled IT architectural and management level staff on business strategy initiatives and committees.

✓ Create a biz-tech ecosystem center of excellence to identify and drive opportunities for cross-fertilization of ideas, staffed from business and IT.

✓ Brainstorm at executive level—cross-functional, including IT— to generate and evaluate opportunities for innovative use and/or monetization of information within the business, with partners and customers.

✓ Working with financial and accounting leaders, innovate with formal valuation models for information, to allow educated and knowledgeable decisions on purchasing, collecting, storing, managing and disposing of information.

✓ Reduce/eliminate organizational barriers within IT between operational, informational and collaborative support functions. Limit and reduce technology differences where possible.

✓ For companies with a strong enterprise data warehousing approach and/or a long history of successful cross-enterprise BI, build biz-tech ecosystem initiatives from these organizations as starting points. Their knowledge and skills in working with loosely defined business needs, across multiple departments and with enterprise-level information integration are invaluable in the broader context and aims of the biz-tech ecosystem.

✓ Tackle real or perceived problems in IT delivery of business needs—such as *"IT is the bottleneck"*, *"IT is unresponsive"*, etc.—to reduce or eliminate the tendency of business departments to unilaterally instigate independent, stand-alone, computer-based solutions to immediate needs. Decommission existing stand-alone solutions as a vital step toward enabling the biz-tech ecosystem.

2.6   CONCLUSIONS

To live is to change, to grow. So, too, it is with business. Without evolution, without adaptation to changing circumstances, the business dies, overtaken by competition or by the changing market itself. The current, ongoing, and, indeed, culminating wave of change is what I have called the biz-tech ecosystem. In this new environment, business and IT work as partners. It has not always been so.

IT has long understood that business needs should be the driving force for all its work. From diligent understanding of requirements to delivery of comprehensive and timely solutions, in this view application development is wholly subservient to the business. This approach has delivered excellent solutions to well-understood needs. However, it seldom delivers full-fledged BI systems. Nor can it develop the innovative ecosystem needed today.

Computer technology is deeply embedded in every aspect of modern business, from initial concept to product delivery and beyond. Success depends as much on engaging and fully exploiting technology, both available and emerging, as on the traditional concepts of serving customers and managing finances. Business and technology comprise a tightly knit and interdependent ecosystem. Technology is driving business as much as business drives technology; they exist in a fully symbiotic relationship.

In this chapter, we've focused on the aspects of the biz-tech ecosystem relating to the relationship between the business and the computer. In particular, we've explored the centralized, mainframe computing environment and seen how the role of IT has emerged to service that environment and act as mediator between the business and this technology. We've also seen how the development of business intelligence has been a key launch-pad for a new relationship between business and technology. You've seen a flavor of the types of applications characteristic of this new ecosystem. You've sampled some of its opportunities and its challenges, both at a detailed implementation level and in its wider societal impact.

In further chapters, we'll see other aspects of this biz-tech ecosystem, including how the structure, meaning and use of information drive its evolution, how personal computing and the Web impacts its development, and the implications for business processes and procedures, as well as the changing role of people, both business and IT, within the emerging ecosystem.

ROADMAP

→ *DIKW fails:* Ackoff's data – information – knowledge – wisdom (DIKW) pyramid, which proposes that each layer is derived from those lower in the hierarchy is untenable

→ *From information to data:* Data is simply a form of *hard information* optimized for computer use; both hard and soft information ultimately derive from the meaning that people ascribe to reality; data modeling was an early approach to capturing meaning

→ *Informal information underlies collaboration:* The informal interaction between people—meetings, phone calls, SMS/Text messages, etc.—is vital for innovative collaboration; increasingly it is being collected and stored

→ *Modern meaning model (m^3):* Three interconnecting layers of information – knowledge – meaning as a new basis for understanding how people really create information

→ *Information structure/context:* Understanding the structural and contextual aspects of information clarifies how it can be used and managed; classes on this continuum are: raw, atomic, derived, compound, textual and multiplex

→ *Metadata is context-setting information:* When recognized as such, we eliminate much business confusion and focus on storing and managing metadata as it deserves: equally with all other business information

→ *From data to information:* The new and emerging focus for IT is information (rather than data) management

CHAPTER 3
DATA, INFORMATION AND THE HEGEMONY OF IT

"Information is an idea that has been given a form, such as the spoken or written word. It is a means of representing an image or thought so that it can be communicated from one mind to another." — Theodore Roszak

"It is a very sad thing that nowadays there is so little useless information." — Oscar Wilde

We live in the information age. Allegedly. *"Information is the oxygen of the modern age,"* according to none other than Ronald Reagan. And yet, even the most cursory discussion on the topic of information and data reveals a depth of confusion in business and IT minds about what exactly is meant by these terms. And that is without even mentioning knowledge and other "higher" forms of information. However, it is impossible to discuss the evolution of the biz-tech ecosystem without some common definition of these terms. This chapter begins to build such a foundation, initially in data and information, particularly from the viewpoint of information technology. We also explore knowledge, meaning and even wisdom based on a clearer view of information and its almost endless variety and uses today.

We begin with a model that permeates IT today—the knowledge pyramid that purports to position data, information, knowledge and wisdom and gives rise to the acronym DIKW. Unfortunately, it turns out to be of little help and its basis suspect. So, we will dig deeper into data, both in its definition and in its historical role as fodder for computers. Here we see how data is both less and more than many would imagine, and also how thinking about data is intimately enmeshed with the concepts and structure of computers, as well as their technological limitations, some long eased.

From there, it is clear that we must focus on information—that's what makes sense to humans. With data we worry about structure and standards; with information we concern ourselves with content and context. And contrary to popular opinion, data emerges from information rather than the other way around. This occurs through the process of modeling, but modeling first appeared to support the design of relational databases; we are in a recursive loop.

So, it's time to open Pandora's Box of data vs. information. We must ask from whence, precisely, information emerges, how it relates to data, how we invest meaning in information, and how such meaning is recorded and managed. This leads us, inexorably, to a conceptual model for information, knowledge and meaning, as well as new answers to the vexed question of metadata. We need a set of definitions for words such as data and information, knowledge and information that can be commonly accepted.

3.1 THE KNOWLEDGE PYRAMID AND THE ANCIENT SERPENT OF WISDOM

Pyramids, it seems, have fascinated humanity since time immemorial. We have been building them for 5,000 years and assigning meaning to them ever since. In information science, too, the pyramid has a long tradition—being a common representation of the *data, information, knowledge, wisdom (DIKW) hierarchy* first described by Russell L. Ackoff (Ackoff, 1989). He posited a hierarchy with wisdom at the top and understanding, knowledge, information, and data below, with each category including those that fall below it. Understanding is omitted from most representations; some authors add or subtract terms to suit their needs.

Ackoff suggested—with minimal justification for the numbers—that *"on average about forty percent of the human mind consists of data, thirty percent information, twenty percent knowledge, ten percent understanding, and virtually no wisdom"*, leading to the pyramid we see today, depicted in Figure 3-1. Most authors draw solid lines between the categories, implying distinct boundaries. The boundaries—as well as the definitions of terms and their relationships—seem very fuzzy indeed.

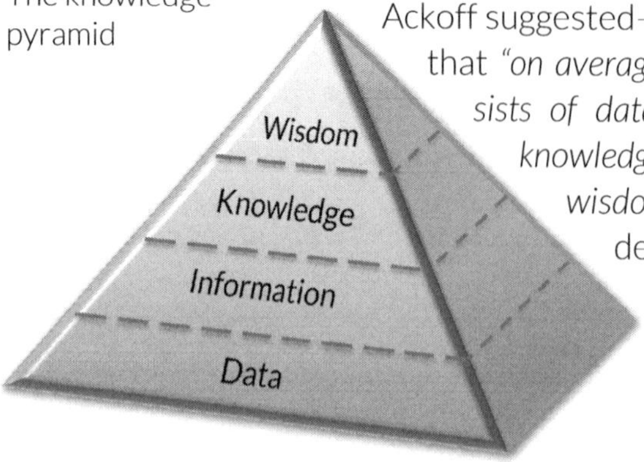

Figure 3-1:
The knowledge pyramid

Ackoff's academic background in operations research and management science, as well as his work as a management consultant, led to this framework specifically in the context of management information systems (MIS) issues of the day. In fact, over 20 years previously, at the very beginning of the computer age, he had identified five false—in his view—assumptions made by the designers of MIS (Ackoff, 1967). Given its early date, it provides a most prescient list; we will return to it in Chapter 4. For the moment, however, the point is that Ackoff's 1989 definitions were based on data and information as it was then produced for and used by MIS. Today, the biz-tech ecosystem deals with a far wider spectrum of information—in the broadest sense of the word. Of course, Ackoff didn't pluck the hierarchy out of thin air. An entire branch of philosophy—epistemology—deals with the nature and scope of knowledge. Debate on the relationship between data, information and knowledge dates to early in the 20th century and continues apace even today, both in information science (Rowley, 2007), (Zins, 2007) and in epistemology (Frické, 2009). We may summarize the situation as follows. Much has been written about data, information and knowledge; rather less about wisdom. And various authors differ to varying degrees about the meaning and relationships of each.

Figure 3-2:
Temptation and Fall,
detail, Michelangelo
Sistine Chapel, Rome.

In information science, the focus is on the better-defined data and information; a definition of knowledge is more elusive. There is a consensus that knowledge derives from information, which derives from data. Data is transformed into information through classification, sorting, aggregating, selection and calculation. Information can be transformed into knowledge through human experience, synsynthesis and contextual understanding. Knowledge is often divided into explicit knowledge, which can be recorded in information systems and tacit knowledge, which cannot. Zins suggests that data and information exist in subjective/personal and objective/universal forms, related broadly to the tacit/explicit division of knowledge. Neither Rowley nor Zins ventures conclusive definitions. Epistemology has a far broader interest and remit than information science and a full discussion is beyond the scope of this book. However, it is of interest that Frické concludes that definitions used in the DIKW hierarchy are poorly differentiated and that the proposition that data begets information begets knowledge is flawed—examples exist where information exists independently of data and where knowledge is similarly independent of information. He further posits that the use of information and knowledge in DIKW overlap, and both equate to what he calls "weak knowledge". Knowledge and wisdom lead us into the realm of belief systems and even moral judgments. Ancient cultures used the snake as a symbol of wisdom, fertility, creativity, healing and regeneration. From there, the serpent moved to become a symbol of the devil or Satan via its role as tempter to eat of the tree of the knowledge of good and evil. There clearly exist important questions and subtle distinctions to be teased out in this area—even in the empire of Mammon called business.

Such questions and distinctions range far beyond the philosophical and academic. They offer a foundation for exploring how human insight—rather than simple information—is the real basis for personal decision making. They suggest how personal and social meaning and intent lead to the tangible innovation that is a *sine qua non* of the biz-tech ecosystem. Chapters 8 and 9, which explore the people layer of the conceptual IDEAL architecture, examine the wisdom and intentions of decision makers within an information-rich, process-supported and collaborative model of how decisions really come about. For now, we conclude that the validity and usefulness of the knowledge pyramid and its underlying DIKW hierarchy are, at a minimum, questionable, despite their popularity in the world of BI, knowledge management, and information science. Much of this chapter explores data and information from a new perspective: how do they apply in our information-overloaded world? This further allows the construction of a new and improved model of information, knowledge and meaning, which I propose as a replacement for Ackoff's pyramid in Section 3.4, and offers useful and usable definitions of these terms and their interrelationships for use in the biz-tech ecosystem.

3.2   WHAT IS THIS THING CALLED DATA?[1]

Before computers corrupted the word—and world—data was the plural of datum. (Despite the efforts of a few diehards, "data is" flows more easily off my tongue than "data are", so I use the singular throughout.) Datum, coming from the Latin meaning "something given" is defined as (1) a single piece of information, such as a fact or statistic and (2) in philosophy, any fact assumed to be a matter of direct observation or any proposition assumed or given, from which conclusions may be drawn[2]. These basic definitions are of interest because they show that thinking about the fundamentals of data is not as straightforward as you might expect. In fact, this first definition equates data to the "singular" of information! This leads us directly into the endless debates we all know about data, information and knowledge, as well as into the assumptions we make about the relationship of data to the real world and how it can be used.

Let's try a new starting point relevant to our so-called Information Age. *Data* is the basic bits and bobs (1s and 0s for the technically minded) we store in computers as a representation of things of interest in the real world. As we know, before we had computers, these bits and bobs were stored first on clay tablets, and eventually on paper; but let's stay with computers. Let's consider a string of numbers on a 1960s punched card: 3128313031303131303313031. Just this and no more. The person who recorded this data also wrote the program that used it, and when that program read this card in the deck, the code was designed to expect the numbers of days per month of a non-leap year, each two digits with no spaces— a very compact way of storing the information. Did you recognize it at first glance? Yes? That's the beauty of being human! This type of early data representation of aspects of reality leads directly to the common definition that data is information without context. However, what we really have here is information where numerical data has been separated from the other information (none other than *metadata*, as we discuss in Section 3.8) that describes its meaning

---

[1] *What is this thing called love?*, a Cole Porter song (1929) and a short story by Isaac Asimov (1969)

[2] Abstracted from http://dictionary.reference.com

Figure 3-3:
Hard and soft
information, sample
structures

(a)

> Number of days per month in a standard year.
> Format: [Month name]: [Number of days],
> January: 31, February: 28, March: 31, …

(b)

Month	January	February	March	…
Days	31	28	31	…

(c)

Month	Days
January	31
February	28
March	31
…	…

and structure. In this first program, the way to extract the meaning from the numeric data is encoded in the lines of the program that read the string and parsed it out, supported by associated comments by the programmer—if you're lucky.

One primary driver for this representation was, as mentioned, minimizing storage and processing. However, this piece of data makes sense only to the program for which it was designed. As application developers began to consider reusing the same data for multiple purposes in different programs coded by different people, it became clear that the data needed some level of definition associated directly with it. There are many different approaches, some of which are shown in Figure 3-3. The first method (a) leads back to "complete" information: the numerical data and the description of the context are all intermixed in a single structure. I call this intermingled structure *soft information* when I need to be explicit, although this is a highly formalized version, written in a way that completely defines the values and structure. We'll delve deeper into this topic in the next section. The other methods, (b) and (c), keep the data and the metadata separate, but in some structural relationship to one another. It is these latter methods that have long been favored by application designers because of their generality and efficiency in use. So, data today usually consists of values and their associated but disjoint descriptors. Unfortunately, common usage of the word *data* usually excludes the metadata descriptions of meaning and structure; so, when I need to be clear, I use the term *hard information* to refer to data values and their related metadata stored in tandem. To database and data administrators and programmers, this may feel like overkill. However, clear definitions are vital in the light of the importance of information and how computers deal with it.

There is another key consideration. How does the data we record and store in computers relate to reality? In all cases, data is at least one, and usually two steps away from what exists in the real world. First there is the object or event in the real world, such as the smartphone you want to buy or the click on the website that found it. At the second level is the specific and very personal human interpretation of the object or event. Is the smartphone an object of desire or simply a communications device? Is that website click an indication of interest in buying or a random slip of the mouse? Depending on the person, their interests and attention, as well as the context, we attribute different meanings and interpretations to everything we see. The variety of descriptions of what happened at an accident scene given by witnesses illustrates this perfectly. However variable, when recorded, we call this material *information*—the human description of our world.

Finally, at the third level is data: the formalization and digital storage of the information we choose or chance to see about the real world. Such data can originate from one of two—and only two—real-world sources: people or machines. As we've just seen, people create information, which is translated into data by various means, from mice and keyboards to audio recorders and cameras. Machines measure and record raw data, such as temperature, velocity and acceleration, using physical sensors that translate these characteristics into electrical signals. Such raw data is only one degree from reality, based on the design of the measuring equipment that fixes the relationship between the measured characteristic, the electrical signal measured, and the numeric digital value stored. Whether sourced from people or machines, we must determine the appropriate data and structure required to give a valid and valuable representation of the information needs of the users. There is usually a variety of trade-offs to be made. The specific data we need to store or display about the smart phone depends on the customer's needs for a fashion statement vs. a communication device vs. an information display unit. Click stream data volumes may be too large to justify keeping long-term historical details. And so on. Thus, the data stored on computers is highly dependent on the information and processing needs of the person who decided to *store* it. And if that person has communicated with the person who

Figure 3-4:
Hermes, Greek messenger of the gods, and associated with information and commerce, *Museo Nazionale Romano*

Data vs. information

In this chapter, I've drawn a very careful distinction between data *and* information. *Where important, I do so throughout this book.*

In common parlance, however, data and information *are used loosely and interchangeably. When in flow, I tend to do the same; old habits die hard.*

needs to use the data and described it effectively in associated metadata, information will be stored and exchanged. However, as we gather and use more and more data from different sources beyond our control, designed for different needs, we face growing challenges in interpreting the data we receive and in understanding the circumstances under which it can be reused. This leads to significant implications for the use of big data and the concept of *analyzing the data exhaust,* as seen in Section 6.2.

In summary then, I am defining data (or hard information) for the purpose of this book as the highly structured and formalized representation of interesting aspects of the real world, collected from people or machines and stored in digital form, with values and descriptions of meaning and structure separately recorded for ease of processing, reduction in storage volumes, or other technical limitations of the storage and processing medium. This positioning stems from consideration of the practice of creating and using data, rather than from the alternative epistemological definition mentioned at the start of this section.

3.3   FROM INFORMATION TO DATA

Long-time experts in BI may look at the above heading and wonder: *"Doesn't he mean 'From data to information'?"* That's long been the challenge for BI—how to get meaningful information for business users out of computer data. But, we must take a step further back, before computers existed, to understand the reality of data and information. Data, even as described above in computing terms, existed before computers. Tables of scientific and mathematical data—do you remember log tables?—predate computers by centuries. But such tables of data were drawn up by people using rules and formulae, which are essentially information. People naturally work with information, either hard or soft; to use it fruitfully is at the core of human intelligence. So, in some sense, information must precede or foreshadow data: the collection of data or observed facts is possible only if somebody has defined what to measure, how to measure it and, indeed, what one might want to do with it. We are in danger of becoming overly philosophical here, but there is an important point to note. Information implies some context that is supplied only by human thought. The common belief that adding context to data creates information puts the cart before the horse. Data is collected or generated only in support of a human need for information within some context. There are two sources. Data is collected from the external world by machines—from simple rulers to complex radio telescopes—designed and driven by human information needs. And data is generated in the basic processes by which we humans record information, as in the electro-mechanical keys I press in sequence to type the information contained in this text. But, let's keep our eye on actual information for now (which is often a challenge for IT professionals...)

Information (or soft information), in the most fundamental sense, we define simply as the way humans communicate with one another. It's commonly called *content* and also unstructured information. (This latter term is actually an oxymoron—information that has no structure is, by definition, noise!) In contrast to data, soft information is rich in meaning and context—fluid, connected and open to interpretation. Its uses are wide-ranging and diverse. Its sequence of use is varied, and its potential interrelationships numerous. And computers struggle to decode it. Returning to the list of the number of days in each month, we see another three examples of this information in Figure 3-5. Each of these is an increasingly less formal type of information. In (d), we see the information that might appear in a formal business requirements document—although I

(d)

> "As used throughout the business, January counts as 31 days, February 28, March 31, …"

(f)

> "You'll be paid in arrears on the last day of each month…."

(e)

> "Thirty days hath September,
> April, June, and November.
> All the rest have thirty-one,
> Excepting February alone,
> That has twenty-eight days clear,
> And twenty-nine in each leap year."

Figure 3-5:
More soft information sample structures

hope that no programmers would need this defined for them! The mnemonic rhyme shown in (e) is ancient and known to children and adults alike, and is both incomplete in one sense, assuming the names of the other seven months are known, and more extensive in adding a (partial) rule defining the number of days in February in leap years. The final example, case (f), is perhaps most interesting in that it simply assumes the receiver of the information knows the number of days in each month. Here we see a progression from highly formalized to completely informal information, all of it fully person-centric. In business, most data begins life as such person-centric information. An address line in a customer database—data—comes from a sign-up form—information. Order in SAP: data; customer call, email or whatever was used to place the order: soft information. The relevance of this line of thought comes from the fact that data processing has to begin with a set of steps that gets from information to data, a process we know now as requirement analysis, modeling, and application design. In this way, human-oriented soft information is transformed into computer-amenable data and the structure to store it.

Other data originates from machines or physical sensors. Although once largely the preserve of scientific work, data collection from sensors and other machines has become increasingly important in all aspects of life. From biometric implants in medicine to RFID scanners throughout the supply chain, from ATMs to automobile engine management systems, and, above all, the about-to-become ubiquitous smartphone, the machines we use daily generate ever-increasing streams of raw data. Data that flows directly to computers, seldom seen by the human eye until it has been processed and compressed back into something approximating to information suitable for human interpretation and use. Such data, as mentioned earlier, was designed according to the information needs of some human-oriented process. The above considerations, taken together, allow us to define data and information in a coherent and useful way that recognizes that information does *not* necessarily flow from data. Some does, but the more interesting and relevant observation is that data is really a formally structured, computer-oriented subset of information.

3.4   THE MODERN MEANING MODEL—M^3

With this understanding of data and information, as well as the inadequacy of the DIKW pyramid as a basis for understanding how people use information in the biz-tech ecosystem, the need for a new model is apparent. The *modern meaning model (m^3)* defines the relationships between information (and data), knowledge and meaning in terms of where we locate them and their level of structuring. Structure is divided into strict and loose, with the understanding that the axis is really a continuum from highly structured and formally defined, to weakly structured and informally defined. Locus, which ranges from physical, through mental, to relational, shows "where" we find each concept. We now build this model in three steps from the familiar (to IT) physical ground of data and information to the higher, more conceptual levels that exist only in the human mind. My positioning of knowledge and meaning as non-physical provides context as to why they prove so difficult to understand, collect and manage in the business environment.

The physical world of information (and data)

The lowest level of m^3 is shown in Figure 3-6. The physical layer here is, by definition, information—all the information we have ever recorded about the real world and our thoughts about it. From tally sticks and Tweets to cave paintings and digital video, we have progressed from the formal structure of counting through writing to

Figure 3-6:
The m^3 modern
meaning model:
physical locus

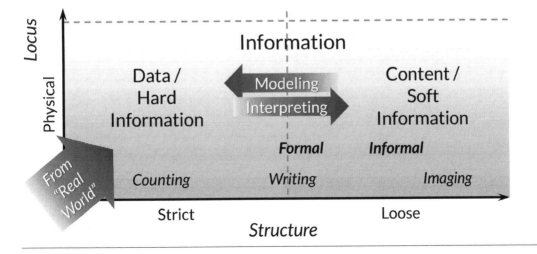

Information—hard or soft

Information: the recorded and stored symbols and signs we use to describe the world and our thoughts about it, and to communicate with each other. Information is mostly digital but also includes paper, books and analogue recordings.

Hard information (data): simple facts—measurements, statistics, the output of physical sensors, etc.—in the form of values, often numeric, and the descriptions of their meaning and usage, distinct from, but explicitly related to, those values. Hard information is optimized for processing by digital computers.

Soft information (content): loosely structured facts, descriptions, meanings and opinions that we as humans use to describe our inner and outer world to ourselves and to one another. Soft information is well matched to how the mind works.

the informal structure of images and video. The spoken word—but only when recorded as audio or transcribed to text—also exists at this level. A key common feature is reproducibility, providing an improved basis for trust that spans discrete interactions as agreements are recorded and provide later proof. As we have seen, data and content are simply subsets of information, hard and soft, optimized for computer processing and human use respectively. And we see the processes by which we can convert—if we wish—from hard to soft information and back again. Interpreting hard data into soft, human-centric information is the essence of business intelligence, but it depends implicitly on human understanding and interpretation of the context in which the data exists, which we explore in Chapter 8. Modeling soft information into data is the opposite process. It also requires careful thought, both as it has evolved—described in Section 3.5—and where it must go, explored in Chapter 8. Both of these processes demand human skill and expertise, characteristics of knowledge, as well as an ability to draw inferences. These more deeply human aspects appear in the higher layers of this model. But first, we must dive even deeper into a seldom recognized characteristic—*information formality*—to understand what really happens when people interact, communicate and exchange information.

Informal precedes the formal

The process of human interaction is seldom fully formalized and the information exchanged often very loosely structured. Consider, for example, a team brought together to investigate and plan the CEO's vision of a new process for engaging customers. The team members come from across the business and IT, bringing their skills and knowledge of process and information needs, approaches and tools. Having been briefed by the CEO, the team members begin to gather documentation on their PCs, or even in a content store or team room tool. As the project progresses, the team members interact with one another, using and creating further information. A new team member is brought onboard. The only information about what has occurred so far is what exists in the team's formal documents. Knowledge about previously discarded options exists only in the heads of the original team, and the new team member wastes time and energy exploring invalid options. But that's just a hint of a bigger problem to come...if only the team could recognize it.

Nonetheless, the team eventually concludes on a new strategy and plan for the process and presents it to the CEO. She declares herself only partially satisfied; in truth, she is very disappointed. Some key information had been lost—the only record of the CEO's briefing is in one participant's handwritten notes and on another's iPad; they are inconsistent and incomplete. The main business participant recalls a conversation with an executive where he picked up a thread that led to the new plan. The CEO bluntly reminds him that she had said the exact opposite in the previous month's business planning call. The team returns to work suitably chastened...

The problem lies in a set of vital information that was somehow undocumented and failed to find its way as a guide for the team's process and progress. We call this *informal information*. It consists almost entirely of soft information generated as part of every process, both formal—project kick-off and plan review meetings, shareholder and board meetings, court proceedings, etc.—and informal—chats at the water cooler, *ad hoc* meetings, phone calls, conferences attended, and so on. In some limited number of these cases, a secretary is appointed and formal notes taken, still often handwritten, which form the agreed record of the meeting—in this case, formal information that is part of the formal process, of which this meeting is a part. But, even in these cases, other meeting attendees may take their own notes, some of which may be important in the future. Court proceedings provide an unexpected clue to what may be required. A stenographer records verbatim everything said by the judge and the lawyers—because it is all potentially important.

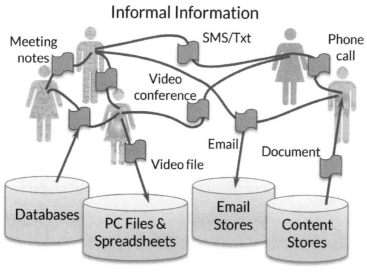

Informal Information

Meeting notes · SMS/Txt · Phone call · Video conference · Email · Document · Video file

Databases · PC Files & Spreadsheets · Email Stores · Content Stores

Formal Information

Figure 3-7:
Formal and informal information

But, in this age of electronic intercourse, communication is increasingly conducted remotely. Phone calls were but a beginning. Instant messages, email, voicemails and webinars all point to the digitization and storage of a growing percentage of our informal communications. Even in cases of physical proximity, digitization is becoming the norm. College students regularly record their lectures on digital recorders. Camera phones snap images or videos of much of the mundane detail of our private lives, while surveillance cameras monitor our public reality. And tablets are replacing handwritten note-taking in meetings. Google Glass, despite significant and real concerns about privacy, is another example of our growing propensity to try to record everything. It is but a small step to imagine that all business meetings could be thus recorded and the informal information stored for reuse and analysis. The specter of Big Brother looms, of course, but in some sense, he already pervades our private and public lives; and the value to be gained in business could be substantial. The legal and ethical issues cannot be underestimated, of course, nor the rights of employees trampled without concern. Real informed consent will be mandatory.

As shown in Figure 3-7, the informal information that is exchanged between consenting adults may exist in both digital and non-digital forms. As physical communication is digitized, the opportunity exists to save (convert) it to formal information, either by the participants themselves or by the system, as in the case of email. Similarly, participants draw formal information from stores, circulate and even modify it in the informal sphere. The boundary between the two categories is thus somewhat blurred. In today's business, informal information is often lost, even when collected, because there is no single place or set of places where it can be collected

ThoughtPoint

The distinction between data and information, which is pivotal to-day as we embrace the biz-tech ecosystem, was almost wholly absent in the early days of computing. Our computing legacy, aptly illustrated in phrases like *data processing* and even *databases*, is deeply data centric. The challenge is to move from an environment where data is structured for computers to a world where information—both formal and informal—is captured and made meaningful to people.

and managed. But, it is the key to understanding and managing the full process by which humans interact, discuss possibilities, and eventually reach consensus, draw conclusions and make decisions. We return to the use (and abuse) of informal information, as well as it potential value for innovation, in Chapter 9.

The mental world of knowledge

The next layer up in Ackoff's pyramid is knowledge. There has been some suggestion in recent years that information is old hat, that knowledge is where IT now needs to focus. The disciples of knowledge management, discussed in Chapter 8, have been at the forefront of such thinking since the mid-1990s. However, the focus has been more on the process of management rather than on what should be managed (Koenig, 2012). Let's focus on what knowledge is and why it's important. Epistemology has long described different types of knowledge (Ryle, 1949), a common classification being:

- Knowledge-that (propositional, descriptive or declarative), e.g. knowing that 2+2 = 4

- Knowledge-how (procedural), e.g. knowing how to play tennis

- Knowledge-of (acquaintance), e.g. knowing of the color blue

Although modern English doesn't distinguish between different forms of knowing, other European languages do. For example, German uses *wissen* for knowing a fact and *kennen* in the sense of knowing by acquaintance or having a working knowledge of something. Knowledge-how and knowledge-of are largely tacit in nature; knowledge-that is closer to explicit. More modern thinking (Bengson & Moffett, 2012) tends to blur the boundaries, but the ideas are discussed in the evolution of the Semantic Web and the role of agents (Thimm, et al., 2012).

Perhaps more familiar to IT practitioners are the concepts of tacit and explicit knowledge (Polanyi, 1966). Tacit knowledge is that which is known but is difficult to explain or communicate to another. The oft-quoted example is riding a bike. You can try to learn by reading a manual or watching a video, but the most effective way is simply through repeated practice. Many valuable workplace skills fall into the same category, including selling, product design, problem solving, and even people management. Explicit knowledge, on the other hand, is more formally structured. If tacit knowledge can be codified and articulated, it becomes explicit, allowing it to be more easily shared and explained. Explicit knowledge is often stated as being easily stored; however, by our definition, it has then become information, either formal or informal. We might thus say that explicit knowledge and soft information are most easily inter-converted, given their similar definitions. But the difference between tacit and explicit knowledge is moot until the explicit knowledge is recorded as information.

Knowledge and learning

In a more practical sense, any discussion of knowledge most usefully begins with how it comes first into existence in its primary locus, the human mind. Figure 3-8 shows knowledge and its relationship to information in the context of m^3, where it forms the mental locus placed in the human mind. With knowledge comes an internally structured understanding of the information we receive about the world, which leads to insights that allow us to piece together various pieces of seemingly unrelated knowledge and practice to be fully human. With the knowledge layer, we are moving closer to forming full-fledged hypotheses about reality and taking action on them. But, we're not there yet. With the unequivocal separation of knowledge as internal from information as recorded, it becomes possible to see the processes that transform one to the other. Explicit knowledge can be documented as information, mostly as soft information such as manuals and books, both hard- and softcopy. Some explicit knowledge can be recorded directly as data in computers. This leads inevitably to learning—seeing, understanding and internalizing information—which is the inverse of documenting.

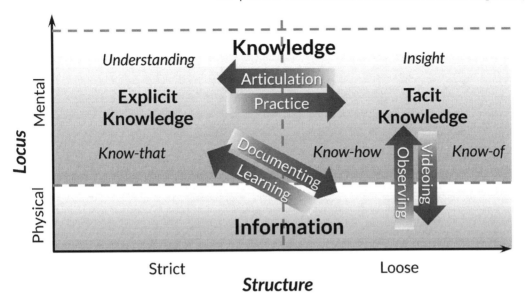

Figure 3-8:
The m³ modern
meaning model:
mental locus

Of particular interest in today's world are the processes of videoing and observing reality that transform tacit knowledge into soft information and *vice versa*. The popularity of video is directly attributable to the removal of formally written information as an intermediate stage and the ability to directly record know-how and know-of. Learning to ride a bike is easier from watching a video than reading a manual, although practice is still the key step. Furthermore, much of what is done in business is a subtle mix of know-that, -how and -of, best shared through a variety of information media and learned through a combination of modalities. Not everything can be communicated solely via YouTube videos! We can apply the adjectives *tacit* and *explicit* to information, but with care. Information in business is explicit; it can be physically stored and managed. Formal and informal information are both forms of explicit information. Tacit information, however, is difficult to position, having defined information as recorded, unless we resort to the quantum zero point field (McTaggart, 2001) as the ultimate source of information. Tacit knowledge, on the other hand, is both unmanaged and unmanageable by an explicit informational environment—at least for the foreseeable future. The existence of such tacit knowledge can be inferred and recorded only from business process and the behaviors of users, but is key to highly innovative, social decision making, as we shall see in Chapter 9.

The interpersonal world of meaning

We come now to the end of our exploration of Ackoff's DIKW pyramid; we are left only with the tip—wisdom. Definitions of the word usually suggest that having experience, knowledge and good judgment are the key contributors to wisdom. We've met experience and knowledge already; judgment—especially good judgment—requires careful consideration. Attributing "good" or "bad" qualities to a judgment leads us far beyond MIS and even knowledge management. To invoke wisdom seems presumptuous. But, if we trace the journey of a decision maker from information gleaned from the environment, through knowledge that internalizes and contextualizes that information to the actual moment of deciding, there are certainly some important steps missing. Knowledge, although certainly internal and personal, still has a connotation of universality to it. We consider—rightly or wrongly—that knowledge has a quality of truth. We believe that knowledge somehow has an objective, justified view of reality embedded in it. But when we move towards the moment of decision making, we also recognize that one person's decision may be very different than another's even though they have equivalent knowledge to hand. We could call that judgment, but it sounds...well, judgmental. Let's just call it *meaning*. The meaning we, individually, apply to the knowledge we have. Simply put, it is the stories we make up and tell ourselves about what we know, what we don't and, more importantly, what we can or should do about it. And note the plural; we may tell ourselves many different and diametrically opposed stories about the same thing.

Figure 3-9:
Athena, Greek goddess of wisdom, *Museo Nazionale Romano*

Consider an agreement on terms and conditions for payment for services provided that was entered into via electronic communications such as instant messaging or email. When the services have been delivered, a disagreement arises over the payment terms—the supplier understands it was to be payment on delivery, the customer believes it was 30 days. Leaving aside legal considerations (the amount involved is less than the lawyer's fee to even write a letter), how can this be resolved? The supplier has a record of the messages sent and may be able to prove they were received, but did the customer read them? Did she understand them? Did she assume that the terms didn't apply because of some prior interaction? Today's IT systems store the information that was physically sent and received. The knowledge that the buyer and seller have may well be equivalent. But, the meanings—the stories they tell themselves—can be very different. Our use of IT systems in the biz-tech ecosystem will have to reflect and deal with this level of subtlety so that support for decision making can be raised to a new level.

As seen in Figure 3-10, meaning transforms the four-quadrant model of Figure 3-8 into something far more complex. What could have been the standard consultant's 2 x 2 becomes quintile. Meaning tops out the structure, independent of the lower divisions between strict and loose structure. Meaning, while still of the mind, transcends the mind to an interpersonal locus, where we recognize the mental processes themselves in operation, the inner observer in relation to the knowledge observed, as well as the social context that relates me to you. We move silently from basic knowing-that,

> ## Knowledge and meaning
>
> *Knowledge: an ever-evolving collection of experience, values, understanding and insight that provides a framework for evaluating and incorporating the input of our senses about the world around us. It originates, is stored and used in the minds of people. In organizations, it can be inferred from the routines, processes, practices and norms of people's behaviors and actions. Knowledge itself cannot be physically recorded and stored; it must first be transformed into information.*
>
> *Meaning: the interpretations that people put on "reality", why things have happened and how other people perceive them. These stories differ from person to person, influenced by their entire knowledge, experience and history. Two people with identical information and knowledge may infer radically different meanings from the same circumstances.*

knowing-how, and knowing-of all the way to knowing-why. At this level in the m^3 model, we are far beyond databases and content stores, query and search. If this were a standard IT text, we would not go there. But, the biz-tech ecosystem demands that we delve more broadly and deeply into the "human" side of IT. The processes linking knowledge and meaning—mentoring and sense-making—are personal and interpersonal. They form part of the diverse topic of sense-making in information science, organizational theory and human-computer interaction that we probe in Chapter 9.

Ackoff's DIKW pyramid has provided a starting point for much of IT's thinking about information since its inception in 1989. In the context of the emerging biz-tech ecosystem, its shortcomings are apparent. I propose the modern meaning model, m^3, as a replace-

Figure 3-10:
The m^3 modern
meaning model:
interpersonal locus

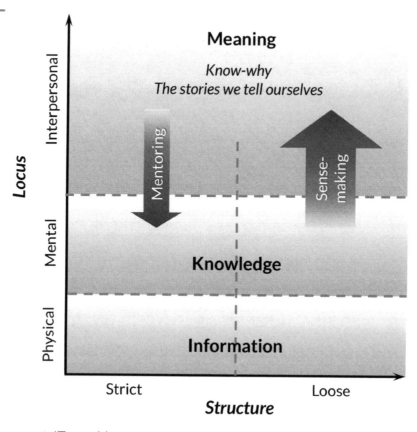

ment. IT provides a more realistic understanding of the relationship between data and information, as well as more useful definitions of the upper layers that enable new approaches to supporting the human processes that lie at the heart of decision making. As such, it underpins the relationship between the information and people layers of the IDEAL architecture.

3.5 DATABASE DAEMONS AND DELICATE DATA MODELS

The preceding section declared, perhaps contrary to popular opinion among IT people, that data is actually a subset of information and that data emerges into view from information almost exclusively today at the behest of computers. That popular opinion is a legacy of the history of computing and how data made the evolutionary leap from flat files to databases. This leap was facilitated and even driven by the switch to random-access storage, beginning in the 1960s. The term *data base* (with a space) originates as far back as 1964 (McGee, 1981) as a collection of data shared by users of time-sharing systems. The ability—and, indeed, the need—to write, find and rewrite individual data items rather than entire files represented a fundamental change in thinking about how data should be handled. Such thinking also included the concept of integrated data processing—consolidating the data requirements of multiple applications onto a common source.

Database management systems (DBMS) grew dramatically through the 1970s, focusing specifically on transaction processing environments and their need for rapid and reliable access to and update of specific, individual data items. These systems, based on hierarchical or network (CODASYL) models, included market leaders Cincom TOTAL and IBM IMS, as well as Cullinane IDMS and Software AG ADABAS (Bergin & Haigh, 2009), and remained the preferred foundation for production systems until the early 1990s. While based in part on an emerging logical, business-oriented view of data structures, these early database implementations often maintained strong links to the physical data storage structure. Such business-oriented views mark an early recognition that the data stored in computers stands for some form of business information at a higher level. Given the limited processing power and storage of that time, the focus remained on data—more efficient both for storage and processing—at the expense of information. It proved difficult to shield users from this tradeoff, and, despite early enthusiasm to make data available directly to managers and analysts, access and usage remained in the hands of programmers and an emerging class of database administrators.

While theoreticians and academics continued to press for a clearer separation of logical and physical models of data, the hierarchical and network database market grew rapidly through the 1970s and well into the next decade. The success of these databases is testified by their continued use even today in systems handling the largest volumes of transactions with the fastest required response times, such as banking ATMs and airline reservation systems. Nonetheless, 1970 saw the development of a new data model, which enabled the logical and physical levels to be finally divorced, with the publication of Dr. E.F. Codd's seminal paper (Codd, 1970) introducing the relational model. The pure mathematical basis of this model allowed the development of a complete, comprehensive relational algebra describing the fundamental operations possible on the data, as well as the mathematically valid outcomes of these operations. Its simple and elegant structure, at least at the highest level—of a table[3] of data arranged in rows and columns—was instantly understandable to many business users, especially those in financial departments, whose daily work consisted of juggling the equivalent structure of rows and columns of numbers.

In 1973, Dr. Eugene Wong and Prof. Michael Stonebraker initiated INGRES, an academic project to build a relational database at UC Berkeley. By the early 1980s, the project had spawned a number of commercial databases including Ingres, Sybase and Informix. IBM set up a relational research project, System R, in the early 1970s, leading to the commercial systems SQL/DS in 1981 and DB2 in 1983. The Oracle database also had its genesis in the early 1970s, with Relational Software Inc. (later renamed Oracle) bringing its first commercial release to market in 1979. In the same year, Teradata was founded with the goal of building a massively parallel relational database, culminating in its first product release in 1984 (White, 2004). This blossoming led directly to the dominance of relational databases in the 1990s and 2000s, some consequences of which we discuss in Chapter 6, when we explore big data.

The first data models take the stage

Of more importance to our current discussion of information and data, Codd's relational model also led to a widely accepted approach to and notation for a more logical level of data representation: entity-relationship (ER) modeling (Chen, 1976). In simple terms, an entity is defined as *"a collection of information about something that the business deems important and worthy of capture"* (Hoberman, 2009). A relationship, as the name implies, represents how two entities relate. Both entities and relationships have attributes, characteristics that can be described or measured. Entities can be considered the *nouns*, relationships the *verbs* defining how the nouns work on each other, and attributes the *adjectives* describing the entities or the *adverbs* qualifying the relationships.

---

[3] Codd wrote in terms of mathematical relations and tuples, as well as rows and columns. The term *table* appeared later in the System R project, also at IBM.

Since Peter Chen's paper, much work has been done in data modeling by Charles Bachman, James Martin, and others, leading to a variety of diagramming styles, shown in Figure 3-11. The original diamond representation of a relationship has collapsed into the line joining the entities—undoubtedly a cleaner convention, but one that deemphasizes the reality that relationships must also be instantiated and may have associated attributes. Other differences relate to how the cardinality of the relationship—one-to-one, one-to-many, etc.—is shown. These concepts and notations continue to provide the basis and methodology for tooling used today to analyze business information and design data structures (Simsion, 2007), (Hoberman, 2009).

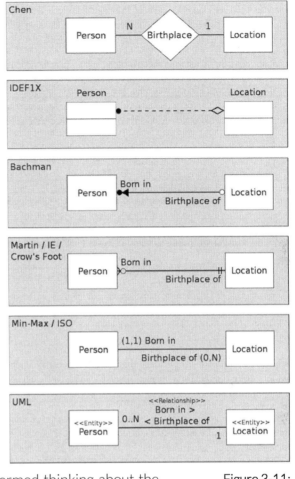

Figure 3-11: Entity-relationship diagramming notations

So, what does this add to our understanding of data and information? First, we see that the technology has evolved to a stage where physical and logical representations of data and information are distinct and separate. This allows informed thinking about the potential differences between them. Second, the theoretical foundation of modeling emerges, providing the language and methods to describe the meaning, structure and relationships required to carry our understanding, description and representation of the real world over into the world of computers. Modeling, beyond transforming soft to hard information, provides a foundation for linking human knowledge of the business to information and provides a method to assure that the thought and expertise at the core of business can be clearly and reliably stored as information.

Third, we see a potentially limiting assumption that has crept from the world of computer storage into our thinking about information meaning, structure and relationships. Sequential data files are very inflexible in structure and even in content: once defined and written, data becomes very difficult to change. In databases, first hierarchical/network and then relational, data content is very flexible, but structural inflexibility persists to varying degrees. This assumption of *persistence* in meaning and structure becomes obvious every time we need to modify a database schema to reflect an unanticipated change in the real world. As described by Chen, entity-relationship modeling was conceived as *"a basis for a unified view of data"* and *"for unification of different views of data: the network model, the relational model, and the entity set model"* (my emphasis); it thus carries a residue of inflexibility as we try to bridge from a highly changeable human world of information to highly inflexible computer representations of data. As we shall see when we revisit modeling and explore the concept of insight in Chapter 8, this last assumption is false; it emerges from the computer orientation that drives IT's view of data and information, and from the restrictions of older technology.

Finally, we note an emerging challenge. Modeling today starts from the soft information of business requirements and creates data structures that can validly represent the content and relationships needed to support the business needs. Most good modelers recognize that this process excludes certain information and context as superflous to current needs. In the exploding world of big data, we are faced with (i) having to extract a "model" from existing data arriving from beyond the enterprise, where the context of its creation differs from ours, (ii) doing such "modeling"—via text analytics, for example—on the fly as variable and changing information structures arrive and (iii) applying the model across a

ThoughtPoint

Data files, databases and data modeling carry within them a belief in persistent, structured data that differs dramatically from the reality of human-oriented information, especially in the context of externally-sourced big data. Such information may often be of unstable and arbitrary structure and subject to ongoing change of meaning and usage in the business. The words *information* and *data* are often used loosely and interchangeably, a practice that must change. A new level of clarity in definition and new tools are required if we are to respond adequately to the ongoing explosion of information types and volumes used in the biz-tech ecosystem.

diverse and changing array of storage environments, ranging from strictly structured databases to loosely structured content stores and Web sources. Current tools and techniques are still struggling to address these challenges, as we see in Chapter 8.

3.6   THE IMPORTANCE OF BEING INFORMATION[4]

Our exploration so far of the meaning and relationship of data and information—and their rather unorthodox relative positioning—aims to uncover some fundamental characteristics of information that will enable its valid, realistic and innovative use in the growing biz-tech ecosystem. We have focused on very traditional business data from common operational processes to provide familiar ground to most IT professionals today. However, to fully explore the implications of the distinction we drew between hard and soft information, we need to look beyond traditional business data to the exploding world of big data. Here we find examples of other types of information that illustrate the range of possibilities today's business must consider.

My earlier *Mind over Matter model* of information (Devlin, 2011) is expanded in Figure 3-12 to provide a novel and unique way of understanding the nuances of hard and soft information, moving from the hardest data at the bottom layer to the softest at the top. The model consists of two triangles placed tip-to-tip. Broadly speaking, the bottom triangle represents data, the hard information ultimately gleaned from the physical world, the world of matter. As we move to the top triangle, we enter the realm of the mind—soft information originating from and representing the way we humans perceive the world and interact socially within it. It is more subtle, however, as these two worlds also cross over, as depicted by the arrows, and will become clear as we define the layers in more detail. The relative widths of the layers very loosely indicate the data volumes and numbers of records in each category.

Starting at the lowest level, we find *raw* data—signals from electronic sensors connected to computers and the Internet. Such

---

[4] *The Importance of Being Earnest, A Trivial Comedy for Serious People* by Oscar Wilde, first performed in 1895 and considered the culmination of his career.

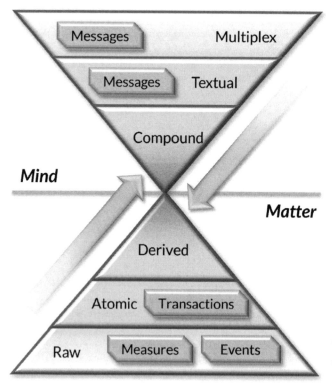

Figure 3-12:
The Mind over Matter model of information

physical event data includes measures and events such as location, temperature, velocity, flow rate, event count, chemical signal, and many more. This data has grown to enormous volumes in scientific research and the Internet of Things in recent years. Beyond the "pure" environmental events/measures mentioned above, raw data also includes physical events generated by human actions, such as mouse clicks or buttons pressed on an ATM. Like environmental data, these too are simple electrical signals to which meaning is eventually assigned, either individually or in combination. Raw data is the hardest of information, at least in its initial production and storage. It consists solely of values whose meaning is determined by and known only to the physical machines (and, of course, their designers) that recorded them. However, when transmitted to an enterprise system, it may be structured into `name : value` pairs in a binary or textual format. This is a basic form of compound information, as discussed below.

When such raw Matter data is interpreted in some meaningful way by the human Mind, it becomes interesting in the commercial world, and is often called transactions. *Atomic* data is thus comprised of physical events, meaningfully combined in the context of some human interaction and represents transactions. For example, a combined set of location, velocity and G-force measurements in a specific pattern and time from an automobile monitoring box may indicate an accident. A magnetic card reading of account details followed by a count of bills issued at an ATM is clearly a cash withdrawal transaction. More sophisticated combinations include call detail records (CDRs) in telecommunication systems, banking transactions and so on. There's nothing new in this type of data. Telecommunications companies, financial institutions and web retailers / service providers have created and gathered it to run their businesses. They have integrated and analyzed it since the early days of data warehousing to report on the business and for insight into customer behavior. Until the advent of big data, atomic data was the lowest level of information most businesses ever considered. Atomic data is hard information, highly structured, with its contextual meaning separately stored for ease of computer use.

Derived data, created through mathematical, logical and programmatic manipulation of atomic data, is generally used to create a more meaningful view of business information to humans. For example, banking transactions can be accumulated and combined to create account status and balance information. Transaction data can be summarized into averages or sums at times of interest, such as month end. Some of these processes—averaging is the most obvious example—result in a loss or distortion of detailed data and must therefore be used with care, and atomic level data preserved. Derived data is also hard information, largely numerical and keyword data, well-structured for use by computers and amenable to standard statistical processing. Derived data, as well as atomic and even raw data, can be transformed into graphs and other visual representations, at which stage they cross the line and become information of the Mind. Similarly, although atomic and derived data is placed below the boundary, it should be clear that human Mindfulness is required to assign meaning to both types of data.

This leads us to a key transitional layer of our double triangle: *compound* information. This could perhaps be seen as a vague boundary class between hard and soft information although—as should be clear by now—this is truly a continuum rather than a binary definition. Compound information is most easily described

> **Measures, events and messages**
>
> *Transactions—legally binding business activities—are the staple of traditional operational and informational systems. The biz-tech ecosystem deals with three additional, antecedent activities.*
>
> ***Measures:*** *the output of devices monitoring the ongoing state of physical systems. Measures are raw, hard information.*
>
> ***Events:*** *instant changes in the state of physical systems, captured by measuring devices as raw, hard information.*
>
> ***Messages:*** *communications created by and for people recorded in any digital format. Messages are textual or multiplex, soft information.*

in terms of the layers below and above it. In contrast to the three data layers in the triangle of matter below, compound information consists of distinct sets of values and structural, syntactic and model definitions in the one structure. This approach provides more flexibility in content than the hard information/data classes below it, while maintaining more processing-friendliness than the textual and multiplex classes above. Compound information actually differs from the other two classes in the triangle of Mind only by the degree and transparency of its structuring into content and description parts. A common format for storing compound information is *XML (eXtensible Markup Language)*, discussed further in Section 8.5. The process of converting XML into relational database records is one example of the transition across the Mind/Matter boundary. An emerging format, particularly for big data, is *JavaScript Object Notation (JSON)*, described in Section 6.4. Metadata is the most significant subset of compound information. This places metadata as part of the data-information continuum; not something to push out to one side of the information architecture as a separate box, as seen in other information architectures. Metadata is discussed in detail in Section 3.8. Compound information is also prevalent in big data. Social media information is a combination of compound relationship information and soft textual (and even image/video) data from sources such as Twitter, Facebook and so on. The query strings—text strings structured as `name : value` pairs and similar constructs—created by web servers and used to analyze user behavior on websites (see Section 6.2), is also compound data.

The next layer up—*textual* information—is exactly as the name implies: documents, emails, Tweets and so on. In textual information, the complexities of language, grammar, style and usage long accessible only to humans are yielding gradually to computer processing. Statistical analysis and content/context extraction in text analytics tools are increasingly used to create the compound information and even atomic data in the lower layers of the model for use in the operational and decision-making processes of the business.

Multiplex information, the top layer, consists of image, video and audio. This is the ultimate in soft information, rich in context, with values and context deeply intermixed. It forms a large part of the big data scene, as we shall see in Chapter 6, much of it generated in the external environment by consumers on smartphones, digital recorders, cameras and so on. However, there are also internal sources such as call center recordings, images of products for websites or damaged goods in insurance claims, security videos, and even the output of BI tools mentioned above. Multiplex information exists in increasing volumes of very large files that often require specialized processing to extract usable content and context. Facial and a wide range of other pattern recognition in image and video is the subject of extensive, ongoing research to create or improve the necessary tools. Voice recognition for audio to create textual representations is another form of content extraction from multiplex information that has seen big advances in recent years.

Multiplex and textual information are often called content or un-structured data/information. The term *content* has some validity, focusing on the rich content and extensive context often found in these types of information. Unfortunately, the more popular *un-structured* terminology is deeply misleading. These information types conform to well-defined structures: at a high level, they contain distinct fields of content and structural information that enable computers and other devices to process them and render them on screens; at a lower level, the content and structure may only be easily discernible to human perception.

The Mind over Matter model clearly shows that information spans a continuum of structural complexity from simple, raw numbers or text at the lowest level to large, intricate compositions at the top. While the level of structuring is important for computer processing, of more interest for understanding the information is the spectrum of support for contextual descriptions that make raw data values meaningful. These characteristics are closely interrelated and form the basis for describing one aspect of the conceptual architecture of the biz-tech ecosystem.

3.7   IDEAL ARCHITECTURE (I): INFORMATION, STRUCTURE/CONTEXT DIMENSION

The discussion of the previous section leads us directly to the first component of the information layer of the IDEAL conceptual architecture introduced in Chapter 1. These components are best described as dimensions or axes of the information, process and people layers, respectively. The information layer consists of a three-dimensional space where each axis is a carefully chosen combination of characteristics that together provide a spectrum of sourcing, usage or management considerations. These characteristics have been combined for two reasons. First, they can be seen to be interdependent to some degree, although in common usage, they are often treated separately. Second, my ability to think about or draw n-dimensional spaces where n>3 is very limited!

The first dimension we consider emerges from the discussion in this chapter around the concepts of hard and soft information, and the way that descriptions, or context, are separated from values when we move from information to data. The resulting *structure/context (SC)* dimension is shown in Figure 3-13, and the classes defined are precisely those described in the previous section. As with the other dimensions we introduce in succeeding chapters, these classes are loosely defined, and this axis actually portrays a continuum of levels of structure and context, rather than discrete, separate categories.

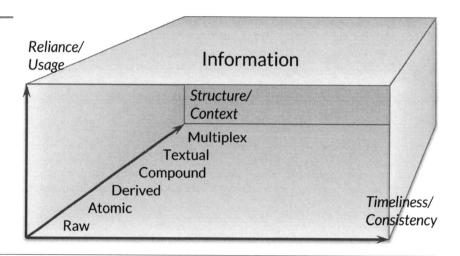

Figure 3-13: Structure/ context dimension of information

Interpreting this figure most simply, we move from hard data to soft information as we travel from left to right along the axis. This is the "structuredness" characteristic of information. Moving from right to left, contextual richness is stripped away (and stored, in part, elsewhere) in the modeling process described in Section 3.5. Simplifying Figure 3-12 into a one-dimensional axis hides some of the richness we saw in the previous section. However, it allows us to broaden our view to include other vital characteristics of information that will be introduced in succeeding chapters.

3.8   METADATA IS TWO FOUR-LETTER WORDS

Finally, we come to metadata. BI gurus and information architects may wonder why it took us so long. My rationale is that the concept is a misnomer, perhaps even a distraction to clear thinking on the topic of information. But, with a clearer understanding of hard and soft information, formal and informal information—as well as data—in the real world, we can begin.

Metadata is at once the overhyped star and lost orphan of information management. Unlike data warehouse and BI, metadata attracts no loud claims of paternity. Apparently born in an obscure research report on extending programming language concepts by Philip Bagley of the University City Science Center, Philadelphia for the US Air Force (Bagley, 1968), metadata first came out in the mid-1980s, a self-effacing debutante with the moniker of "data about data", as data dictionaries became popular (Dolk & Kirsch, 1987). As a definition, this is at best overly simplistic. In the context of the earlier discussion on DIKM, it is misleading. Data, as a very restricted class of information, is ill-suited to the type of description we expect about data. My own early definition, *"Data that describes the meaning and structure of business data, as well as how it is created, accessed and used,"* (Devlin, 1997) attempted more clarity on the scope and content of three types of metadata:

- *Build-time:* created and used in application and database design and development

- *Control:* actively controlling the operation of the warehouse environment, particularly timeliness and utilization metadata

- *Usage:* supporting business users' understanding and use of data for business purposes

David Marco went further a few years later, declaring that metadata (or meta data, as Marco prefers) covers: *"...all physical data (contained in software and other media) and knowledge (contained in employees and various media) from inside and outside an organization, including information about the physical data, technical and business processes, rules and constraints of the data, and structures of the data used by a corporation"* (Marco, 2000). Here we see the introduction of knowledge in employees' heads as a metadata component—perhaps extreme, and posing some difficulties in its extraction and use! Clearly, a well-formed definition of metadata is difficult to pin down. And yet, there clearly exists a set of information that describes and defines some other information, as we saw in Section 3.2. Therein lies the problem. The thinking in that section is characteristic of data management professionals, database designers and programmers who must build the technology; and, as we also saw, who struggled with severe restrictions in the storage and processing power available in the computer systems of the 1960s, when most of this foundational thinking occurred.

Metadata emerges as a separate, if ill-defined, concept when we try to (i) understand and document—model—the meaning of information and (ii) create structures—files and databases—in which to store and process that information. It also appears when we build and run all the processes that create, manage or use information in a technical or business context. Making a physical reality of an ill-defined concept is challenging. In the case of simple files, metadata is actually stored in design documents for the programs that act on the information and, if you're lucky, in the comment fields in the code. Of course, it is also inherent in the code itself. In relational databases, metadata resides in system tables as table and column names of business information, augmented by any descriptive information the database administrators deign to enter. In other types of databases, such as XML stores discussed in Chapter 8, the metadata is mixed (in an easily recognizable way) with the business information values. And of course, much metadata about hard information is stored in data dictionaries and metadata repositories.

But the problem is bigger. Digital photographs, for example, are documented by metadata (called Exif—exchangeable image file format—data) that covers everything from date and time, camera settings, and user-entered descriptions to geolocation data. One may reasonably ask which of these characteristics are metadata and which are "business information" for the photographer. As defined, metadata also exists implicitly in soft information; recognizing it depends on context and on people. In a movie, for example, a series of opening shots of the

> ## Context-setting information
>
> *Context moves us from information, through knowledge, to meaning. Context-setting information provides the background to each piece of information, to every process component and to all the people that constitute the business. Every piece of information adds context to something else; it is all context setting.*

Eiffel Tower, the Seine, and Notre Dame easily sets the location metadata as Paris for the majority of Western people but may fail abysmally for the residents of an African township. The increasingly sophisticated algorithms for mining text and images automatically extract metadata, isolating names, addresses, and so on from freeform text, or identifying people via facial recognition. The list is long and growing. And the distinction between metadata and information becomes well-nigh impossible to justify or even articulate. Metadata is clearly important. But, as defined today, it presents us with several problems:

- Business users and other laypeople don't understand how or, indeed, if it differs from the business data they really need

- Data management professionals debate its scope in the manner of Scotus and Ockham in medieval Scholasticism

- Segregated from business data, architects and vendors have devised separate approaches to gather, store and manage it

- Knowing which of these separate systems contains a specific item of information can be a challenge, as can any requirement to use them together beyond their original design

- BI implementations have included distinct metadata projects that, often as not, fail for lack of time or business support

The solution sounds perhaps too simplistic: reintegrate metadata—descriptive information—into the larger information scope. Looking

Figure 3-14
The Mars Climate Orbiter, lost in 1999, in perhaps the costliest metadata failure in history

at its structure, we should recognize that it is certainly not data. It is information. We must stop thinking of it as conceptually different from the other information it describes. Let's call it *context-setting information (CSI)* because that's exactly what it does. Metadata is simply one part, comprised of many components, of the information resource of the business. We must treat its management and storage, use and access with exactly the same approaches we use for "business information". Metadata is a combination of two four-letter words that confounds business users and confuses IT. It is unlikely to die, but I will use it only with great care in the rest of the book and reiterate that it is simply context-setting information.

The costs—hardware, software and project—of gathering metadata can be significant. The benefits, particularly in BI projects, have often been difficult to quantify. Recognizing and treating it as the business information it truly is can help to emphasize both its costs and benefits. The catastrophic consequences of one organization's failure to manage metadata offer a salutary lesson. On September 23rd, 1999, NASA's Mars Climate Orbiter broke up in the Martian atmosphere when a braking maneuver took the spacecraft too close to the planet. The cause of the accident was identified shortly afterwards as metadata. The orbiter software was designed to accept instructions for maneuvering in the metric system; the command software on Earth sent instructions in imperial units. The cost exceeded $325 million (NASA, 1999).

It is also deeply ironic that as I finalized this section in June, 2013 metadata finally achieved public notice and notoriety when it was reported widely that the National Security Agency (NSA), an arm of the US Government, was collecting the metadata—originating and dialed numbers, time and duration of calls, cell phone identification numbers and more—about all calls carried by Verizon in the United States and abroad (Greenwald, 2013). By designating the material as metadata rather than communications (information), the government was able to legally argue that no individual warrants were required for its access. Must I reiterate that metadata is—purely and simply—information, used in in some circumstances to define context? And at other times, like any other business information.

3.9   IN PRACTICE—FOCUSING IT ON INFORMATION

The data processing department has long ago reimaged itself as the information technology, IT, function. Unfortunately, the focus has been on the *T* and for all the difference it has made, *data* and *processing* might as well still be part of the name. The historical weight of highly structured data files and databases seems too heavy to easily put down. To begin walking the path of Business unIntelligence, both business and IT must now place their attention on information in all its forms. The initial emphasis is mainly for IT:

✓ Expand the focus of data management to include all soft information generated in internal processes, especially information that supports or enhances traditional data stores. Explore sources, document ownership and relationships. Focus on how the information is used in decision making, especially at senior levels of the organization in tactical and strategic decisions.

✓ Based on the experience gained in the previous point, expand the exercise to externally sourced information. Document how and where information crosses organizational boundaries, noting how misunderstandings can be introduced.

✓ Build a high level model for soft information and integrate it with any existing enterprise data model(s).

✓ Study the creation and use of informal information in teams across the enterprise and note best practices. Prototype new approaches around team rooms, content stores, collaborative and other software.

✓ Instigate formal processes around gathering and managing metadata—context-setting information—spanning all areas of the business (not just BI). A center of excellence may be appropriate in the early stages to create focus. However, in the medium to long term, this should be merged into activities that focus today on "business information", recalling that metadata is simply a subset of information.

✓ Refocus and reenergize any existing data governance activities to include all soft information. This may be the time to rename it to *information governance*, especially if previous data governance initiatives have proven unsuccessful.

✓ Educate personnel across all levels in both business and IT on the growing importance and value of information. Enhancing and expanding such education should be an ongoing exercise as business goals shift and/or technologies advance.

3.10   CONCLUSIONS

The old DIKW hierarchy and knowledge pyramid have been widely used over the past two decades to depict the information continuum dealt with by IT. They proved sufficient when IT dealt only or mainly with data—the most basic and formalized representation of reality. The emerging biz-tech ecosystem demands a broader and more nuanced view of information and data, and how humans define and describe the world around them. It becomes clear that the old idea that information emerges from data is no longer tenable. Data, it turns out, is a stripped-down, highly structured form of information best suited to the needs of arithmetic and logical calculation that is the forte of computers. Data is but a very particular—hard—subset of information, and metadata an even more constrained—but softer—subclass of the same superset. Information, in all its forms, formal and informal, as the recorded and stored symbols and signs we use to describe and communicate our thoughts about the world, is the foundation.

The role reversal of data and information is driven by the fact that we are moving from a world where computers were primarily extraordinary calculators for accountants to one where information systems also do precisely that—*systematize information*—as the physical storage mechanism for all formal and informal information. Both ordered and orderly, as well as messy and disordered. With m^3, we introduce a modern model of the definitions and interrelationships of data and information, knowledge and meaning. This model recognizes these as different constructs, and although it is possible and often desirable to transform between them, they do not exist in a hierarchy, either by containment or by relative percentages.

As we begin to explore the structure and context that exists within and around information and data, it becomes clear that these inter-related characteristics form one of the key dimensions by which information is classified. The Mind over Matter model, and its sim-plification as one dimension of the information space in the IDEAL conceptual architecture, provides a novel approach to understand-ing information and a basis for developing practical tools and tech-niques to manage and process it.

ROADMAP

→ *BI's centralized legacy:* MIS and DSS thinking emerged in the 1960s and 1970s based on the premise that the data needed could be sourced from strictly controlled operational applications and managed in a centralized manner

→ *Personal computing triumphs:* The growth of PCs and spreadsheets beginning in the 1980s gave business users the power to create new data and to control its manipulation and distribution

→ *Mobile and Web complete the transition:* Sourcing and processing of management support information is now largely distributed and decentralized, raising questions of reliability

→ *The information reliability matrix:* The trust than we can place in information depends on its sourcing and processing prior to our use of it

→ *Information reliance/usage and trust horizon:* Positioning information on this axis allows us to judge the types of decisions that should be based upon it, potential problems that might arise and the costs of mitigating them; reliance/usage classes are: universal, global, enterprise, local, personal, vague and unknown

CHAPTER 4
FACT, FICTION OR FABRICATION

"Anyone who says businessmen deal in facts, not fiction, has never read old five-year projections."	Malcolm Forbes
"In this treacherous world nothing is the truth nor a lie. Everything depends on the color Of the crystal through which one sees it"	Pedro Calderón de la Barca

In Chapter 3, we probed the DIKW pyramid for today's understanding of the relationship between data and information and found it wanting. We now poke at data from a different direction to question how accurately it represents reality and how we come to believe it to be so. This has much to do with its provenance. Information is quite literally food for thought, and, as information becomes ever more central to our business and personal lives, we ignore questions of its source and reliability at increasing risk. In the developed world, we take growing notice of the provenance of the food we consume for bodily sustenance, from farm and factory to the fork that feeds us. Where did it originate and how was it processed? By what means did it get to us and through whose hands did it pass? Is it still pure, or has it been somehow contaminated? Will it nourish or poison, feed us or fail us?

Our current diet of data/information to support decision making dates to the 1960s, and it's there we must start to examine its sources and analyze its processing on its way to managers' tables. In those halcyon days, it all seemed so simple to build management information systems from the burgeoning centralized operational databases to mainframe-based reporting and analysis systems. But with the spread of PCs in the early 1980s, followed by the emergence of laptops and the Internet in the 1990s and fully mobile devices in the 2000s, fast food rapidly became the norm. The issues of information provenance were growing rapidly; they continue to loom large today. The ongoing information explosion on the Web increases the urgency to address this issue. Information governance and management in the biz-tech ecosystem move from nice-to-have programs to live issues that can, in some instances, determine if business executives end up behind bars—of the iron variety, rather than those stocked with good malt whiskey.

The issue is not confined to business, of course. Social networking and Web 2.0 have enabled millions of us to become publishers of everything from records of the mundane events of our daily lives to our unedited and uncensored opinions about each and every event or person we wish to praise or, more often, put down. But, as fast as we have become publishers, even faster have we become consumers of this junk food—an uncontrolled, unlimited data feed.

This chapter explores the reliability of information as a representation of reality from mainframe to mobile device. From corporate-controlled asset to personal property. From a reliable, trustworthy and, arguably, always one-sided view of reality to a multi-faceted but unreliable kaleidoscope of conflicting truths...or opinions. What we seek is nothing less than a model of trust in information.

4.1   QUESTIONS AND ANSWERS

D ecision support systems (DSS), a term dating from 1971, is the discipline that covers all aspects of supporting decision makers with the relevant facts and tools they need via information technology. Prof. Dan Power provides a comprehensive history of the evolution of DSS (Power, 2009) from its definition by Michael Scott Morton in 1964 at Harvard University (Scott Morton, 1967) to recent times. He defines five classes: model-, data-, communications-, document- and knowledge-driven. Among these, model-driven DSS—access to and use of optimization and/or simulation models—and data-driven DSS—access to and manipulation of time-series data—both dating to the mid-1960s, are our initial focus. In these two categories, we can see the nascent shapes of today's analytics and BI, respectively. Model-driven DSS focuses on models for production planning and scheduling, financial planning and budgeting, and so on, characterized by the use of interactive tools applied over limited data volumes. In the mainframe era, interactivity was rare, confined to the largest and most research-oriented organizations. As a result, it was only with the emergence of PCs and spreadsheets in the 1980s that this aspect of DSS blossomed, as we shall see in Section 4.3. Document-driven DSS relates to document retrieval and analysis, while knowledge-driven DSS focuses on recommendation and so-called *expert systems*. Communications-driven DSS uses networks and communications to facilitate collaboration and communication in support of decision making. We return to these three types in Chapters 8 and 9.

Management information systems

Management information systems (MIS), a term that closely corresponds to Power's data-driven DSS, became a *"growing preoccupation of operations researchers and management scientists"* (Ackoff, 1967) and a favored solution to management problems in the mid-1960s. In its heyday through the 1970s and early 1980s, MIS could be described in three steps: (i) collect all significant data from existing operational applications, (ii) distribute comprehensive, printed reports of that data to managers, and (iii) provide specific skilled business specialists with *ad hoc* data exploration facilities to support management as needed.

> ### Operational or informational
>
> *Terms used to denote two types of usage, data, systems and applications.*
>
> *Operational: running the business in real time, based on current data, handling large volumes of simple read/write transactions. Also known as transactional, systems of record, and online transaction processing (OLTP).*
>
> *Informational: managing the business based on reliable, stable and historical, data using unplanned, complex, read-only queries. Also called BI, analytical and online analytical processing (OLAP).*
>
> *In the biz-tech ecosystem and with the growth of big data, the distinction between the two is rapidly fading.*

By the early 1970s, with ever increasing volumes of business transactions stored in numerous and diverse files and burgeoning hierarchical and network databases, it's unsurprising that assorted managers, analysts and bean counters began to imagine new possibilities for assessing business performance and supporting decision making. As we saw in the previous chapter, these data structures were neither easily understood by users nor particularly amenable to *ad hoc* query. Furthermore, with the limited processing power and memory of even the largest computers of the time, applications were tightly tuned to maximize performance and minimize response times. IT departments were thus understandably reluctant to allow MIS users direct access to the operational data, even had

```
**************************************************
* PROGRAMA EXEMPLO 001
**************************************************
PARM DEBUG(PMAP, DMAP)
*-------------------------------------------------
* DECLARACAO DE ARQUIVOS E RESPECTIVAS AREAS DE I/O
*-------------------------------------------------
FILE SYSREL PRINTER
FILE ENTRA
AL            1 80 A
AL-NOME       1 15 A
AL-DATA      16 08 N
AL-SALDO     24 10 N 2
FILE SAIDA
AG            1 80 A
*-------------------------------------------------
* DECLARACAO DE VARIAVEIS DE TRABALHO
*-------------------------------------------------
WLL      W   7   N
WGG      W   7   N
*-------------------------------------------------
* DECLARACAO DE PROCEDIMENTOS
*-------------------------------------------------
*-------------
* ROTINA PRINCIPAL
*-------------
JOB INPUT ENTRA FINISH ESTATIS
WLL = WLL + 1
PRINT RELAT
AG = AL
PUT SAIDA
WGG = WGG + 1
GO TO JOB
*-------------
* ROTINA DE FINALIZACAO
*-------------
ESTATIS. PROC
DISPLAY  '***********************************'
DISPLAY  'COPIA OK ! '
DISPLAY  '***********************************'
DISPLAY  WLL '/' ENTRA:RECORD-COUNT ' REGISTROS LIDOS.'
DISPLAY  WGG '/' SAIDA:RECORD-COUNT ' REGISTROS GRAVADOS.'
DISPLAY  '***********************************'
END-PROC
*-------------
* DECLARACAO DO RELATORIO
*-------------
REPORT RELAT PRINTER SYSREL NOADJUST
SEQUENCE AL-DATA
CONTROL  FINAL
TITLE 1 '                 PROGRAMA EXEMPLO 001'
LINE 1 AL-NOME AL-DATA AL-SALDO
**************************************************
* FIM ********************************************
**************************************************
```

Figure 4-1:
Easytrieve report
generation program

the tools been capable of it. The original approach to collecting the facts about business performance was for operational applications to produce regular, standard printed reports. These reports were often inadequate and more flexible report generators began to appear, either closely associated with particular databases or as stand-alone systems. It's seldom recalled that one of the most successful programs of the time was Pansophic (now Computer Associates) Easytrieve (Bergin & Haigh, 2009). Despite its popularity, this is clearly a programmer's language, as shown in Figure 4-1. Reports—increasingly electronic rather than printed—and their (more user-friendly) generators continue to play an important role in many BI implementations and operational reporting needs. However, reports alone often fail to answer really novel or interesting questions. The challenge was how to enable business users to explore the facts underlying the reported numbers.

The early support required for such analysis was rather simple—the ability to perform simple queries or drill-downs on reported data. Although perhaps difficult to believe today, business users of the time didn't actually want live data in most circumstances. Managers were more interested in longer-term trending—monthly or weekly in many cases, or occasionally daily after close of business or day-end processing. These were deemed to be the *facts* of interest for managing the business. More frequent samples simply generated too much data to process and too much random variability to see overall trends on printed results or character-based output devices. Managers, sometimes described as *dependent users* (Devlin & Murphy, 1988), would often turn to more skilled, *independent* or power users to dig beneath the reports whenever a query or problem arose. Today's managers are more likely to do their own digging, a fact that has led to a convergence of reporting and exploring in modern BI tools. However, it is a distinction worth keeping in mind.

These business needs, in combination with the technical concerns mentioned earlier, led directly to the approach that became common, and continues to be widespread today for supporting DSS: first, extract the data from the source system, and second, convert it to a format more amenable to the needs of reporting tools and power users, alike. This early decision to extract and format operational data into a special area for DSS—later termed informational—usage has had a lasting impact in the IT world. Reporting tools used this copied data rather than working against operational sources. Query and analysis tools were designed to use it. The approach continues to this day in "traditional" BI for numerical analysis of data from operational systems, and has also extended into the design of almost all information analytics, irrespective of the sources or structures of the information involved. Until very recently, the default starting point for all MIS work has been, to put it simplistically: *first, make another copy of the data*. Although useful, especially in the early days, this approach leads to significant data management issues in the longer term: maintenance of multiple, overlapping copies of data and a spaghetti-like tangle to extraction programs containing often complex selection and manipulation logic. In this situation, once-clear facts become increasingly unreliable over time; it would be the mid-1980s before IT figured out how to tackle this problem.

Back in the 1970s, the more pressing issue was how to represent raw MIS data to business users and to support the basic querying and analysis functions power users required for problem solving. A data structure of rows and columns was seen as most suitable, ech-

Figure 4-2:
APL keyboard layout

oing the multi-column ledger systems long used by accountants and analysts. In some early systems, the advanced array-handling of APL—an interactive programming language with rich mathematical function represented by esoteric symbols and Greek letters shown in Figure 4-2—was used to represent rows and columns and to create inverted file structures optimized for query (Alter, 1980)[1]. This structure, where columns rather than rows are stored together, is used in columnar databases for the same reason, as discussed in Section 5.2. However, by the early to mid-1980s, a consensus had emerged that relational databases could provide the most appropriate tabular format of rows and columns, as well as the technological base for querying and analyzing data in MIS. This technology was also seen as a base from which to tackle the growing inconsistency observed among the plethora of MIS files that were being regularly produced in larger organizations. That will lead us to data warehousing, which is the subject of Chapter 5.

Management misinformation systems

Management information systems were the earliest attempt to collect the facts of the business from its operational sources, and were seen as an antidote to the fiction of gut-feeling that managers typically applied (and still do) in decision making. In a contrarian view, Russell Ackoff, whose knowledge pyramid we met earlier, produced a feisty critique of "management misinformation systems" (Ackoff, 1967), that should still be required reading for all BI vendors and implementers today, almost fifty years later. He identified five erroneous assumptions (for consistency with our current terminology, I substituted *data* for *information* as needed):

[1] APL, *A Programming Language*, an interactive coding environment dating from 1966, is based on a book of the same name describing a mathematical notation for array handling (Iverson, 1962). The language was so concise that it was not uncommon for programmers to write a powerful function in half-a-dozen lines and then find, a short time later, that they could no longer understand their own code!

- *Give them more*—managers suffer far more from an over-abundance of irrelevant data than from a lack of relevant data. Addressing the over-abundance problem would reduce our tendency to gather ever greater volumes of data.

- *The manager needs the data he wants*—managers can seldom predict in advance the decisions they will need to make, so they tend to want more data than they actually need.

- *Give a manager the data he needs and decision making will improve*—this assumption is disproven by ongoing experience.

- *More communication means better performance*—when organizations have inappropriate performance measures that create conflict, communication usually damages the overall outcome.

- *A manager does not have to understand how an information system works, only how to use it*—ease-of-use MIS designs keep managers ignorant. This disempowers them in decision making, because they must depend blindly on the system as designed.

Unfortunately, Ackoff's criticisms went largely unheard. MIS has proceeded on an almost diametrically opposed trajectory since then. The focus has been on ever more data, rather than its relevance to its users and its impact on decision making. Perhaps Ackoff didn't go far enough. Gut-feeling, although long derided by proponents of rational decision making, may be less of a fiction than we think; Chapter 9 will show that modern psychology and neurobiology suggest it has an important role. Misinformation (in Ackoff's meaning here) is at the core of today's business intelligence; hence our search for its opposite, unintelligence.

We assume we can collect the facts of the business. We imagine they may be relevant. We make up the story that decisions are improved through their use. These are the facts, fictions and fabrications that lie at the foundation of MIS. It's a reality and it's fine, provided we recognize their relative contributions, understanding how the sources of data have expanded and changed in the biz-tech ecosystem, starting with centralized sources, moving to the PC and mobile explosion, and ending up with the World Wide Web.

ThoughtPoint

4.2　Where do you come from (my lovely)? [2]

B ack in the "good old days" of the 1960s and 1970s, you could be sure of one thing about your business information—it all came from one place: your mainframe. And it stayed there, too. Furthermore, because mainframes were not cheap, you could be relatively certain that a lot of data modeling and administration effort had gone into making such traditional business data as clean, accurate and consistent as possible. Not that it was always completely successful, or we would never have needed data warehousing. This traditional business data is essentially a record of the financially relevant transactions of the business and the parties involved in them. But, where does this information *ultimately* originate? In short, the vast majority comes from people recording business transactions through *systems of record.*

Systems of record

Figure 4-3:
Ledger Book from 1933, Cullen's Mill at Mullinderry Bridge, New Ross, Ireland

In Section 3.5, we saw how modeling gives an understanding of these transactions and parties and what data should be collected to faithfully record the business consequences. In the past, this data was collected by clerks—employees of the business—who entered the relevant data first into ledgers, such as that shown in Figure 4-3, and then into computer applications, the systems of record or operational systems, designed and built by the IT department of the business. This transactional data is manipulated and codified into a variety of status files, reference databases, master data, and so on—traditional business data that has long been the bread and butter of IT work. We call this *process-mediated data* because it is created and used in the formal processes of running and managing a business. It consists of hard information, defined earlier, and is found throughout the operational and informational sys-

---

[2] *Where Do You Go To (My Lovely)?* the 1969 UK hit song by Peter Sarstedt

tems of all businesses. In recent years, customers have begun entering the required data on business websites. Such websites are also business applications, perhaps developed and maintained today by vendors on behalf of the business. In either case, the purpose of these applications is to record process-mediated data in a controlled and managed environment as hard, computer-oriented data. Once recorded, this hardened information is accepted as a true and reliable record of the business transactions that have occurred. Responsibility for the quality of the data—both definition and content—

> **Systems of record and systems of engagement**
>
> *Systems of record: traditional operational systems track reliably confirmed outcomes of business interactions of value or legal substance. They focus on the past.*
>
> *Systems of engagement: based on social media and networking, these emerging systems track behaviors that indicate the likelihood of a future interaction of value or substance. They are future oriented.*

resides with the business and its IT department. Process-mediated data, being systemically generated and controlled, is thus *intentionally-governed*, in contrast to softer information and much external data, which often lacks such attention.

Records of systems events

Data originating from sensors on machines also has a long history within business, although its use was originally more limited. A common example is telephone exchanges that have been generating electronic records of calls—call detail records—since the 1960s, for automatic generation of phone bills. Machines on manufacturing production lines have also been generating electronic status messages since the 1960s. Retailers began using barcode readers at checkouts in the mid-1970s, leading eventually to the revolution in retailing described in Section 2.2. In banking, perhaps the first automated teller machine (ATM) went into service in the UK in 1967, although it was the mid-1980s before they became commonplace. All of the above is *machine-generated data*, and specifically, *sensor-generated data*. As the phrase *automated teller machine* suggests, these devices—as actors and sensors—replace humans in a particular process, in banking and elsewhere. The information they create is predefined and well-structured, and, to the extent that engineering permits, it is accurate and reliable. In this respect, it is of higher quality than that input by people in the data entry

Figure 4-4:
Commemorative plaque for first ATM in the UK

screens of operational systems. Such data is thus fed into business systems of record with more limited checking and pre-processing. Like process-mediated data, control and ownership of sensor-generated data resides in the business; it is thus also intentionally-governed.

Outsourcing and supply chain management move responsibility for traditional business data to suppliers of goods or services, but the governance of the definition and content of such *commercially-shared* data is covered by legally binding agreements. The point to note with both internally-generated and commercially-shared data is that they are both intentionally-governed: their sources and processing are known, well defined, and carefully, systemically controlled. So, too, are the networks which deliver this data to the systems of record. As a result, such data can be used with a high level of confidence and trust that it is a valid representation of events that have occurred. Any errors or willful misrepresentations it may contain can, in principle and often in practice, be traced and corrected.

Fortunately, the information described thus far, whether process-mediated or machine-generated, has the common characteristic that it arises and exists in a well-controlled environment throughout its lifecycle. This means that controls—technical, organizational and legal—are in place to monitor and guarantee its accuracy and integrity. Such information is created internally in the enterprise (or commercially shared under legal agreements) and is subject to cleansing on initial storage and control throughout its existence. In practice, IT has always taken responsibility for these controls, most particularly for hard information such as transactions, status and reference data. However, this applies only to information stored on machines or traversing networks that IT controls. In the past, this covered all business-critical information and much of the rest too. Today, there exist considerable amounts of information where this is not the case. Such information raises issues of confidence and trust because the sources of the data and any intermediate processing are less well known, poorly defined, or uncontrolled. *Ungoverned information* brings substantial challenges to the reliability of the information involved and the uses to which it can be put. The first source of such information, dating back to the 1980s, emerged on PCs and has since spread like a plague to mobile devices of every sort. Mention spreadsheets to most BI or data governance groups and they run for cover! But this is the territory into which we must next venture.

4.3   It's my data, and I'll play if I want to[3]

As we've seen, the complexity of the technology and its truly experimental nature in the earliest days led to the emergence of a "high priesthood" of computing. These designers, programmers, and later, database administrators took responsibility for all aspects of the data resource. The relational databases described in Chapter 3, whether on mainframe or minicomputer environments, remained true to this paradigm of data managed and monitored by IT on behalf of the business. Even through the 1980s, this view continued to hold, especially in complex and largely centralized organizations with strong IT shops.

Figure 4-5:
Apple II, 1977

However, the seeds of change, in both hardware and software had already been sown in the late 1970s. In 1977, after some years of development by kit makers and electronics enthusiasts, three microcomputers—the Apple II, the Commodore PET, and the Tandy Radio Shack TRS-80—were released. These machines, despite their primitive features (typically 4KB of RAM, 40x24 character display, and an audio cassette recorder for storage), were arguably the first computers the "man on the street" could afford or put to some pro-

Figure 4-6:
IBM PC, 1981

ductive use (Weyhrich, 2010), (Matthews, 2004), (Sysop, 2003-2010). Between them, they sold millions of units over the next few years (Reimer, 2005). While the market for microcomputers grew rapidly, it was 1981 before business began to take a real interest in this technology, with, predictably enough, the launch of the IBM personal computer (IBM PC), and subsequently in 1983, the IBM PC/XT (IBM, 2003). The technology had advanced to include up to 128KB of memory, an 80x25 character display, a 360KB 5¼" floppy disk drive,

---

[3] *It's My Party* (1962) by John Gluck, Wally Gold and Herb Weiner, was Lesley Gore's first hit in 1963.

and a 10MB hard drive. This level of power and storage would have been considered substantial in a computer room of the mid-1960s; now it was in the hands of business users. All that was needed was some intuitive software to unleash its potential.

Such software was already waiting in the wings. The rise of personal computers, especially in business, and spreadsheets have long been seen as inextricably linked. Developed by Dan Bricklin and Bob Frankston in 1979 (Bricklin, 2009), Visicalc was first released on the Apple II. It has been widely described as the "killer app" that drove the personal computer revolution in business throughout the 1980s. By today's spreadsheet standards, Visicalc—especially in its original Apple II version, as re-created in Figure 4-7—had limited function and usability, largely a consequence of the hardware of the time. A 40x24 character display and a few KB of RAM don't leave much room for frills. Navigation around the cells was by the arrow keys, an approach somewhat limited by the fact that the Apple II had only left and right arrows. The developers were undeterred; the spacebar was co-opted to convert the direction of cursor movement between left-right and up-down! However, the concept was revolutionary. The layout is instantly recognizable to any financial person, but the real magic lay in the automatic update of the results of any calculation whenever a relevant cell was changed. Anybody who needed to play with numbers—from totting up sales to creating financial projections with varying assumptions—could see almost endless possibilities.

Figure 4-7:

Visicalc as seen on the Apple II, 1979

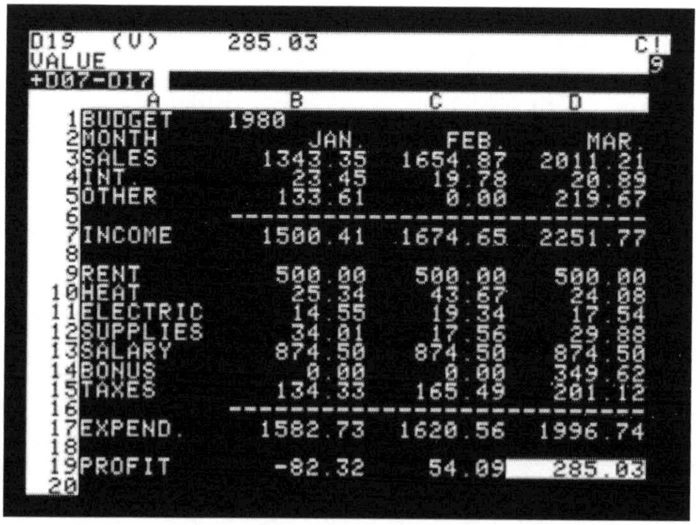

Throughout the 1980s, PCs and spreadsheets evolved together in leaps and bounds, each enabling and driving the other to greater heights of power, size and usability. New, improved products were developed, including one-time contender, Lotus 1-2-3 (1983) and the eventual champion, Microsoft Excel (1985), whose name is now almost synonymous with spreadsheets. PC-based databases, of which dBase II (1980) was the forerunner, also play a role in data use by business users. However, the spreadsheet has proven to be more amenable to both casual use and complex, iterative calculations performed by business analysts. PCs offer a wide variety of other functions, of course, but in the land of hard information, spreadsheets continue to be king. PCs and spreadsheets should, perhaps, have caused IT organizations to stand back and review their role *vis-à-vis* data governance as far back as the 1980s. Business users clearly saw a need to play with data; spreadsheets gave them that possibility, and they grasped it with both hands. Today, a large proportion of data innovation occurs in spreadsheets and their successors. Many users and vendors of PC-based solutions believe passionately in the power of this approach to deliver impressive business results. Meanwhile, IT correctly mourns the impact on data quality and management. As Wayne Eckerson lamented: *"Spreadsheets run amuck in most organizations. They proliferate like poisonous vines, slowly strangling organizations by depriving them of a single consistent set of information and metrics..."* (Eckerson, 2003). Hidden among facts, therefore, we may find unintended fictions as users generate and manipulate data. More dishonestly, data may be fabricated for personal gain or protection. Spreadsheet data, although internally generated, is not systemically controlled. It thus counts as ungoverned information.

The creation and use of soft information—documents, presentations, etc.—never fully centralized in any case, moved completely and almost immediately to the PC environment. Responsibility for document management, version control, and so on was casually taken on by business users—an approach suited to the apparently less onerous data governance needs of such information. IT stood back, largely unaware of the longer-term consequences of ignoring soft information governance, as personal computing went fully mobile. *Enterprise content management (ECM)*, a term that emerged in the early 2000s, now covers the management of soft information. Its origins were in the electronic document management systems of the 1980s—physical documents were scanned and stored, on laser disk and other media, with search and indexing functions providing management and access. It was thus a largely centralized and managed process, characteristics far from those of an increasingly mobile world. We deal with the business value, use and contents of soft information in depth in Chapter 8. For now, our focus is on its trustworthiness. As in the case of hard information, its creation and management on user-controlled PCs means that we must assign to it a far lower level of trust than information that is intentionally governed by IT. And, being soft information, it is easier for it to be a fictional or fabricated artifact of the user who controls it.

ThoughtPoint

Ultimately, business depends on the integrity and honesty of those who create and manage the information. With centrally created and managed information, the processes are more transparent and easily controlled. Business and IT have largely neglected the risks associated with personally generated information. This is a situation which will have to be addressed as more and more information comes from personal sources.

4.4   I'M GOING HOME...AND I'M TAKING MY DATA WITH ME

If the dispersal of corporate data from the mainframe to PCs beneath users' desks was uncomfortable for IT, the additional possibility that they could take it home with them seems to have come as an even greater surprise. The first commercially successful portable computer, the Osborne 1, was released in April, 1981. Weighing in at nearly 24 lbs (11 kg), it and its contemporaries quickly gained the name "luggables" but also widespread popularity despite a number of technical limitations, most notably a 5" screen. (The IBM Model 5100, launched in 1975, selling for up to US$ 20,000 depending on memory size, is often deemed to be the first portable computer; although weighing some 55 lbs (25 kg), even *luggable* sounds considerably like marketing-speak!) It would be the best part of a decade before the first truly portable computers, such as the Compaq LTE (1989) and Apple PowerBook 100 (1991), adopted the clamshell format, earning the names notebooks and laptops. Running the common operating systems and applications of the day, these machines finally took corporate data out of the office onto the road and into the home. For business users, from salespeople to managers, no longer dependent on access

Figure 4-8:
Osborne 1 portable computer, 1981

to mainframe terminals or tethered to their desks, they represented the ultimate break for freedom. Until, of course, tablets arrived on the scene.

For IT departments, notebooks were the beginning of the end of their control of corporate data, although strangely enough, little attention was paid to the implications for data governance at the time. Back in the late 1980s, it's probably fair to say that most of the business data found on PCs and laptops originated directly or indirectly on enterprise mainframes. But, as business users became more familiar with spreadsheets, in particular, increasing quantities of data began to originate in this new, distributed and uncontrolled environment. Brand-new data was created, especially in planning applications. Existing corporate data, downloaded from mainframes, was edited and extended to suit departmental or personal needs. Data definitions were changed or extended. Business rules and calculations were embedded in spreadsheet cells; errors of understanding or logic became widespread, and manual data entry took a further toll on data quality (EuSpRIG, 2012). A recent example shows that no one is immune, not even Harvard economics professors, Carmen Reinhart and Ken Rogoff (also a former chief economist of the International Monetary Fund). Their paper *Growth in a Time of Debt* (Reinhart & Rogoff, 2010), which has been extensively used to support austerity strategies in Europe and elsewhere, was shown to be based on a spreadsheet containing a simple calculation error. Their conclusions were built on a much shakier foundation than anybody thought (Alexander, 2013).

As technology has become ever faster, smaller and more mobile, with mobile devices from smartphones to tablets becoming pervasive in the past few years, this trend has accelerated rapidly. Furthermore, an ever broadening variety of data types is now being generated on mobile devices. Traditional, numerical data and text documents are being supplemented with softer information such as images, audio and video, geolocational data, and more. Such novel information, generated directly by business users and their devices, is already outstripping traditional business data volumes. And its value to the business is increasing dramatically as new applications and business processes are developed in the biz-tech ecosystem. Management and governance of such information is at best basic and, in some instances, nonexistent. Taking an overall view of hard and soft information in the mobile environment now pervasive in most enterprises, and even within well-managed information assets, an integrated, consistent view of the business' information has become well-nigh impossible to achieve. Even basic data governance presents a considerable challenge. And this is before we even begin to consider digital information originating beyond the boundary of the enterprise and its employees and agents.

4.5 INFORMATION FROM BEYOND THE PALE[4]

In most types of business, computerization was centered on the processes for running and managing the business, leading to the development of systems of record to collect and manage the internally-generated data required for these operational processes. IT has thus long been focused on internal information, particularly hard information, to the exclusion of all else. However, no business operates in a vacuum. The reality is that all businesses require some information of varying importance originating beyond the enterprise. Many IT professionals had successfully ignored this information until the advent of big data—largely externally sourced—in the past few years. Today, it's well-nigh impossible to avoid the term, and we will address this topic in depth in Chapter 6. However, we can come to an initial understanding of the important characteristics of external information from its more traditional sources and uses, combined with a brief foretaste of the most heavily hyped category of big data today. But first...

Here is the news

Among the readers of the earliest newspapers in the 17th century were businessmen who needed information about events near and far that could affect their business interests. This led to the emergence of titles directly addressing their needs, such as *Lloyd's List* in England in 1734, detailing general commercial news, stock prices, and ships arriving at ports...or not. Such information was very

---

[4] *Beyond the Pale* meaning *unacceptable behavior* refers to the rebellious Irish who lived beyond and raided the English-controlled Pale of Dublin in the 1400s. It derives from the Latin *palus*, meaning stake, a component of the boundary fence.

loosely structured, as can be seen in Figure 4-9 and, more importantly, of varying relia- bility and timeliness; reporting was erratic and communica- tions slow. But, we can imag- ine gentlemen of the era, stockinged and bewigged, making the decisions to buy or sell, expand or hold, starting from this very information, uncertain as it may have been, and spicing it with liberal dos- es of gut feel. The shipping data available from *Lloyd's List* and others today is far more accurate and timely, as we'll see shortly, but a considerable proportion of business news is still heavily dependent on opinions and interpretations of observers and declared

Figure 4-9: *Lloyd's List*, clippings from an early edition

experts in the field. Such human-sourced, soft information contin- ues to play an important role in decision making for higher-level executives, but is seldom formally channeled through IT processes or subject to formal quality governance programs.

Enumerating people

"In those days a decree went out from Emperor Augustus that all the world should be registered...Joseph also went...to the city of David called Bethlehem...to be registered with Mary...who was expecting a child."[5] The word *census* comes from the Latin *censere*, to estimate, but the practice of counting the population dates back to the Egyp- tian civilization some thousands of years earlier. Early censuses were used by governments for tax collection, conscription into armies, and so on, but represented some of the first collections of statistical information about the distribution and density of the population. Fast forward to the 20th century, and businesses are

---

[5] Luke 2:1-7, New Revised Standard Version of the Bible

making extensive use of the statistical data gathered by governments, most often via third parties, to plan retail store locations, understand consumer behavior, and predict and even drive sales. Since the 1930s, Nielsen has been gathering behavior information from consumer panels, radio and TV monitoring devices, online tagging, and more. Such marketing research companies also gather information from the census, telephone directories, driver's license and automobile registrations, birth and marriage records, and credit reporting bureaus, to name just a subset of the sources. The result is a detailed set of demographics—some actual, such as age and marital status, and others inferred, among them income and occupation—for varying size areas depending on country privacy legislation and data sources available. This external information is used extensively by a range of industries including retail, telecommunications, consumer packaged goods, and media worldwide.

There exist many other external sources of information used by particular industries or geographies. In finance, for example, agencies such as Moody's and Standard and Poor's provide credit rating information. Eurostat provides statistical information in the European Union. The list is extensive, but the principles remain the same in all cases. In contrast to the softer news information, this demographic and statistical data is process-mediated data; although, in this case, the processes are those of the market research companies that produce the data, rather than the businesses that buy and use it. These production processes are statistics-based, as opposed to the more common processes oriented towards individual people and events seen in most businesses.

Facts from on high

From the value of π to ISO (International Organization for Standardization) country codes, from tax rates to safety regulations, from currency conversion rates to the great-circle distance from New York to London, all businesses rely on a wide variety of standard information to underpin many business processes. Such information is often embedded in them. As a result, it often appears that such information is part of the process-mediated data of the business. In fact, this information is actually external, sourced from standards authorities, governments and regulatory bodies, both industry and more broadly based. The reliability of this type of information should thus be assessed separately from internally generated information.

It is generally assumed, usually correctly, that standard information is of high quality. It is created through well-defined procedures in reputable organizations so that, although external, it satisfies the criteria for process-mediated data. It is also accepted to be constant in meaning and value (π hasn't changed much in several thousand years) or with a well-defined meaning and value changing infrequently according to a known process. It is also generally limited in volume. Therefore, the reliability of standard information is usually considered to be higher than internal process-mediated data. Physical constants are a good example of highly reliable standard information. However, given that standard information is externally sourced, businesses must remember that its governance is outside their control and its quality may be compromised. The still-ongoing—as of mid-2013—scandal where the British Bankers' Association's LIBOR (London Interbank Offered Rate) and other key interest rates in the world financial system were being manipulated by vested interests at a number of large banks, shows the issues arising when standards are compromised.

Figure 4-10: Archimedes first calculated π using geometry c. 250BC, *Domenico Fetti, Alte Meister Museum, Dresden*

Becoming socially adept

The external information *du jour* today is, without question, social media data, from sites such as Facebook, YouTube, Twitter and more. This information has become the statistical Disneyland of marketers searching for the golden El Dorado of perfectly targeted selling. The content is human-sourced—entirely dictated by the whims of individuals. Even its structure is highly variable and volatile. In terms of volume, it is huge. But its value lifetime may be as brief as minutes, in some cases. Its processing is statistical and analytical, the aim being to detect patterns and build models that enable prediction of future behavior or outcomes. The use of such information is largely confined to marketing for now, or at an early stage of assimilation into enterprise data by some traditional IT departments. From the viewpoint of the reliability of such information, this is probably good news. The accuracy of such information in terms of demographics, for example, is questionable, given that it is self-declared. And while the wisdom of crowds is widely promoted, the effects of mass hysteria have also been noted. The longer-term effects of highly focused, data-driven recommendation systems are still unknown. Despite an extraordinary level of current interest and activity, how well such information represents reality—and even influences it—is still undetermined.

4.6   TALES OF SAILS AND SALES

The extent and nature of facts, fiction and fabrication as it applies to externally-sourced big data becomes very clear when we examine two specific incidents reported within a month of one another in early 2012. They involve very different industries and data types, but they illustrate very similar points about how far we can trust information and the consequences that arise from its collection.

Plain sailing...or not

At approximately 9:40 p.m. on Friday, January 13th, 2012, the *Costa Concordia* struck a reef close to Isola del Giglio, off the coast of Italy, leaving a huge gash more than 50 meters long in her hull, well below the waterline. Within some 40 minutes, the giant cruiser was lying on her side, half-submerged, with passengers and crew scrambling to evacuate. In London, data streaming into *Lloyd's List* Intelligence's computer from its proprietary network of land-based receivers confirmed the event. While the media focused on the chaos of the evacuation, the enormity of what could have happened, and who to blame, Lloyd's List Intelligence reviewed their data and publicly confirmed within a few days that the liner had also passed as close to shore only five months previously, as shown in Figure 4-11. For the general public, it was probably one of the first indications of just how much data is gathered and stored about maritime movements. To recall another—far more tragic—disaster, such data collection is but the tip of an ever-growing iceberg.

Many organizations collect and process data from the automatic identification system (AIS) devices now mandatory on internationally voyaging ships with gross tonnage of 300+ tons and all passenger ships. Lloyd's List Intelligence, for example, receives over 60 million position reports per day from more than 72,000 vessels. Position reports, consisting of location, speed, heading, rate of turn, as well as other optional information, are transmitted every few seconds. Increasingly, land-based receivers are being supplemented by satellite receivers to increase coverage. The primary purpose of AIS is real-time for collision avoidance; but the data is also used as an aid to navigation, to track the progress of shipments, and for search and rescue. Furthermore, the historical record is used for

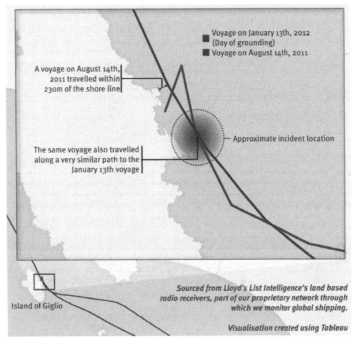

investigation of accidents and insurance claims, as well as loss adjusting. All of these applications depend on reliable and proven data about ship positions, times and more—in short, facts. Errors in one or more of these measures could result in financial losses through litigation or, more seriously, loss of life. Fabrication of any of this data, if it were possible, risks accusations of negligence, criminal intent, and beyond. In short, for machine-generated data of this type, even though it comes from third parties via unsecured network links, we must be able to trust it to be fully factual.

Figure 4-11
Two voyages of the stricken cruise liner, *Costa Concordia*

Plain sales

Headquartered in Minneapolis, Target Corporation is the second-largest discount retailer in the United States, behind Walmart. For Target, as for all retailers, success comes from driving sales, which depends on predicting when a potential customer is likely to buy or at least be most receptive to advertising. It was with the latter intention that Target, notoriously adverse to such publicity, made the *New York Times* newspaper in mid-February of 2012, when it was reported that Target could predict the likelihood that you were pregnant (assuming you're a woman, of course) and your probable date of delivery by noting changes in your shopping patterns— unscented soaps and lotions, vitamin supplements, cotton balls, and hand sanitizers—in the first trimester of your pregnancy (Duhigg, 2012). The author's book, *The Power of Habit: Why We Do What We Do in Life and Business* (Duhigg, 2012a), a fascinating study of the power of habitual behavior, points out that there are times in our lives when we are particularly open to changing our habits— marriage, divorce and starting a family are all high on the list—and that identifying such events earlier than a competitor is often a key goal of marketers. However, our interest here is on the information gathered and analyzed by business about consumers with the aim of influencing their buying patterns. Among US retailers, infor- mation that is regularly gathered includes items bought or re- turned, credit card used, coupons redeemed, emails opened, and web site visits. In addition, retailers purchase a wide range of de- mographic information such as age, gender, marital and family sta- tus, address, financial status—from estimated salary to declarations of bankruptcy—not to mention political leanings, brand prefer- ences, reading habits, and more. And retailers are not alone; banks, airlines, insurers, telecommunications companies and more also gather and purchase such data. Literally thousands of variables are now continuously recorded and stored about every consumer in the US. Businesses in other countries worldwide are not far behind.

How Target stumbled into the limelight, according to Duhigg, was that they used their newfound information to target (ironically) expectant mothers with personalized catalogs that demonstrated the retailer knew they were pregnant, sometimes before their ex- tended families or friends. The facts of the women's shopping bas- kets had been converted to stories about their lives, fictions with a high probability of being true. The information collected was being used to both understand and manipulate consumer behavior, and therein lies the potential for extensive fabrication. When we begin to disentangle fact, fiction and fabrication within the information we record and use, we address more than dry data governance. We affect people's lives and companies' futures.

Fact, fiction or fabrication—the bottom line

With this review and tales of external information use in business, as well as the discussion of PCs and mobile devices as data sources, we can begin to discern important patterns in sourcing and pro- cessing that have significant implications for information reliability.

External information typically arrives in enterprises through individual functions such as marketing, finance and research departments. In some cases, particularly for business news stories of interest to executives, it is loaded directly onto PCs at the behest of individual users. There may be multiple copies purchased. Information from different sources may be inconsistent or even contradictory. Management and control is cursory.

As the Web has become ubiquitous, sources of external information have expanded and multiplied. Some are correct, others mistaken or downright false. Often, the original sources are untraceable or simply unknown. Social media data, in particular, has a high level of uncertainty and unreliability and must be treated with special consideration. In many cases, IT may be completely unaware of the existence of such external information arriving in the enterprise, how it is being combined with the internal process-mediated data and how it is eventually used by the business. Even when the original quality and reliability of process-mediated data is largely guaranteed, the informal processes through which it passes within the enterprise leave it open to misinterpretation or misuse. Copying it to PCs leaves it open to manipulation. The same data may be understood and applied differently in different departments and by different people. In short, we need a new way of looking at the level of trust we can place in different types of information.

ThoughtPoint

While big data excites business with its promise of new opportunities and stimulates IT with novel technologies, where both sides need to really focus is *information governance*. The balance of probability between data as fact or fiction, information as truth or fabrication, has shifted dramatically. A dedicated, independent, powerful and well-funded information governance department reporting to the CEO—on a par with finance—becomes mandatory.

4.7   A NEW MODEL FOR INFORMATION TRUST

The same two factors determining the underlying reliability of information, and thus its trustworthiness, are apparent in all of the information we have reviewed. These two factors are: (i) the original sourcing of the information—how and where it was generated—and (ii) its pre-processing—any possible manipulation it may have undergone—prior to its use by the business. Figure 4-12 shows these two factors and their applicability to a sample set of common information types, both internally and externally sourced.

On the horizontal axis, certified sources are designed and operated to the highest standards of reliability. Described sources are well-defined and understood but their content is more loosely controlled, and sources of uncertain origin are the least reliable in terms of definition and content. On the vertical axis, regulated information is fully controlled and managed through all processing steps. At the next level, information processing is understood and defined but not closely controlled, while chaotic processing is neither defined nor controlled.

Figure 4-12:
The information reliability matrix

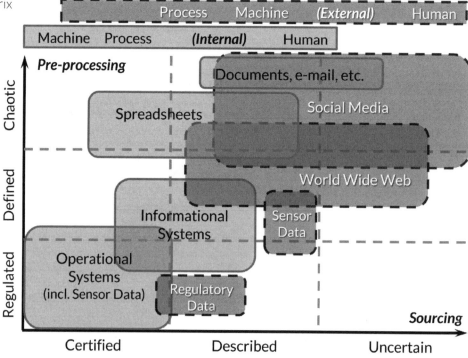

These categories apply slightly different-ly to internally and externally sourced data. We divide both types into machine-, process- and human-sourced classes. We've met these already, and will define these classes formally in Section 6.5. In general, internally sourced information can be, and often is, more tightly con-trolled in generation and processing than its external counterpart. However, we see that it is only in the traditional opera-tional systems, and to a lesser extent, in centrally controlled informational sys-tems, where IT retains a significant level of control that reliability is assured—even in internally-sourced data. The inclusion of external information in the information pro-cessing environment of a business introduces a significantly higher level of unreliability in the data.

> ## Trust horizon
>
> *The extent to which a set of information can be relied upon by business users in a particular set of circumstances.*
>
> *The trust horizon of information is a vari-able that must be calculated at the time of use, based on (i)the reliability of each information set used, (ii)how multiple sets are combined, and (iii) the business out-come under consideration.*

Trust as an horizon

As just described, the reliability of any information source is de-termined by its sourcing and prior processing. The trust that a business user should place in it builds upon the reliability of the information and the organizational breadth within which it can be safely used. We call this quality the *trust horizon* of the information. Use of data beyond its trust horizon carries significant risk of misin-terpretation and errors of judgment. We've seen this already with spreadsheets created in whole or in part from personally generated data that are subsequently used in enterprise level decision-making processes, leading to serious financial and legal exposures. Figure 4-13 shows the trust horizon of information as it relates to its reli-ability, going from extremely limited conditions of safe usage to the broadest and most reliable data possible. As we move to higher trust levels, the volume of such data decreases. An *unknown* hori-zon is the starting point for all data; in most cases we hope to de-clare a narrower horizon for the data after some analysis. However, some information—much of social media, for example—is such that its provenance is unknowable; use of such data within any narrow-er horizon carries substantial and often unacceptable risk.

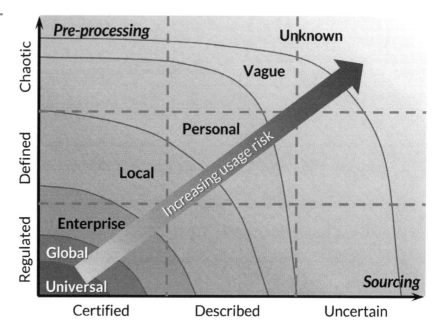

Vague data comes in enormous volumes from the Internet, or is personally generated within the organization. Its source and subsequent manipulation is poorly defined. It carries many risks, but may be the best that can be obtained in some circumstances, and may still be deemed useful in the absence of more reliable data. Examples include competitive intelligence, information from credible Web sources, and internal documents or emails from less-experienced staff.

Personal information comes from a known, trusted personal source. Known and trusted is, of course, a value judgment; in practice, it generally means a respected employee or contractor of the enterprise. Spreadsheet data, mentioned earlier, originates on this horizon, but can be moved to a narrower horizon through peer review or more formal expert evaluation processes. In fact, a great deal of personal spreadsheet data actually originates from a narrower horizon—such as centrally managed systems—but is "degraded" by unmanaged personal manipulation.

Local data is the next level down; it originates from a system formally designed and constructed to perform a particular task or capture a specific measurement, often within a business function or department. It thus includes data generated by operational systems and machine-generated data. Such data has a well-defined scope and application, within which it can be relied upon. Users, and IT, must be aware that use at a narrower horizon or in a different application requires care. For example, consider RFID sensor data that has been gathered for the purpose of tracking the speed of goods through the supply chain from manufacturing to store. Reusing this data for detecting "shrinkage" (theft) may give invalid results when the routing is changed, even though the original application results remain true.

The *enterprise* horizon represents data that is reliable across the breadth of the enterprise, including systems such as enterprise resource planning (ERP) and master data management (MDM). Local data can be moved to the enterprise horizon—in the design and delivery of an enterprise data warehouse (EDW), for example. It is an expensive process involving widespread modeling, cleansing and reconciliation of data from different local scope sources. It illustrates the general principle that moving data from a wider to a narrower horizon involves substantial human expertise, technology and investment. The *global* horizon takes this one step further, indicating data that can be used broadly across enterprise boundaries, between multiple trading partners, or for release to regulatory bodies or the public record.

The final horizon, enclosing the least amount of information, is *universal*, indicating data that can be relied upon irrespective of time or place. It includes universal physical constants, as well as data that is declared by a relevant authority as final and fixed, such as a standard code or measure, a tax rate or the inflation rate for a country for some year past.

In general, the use of information at a wider horizon than that at which it is evaluated is perfectly fine. The problem arises going in the opposite direction; creating data with a narrower horizon is more expensive—often considerably more so—than at a wider level. Consider the trust vs. cost equation for Wikipedia vs. *Encyclopædia Britannica*, for example. There would be few arguments over the relative placement of the two works on the trust scale: Wikipedia probably rates vague, *Britannica* perhaps global. In its day, the latter employed 100 full-time editors and over 4,400 freelance contributors to create a work that sold for thousands of dollars. *Britannica 3*, published in 1974 after ten years of work cost some $32 million to

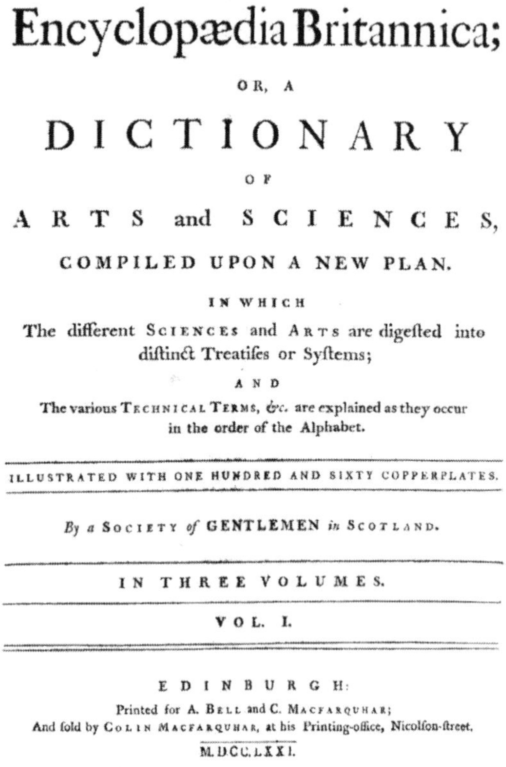

Encyclopædia Britannica;

OR, A

DICTIONARY

OF

A R T S and S C I E N C E S,

COMPILED UPON A NEW PLAN.

IN WHICH

The different SCIENCES and ARTS are digested into
distinct Treatises or Systems;

AND

The various TECHNICAL TERMS, &c. are explained as they occur
in the order of the Alphabet.

ILLUSTRATED WITH ONE HUNDRED AND SIXTY COPPERPLATES.

By a SOCIETY of GENTLEMEN in SCOTLAND.

IN THREE VOLUMES.

VOL. I.

E D I N B U R G H:
Printed for A. BELL and C. MACFARQUHAR;
And sold by COLIN MACFARQUHAR, at his Printing-office, Nicolson-street.
M.DCC.LXXI.

Figure 4-14:
Encyclopædia Britannica, title page, 1st edition, 1771

produce. Wikipedia's production costs, with its army of volunteer contributors and editors, are minimal. *Brittanica*'s financial decline, beginning in the 1990s, to the announcement that there would be no further print editions in 2012, as it competed first with CDs and then with online encyclopedias, is simply the business outcome of the trust vs. cost equation. In this case, the value placed on the higher reliability of *Britannica* weighed less than free access to Wikipedia.

In business, the balance tilts mostly in the opposite direction. Information created has a (usually implicit) trust horizon. In most systems of record, that horizon is local. For spreadsheets, it's usually personal. To raise the trust level to enterprise or global use, relatively expensive cleansing, quality and governance programs are required. This is regularly seen in the delivery of enterprise data warehouses. It is also regularly ignored when spreadsheets are promoted to departmental—or broader—use. The consequences of misplaced trust in wider horizon data for use in a narrower context can be catastrophic, ranging from embarrassing financial reporting errors to executives being jailed under the Sarbanes-Oxley or similar acts in many jurisdictions.

Managing information trust

Risk is the negative side of this equation, of course. But, in a more positive view, one may ask how we can deal with the fact that information comes increasingly from diverse sources and thus with very different trust levels. The answer is twofold. First, we must define these different usage horizons and categorize and tag information accordingly, providing users with an understanding of the limits of usage of particular information and the risks of exceeding them. This involves the creation and use of business metadata, a process that is neither simple nor inexpensive. However, it is the minimum that should be done in response to the explosion of information we are currently seeing in big data. Second, we can undertake the necessary steps to certify the information at a narrower usage horizon. This will certainly involve costs, some of them significant, to investigate data provenance, cleanse the incoming data if possible, or find alternative and more reliable sources. Such costs may be justified, depending on the use to which the data is put. Again, the emergence of big data, as we'll see in Chapter 6, is a key consideration because many of its characteristics differ so dramatically from those known and understood by IT.

4.8   IDEAL ARCHITECTURE (2): INFORMATION, RELIANCE/USAGE DIMENSION

As we return to the conceptual architecture, the categories of trust discussed in the previous section—from universal through to unknown—become the classes on the second dimension of information, *reliance/usage (RU)*, shown in Figure 4-15. These characteristics of information are seldom considered in any depth by business or IT even today, despite the long history of business users creating or using PC-based and externally sourced information within every enterprise. As big data becomes ever more important, this lack of focus becomes increasingly dangerous. Business users, in common with the population at large, often place an unwarranted level of trust in information once it has been transformed into the "facts and figures" of data. They rely on it and use it in situations where it may be unsafe to do so. IT should know bet-

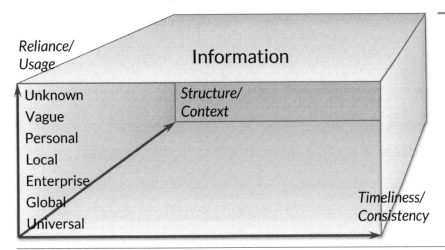

Figure 4-15:
Reliance/usage
dimension of
information

ter, but are often misled by their own historical role as creators and guardians of data. As we've seen, operational systems were developed within well-defined boundaries, with known users and use cases and well-defined processes that generated and managed that data. Even the data warehouse, which had a considerably wider scope, used data from operational sources, so reliance/usage was implicitly strong. Consideration of the reliance/usage dimension of information is required to bring these aspects into sharp focus.

As is the case for all dimensions, these classes are loosely defined, and this axis actually portrays a continuum of levels of trust, rather than discrete, separate categories. This lack of precision is a result of the fact that we are combining attributes—in this case, sourcing and pre-processing—which are themselves open to interpretation. Information that is required to be certified and regulated in one context may be uncertain and chaotic in another. Unlike the other two information dimensions, technology has only a minor role to play in the management of this dimension. While various tools are used to transfer data to/from PCs, little or no attention is paid to any aspect of reliance or usage. Information coming into the enterprise may be cleansed using data quality tools to remove inconsistencies, missing values or outliers, to match field names to internal standards, and so on. While this is a good starting point, there are few, if any, tools that attempt to characterize the reliance/usage characteristics. It is thus the responsibility of IT in general, in conjunction with the data governance organization, wherever that may sit in the business, to understand where particular information sets lie on this axis for the enterprise as a whole, and manually annotate the information with appropriate business context-setting information. This is no small task, requiring action not just at an enterprise level—where most data governance occurs today—but also at departmental and personal levels where much of this ill-defined information is created or imported. It is also required at inter-enterprise and governmental levels to set and enforce standards for definition and guidelines for use across company and country boundaries.

4.9   IN PRACTICE—(RE)BUILDING TRUST IN DATA

T he "data warehouse good, spreadsheets bad" approach to data reliability is long beyond its use-by date. Data and information provenance has become much more varied and complex; a more nuanced response is required. These issues fall within the broad remit of data governance and data quality:

✓ Take data governance to the business users' offices... as well as their pockets and purses. While the traditional starting point for data governance is the centrally controlled and managed data from systems of record, many modern data governance issues arise from data that is copied to or created on users' personal computing devices—from PCs to smartphones. Document how data is manipulated and shared. Investigate why personal and peer data is used in preference to centrally supplied data. Establish guidelines or rules where appropriate.

✓ Extend data governance to externally-sourced information. Document sources and pre-processing. Create a process for vetting and approving new information sources. Remove duplicate and redundant sources. Define minimum metadata requirements for external data. Track how external data is combined with internally-generated and intentionally-governed data and how it is incorporated—perhaps unknowingly or unintentionally—into highly regulated processes.

✓ Investigate the extent to which the data provided through your (expensive) BI environment is actually being used by managers and other decision makers. If it is unused, document why and, if appropriate, stop generating it. In some cases, it may be an interesting experiment to simply turn off some old MIS systems—temporarily, at first—and see who complains.

✓ Create a management process around novel uses of personal and other potentially sensitive information from social media and external machine-generated data sources. Ensure that staff involved in these areas is trained in legal and privacy matters.

4.10   CONCLUSIONS

The early history of information technology, with its cadres of experts on data storage and use, as well as the continuing focus of traditional IT departments on the operational processes and systems of businesses, created a skewed perception of the reliability of computerized information. In brief, all was not as it seemed.

The first hints of trouble emerged on two fronts in the 1980s. PCs enabled business users to create their own data, and the perennial problem of spreadsheet consistency and accuracy was born. Data warehousing introduced the issue of quality from the opposite direction, highlighting the cost of creating data fit for enterprise use from the functionally based operational data of the day. More recently, the twin explosions of powerful mobile devices and ubiquitous social media on the Web pose serious questions about data reliability and trustworthiness to anyone who cares to probe into these issues. Unfortunately, few do.

By examining the emergence and characteristics of a variety of information types, we can see that the reliability of information is directly related to its original sourcing and processing prior to its use for any particular business task. The trustworthiness of any information is dependent on this base reliability and the scope of its use within the enterprise. We can then determine the trust horizon of particular information, decide if it is fit for purpose, and if not, what mitigating measures are possible and affordable.

The IDEAL architecture reliance/usage dimension of information addresses this need. Of course, we can only go so far in labeling information as fact, fiction or fabrication—sometimes it's a human judgment call. But we have long talked in BI of something called a "single version of the truth", and it's there we turn next on this somewhat tortuous but enlightening journey.

ROADMAP

→ *Consistency is the purpose of the data warehouse:* Although often forgotten, the *raison d'être* of the enterprise data warehouse (EDW) is to reconcile business data from diverse and inconsistent sources in a historical context

→ *Appliances are all about timeliness:* Data marts and, more recently, appliances are designed and sold for speed to results, irrespective of underlying data quality

→ *Playtime with BI and analytics:* The core function of business intelligence and analytics tools (including spreadsheets) is to allow business people to manipulate hard data mathematically and pictorially... nothing more

→ *Seven outmoded postulates:*
  (i)   Operational and informational systems are separate
  (ii) Data integration is possible only in the warehouse
  (iii) The enterprise data model can exist only in the EDW
  (iv) Layering is obligatory for speedy and reliable querying
  (v)   Information is just a super-class of data
  (vi) Data quality is only possible with centralization
  (vii) Innovative business usage of data threatens quality

→ *Information timeliness/consistency:* The balance between timeliness and consistency drives storage and processing choices; classes on the timeliness/consistency axis are: in-flight, live, stable, reconciled and historical

→ *Core business information:* Existing data warehouse and data mart components are key to consistency at the heart of information in the new architecture

"Most executives, many scientists, and almost all business school | Edward de Bono
graduates believe that if you analyze data, this will give
you new ideas. Unfortunately, this belief is totally wrong.
The mind can only see what it is prepared to see."

"The purpose of computing is insight, not numbers." | Richard W. Hamming

By the mid-1980s, corporate IT figured that they had a reasonably good handle on building and running the operational systems responsible for the day-to-day processes of increasingly automated businesses. The majority of companies programmed their own systems, mostly in Cobol, computerizing the financially important and largely repetitive operational activities, one business activity at a time. Of course, the applications IT built weren't perfect and there were backlogs in development, but the problems were understood and solutions seemingly in sight. We will return to the illusion that the operational environment was largely complete in Chapter 7, but for now we'll focus on data.

Attention thus turned to a rather different business need: MIS or decision support. We've already seen how MIS grew in the 1970s through point solutions. IT saw two problems worth tackling. First, from the business view, there was growing inconsistency among the results they were getting. Second, the explosion of extracts from the operational systems was causing IT serious headaches. An integrated solution to ensure consistency and reduce extract loads was required. And a modern technology—relational databases—was seen as the way to do it.

In 1985, I defined an architecture for business reporting and analysis in IBM (Devlin & Murphy, 1988), which became a foundation of data warehousing. At the heart of that architecture and data warehousing in general, is the need for a high-quality, consistent store of historically complete and accurate data. Defining and delivering it turned out to be tougher and slower than anybody imagined. Over the succeeding decades, the focus shifted back and forth between these consistency goals and timeliness—another eternal business need. The enterprise-oriented data warehouse was praised for quality or excoriated for never-ending, over-budget projects. Data marts were introduced for immediate business value but soon derided as quick and dirty. The pendulum continues to swing. Data warehousing soon begat business intelligence, drove advances in data management, benefited from developments in information technology, and is now claimed to be replaced by business analytics. But analytics and big data still focus on data rather than information, numbers rather than insight. And even there, the increasing role of simulation and modeling poses questions about what we are trying to achieve.

Ackoff's issues with MIS have not gone away. Does better and more data drive "improved" decisions? Is de Bono wrong to say that new thinking never emerges from analyzing data? We focus on bigger, faster and better data and continue to dream of a *single version of the truth*. Behind a superficially unchanging architecture, we are forced to address the conundrum of consistency vs. timeliness—accepting the fundamental inconsistency that characterizes the real world and the basic inability of humans to think and decide at the speed of light. We must reexamine the postulates at the foundation of data warehousing and business intelligence. We find them wanting.

With this, we reach the third and final dimension of information in the IDEAL architecture. The evolution of data-based decision making has reached a punctuation point. A focus on data—in its old restricted scope—as the basis for all decision making has left business with increasingly restrictive tools and processes in a rapidly evolving biz-tech ecosystem. It's time to introduce the core components of a new logical architecture—a consolidated, harmonized information platform (REAL)—that is the foundation for a proper balance between stability and innovation in decision making.

5.1 TURNING THE TABLES ON BUSINESS

What do you recall—or, if you're somewhat younger than me, imagine—of 1984? Other than George Orwell's dystopian novel. Los Angeles hosted the Olympic Games. In the UK, a year-long coal miners' strike began. The Space Shuttle Discovery made her maiden voyage. More than 23,000 people died of gas poisoning in the Bhopal Disaster. *Terms of Endearment* won five Oscars. The Bell System of companies was broken up by the U.S. Justice Department after 107 years. The Sony Discman was launched. Ronald Regan won a second term as President of the United States. The first Apple Macintosh went on sale with 128kB of RAM and a single floppy disk drive. I've focused in on this year because it was in 1984 that Teradata released the DBC/1012, the first relational database MPP (massively parallel processing) machine aimed squarely at DSS applications. Oracle introduced read consistency in its version 4. And 1984 also marked the full year hiatus between the announcement of DB2 for MVS by IBM and its general availability in April, 1985. In summary, this was the year that the technology required to move MIS to a wider audience finally arrived.

Figure 5-1: DBC/1012 Data Base Computer System, *1987 Teradata Brochure*

Until that time, MIS were hampered by a combination of hardware and software limitations. As John Rockart noted in a paper introducing critical success factors (CSFs), the most common approach to providing information to executives was via a multitude of reports that were by-products of routine paperwork processing systems for middle managers and, most tellingly, *"where the information subsystem is not computer-based, the reports reaching the top are often typed versions of what a lower level feels is useful"* (Rockart, 1979). My experience in IBM Europe in 1985 was that use of the existing APL-based system (Section 4.1) was mainly through pre-defined reports, that business users needed significant administrative support, and that tailoring of reports for specific needs required IT intervention. The new relational databases were seen as the way to rejuvenate MIS. Business users were initially offered SQL (Structured Query Language), a data manipulation language first defined as SEQUEL at IBM in the 1970s (Chamberlin & Boyce, 1974) and QMF (Query Management Facility), because the language was well defined and basic queries were seen as simple enough for business analysts to master. Views—the output of relational queries—provided a means to restrict user access to subsets of data or to hide from them the need for table joins (Devlin & Murphy, 1988) and the more arcane reaches of SQL. Simpler approaches were also needed, and QBE (Query by Example), developed at IBM (Zloof, 1975), presaged the graphical interfaces common today.

This consensus was not driven by user requirements or technological fit alone. Relational database vendors of the time were in need of a market. Their early databases performed poorly vs. hierarchical or network databases for operational applications, in many cases. MIS, still a relatively immature market, offered an ideal opportunity. From the start, a few new vendors—notably Teradata—optimized their technology exclusively for this space, while other RDBMS vendors chose a more general-purpose path to support both types of requirements. However, given their deeper understanding of transactional processing, these vendors were more successful in improving their technology for operational needs, such as update performance, transactional consistency, and workload management, already well understood from hierarchical or network databases. The relational database market thus diverged in the 1980s, with large-scale, data-driven DSS, pioneered mainly by Teradata, and other vendors successful at small- and medium-scale. A continued focus on transactional requirements allowed RDBMSs to eventually overtake hierarchical and network databases for new operational developments, in a classical example of the working of a *disruptive technology* as defined in *The Innovator's Dilemma* (Christensen, 1997). The outcome was that ERP, SCM, and similar enterprise-wide initiatives throughout the 1990s were all developed in the relational paradigm, which has become the *de facto* standard for operational systems since then. From the late 1990s on, the major general-purpose RDBMS vendors increased focus on MIS function to play more strongly in this market.

Specialized multidimensional cubes and models also emerged through the 1970s and 1980s to support the type of drill-down and pivoting analysis of results widely favored by managers. The term *online analytical processing (OLAP)* was coined in the early 1990s (Codd, et al., 1993) to describe this approach. It is implemented on relational databases (ROLAP), specialized stores optimized for multidimensional processing (MOLAP), or in hybrid systems (HOLAP). As a memorable contrast to OLTP (online transaction processing), the term OLAP gained widespread acceptance and continues to be used by some vendors and analysts as a synonym for BI, MIS or DSS to cover all informational processing.

To this day, there continues to exist a tacit assumption that the correct, and perhaps only, approach to providing data for decision making is through a separate set of data copied from the operational and other source environments. Now, knowing the business and technical reasons for the original separation, we must surely ask if the assumption is still valid.

ThoughtPoint

5.2   THE DATA WAREHOUSE AT THE END OF THE UNIVERSE[1]

Beyond the report generation culture and lack of easily used or understood tools for exploring data that relational technology was expected to address, another key issue that had emerged was the multiplicity of inconsistent analytic data sets being created throughout the organization. Both business and IT were struggling with this. Over time, the problem and the solution became a mantra for BI: a *single version of the truth*.

Operational applications are optimized for particular tasks within the functional or divisional context in which they were built. Banks have separate systems for checking (current) accounts and credit cards. Accounts receivable and accounts payable run on different databases. However, they also contain overlapping data, which may be defined differently or may be inconsistent at certain moments in the process. Acquisitions lead to multiple systems across geographical regions doing the same tasks. Furthermore, data sourced from the same operational system through different pathways may give

---

[1] *The Restaurant at the End of the Universe* (1980) is the second book in the series *The Hitchhiker's Guide to the Galaxy* by Douglas Adams.

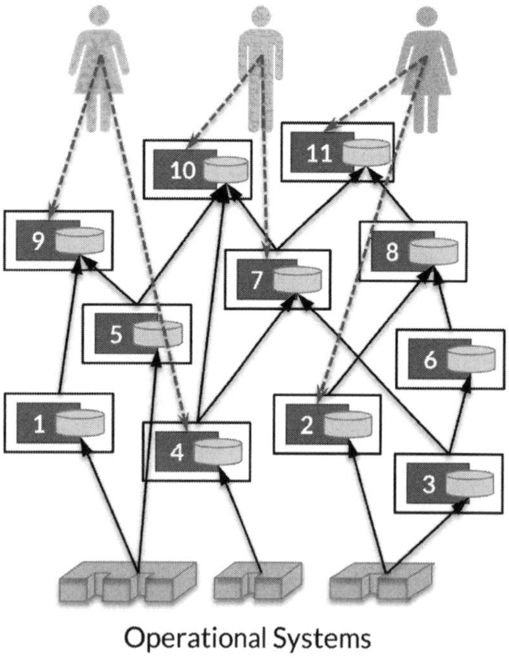

Operational Systems

Figure 5-2:
A typical MIS
environment

differing results. Figure 5-2 is a simplified view of a typical environment; tracing the flow of data fragments via the various numbered management information systems (developed by different teams for divergent purposes) to the business users gives some idea of the potential for data disorientation. All of this leaves the business with difficult reconciliation problems—even getting a single, consistent list of customers can be a challenge. The result is inconsistent and incorrect business decisions. Unseemly disputes arise in management meetings over the validity of differing reports. IT is blamed and tasked by irate executives to explain and fix these inconsistencies and simultaneously required to deliver ever more extracts for new MIS and reporting needs. Add the inefficiency of the same data being extracted from overworked operational systems again and again, and the IT cup doth flow over (Devlin, 1996).

Enter the data warehouse

BM faced the same problems in its internal IT systems, and in 1985, Paul Murphy and I were tasked to define a solution. The term *data warehouse* was conceived in this internal work, and based upon it, we published the first data warehouse architecture in 1988, shown in Figure 5-3 (Devlin & Murphy, 1988). It proposed a *"Business Data Warehouse (BDW)... [as] the single logical storehouse of all the information used to report on the business... In relational terms, a view / number of views that...may have been obtained from different tables."* The BDW was largely normalized, its data reconciled and cleansed through an integrated interface to operational systems. Among the first things that we and other data warehouse builders discovered was that cobbling together even a single, consistent list of customers or products, for example, was hard work. Operational systems that were never designed to work together didn't. Even when individually reliable, these systems failed to dependably deliver consistency. With different meanings, contexts and timings for multiple sources, data reconciliation was expensive. The conclusion was that operational applications could not be fully trusted; they contained data that was incomplete, often inaccurate, and usually inconsistent across different sources. As a result, the data warehouse was proposed as the *sole* place where a complete, accurate and consistent view of the business could be obtained.

A second cornerstone of the architecture was that in order to be useful to and usable by business people, data must have a frame-framework describing what it means, how it is derived and used, who is responsible for it, and so on—a business data directory. This is none other than metadata, sourced from operational systems' data dictionaries and business process definitions from business people. Data dictionaries were components of or add-ons to the hierarchical and network databases of the time (Marco, 2000). However, they typically contained mostly technical metadata about the fields and

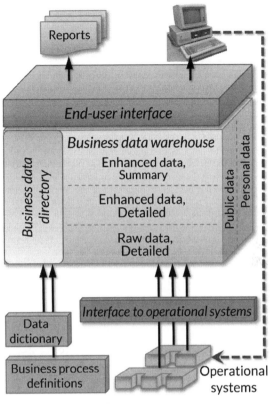

Figure 5-3: First data warehouse architecture, based on Devlin & Murphy, 1988

relationships in the database, supplemented by basic descriptions, written by programmers for programmers. Making data as reliable as possible at its source is only step one. When information about the same topic comes from different sources, understanding the context of its creation and the processes through which it has passed becomes a mandatory second step.

For this process, enterprise-level modeling and enterprise-wide IT are needed. Over the same period, the foundations of information architecture were established (Zachman, 1987), (Evernden, 1996), leading to the concept of enterprise data models (EDM), among other model types. An enterprise data model has become a key design component of data warehousing metadata, although its definition and population has proven to be somewhat problematic in practice. A key tenet was that the EDM should be physically instantiated as fully as possible in the data warehouse to establish agreed definitions for all information. It was also accepted that the operational environment is too restricted by performance limitations and too volatile to business change to allow instantiation of the EDM there. The data models of operational applications were fragmented, incomplete and disjointed, so the data warehouse became the only reliable source of facts.

The final driver for the data warehouse was also the reason for its name. It was a place to store the historical data that operational systems could not keep. In the 1980s, disk storage was expensive, and database performance diminished rapidly as data volumes increased. As a result, historical data was purged from these systems as soon as it was no longer required for day-to-day business needs. Perhaps more importantly, data was regularly overwritten as new events and transactions occurred. For example, an order for goods progresses through many stages in its lifecycle, from provisional to accepted, in production, paid, in transit, delivered and eventually closed. These many stages (and this is a highly simplified example) are often represented by status flags and corresponding dates in a single record, with each new status and date overwriting its predecessor. The data warehouse was to be the repository where all this missing history could be stored, perhaps forever.

ThoughtPoint

The trustworthiness of operational data—its completeness, consistency and cleanliness—although still a concern for many BI implementations, is much improved since the 1980s. Enterprise data modeling plays a stronger operational role, with enterprise-scope ERP and SCM applications now the norm. The data warehouse is no longer the only place where the EDM can be instantiated and populated with trustworthy data. And yet, the goal of a single version of the truth seems to be more remote than ever, as big data brings ever more inconsistent data to light.

The data mart wars of the 1990s and beyond

While envisaging a single logical data repository accessed through relational views is straightforward, its physical implementation was—certainly in the 1990s, and for many years—another matter. Database performance, extract/transform/load (ETL) tooling, data administration, data distribution, project size, and other issues quickly arose. The horizontal divisions in the BDW in Figure 5-3 became obvious architectural boundaries for implementation, and

vendors began to focus on the distinctions between summary/enhanced data
and raw/detailed data. The former is seen
by users and typically provides obvious
and immediate business value. The latter
is, at least initially, the primary concern of
IT and delivers less obvious and immediate business value, such as data integration and quality. In contrast to the user-
unfriendly concept of a warehouse, a *data
mart*—optimized for business users—
sounded far more attractive and inviting.
As a result, many vendors began to promote *independent data marts* in the 1990s
as largely stand-alone DSS environments
based on a variety of technologies and
sourced directly from the operational
applications.

Their attraction was largely based on the
lengthy timeframe for and high cost of
building the integrated data store, by
then called the *enterprise data warehouse
(EDW)*. Business users with urgent deci-

> ## Warehouse or mart
>
> *The terms* data warehouse, enterprise
> data warehouse *and* data mart *are
> much confused and abused in common
> parlance. For clarity, I define:*
>
> *Data warehouse: the data collection,
> management and storage environment
> supporting MIS and DSS.*
>
> *Enterprise data warehouse (EDW): a
> detailed, cleansed, reconciled and mod-
> eled store of cross-functional, historical
> data as part of a data warehouse.*
>
> *Data mart: a set of MIS data optimized
> and physically stored for the convenience
> of a group of users.*
>
> *In a layered data warehouse, dependent
> data marts are fed from the EDW and
> independent marts are discouraged.*

sion-support needs were easily convinced. Architecturally, of
course, this approach was a step backwards. If the data warehouse
was conceived to reduce the number and variety of extracts from
the operational environment—often described as *spaghetti*—
independent data marts significantly reversed that goal. In fact,
except perhaps in terms of the technology used, such marts were
largely identical to previous copies of data for DSS.

Many data warehouse experts consider independent data marts to
be unnecessary political concessions that drain the IT budget. Vendors promote them for speed and ease of delivery of business value
in a variety of guises. Data warehouse appliances, described below,
are often promoted by vendors with data mart thinking. Similar
approaches are often used to sell data analytic tools that promise
rapid delivery of reports, graphs and so on without having to "both-
er with" an enterprise data warehouse. Independent data marts

often deliver early business value. However, they also drive medium and longer term costs, both for business users, who have to deal with incompatible results from different sources, and for IT, who must maintain multiple data feeds and stores, and firefight extensively on behalf of the business when inconsistencies arise. On the other hand, independent data marts may be seen as complementary to an EDW strategy, allowing certain data to be made available more quickly and in technologies other than relational databases—a characteristic that is increasing in importance as larger and more varied data sources are required for decision support.

Another approach, known as *dependent data marts*, is to physically instantiate subsets of the EDW, fed from the consistent raw data there and optimized for the needs of particular sets of users. This approach was adopted by practitioners who understood the enormous value of an integrated and well-modeled set of base data and favored centralized control of the data resource (Inmon, 1992). From the early 1990s, many data warehouse projects attempting to adhere to the stated data quality and management goals of the architecture were severely limited by the performance of general purpose databases and moved to this hybrid or layered model (Devlin, 1996), as depicted in Figure 5-4, where dependent data

Figure 5-4:
Layered DW architecture, based on Devlin, 1996

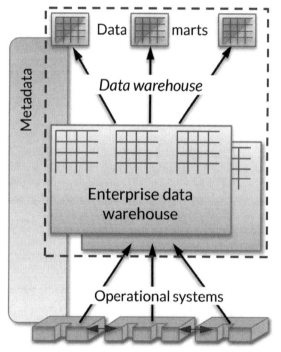

marts are sourced from the EDW and treated as an integral part of the warehouse environment. While addressing query performance needs, as well as providing faster development possibilities, the downside of this approach, however, is that it segments the data resource both vertically—between EDW and data marts—and horizontally—between separate marts. Furthermore, it adds another ETL layer into the architecture, with added design and maintenance costs, as well as additional runtime latency in populating the data marts. However, many vendors and consultants continue to promote this layered approach to ensure query performance as a way to isolate data in a mart, and/or shorten development project timelines. A few vendors, notably Teradata aided by its purpose-built parallel database, pursued the goal of a single, integrated physical implementation of the original architecture with significant success.

The ODS and the virtual data warehouse

The simple and elegant layered architecture shown in Figure 5-4, despite its continued use by vendors and implementers of data warehouses, was further compromised as novel business needs, technological advances, and even marketing initiatives added new and often poorly characterized components to the mix. In the mid-'90s, the operational data store (ODS[2]) was introduced as a new concept (Inmon, et al., 1996) integrating operational data in a subject-oriented, volatile data store, modeled along the lines of the EDW. First positioned as part of the operational environment, it became an integral part of many data management architectures, supporting closer to real-time, non-historical reporting. Although still seen regularly in the literature, the term *ODS* has been appropriated for so many different purposes that its original meaning is often lost. Nonetheless, the concept supports an increasingly important near real-time data warehouse workload, albeit one that is implemented more like an independent data mart and with limited appreciation of the impact of the extra layering involved.

Another long vilified approach to data warehousing is the virtual data warehouse—an approach that leaves all data in its original locations and accesses it through remote queries that federate results across multiple, diverse sources and technologies. An early example was in IBM's Information Warehouse Framework announcement in 1991, where EDA/SQL[3] from Information Builders Inc. (IBI) provided direct query access to remote data sources. The approach met with fierce opposition throughout the 1990s and early 2000s from data warehouse architects, who foresaw significant data consistency—both in meaning and timing—problems, security concerns, performance issues, and impacts on operational systems. The concept re-emerged in the early 2000s as Enterprise Information Integration (EII), based on research in schema mapping (Haas, et al., 2005), and applied to data warehousing in IBM DB2

---

[2] It has long amused me that ODS spoken quickly sounds like *odious* ☺

[3] Since 2001, this technology is part of iWay Software, a subsidiary of IBI.

Information Integrator (Devlin, 2003). The approach has been recently rehabilitated—now called *data virtualization*, or sometimes *data federation*—with an increased recognition that, while a physical consolidation of data in a warehouse is necessary for consistency and historical completeness, other data required for decision support *can* remain in its original location and be accessed remotely at query time. Advantages include faster development using virtualization for prototyping and access to non-relational and/or real-time data values. This change in sentiment is driven by growing business demands for (i) increased timeliness of data for decision making and (ii) big data from multiple, high volume, and often web-based sources (Halevy, et al., 2005). Technologically, both of these factors militate strongly against the copy-and-store layered architecture of traditional data warehousing. In addition, the *mashup*, popular in the world of Web 2.0, which promotes direct access from PCs, tablets, etc., to data combined on the fly from multiple data sources, is essentially another subspecies.

Gartner has also promoted the approach as a *logical data warehouse* (Edjlali, et al., 2012), although the term may suggest the old *virtual DW* terminology, where physical consolidation is unnecessary. In modern usage, however, more emphasis is placed on the need for an underlying integration or *canonical model* to ensure consistent communication and messaging between different components. In fact, it has been proposed that the enterprise data model can be the foundation for virtualization of the data warehouse as well as, or instead of, its instantiation in a physical EDW (Johnston, 2010). By 2012, data virtualization achieved such respectability that long-time proponents of the EDW accepted its role in data management (Swoyer, 2012). Such acceptance has become inevitable, given the growing intensity of the business demands for agility mentioned above. Furthermore, technology has advanced. Virtualization tools have matured. Operational systems have become cleaner. Implementations are becoming increasingly common (Davis & Eve, 2011) in operational, informational and mixed scenarios. Used correctly and with care, data virtualization eliminates or reduces the need to create additional copies of data and provides integrated, dynamic access to real-time information and big data in all its forms.

The advance of the appliances

The data mart wars of the 1990s were reignited early in the new millennium under the banner of analytic / data warehouse / database appliances with the launch of Netezza's first product in 2002. By mid-decade the category was all the rage, as most appliance vendors, such as Netezza, DATAllegro, Greenplum, Vertica and ParAccel (before their acquisitions) sold their appliances as typical independent data marts. As we entered the teens, the appliance had become mainstream as the main players were acquired by hardware and software industry giants. More user-oriented analytic tools, such as QlikView and Tableau, can also be seen as part of the data mart tradition supporting substantial independent data stores on PCs and servers. All these different appliances were enabled by—and further drove—a combination of advances in database hardware and software that provided substantial performance gains at significantly lower prices than the traditional relational database for informational processing. These advances have occurred in three key technology areas, combining to create a "perfect storm" in the data warehousing industry in the past decade.

Parallel processing—SMP and MPP hardware

The growth in processing power through faster clock speeds and larger, more complex processors (scale-up) has been largely superseded by a growth in the number of cores per processor, processors per blade, and servers per cluster operating in parallel (scale-out). Simplistically, there are two approaches to parallel processing. First—and most common, from dual-core PCs all the way to IBM System z—is symmetric multi-processing (SMP) where multiple processors share common memory. SMP is well understood and works well for applications from basic word processing to running a high performance OLTP system like airline reservations. Problems amenable to being broken up into smaller, highly independent parts that can be simultaneously worked upon can benefit greatly from massively parallel processing (MPP), where each processor has its own memory and disks. Many BI and analytic procedures, as well as supercomputer-based scientific computing, fall into this category.

MPP for data warehousing was pioneered by Teradata from its inception, with IBM also producing an MPP edition of DB2, since the mid-1990s. Such systems were mainly sold as top-of-the-range data warehouses and regarded as complex and expensive. MPP has become more common as appliance vendors combined commodity hardware into parallel clusters and took advantage of multi-core processors. As data volumes and analytic complexity grow, there is an increasing drive to move BI to MPP platforms. Programming databases to take full advantage of parallel processing is complex but is advancing apace. Debates continue about the relative advantages of SMP, MPP and various flavors of both. However, a higher perspective—the direction toward increasing parallelization for higher data throughput and performance—is clear.

Solid-state storage—disks and in-memory hardware

Advances—and price reductions—in solid-state memory have allowed core memory sizes to grow enormously, and allow at least some disk storage to be replaced with solid-state devices. Larger volumes of data can be accessed at speeds orders of magnitude faster than possible on spinning disks. This trend splits further into in-memory and solid-state disk (SSD) approaches. The former enables higher-speed performance, but may require redesign of the basic hardware and software architecture of the computer. The latter provides significant, but lower, performance gains without re-architecting the access methods by presenting the solid-state device as a traditional disk. BI and analytic applications, with their need for large volumes of data, benefit greatly from this direction. OLTP systems also benefit from increased processing speed. Because current solid-state devices are volatile and lose their data when power drops, this technology is seen as more appropriate for BI, where there exists another source for any data lost, as opposed to operational systems where the risk of data loss is higher.

Because spinning disk remains substantially cheaper than solid-state storage, and is likely to remain so for the foreseeable future, most solid-state storage is used for data that is accessed regularly, where the benefit is greatest. This leads to temperature-based—hot, warm and cold data is defined on frequency of access—storage hierarchies. Some vendors, however, opt for fully in-memory databases, redesigned to take maximum advantage of the solid-state approach, using disk only as a disaster recovery mechanism. Because solid-state stores remain significantly smaller than the larger disks, solid-state is favored where speed is the priority, as opposed to large data volumes, which favor disk-based approaches. The general trend, therefore, is towards hybrid systems containing a substantial amount of solid-state storage combined with large disk stores. SSDs, with their hybrid design, will likely continue to bridge fully integrated, in-memory databases and large disk drives with high speed, mid-size, non-volatile storage.

Row-based and columnar database design

In the relational model of tables consisting of rows and columns, row-based storage—physically storing the fields of a single database record sequentially on disk—was the physical design of choice of all early relational database designers because it performed well for the typical single record, read/write access method prevalent in OLTP applications. Since the start of the 21st century, relational database and appliance designers have begun experimenting with column-based storage—storing all the fields in each column physically together. Both types are shown in Figure 5-5. The columnar structure is very effective in reducing query time for many types of BI application, which are typically read-only and require only a subset of the fields in each row. In disk-based databases, the resulting reduction in I/O can be significant. Columns also enable more efficient data compression because they contain data of the same structure. Together, these factors enable substantial performance improvements for typical BI queries. Again we see a trade-off in performance. Row-based is optimal for OLTP; columnar is better suited to certain classes of BI application. Loading data into a columnar database requires restructuring of the incoming data, which generally arrives in row-based records. This and other performance trade-offs between row and column storage have led increasingly towards hybrid schemes,

Figure 5-5:
Physical layout of row-based and columnar databases

Row

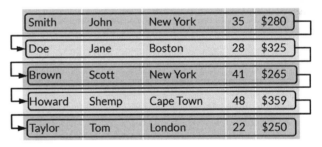

Column

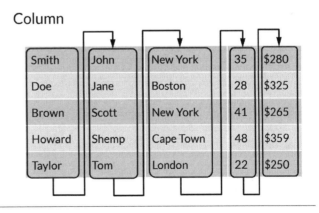

where the DBMS decides which type or even multiple types of storage to use for which data to optimize overall performance.

Summary of technology advances

The major driver for the advances above has been the business demand for faster query and analysis performance for ever larger sets of data. Performance and price/performance measures for analytic databases in TPC-H benchmarks and in quoted customer examples over the past few years show gains of 10X to 100X—and in some cases considerably more—over general-purpose databases. Of course, performance optimization is not new in relational databases. Indexes, materialized views, caching and specialized table designs have been the stock in trade for 20 years now. However, these traditional approaches are often highly specific to the data model in use and anticipated query patterns. Tuning and optimization is thus a labor-intensive process that delays initial use of the data and often requires rework as usage patterns change. And complete *ad hoc* usage cannot be optimized by these means. In contrast, the performance gains in analytic DBMSs step from fundamental hardware/software improvements and are model-independent and generally applicable to all data and most analytical query patterns. This improved performance has also allowed vendors to simplify database design and management. Physical design trade-offs are reduced. The need for indexes can be limited or removed altogether, simplifying both initial and ongoing tuning and maintenance work for database administrators, thus lowering DBA involvement and costs over the entire lifetime of the system.

ThoughtPoint

Data warehouse implementation has strayed far from the ideals of the original architecture. The concept of a single source for DSS was quickly overthrown by technology limitations, practical/political issues for buyers and the needs of vendors to close sales quickly. It is often assumed that data layers are mandatory in any large-scale warehouse implementation. However, the original main driver for layering—query performance of relational databases—has been at least partially overcome in modern technology. Perhaps the key question posed by this history is: why do we persist with the highly fragmented data structure that has evolved?

So far, much of the impact has been on traditional BI—running faster queries over larger data sets. However, as we shall explore in Section 5.7, these advances also enable new ways of thinking about the overall operational/informational architecture that has evolved over nearly three decades. Today, the focus is shifting to the relationship between operational and informational needs. In the future, the emphasis will likely extend to operational processing.

Well, here's another fine[4] mess you've gotten me into

The outcome has been that most data warehouse implementations have become increasingly complex, with combinations of independent and dependent data marts, marts fed from other marts, and even read/write marts added to the mix. These added types and layers of marts lead to an extensive set of ETL that is difficult to maintain as users' needs change. All of this harks back to the earliest days of decision support, when many users made specialized copies of any data they needed, while others—with sufficient technical *nous*—dived directly into the actual sources, irrespective of any ensuing data management chaos. The resulting data warehouse "architecture" today, depicted in Figure 5-6, has lost its original simplicity and provides implementers with little guidance on how to structure DSS in a modern business. As the layers and silos increase, many problems become more pressing. Data duplication leads to ever-growing levels of inconsistency that have to be manually reconciled in the reporting process, reducing users' confidence in the data warehouse. Hardware, software and labor costs grow, and maintenance becomes ever more complex, constraining the provision of new functionality and information

Figure 5-6:
A modern data
warehouse
"architecture"

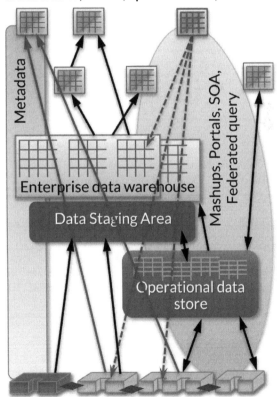

Data marts, cubes, spreadsheets, etc.

Metadata

Mashups, Portals, SOA, Federated query

Enterprise data warehouse

Data Staging Area

Operational data store

Operational systems and more

---

[4] Ollie's catchphrase in the Laurel and Hardy films was actually "...another *nice* mess..."! See http://bit.ly/kARK1

to meet business demands. Customer and partner interactions suffer because of siloed and inconsistent information. And despite demands for more timely information, the added layers actually delay data supply to the users.

It is now mandatory to address these issues. From a business viewpoint, increased competition and higher customer expectations are driving demands that both hard and soft information from all sources—human-sourced, machine-generated and process-mediated, both internal and external—is integrated and internally consistent as far as possible and necessary across the organization, and delivered at ever increasing speed. Data warehousing as originally conceived, with its almost exclusive focus on hard information and internally generated, process-mediated data, fails these business demands. On the technology front, we've seen the advances in databases that have changed the computing landscape. Still to come, we will see how Service Oriented Architecture (SOA) and mobile computing approaches are dramatically changing the data and process structures of the operational environment, while Internet technologies are redefining how users expect to interact with all applications. Big data has added a further, and perhaps final, twist to the story: the data volumes and velocities involved are incompatible with a dependent data mart approach that involves passing such data through the EDW. This, together with the new storage technologies needed, leads to the conclusion that these data sets can be supported only in an architecture that allows independent data marts in addition to an EDW. All of these changes in technology press in upon the data warehouse environment from above and below, within and without, challenging the fundamental assumptions upon which data warehousing was originally defined.

ThoughtPoint

The data warehouse may be at the end of its own universe. Its original *raison d'être* as the one, true, consistent past and present state of the business is no longer possible nor, arguably, needed. However, it is the only approach to data management that has even considered many of the information issues raised so far. The bottom line is that the data warehouse architecture, as originally conceived and eventually delivered, is in need of a radical overhaul.

5.3   BUSINESS INTELLIGENCE—REALLY?

The previous section focused on the data aspect of data-based decision making, particularly on the preparation phase. While this is probably the IT comfort zone in decision support, it is also fair to say that without meaningful and consistent data, promoting data-based decision making to the business is a recipe for disaster. It takes only a single set of erroneous information for the entire approach to be discredited in the users' eyes. So it was that in data warehousing, although originally defined as covering the entire process of data-based decision support—from defining, collecting and preparing the needed data to the user-facing tooling required by business users—much of the early focus was on data management issues. *Plus ça change, plus c'est la même chose.*

By the early 1990s, the data warehouse was perceived much as its physical counterpart—a user-unfriendly place, cavernous, poorly lit and infested with deadly fork-lift trucks. As a result, the phrase *business intelligence (BI)* was adopted by Gartner analyst, Howard Dresner, when he moved from Digital Equipment Corporation (DEC), where the phrase was in use internally from 1989[5]. The term was also in use in the early 1990s in the intelligence—meaning spying—community in the context of industrial espionage. However, Dresner's stated aim was to emphasize the business aspect of data warehousing, summarized in a common definition of BI as *"a set of concepts and methods to improve business decision making by using fact-based support systems"* (Power, 2009). In practical terms, this translated into a set of reporting and *ad hoc* query tools with attractive presentation capabilities. Spreadsheets clearly meet these criteria and are widely used to support decision making, but, as we saw in Chapter 4, they are seen as anathema to the data management foundation of data-based decision making.

One might argue that *business intelligence* is actually an oxymoron. Those of us who've worked in large enterprises have seen enough evidence to conclude that many decisions have limited relevance to stated business goals and a shaky relationship with intelligence. How many successful decisions have been declared as based on

---

[5] Private communication

"gut feeling"? And unsuccessful ones blamed on "lack of *reliable information*"? How often does political expedience override a strongly argued rationale? How many business analysts have been asked to "just take one more look at the figures" when the numbers seemed to contradict the group wisdom of the boardroom? So, what does the term really mean?

Pharaoh's tomb—the BI usage pyramid

The meaning of BI may be best explored through its support of decision making as it relates to business roles and organization, depicted in the second ubiquitous pyramid in the BI literature and shown in Figure 5-7. Classical Egyptologists identify pyramids as the Pharaohs' tombs; alternative historians propose an array of far more interesting possibilities. Their original purpose remains ob-scure. The BI usage pyramid has a simple and obvious purpose, but is weighed down with added—and often misleading—connotations. In its most basic form, it describes three broad levels in the organi-zation where BI plays. The original, and still most widely practiced, form is *tactical BI*. Mid-level managers and supervisors of ongoing activities, as well as the more numerically savvy (often termed *inde-pendent*) business analysts, who support them, are the target audi-ence. The goal of tactical BI is three-fold: (i) to ensure ongoing operational processes and their operators are running optimally, (ii) to find and encourage speed or productivity improvements in these processes and (iii) to investigate and fix any anomalies that may arise from either internal or external causes. Typically operating in a timeframe of days to weeks, tactical BI uses historical, often rec-onciled, data sourced from operational systems through the data warehouse environment, usually via data marts. Tactical BI is well suited to the traditional data warehouse architecture shown in Section 5.2 and well supported by the BI query, analysis and reporting tools that emerged in the 1980s and beyond. In fact, the first two goals above drove tactical BI to-wards the current preponderance of report gener-ation and, more recently, dashboard creation at this level. The investigative third goal above has, in many cases, been taken over by spreadsheets and thus deemed not worthy of consideration as BI by some purists.

Figure 5-7:
The BI usage pyramid

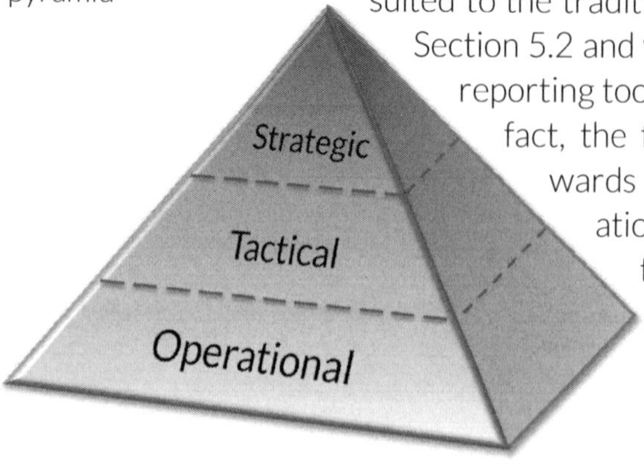

Strategic

Tactical

Operational

Historically, *strategic BI*—aimed at supporting senior managers and executives in long-term, strategic decision making—was the next target for proponents of BI. This need had been identified as early as 1982 in a Harvard Business Review paper *The CEO Goes On-Line* (Rockart & Treacy, 1982), where the authors reported on the shocking discovery that some C-level executives were using desktop computer terminals to access status information—reports—about their businesses and even analyzing and graphing data trends. One executive even reported that *"Access to the relevant data to check out something...is very important. My home terminal lets me perform the analysis while it's at the forefront of my mind."* The paper also introduced the term *executive information system (EIS)* to an unsuspecting world; a reading some 40 years later reveals just how little has changed in the interim in senior managers' needs for data about their businesses and their ability to probe into it. An intriguing and earlier reference to a system on a boardroom screen and computer terminals declares *"Starting this week [the CEO of Gould] will be able to tap three-digit codes into a 12-button box resembling the keyboard of a telephone. SEX will get him sales figures. GIN will call up a balance sheet. MUD is the keyword for inventory"* (Business Week, 1976). At least the codes were memorable!

These executive-level, *dependent* users needed extensive support teams to prepare reports. However, the thought of an executive analyzing data no longer surprises anyone, and today's executives have grown up in an era when computer, and later Internet use was becoming pervasive. Driven by the iPad revolution, *independent* executives probably outnumber their dependent colleagues today, although extensive backroom data preparation and support remains common. Driven in large part from business management schools, the concept of EIS developed largely independently from data warehousing through the 1980s (Thierauf, 1991), (Kaniclides & Kimble, 1995). With the growing popularity of data warehousing and BI, and the recognition that data consistency was a vital prerequisite, IT shops and vendors gradually began to include EIS within BI as the top layer of the pyramid.

I speak of *data* above because despite the *information* in its name, EIS focused more on data, mainly originating from the financial and operational systems. External data sources such as Standard and

Poor's were also seen as important to executives. However, it has long been recognized that soft information—press and TV reports, analyst briefings, and internal documents and presentations, as well as informal information from face-to-face meetings—forms a high percentage of the information needs of the majority of executives, especially when strategizing on longer-term (months to years) decisions. Its absence from EIS implementations, especially those fed from enterprise data warehouses, is probably an important factor in their relative lack of commercial success in the market. Strategic BI also maintained an emphasis on historical data and was differentiated from tactical BI largely by the longer business impact timeframe—months to years—expected at this level. Strategic BI implementations have struggled to gain widespread traction for two main reasons. First, they usually exclude soft information, of both the formal and the collaborative, informal varieties. Second, they typically require the reconciliation of all hard information across the full range of operational sources, pushing them far out on any reasonable data warehouse implementation timeline.

The final layer of the usage pyramid, *operational BI*, emerged from the development of the ODS and operational BI, described above. The focus is on intra-day decisions that must be made in hours or even seconds or less. Operational analytics is today's incarnation, emphasizing the use of hard information in ever increasing amounts. The initial users of operational BI were seen as front-line staff who deal directly with customer, supplier, manufacturing and other real-time processes of the business, supported through live dashboards. Increasingly, operational applications use this function directly through exposed APIs. Based on detailed, near real-time, low latency data, operational BI poses significant technical challenges to the traditional data warehouse architecture, where reconciling disparate data sources is often a prolonged process. Nonetheless, operational BI has grown in stature and is now of equal importance to the tactical BI layer for most businesses.

Figure 5-7 is used widely to represent several aspects of BI usage. It reflects the traditional hierarchical structure of organizations, both in terms of the relative importance of individual decisions and the number of decisions and potential BI users at each level. It is also often used to illustrate data volumes needed, although this can be misleading for two reasons. First is an assumption about the level of summarization vs. detail in the three layers. Operational BI demands highly detailed and ongoing data feeds, clearly requiring the largest possible volume of data. As we move to the tactical layer, it is often reasonable to summarize data. Even with lengthy historical periods involved, this seldom offsets the summarization savings. However, some business needs do require substantial levels of detail for tactical BI. At the strategic level, significant summarization is common. However, the second factor, the need for soft information for strategic BI mentioned earlier, must also be taken into account. Soft information can be voluminous and is difficult to summarize mathematically. In short, the shape of the pyramid indicates information volumes poorly.

The relationship of the pyramid to the organizational hierarchy may suggest that data flows up and decisions down the structure. Again, while this may be true in some business areas, it is certainly not universally the case. Many individual operational, tactical and strategic decisions have an existence entirely independent of other layers. A strategic decision about a merger or acquisition, for example, is highly unlikely to require particular operational decisions in its support. The IT origins of the BI pyramid and its consequent focus on data rather than information shed little light on the process of decision making. The visual resemblance of the BI usage pyramid to the DIKW version we met in Chapter 3 promotes these further assumptions: that data is the prevalent basis for operational BI (only partly true), while strategic BI is built on knowledge (likely) or even wisdom (probably untrue). However, the BI usage pyramid is more resilient than its DIKW counterpart. It identifies three relatively distinct uses of BI that relate well to particular roles and processes in the organization, to which we return in Chapters 7 and 9. What it misses, because of that very focus on roles and processes, is the topic we now call *business analytics*.

Analytics—digging beneath the pyramids

Data mining, known academically as knowledge discovery in databases (KDD), emerged at the same time as BI in the 1990s (Fayyad, et al., 1996) as the application of statistical techniques to large data sets to discover patterns of business interest. There are probably few BI people who haven't heard and perhaps repeated the "beer and diapers (or nappies)" story: a large retailer discovered through basket analysis—data mining of till receipts—that men who buy diapers on Friday evenings often also buy beer. The store layout was rearranged to place the beer near the diapers and beer sales soared. Sadly, this story is now widely believed to be an urban legend or sales pitch rather than a true story of unexpected and momentous business value gleaned from data mining. Nevertheless, it makes the point that there may be nuggets of useful information to be discovered through statistical methods in any large body of data, and action that can be taken to benefit from these insights.

In the past few years, the phrase *business analytics* has come to prominence. Business analytics, or more simply, analytics, is defined by Thomas Davenport as *"the extensive use of data, statistical and quantitative analysis, explanatory and predictive models, and fact-based management to drive decisions and actions"* (Davenport & Harris, 2007) and as a subset of BI. Other authors suggest it is either an extension of or even a replacement for BI. It also clearly overlaps with data mining. Often discussed as *predictive analytics* or *operational analytics*, the market further tries to differentiate analytics from BI as focused on influencing future customer behavior, either longer term or immediately. A common pattern of operational analytics is to analyze real-time activity—on a website, for example—in combination with historical patterns and instantly adapt the operational interaction—offering a different or additional product or appropriate discount—to drive sales. Thus, none of these ideas are particularly novel. BI included similar concepts from the beginning.

If we position business analytics in the BI usage pyramid, we can immediately see that operational analytics is, at most, an extension of operational BI. Similarly, predictive analytics enhances and extends the investigative goal of tactical BI that has mainly migrated into spreadsheets. Davenport's definition above is often quoted to emphasize the role of statistics and predictive models, but perhaps the most important aspect is its underlining of the goal of driving decisions and actions. Beyond that, what have changed are the data sources and volumes available in big data, as well as the faster processing demanded by users and provided by modern hardware and software advances. For example, logistics firms now use analysis of real-time traffic patterns, combined with order transaction data and traditional route planning, to optimize scheduling of deliveries to maximize truck utilization, and to improve customer satisfaction by providing more accurate estimates of arrival times. While one might be tempted to think that this is simply a matter of speed or scale, in fact, the situation is more of a *step change in what is possible*, enabling new ways of making decisions and driving the new ways of doing business defined as the biz-tech ecosystem.

Data scientists or Egyptologists?

As digging beneath pyramids of data has become an increasingly popular pastime, we've seen the emergence of a new profession: the data scientist. Although the term *data science* has a long history, both it and the role of data scientist have been taken to heart by the big data movement. And given the breadth of definitions of big data itself (see Chapter 6), you won't be surprised to discover that data scientists are equally forgiving about the scope of their job. Unlike Egyptologists.

Figure 5-8:
Khafre's Pyramid,
Giza, Egypt

IBM's Swami Chandrasekaran has built a comprehensive visual Metro map of the skills required of a data scientist (Chandrasekaran, 2013). The visual metaphor is appropriate for a budding data scientist but, with disconnected lines and a technical, big data point of view, the overall picture is disappointing for a business trying to grasp precisely what a data scientist is. In the simplest terms, I believe that a data scientist is best thought of as an advanced, inspired business analyst and power user of a wide set of data preparation and mining, business intelligence, information visualization, and presentation tools. Added to this he or she needs to understand the business, both process and information, and have the ability to present a convincing case to managers and executives. A very broad skill set and unlikely to be found in one person. Bill Franks, Chief Analytics Officer at Teradata, provides a comprehensive recipe for the making of an analytic professional or data scientist (Franks, 2012).

A step beyond the pyramid

Looking forward, a change in thinking of particular interest considers how we analyze and interpret reality. BI tools and approaches have generally followed the basic premise of the *scientific method* in their use of information, where hypotheses and theories are proposed and subsequently verified or discarded based on the collection and analysis of information. It has been suggested that business analytics, when used on big data, signals the end of the scientific method (Anderson, 2012). The statistician, George E. P. Box said, over thirty years ago, that *"all models are wrong, but some are useful"* (Box, 1979). Anderson reported that Peter Norvig, Google's research director, suggested that today's reality is that *"all models are wrong, and increasingly you can succeed without them."* With the petabytes of data and petaflops of processing power Google has at its disposal, one can dispense with the theorizing and simply allow conclusions to emerge from the computer.

Correlation trumps causation, declare the authors of *Big Data: A Revolution That Will Transform How We Live, Work and Think* (Mayer-Schonberger & Cukier, 2013). Clearly, the emergence of big data has reemphasized the analysis of information and the excitement of discovering the previously unknown in its midst. But what becomes "known" if it is a mathematical model so complex that its only explanation is that the simulation works? At least until the arrival of a giant dinosaur extinction event asteroid that wasn't—and couldn't be—in the equations because it wasn't in the underlying data (Weinberger, 2012). The problem is not confined to asteroids or, indeed, black swans—a metaphor for unexpected events that have a major effect, and are often inappropriately rationalized. As we gather ever more data and analyze it more deeply and rapidly, we begin to fall prey to the myth that we are increasingly predicting the future with ever greater certainty. A more realistic view might be that the computers and algorithms are making sophisticated guesses about future outcomes. As Alistair Croll opines, *"Just because the cost of guessing is dropping quickly to zero doesn't mean we should treat a guess as the truth"* (Croll, 2013).

The above radical thinking may be the ultimate logical conclusion of data-based decision making, but I also seriously question if we can trust the Beast in the computer that far, basing decisions solely on basic data. Chapter 8 expands the scope of thinking about soft information and knowledge—using the full scope of information stored digitally today. And that, of course, is only a staging post on the quest for a full understanding of how human and team decisions can be fully supported by computers, as we'll explore in Chapter 9. But for now, it's back to the present, where the data warehouse has faced its biggest challenge for quite a few years now: the timeliness of its data.

5.4   TODAY'S CONUNDRUM—CONSISTENCY OR TIMELINESS

I *want it all and I want it now..."* Queen's 1989 hit[6] sums it up. So far, we've been dealing with the demand for it all. Now we need to address delivering it now. Speed is of the essence, whether in travel, delivery times, or news. For business, speed has become a primary driver of behavior. Shoppers demand instant gratification in purchases; retailers respond with constantly stocked shelves. Suppliers move to real-time delivery via the Web and just-in-time manufacturing. In short, processes have moved into overdrive. Within the business, data needs, already extensive, are thus becoming ever closer to real-time. Sales, front-office, and call center personnel require current information from diverse channels about customer status, purchases, orders and even complaints in order to serve customers more quickly. Marketing and design functions operate on ever-shortening cycles, needing increasingly current information to react to market directions and customer preferences and behavior. Just-in-time manufacturing and delivery demand near real-time monitoring of and actions on supply chains. Managers look for up-to-the-minute and even up-to-the-second information about business performance internally and market conditions externally.

At a technology level, faster processors, parallel processing, solid-state disks and in-memory stores all drive faster computing. Databases and database appliances are marketed on speed of response to queries. Dashboard vendors promise to deliver near real-time KPIs (key performance indicators). ETL tools move from batch de-

---

[6] *I Want it All*, Queen's 1989 hit written by Brian May.

livery of data to micro-batches and eventually to streaming approaches. Complex event processing (CEP) tools monitor events as they stream past on the network, analyze correlations, infer higher-order events and situations—then act without human intervention. In business intelligence, IT strives to provide faster responses to decision makers' needs for data. Timeliness manifests most obviously in operational BI, where information availability is pushed from weekly or daily to intra-day, hourly and lower. Near instantaneous availability of facts and figures is supported by streaming ETL, federated access to operational databases or CEP.

But as we've seen, before e-commerce made speed and timeliness the flavors *du jour*, correctness and consistency of data and behaviors were more widely valued. Data consistency and integration were among the key drivers for data warehousing and business intelligence. Users longed for consistent reports and answers to decision-support questions so that different departments could give agreed-upon answers to the CEO's questions. Meetings would descend into chaos as managers battled over whose green lineflow report depicted the most correct version of the truth. Decisions were delayed as figures were reworked. And IT, as provider of many of the reports, often got the blame—and the expensive, thankless and time-consuming task of figuring out who was right. Unfortunately, within the realm of business information, timeliness and consistency, while not totally incompatible, make uncomfortable bedfellows. Business information is generated by and changed in widely disparate processes and physical locations. The processes often consist of a mix of legacy and modern applications, often built independently at different times and by different departments. The result is inconsistent information at its very source. Increasingly, different parts of business processes are highly distributed geographically. Despite companies' best efforts, such distribution, often predicated on staff cost savings, usually introduces further inconsistencies in the data.

Typically, IT has carried out some level of integration over the years to improve data consistency, but it is often piecemeal and asynchronous. Master data management is but one more recent example of such an effort. However, integration takes time—both in initial design and implementation, as well as in operation. In such an environment, achieving simultaneous timeliness and consistency of information requires: (i) potentially extensive application redesign to ensure fully consistent data definitions and complete real-time processing and (ii) introduction of synchronous interactions between different applications. This process becomes more technically demanding and financially expensive in a roughly exponential manner as information is made consistent within ever shorter time periods, as shown in Figure 5-9.

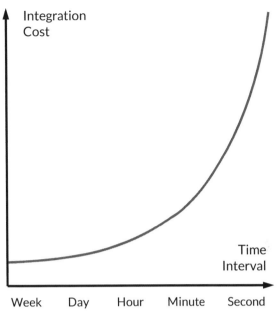

Figure 5-9: Integration cost as a function of timeliness

Despite some consultants' and vendors' claims to the contrary, neither timeliness nor consistency have ever been absolutes, nor are they now. Each has its pros and cons, its benefits and costs. Different parts of the business value them to varying degrees. Finding a balance between the two in the context of both business needs and IT architectural decisions is increasingly important. And adopting technological solutions that ease the conflict becomes mandatory. The solution, however, entails making choices—potentially difficult ones—about which applications prefer timeliness over consistency and *vice versa*, as well as creating different delivery mechanisms. An EDW-based approach maximizes consistency; virtualization maximizes timeliness. Some classes of data might need to be delivered through both methods so that, for example, a report that is delivered with consistent data in the morning might be supplemented by timely data during the day. In such these cases and as a general principle, metadata informing users of the limitations that apply to each approach is required.

Delivering a wrong answer early can have a longer-term and greater impact as incorrect decisions, based on the initial error, multiply in the time period before the correct answer arrives—especially if the error is only discovered much later. Timely, but (potentially) inconsistent, data may be better delivered as an update to a prior consistent base set.

ThoughtPoint

De-layering the operational and informational worlds

As already noted, the need for consistency was the primary driver of the data warehouse architecture, leading to a layered structure, due—at least in part—to limitations of the technology used to implement it. The question thus arises of whether advances in technology could eliminate or reduce layering to gain improvements in timeliness or maintainability. There are two related, but different aspects: (i) removing layering within the data warehouse, and (ii) reuniting the operational and information environments. The possibility of the former has been increasing for nearly a decade now, as increasing processor power and software advances in relational databases have driven gains in query performance. Mainstream RDBMSs have re-promoted the concept of views, often materialized and managed by the database itself to reduce the dependency of dependent data marts on separate platforms populated via ETL tools. The extreme query performance—rated at up to two or three orders of magnitude higher than general purpose RDBMSs—of analytic databases has also allowed consideration of reducing data duplication across the EDW and data mart layers.

We are now seeing the first realistic attempts to merge operational and informational systems. Technically, this is driven by the rapid price decreases for memory and multi-core systems, allowing new in-memory database designs. The design point for traditional RDBMSs has been disk based, with special focus on optimizing the bottleneck of accessing data on spinning disk, which is several orders of magnitude slower than memory access. By 2008, a number of researchers, including Michael Stonebraker and Hasso Plattner, were investigating the design point for in-memory databases, both OLTP (Stonebraker, et al., 2008) and combined operational/informational (Plattner, 2009). The latter work has led to the development of SAP HANA, a hardware/software solution first rolled out for informational, and subsequently for operational, applications. The proposition is relatively simple: with the performance gains of an in-memory database, the physical design trade-offs made in the past for operational vs. informational processing become unnecessary. The same data structure in memory performs adequately in both modes.

In terms of reducing storage and ongoing maintenance costs, particularly when driven by a need for timeliness, this approach is attractive. However, it doesn't explicitly support reconciliation of data from multiple operational systems as data warehousing does. Building history is technically supported by the use of an insert-based update approach, but keeping an ever-growing and seldom-used full history of the business in relatively expensive memory makes little sense. Nor does the idea of storing vast quantities of soft information in a relational format appeal. Nonetheless, when confined to operational and near-term informational data, the approach offers a significant advance in delivering increased timeliness and improved consistency within the combined set of data.

5.5 MOST OF OUR ASSUMPTIONS HAVE OUTLIVED THEIR USELESSNESS[7]

The questions posed throughout this and the previous chapters lead directly to an examination of how our thinking about data management in business, both in general and with particular reference to decision support, has evolved. Or in many cases, has not moved very far at all. An earlier paper (Devlin, 2009) identified four "ancient postulates" of data warehousing based on an analysis of the evolution of the data warehouse architecture. An additional three postulates now emerge.

1. Operational and informational environments should be separated for both business and technical reasons

Dating from the 1970s, this first postulate predates data warehousing, but was incorporated without question in the first data warehouse architecture. At that time, both business management and technology were still at a comparatively early stage of evolution. Business decision makers operated on longer planning cycles and often deliberately ignored the fluctuating daily flow of business events—their interest was in monthly, quarterly or annual reporting; understanding longer trends and directions; or in providing input to multi-year strategies. On the technology front, applications

---

[7] Marshall McLuhan

were hand-crafted and run in mainframes operating at the limits of their computing power and storage.

These factors led to one of the longest-lived postulates in IT—the need to separate operational and informational computing and systems. From its earliest days, DSS envisaged extracting data from the operational applications into a separate system designed for decision makers. And, at the time, that made sense: it was what business users needed, and the technology could support it more easily than allowing direct *ad hoc* access to operational databases. Of all seven postulates, this is the one that has never been seriously challenged…until now, as we saw in the previous section.

2. A *data warehouse is the only way to obtain a dependable, integrated view of the business*

This postulate was clearly visible in the first architecture paper (Devlin & Murphy, 1988) and in the prior work carried out in IBM and other companies in the mid-1980s. As we've already seen in the previous section, a basic assumption of this architecture was that operational applications could not be trusted. The data they contained was often incomplete, inaccurate, and inconsistent across different applications. As a result, the data warehouse was the only place where a complete, accurate and consistent view of the business could be obtained.

This postulate is now under challenge on two fronts. First, the data quality of operational systems has improved since then. While still far from perfect, many companies now use commercial off-the-shelf applications in house or in the Cloud, such as SAP or Salesforce.com, with well-defined, widely tested schemas, and extensive validation of input data. These factors, together with extensive sharing .of data between businesses electronically and between process stages, have driven improved data quality and consistency in the operational environment. Second, the growth of big data poses an enormous challenge to the principle that a dependable, integrated view of the business is achievable in any single place. Going forward, we move from the concept of a single version of the truth to multiple, context-dependent versions of the truth, which must be related to one another and users' understanding of them via business metadata.

3. The data warehouse is the only possible instantiation of the full enterprise data model

Another cornerstone of the data warehouse was that data is use-less without a framework that describes what the data means, how it is derived and used, who is responsible for it, and so on. Thus arose the concept of metadata and one of its key manifestations: the enterprise data model. By 1990, this concept had been adopted by data warehousing from information architecture (Zachman, 1987) as the basis for designing the EDW and consolidating data from the disparate operational environment. A key tenet was that the EDM should be physically instantiated as fully as possible in the data warehouse to establish agreed definitions for all information. It was also accepted that the operational environment is too re-stricted by performance limitations; too volatile to business change and its data models too fragmented, incomplete and disjointed to allow instantiation of the EDM there. Thus, the data warehouse became the only reliable placement for the EDM. However, imple-mentation has proven rather problematic in practice.

With the increasing pace of business change and the growing role of soft data in business, it is increasingly difficult to envisage the type of enterprise-scope projects required to reach this goal. The EDM and its instantiation in the data warehouse thus remain aspi-rational, at best, and probably in need of serious rethinking.

4. A layered data warehouse is necessary for speedy and reliable query performance

As discussed in Section 5.2, data marts and, subsequently, other layering of the data warehouse were introduced in the 1990s to address RDBMS performance issues and the long project cycles associated with data warehouse projects. The value of this postu-late can be clearly seen in the longevity of the architectural ap-proach. However, this layering presents its own problems. It delays the passage of data from operations to decision makers; real-time reaction is impossible. Maintenance can become costly as impact analysis for any change introduced can be complex and far reaching across complex ETL trails and multiple copies of data.

The emergence of analytic databases in the early to mid-2000s, with their combination of software and hardware advances demonstrated that query speeds over large data volumes could be improved by orders of magnitude over what had been previously possible. Even more clearly than the split between operational and informational in postulate 1, the layering in the warehouse itself is becoming, in many cases, increasingly unnecessary.

5. Information can be treated simply as a super-class of data

Since the beginning of computing in the 1950s, the theoretical and practical focus has largely been on data—optimized for computer usage—and information has been viewed through a data-centric lens. Chapter 3 discussed at length why this is completely back-to-front, placing an IT-centric construct at the heart of communication that is essentially human—however imprecise, emotionally laden, and intimately and ultimately dependent on the people involved, their inter-relationships, and the context in which they operate. As the biz-tech ecosystem comes to fruition, we must start from meaning—in a personal and business context—and work back through knowledge and information all the way to data. In this way, we can begin to reorient decision making to its business purpose and the people who must make the decision and take action.

6. Data quality and consistency can only be assured by IT through a largely centralized environment

This postulate had its origins in the complexity and experimental nature of early computers, but it continues to hold sway even though modern PCs and an ever-increasing number of mobile devices are now used extensively by business users, and hold far more data in total than centralized systems. While centralized control and management are the ideal approach to assure data quality and consistency, the real world of today's computing environment makes that impossible.

Management of data quality and consistency must now be automated and highly distributed. In addition, they must be applied to data based on careful judgment, rather than seen as a mandatory requirement for all data.

7. Business users' innovation in data / information usage is seen by IT as marginal and threatening to data quality

This belief can be traced to the roughly simultaneous appearance of viable PCs and RDBMSs in the 1980s. As we observed in Chapter 4, IT was used to managing the entire data resource of the business, and as data became more complex and central to the business, the emerging relational and largely centralized databases were seized with both hands. PCs and spreadsheets were first ignored and then reviled by the IT arbiters of data quality. This postulate has continued to hold sway even until today, despite the growing quantity and role of distributed, user-controlled data. Properly targeted and funded data governance initiatives are required to change this situation. Such initiatives are now widely recognized as a business responsibility (Hopwood, 2008), but in many companies, the drive and interest still comes from IT. In the biztech ecosystem, business management must step up to their responsibility for data quality and work closely with IT to address the technical issues arising from a highly distributed environment.

All these commonly held assumptions have contributed to the relative stasis we've seen in the data warehousing world over the past two decades. The time has come to let them go.

5.6   IDEAL ARCHITECTURE (3): INFORMATION, TIMELINESS/CONSISTENCY DIMENSION

As we've seen throughout this chapter, the original business drive for consistency in reporting has been largely supplanted by a demand for timeliness. However, from a conceptual point of view, in a highly distributed computing environment where information is created in diverse, unrelated systems, these two characteristics are actually interdependent. Increase one and you decrease the other. In our new conceptual architecture, we thus need a dimension of the information layer that describes this. In fact, data warehouse developers have been implicitly aware of this dimension since the inception of data warehousing. However, it has been concealed by two factors: (1) an initial focus only on consistency and (2) the conflation of a physical architecture consisting of discrete computing systems with a conceptual/logical architecture that separated different business and processing needs.

As shown in Figure 5-10, the *timeliness / consistency (TC)* dimension of information at the conceptual architecture level consists of five classes that range from highly timely but necessarily inconsistent information on the left, to highly consistent but necessarily untimely on the right. From left to right, timeliness moves from information that is essentially ephemeral to eternal.

In-flight information consists of messages on the wire or on an enterprise service bus; it is valid only at the instant it passes by. This data-in-motion might be processed, used, and discarded. It is guaranteed only to be consistent within the message or, perhaps, the stream of which it is part. In-flight information may be recorded somewhere, depending on process needs, at which stage it becomes live.

Live information has a limited period of validity and is subject to continuous change. It also is not necessarily completely consistent with other live information. In terms of typical usage, these two classes correspond to today's operational systems.

Stable information, the mid-point on the continuum, represents a first step towards guaranteed consistency by ensuring that stored data is protected from constant change and, in some cases, enhanced by contextual information or structuring. In existing systems, the stable class corresponds to any data store where data is

Figure 5-10:
Timeliness/
consistency
dimension of
information

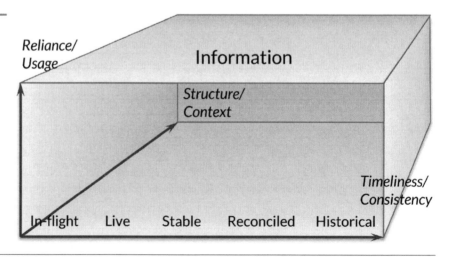

not over-written whenever it changes, including data marts, particularly the independent version, and content stores. This class thus marks the transition point from operational to informational.

Full enterprise-wide, cross-system consistency is the characteristic of *reconciled* information, which is stored in usage-neutral form and stable in the medium to long term. Its timeliness, however, is likely to have been sacrificed to an extent depending on its sources; older, internal, batch-oriented sources and external sources often delay reconciliation considerably. The enterprise data warehouse is the prime example of this class. MDM stores and ODSs can, depending on circumstances, contain reconciled information, but often bridge this and the live or stable classes.

Historical information is the final category, where the period of validity and consistency is, in principle, forever. But, like real-world history, it also contains much personal opinion and may be rewritten by the victors in any power struggle! Historical information may be archived in practice, or may exist in a variety of long-term data warehouse or data mart stores. It is, of course, subject to data retention policies and practices, which are becoming ever more important in the context of big data.

Many of the examples used above come from the world of hard information and data warehousing, in particular. This is a consequence of the transactional nature of the process-mediated data that has filled the majority of information needs of business until now. However, the classes themselves apply equally to all types of information to a greater or lesser extent. For softer information, they are seldom recognized explicitly today but will become of increasing importance as social media and other human-sourced information is applied in business decisions of increasing value.

The timeliness/consistency dimension broadly mirrors the lifecycle of information from creation through use, to archival and/or disposal. This spectrum also relates to the concept of hot, warm, and cold data, although these terms are used in a more technical context. As with all our dimensions, these classes are loosely defined with soft boundaries; in reality, these classes gradually merge from one into the next. It is therefore vital to apply critical judgment when deciding which technology is appropriate for any particular base information set. The knowledge and skills of any existing BI team will be invaluable in this exercise, but will need to be complemented by expertise from the content management team.

5.7   BEYOND THE DATA WAREHOUSE

Given the extent and rate of changes in business and technology described thus far, it is somewhat unexpected that the term *data warehouse* and the architectural structures and concepts described in Sections 5.2 and 5.3 still carry considerable weight after more than a quarter of a century. However, this resistance to change cannot endure much longer. Indeed, one goal of this book is to outline what a new, pervasive information architecture looks like, within the scope of data-based decision making and the traditional data sources of BI for the past three decades.

Reports of my death have been greatly exaggerated[8]

Of course, the data warehouse has been declared terminally ill before now. BI and data warehouse projects have long had a poor reputation for delivering on-time or within budget. While these difficulties have clear and well-understood reasons—emanating from project scope and complexity, external dependencies, organizational issues, and more—vendors have regularly proposed quick-fix solutions to businesses seeking quick and reliable solutions to BI needs. The answers, as we've seen, range from data marts and analytic appliances to spreadsheets and big data. As each of these approaches has gained traction in the market, the death of the data warehouse has been repeatedly—and incorrectly—pronounced. The underlying reason for such faulty predictions is a misunderstanding of the consistency vs. timeliness conundrum described in section 5.4 above. The data warehouse is primarily designed for consistency; the other solutions are more concerned with timeliness, in development and/or operation. And data consistency remains a valid business requirement, alongside timeliness, which has growing importance in a fully interconnected world. Nonetheless, as the biz-tech ecosystem evolves to become essentially real-time,

---

[8] Mark Twain's actual written reaction in 1897 was: *"The report of my death was an exaggeration."*

the data warehouse cannot retain its old role of all things to all informational needs, going forward. As a consequence, while it will not die, the data warehouse concept faces a shrinking role in decision support as the business demands increasing quantities of information of a structure or speed that are incompatible with the original architecture or relational technology.

5.8   REAL ARCHITECTURE (I): CORE BUSINESS INFORMATION

In essence, the data warehouse must return to its roots, as represented by Figure 5-3 on page 121. This requires separate consideration of the two main architectural components of today's data warehouses—the enterprise data warehouse and the data mart environment. In the case of the EDW, this means an increasing focus on its original core value propositions of consistency and historical depth, where they have business value, including:

1. The data to be loaded is process-mediated data, sourced from the operational systems of the organization

2. This loaded data provides a fully agreed, cross-functional view of the one consistent, historical record of the business at a detailed, atomic level as created through operational transactions

3. Data is cleansed and reconciled based on an EDM, and stored in a largely normalized, temporally based representation of that model; star-schemas, summarizations and similar derived data and structures are *defined* to be data mart characteristics

4. The optimum structure is a "single relational database" using the power of modern hardware and software to avoid the copying, layering and partitioning of data common in the vast majority of today's data warehouses

5. The EDM and other metadata describing the data content is considered as an integral, logical component of the data warehouse, although its physical storage mechanism may need to be non-relational for performance reasons

The first business role of any "modern data warehouse" is thus to present a historically consistent, legally binding view of the busi-

Core business information

The set of strictly defined, well-managed and continuously maintained information that defines the business—its identity, activities and legally relied-upon actions—from its time of inception to the present moment.

Core business information combines hard information traditionally found in operational, MDM and EDW systems with legally recognized soft information, as well as context-setting information, to provide the most accurate, complete and reliable picture of the business possible.

ness to both the internal and outside worlds, including finance and audit departments, regulatory bodies for reporting results, and business partners for committed business transactions. This corresponds to the original positioning of the enterprise data warehouse, before it became "report generation central" in broad usage. I discussed the meaning, extent and limits of *largely normalized* in Chapter 8 of my book on data warehousing (Devlin, 1996). A detailed description of the temporal database concept is best left to Chris Date, Hugh Darwen, and Nikos Lorentzos (Date, et al., 2002), and Tom Johnston and Randall Weis (Johnston & Weis, 2010). The second business role is as the source of consistent data used to "anchor" other less reliable or rapidly changing data used in reporting, exploration and other BI applications. In some sense, this is an expansion of the concept of master data management, as applied in the purely operational world to the real-time informational needs of the biz-tech ecosystem, and reflects the fact that operational and informational data usage are rapidly converging.

These two roles suggest that a name distinct from the wider and multiple interpretations of the *data warehouse* brand may be more appropriate. While some traditional BI / data warehousing activities focused on regulatory and business reporting certainly continue to be supported here, more operational, legally guaranteed activities with external business entities are equally important. With the added consideration that context-specific information, including its model and other metadata, are also explicitly included in its scope, this component is called the *core business information repository (CBIR)*, shown in Figure 5-11.

Despite the earlier discussion in Section 5.4 above of the emerging possibility of physical re-integration of the operational and informational environments using in-memory database technology, the

CBIR remains a valid, long-term component of any new information architecture for two distinct reasons. First, historical data is being stored for increasing periods of time, but as it ages, access usually diminishes. Keeping the full historical record in memory becomes impractical or financially unviable as data volumes grow. Second, despite some vendors' desire to integrate the entire gamut of business information processing within a single system, many businesses will continue to run multiple operational applications, albeit in smaller numbers than before. Given both considerations, a physically separate instantiation of the CBIR remains a necessity. In that case, data in the combined operational/informational in-memory store that meets the requirement of cross-functional consistency are considered part of the logical scope of the CBIR.

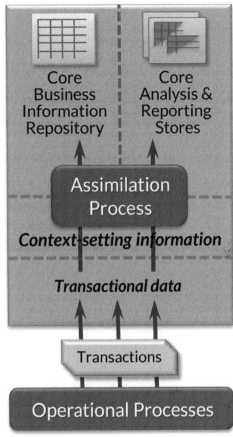

Figure 5-11:
REAL architecture
for core business
information

While the role and content of the EDW are thus transformed significantly by this evolution, data marts are rather differently affected. Their content and purpose remain the same, but their sourcing changes. For consistency with the CBIR, we call these components *core analysis and reporting stores (CARS)*. In the purer architectural form of the data warehouse, experts recommended that data marts should be dependent, i.e. sourced from the EDW. Independent data marts were often frowned upon. As shown in Figure 5-11, the new architecture reverses this advice, feeding all such data marts as directly as possible from their original sources. The reasons are two-fold: to minimize the number of copies of data held and to maximize timeliness. Done indiscriminately, however, such multi-sourcing leads to a spaghetti dish of feeds; a common, model-defined, and CSI-driven information pre-integration function is thus mandatory. In addition, these two components share data—via the *assimilation process* described in Chapter 7—to create and maintain ongoing semantic and temporal consistency.

The lower part of Figure 5-11 also shows a necessary change in thinking about operational systems. In expositions of data warehousing, the data and process components of an operational application are generally presented together and positioned outside the architectural boundary of interest of the warehouse. As we've already seen, this separation is no longer logically tenable; the needs of the biz-tech ecosystem for (near) real-time information in analytics and for analysis results to be applied immediately in production mean that informational and operational needs must be designed, developed and maintained strictly in tandem. The emergence of in-memory database approaches further supports this direction. In terms of physical implementation, relational databases are the most likely platform for all three components. With the convergence of operational and informational systems in the biz-tech ecosystem, we must therefore separate operational data and process and bring the operational data within the boundary of interest of REAL information. Operational processes are likewise identified explicitly as the components that generate transactions, the legally defined and binding interactions of the enterprise. The CBIR, CARS and transactional data are represented as a single logical component, indicating that they must be considered as a whole. Together and individually, they create, store and manage the definitive, transactional reality—current and historical—of the business.

These components represent the first tranche of a new REAL logical architecture, which will unfold in subsequent chapters. First in the sense of this initial introduction, but also first in the sense of a starting point for any migration from a current BI environment to one that fully supports the biz-tech ecosystem—in both informational and operational needs..

5.9   IN PRACTICE—UPGRADING YOUR DATA WAREHOUSE

The principles of Business unIntelligence and the needs of the biz-tech ecosystem are, in reality, a significant extension of those that drove data warehousing. Therefore, any business that has adhered to and invested in an enterprise data warehousing approach is well-positioned to take advantage of this new thinking. The following steps will upgrade your warehouse environment:

✓ Use the dimensions of the IDEAL information layer as a framework for analyzing and documenting the hard information currently in the data warehouse, distributed on departmental servers, and even users' PCs. Use this analysis as the basis for planning next actions in the warehouse and justifying investment in bringing more dispersed data under control and management.

✓ Reduce data mart proliferation. With modern, powerful RDBMS technology, dependent data marts can be largely eliminated by returning to the original concept of views, both virtual and materialized. This step makes mart data timelier and reduces ETL design, runtime and maintenance costs. Consolidate independent data marts on fewer, faster appliances.

✓ Streamline the EDW. Most businesses run multiple EDW systems, despite consistent advice from consultants and experts. This is costly, confusing and unnecessary. Identifying and consolidating multiple instances of core business data will, of course, cost time and money. But, the medium and longer term savings are significant and can be applied to upgrading the warehouse with extensions of high business value.

✓ Ensure business awareness of savings made and ring-fence for use in addressing soft information (see Chapter 8).

✓ Rationalize ETL with particular focus on historical data (as opposed to operational BI demands). Ensure consistent, integrated sourcing for data that must be retained for regulatory and other legal reasons. Eliminate programmatic ETL in favor of rules- and metadata-driven tools.

✓ Expand the role of the data warehouse and its supporting organization to cover all three types of BI—strategic, tactical and operational. Future needs will come from business areas that currently need little support.

✓ Enable the data warehouse to support programmatic access from applications as well as people, in order to support integration with data and information in non-relational technologies.

✓ Integrate metadata into the data warehouse by including it formally in planning and design and by storing it as a recognized part of the warehouse. Make it available to business users and encourage its use through the addition of business context-setting information.

✓ In business areas where operational BI is of particular importance, evaluate in-memory solutions that offer combined operational-informational environments and compare costs and benefits with more traditional approaches of near real-time and micro-batch ETL.

5.10   CONCLUSIONS

Data-based decision making was a pivotal concept in the evolution of computer use in business. It moved IT thinking from the well-bounded world of process automation and improvement into the highly variable universe of business management. From it sprang the data warehouse and its implications for data management, both centrally managed and distributed. It begat BI and encouraged IT to begin dealing with the vagaries of human thinking. But ultimately, its roots in data-based thinking and its origins in the highly managed data that can be extracted from operational applications are fundamental limitations that the industry has struggled, and failed, to overcome. Data—hard information—with its unique, characteristic structure that allows slicing and dicing, summarizing and subsetting, tabulating and graphing, has lured many into the false belief that all the answers needed by decision makers can be found in ever more data and increasingly better visualizations.

A second lesson emerging from the evolution of data warehousing to address the need for more urgent decisions is the interdependence of the concepts of consistency and timeliness. This allows us to define the final dimension of the information space in the IDEAL conceptual architecture. With this model, we can now shape the broader information resource required by the biz-tech ecosystem to better balance these two often-conflicting needs.

Despite claims of its imminent demise, data warehousing will not disappear, although the concept of a single version of the truth has much narrower relevance. With its original focus on consistency at the expense of timeliness, the data warehouse moves to a role as the repository of the historical and broadly agreed core version of hard information that is the relied-upon record of key business data. While its outward use focuses on regulatory reporting and inter-enterprise data consolidation, it takes the internal role of a hub of consistent data with meaning that unifies and underpins other aspects of regular data use, where speed trumps consistency for the business. This is the core business information of the REAL logical architecture.

ROADMAP

→ *Big data is neither necessarily big nor data:* Much of the current discussion about big data is driven by marketing hype and technology-driven thinking

→ *Real big data comes from the Internet of Things:* Machines—from sensors to computers—generate large and increasing volumes of variably structured hard data

→ *Social media generates big information:* From tweets to videos, soft information in large volumes is today's focus of much big data hype, with possible serious societal impact

→ *Remember the internal too:* Big data also comes from within the business

→ *The tri-domain information model:* Three distinct types of information exist—process-mediated data, human-sourced information and machine-generated data; IT used to focus exclusively on the first, while the latter two are reinventing business and IT today

→ *Pillars—not layers:* A new architecture requires multiple types of storage for different kinds of information, so passing it through a series of layers is unsustainable; information pillars, linked via metadata and virtualization, are required

CHAPTER 6
DEATH AND REBIRTH IN THE INFORMATION EXPLOSION

"There are many things of which a wise man might wish to be ignorant." | Ralph Waldo Emerson

"No one has ever failed to find the facts they are looking for." | Peter Drucker

As far back as 1971, Herbert A. Simon, Nobel Laureate in Economics and highly influential polymath, wrote: *"...in an information-rich world, the wealth of information means a dearth of something else: a scarcity of whatever it is that information consumes. What information consumes is...the attention of its recipients. Hence a wealth of information creates a poverty of attention."* (Simon, 1971). I wonder if he imagined just how far we could go.

Google CEO, Eric Schmidt, declared in 2010 that we were creating as much information every two days as we did from the dawn of civilization until 2003. The source of this statistic proved elusive. But, it's probably irrelevant now, two years later, given the exponential growth curve we seem to be on. The elusiveness of its source may be more significant. In all likelihood, we don't know how much information we are creating or, more importantly, its value to humankind. But, there is little doubt that society and business is swimming in an unprecedented flood of data.

This chapter explores in a finite space the almost infinite amount of information that goes by the mundane title of *big data*. From a brief review of the estimated and predicted volumes of information in the world, we move to explore the meaning of the term *big data* and the wide variety of types of information it now covers, much of it from sources beyond the enterprise and seldom previously considered by IT. While much of this information originates externally, businesses are also becoming aware that some internal sources of information have similar characteristics to big data.

During its meteoric rise to fame over the past few years, big data has spawned a variety of new technologies—from the Hadoop zoo to a variety of novel database structures—which we review briefly to understand why the old monolithic approach of using relational databases for everything no longer makes sense. This immediately poses the question of how to match different types of information to the most suitable technology. A new, comprehensive logical model of the full scope of the information used in business and the world at large thus emerges. It identifies three domains of information based on its sourcing: machine-generated, human-sourced and process-mediated. From this basis, we can flesh out the information components of the REAL logical architecture.

Much of the commentary thus far on big data has consisted of breathless paeans on its enormous size and growth, its exciting technologies, and its potential to reinvent marketing. True though these may be, our interest in big data is more fundamental. What big data shows is just how limited was our previous, data-based view of business and the information it uses. It's time to open our eyes and see the big picture.

6.1   DATA DELUGE, INFORMATION TSUNAMI

We are living through the greatest explosion of data ever seen on this planet. An explosion that is set to continue at an ever increasing pace for the foreseeable future. This deluge goes by the anodyne name of *big data*. According to International Data Corporation (IDC, 2012) the volume of data generated in the digital world in 2012 was 2,900 Exabytes (EB), or 2,900 million Terabytes, and set to grow at an average 40% compound growth rate in the coming years. By 2020, we will have reached 40,000 EB, 40 Zettabytes (ZB), and apparently there exists insufficient disk space to store it all, now and in the future! Such figures defy comprehension. Of course, much of this data is comprised of video, audio and image data generated by a general public waving smartphone cameras wherever they go; perhaps we can sensibly argue that IT managers don't need to worry so much. But even in the relatively staid world of enterprise IT, the numbers are large enough to create considerable fear, uncertainty and doubt, or

Exabytes

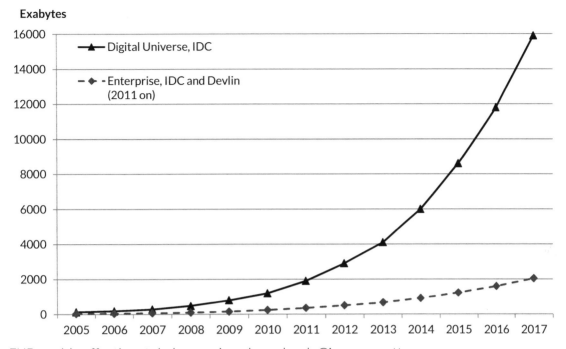

FUD, as it's affectionately known in sales school. Given our attention is on business, let's narrow the focus to the data and information of most interest to the enterprise. Figure 6-1 also shows enterprise data volumes[1] for comparison. IDC provided enterprise figures only on their earlier reports (IDC, 2007), (IDC, 2008), where enterprise data represented approximately 25-30% of the total. For want of better statistics, I've extrapolated the numbers at 80% of the growth rate of the total data, on the basis that consumer creation of image and video will outpace that of the enterprise. However, of more interest in the context of the information resource of companies in the biz-tech ecosystem is the relationship between the total enterprise data and the traditional enterprise data—the largely numeric, highly structured data, discussed in Chapter 3—that we've been storing in files and databases since the 1960s and more recently in spreadsheets on PCs.

Unfortunately, such figures are difficult to unearth; even the definitions of what is included and excluded in such numbers is usually vague and unsatisfactory. In 2008, IDC estimated that less than 5%

Figure 6-1:
Overall and enterprise data size, 2005-2017

---

[1] IDC have not made the definitions or underlying data of the study widely available, so some of my figures are estimates and extrapolations from the published work. I believe they are within the correct order of magnitude.

of the digital universe emanated from the datacenter. Ask the percentage of "structured" vs. "unstructured" data in the enterprise and you'll get something in the range of 10-20%. The numbers I found are undated and undefined and the research supporting them is missing in action. Nor did I find estimates of the growth rate, which I would place in the range of 5-10%, based on the assumption that traditional data, which directly reflects the level of business being performed, should not grow much faster than the worldwide gross world product. The latter figure is highly variable, of course, but averaged approximately 3.5% since the turn of the millennium (IMF, 2013). While clearly guesswork, the numbers shown in Figure 6-2 (based on a 5% growth rate from the 2008 base for datacenter sourcing above) illustrate graphically the magnitude of the shift in volumes from traditional to the new types of data that form part of big data. Three key implications emerge.

First, the constant 5-15% ratio of "structured" to "unstructured" data is meaningless, unless both types of data are growing at the same rate—an unlikely assumption.

Second, the shift from traditional to emerging data types threatens data professionals' ability to manage the entire information re-

---

Figure 6-2:
Emerging vs. traditional enterprise data growth, 2005-2017

Exabytes

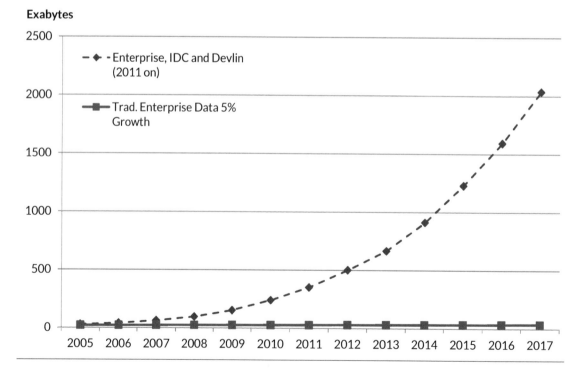

source of the enterprise—an approach founded in traditional data types as we saw earlier. It is likely that emerging data types exceeded traditional types around the turn of the millennium, as the former are closely associated with use of the Internet, which took off for business in that timeframe. By this year (2013), traditional data types—the comfort zone of data warehouse and operational systems experts—comprise perhaps 5% of the enterprise total; by the end of the decade, it is likely to be down to 1% and shrinking.

Third, and more worrying, perhaps, the overall enterprise data growth rate will put many IT budgets under severe pressure. While storage costs are dropping, the personnel cost of managing these growing volumes is actually growing. The implication is that businesses can no longer afford all the data they might desire. On the other hand, the broad consensus among analysts and experts is that businesses cannot afford to ignore it either. Significant change in how data is managed is inevitable.

However, these figures they tell only part of the story. The enormous growth in volumes and proportion of emerging data types shows up explicitly. What doesn't appear is more important for data management. The main sources of data are migrating dramatically from internal and operational to external and user-generated, data quality from known to unknowable, from pre-defined conditions of use to conditions that have to be inferred at use time. The figures also say very little about the intrinsic value of the data. The above 5% of traditional data in 2013 still represents probably 75% of the long-term value of data, simply because it describes the fundamentals of any business: customers, products, sales, profits and every other core measure of interest. The other 99% may be mostly dross, but potentially hidden in it are a large but unknown number of insights that, once discovered and acted upon, have the potential to dramatically change everything, from the bottom line of a business to the world we live in. Or so we are told.

The discussion around the actual numbers above is disconcerting. The industry does not appear to have a firm grasp of the shape or scale of big data, especially as it impacts and overlaps with traditional types of data. Additional and substantial market research is required. But, our first task is to determine exactly what it is we're talking about.

6.2   WHAT IS BIG DATA AND WHY BOTHER?

You might think that with a name as simple as big data, its definition would be clear and unambiguous. You would also be wrong. A search for a definition at the fount of all modern knowledge, Wikipedia, provided, *"Big Data is a term applied to data sets whose size is beyond the ability of commonly used software tools to capture, manage and process the data within a tolerable elapsed time. Big data sizes are a constantly moving target currently ranging from a few dozen terabytes to many petabytes in a single data set"* (Wikipedia, 2012). As definitions go, this is pretty vague. Not only does the size span four-plus orders of magnitude, but it's also a moving target and defined on the basis of "tolerable" (what does that mean?) performance of common (to whom?) software tools. Small wonder the term generates fear and excitement in equal measure.

Another popular definitional approach is the v-word blizzard. Although actually dating back over a decade (Laney, 2001), volume, velocity and variety have become almost synonymous with big data since 2010. Veracity, value, virality, validity and viscosity—and probably more—have been added by analysts and vendors (hey, another v-word!) since then. Unfortunately, each of these words stands for a continuous variable, the value for which is never explicitly stated. So, when is velocity (speed of data arrival) fast enough to qualify as big data? And what has velocity, or any of the other v-words for that matter, got to do with size? Even with volume, we're left with a question: tera-, peta-, exa-, zetta- or yottabyte—which is big? Add to that the various combinations of v-words possible and a clear definition eludes everyone. Great for marketers of hardware and software who can claim every product, old and new, is big data enabled or mandatory for success.

Figure 6-3:
Sad little elephant,
Katherine Devlin

And then there's Hadoop—friendly yellow elephant or parallel programmers' paradise—the use of which some consider to indicate big data. Confused? Don't worry. As of July, 2012, big data was cresting Gartner's Emerging Technologies Hype Cycle (LeHong & Fenn, 2012), so clarity—or disillusionment—is coming soon. While we wait, let's explore the history of big data and its business uses.

Big data through the ages

Big data has been talked about since at least the mid-1990s. The original source of the term—and the fear of it—was the scientific community. Modern scientific instrumentation has, for many years, been capable of producing large quantities of digital data on an ongoing basis. The volumes continue to grow astronomically. Speaking of which, back in 2000, when the Sloan Digital Sky Survey began operations in New Mexico, it reportedly collected more data in its first few weeks than had been gathered in the entire history of astronomy. Sloan's archive after a decade of operation was 140 terabytes. The Large Synoptic Survey Telescope being built on Cerro Pachón, a mountain in northern Chile, will begin full survey operations by 2016, producing the same amount of raw data every ten days and 150 petabytes over its lifetime. The Square Kilometre Array (SKA), a radio telescope planned to be in operation in South Africa and Australia / New Zealand by 2024 is expected to collect 1 exabyte of raw data per day. Particle physics, genetics and meteorology—to name but a few other areas of scientific research—are all producing data at large and ever-increasing rates.

The volumes of data above and, in particular, their growth rates point to the key conundrum of defining big data—what was big yesterday is small today, and miniscule in the context of what is anticipated tomorrow. Furthermore, volume itself is not the issue. The interesting number is the volume relative to the storage and processing capacity of the computer equipment available and affordable at that time. What's affordable to a government agency is likely very different from what makes sense in a retailer's budget. But, irrespective of budgetary considerations, a key issue for big data is technological—can it be stored on and processed by the

Figure 6-4:
Artist's impression of part of the Square Kilometre Array

hardware and software of its era? The volumes and acquisition rate of data at the SKA, for example, is driving research at IBM and ASTRON (Netherlands Institute for Radio Astronomy) into 3D stacked chips, phase-change, and racetrack memory, as well as revolutionary tape systems (Cooper, 2012).

The Internet of Things

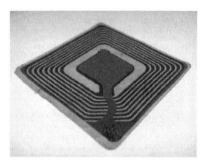

Figure 6-5:
A typical RFID tag found on many products and packages

While much of this scientific research may seem rather far from daily life, it's a fact of the modern world that what is common in pure research doesn't take too long to get incorporated into everyday engineering. Today, we are increasingly instrumenting machines to enable them to measure and report continuously on their performance. For example, only a few years ago, ongoing telemetry of engine performance was confined to jet aircraft valued at millions of dollars. Now, automobile manufacturers are embedding monitors throughout their vehicles, providing continuous information on performance of all aspects of the mechanical systems of the vehicle. Tablets and smartphones now contain multiple sensors from GPS receivers to gyroscopes, all recording events and statuses, and generating data of interest. And, of course, once data is available, businesses will look for ways to profit from it and governments for ways to tax it or use it to monitor the populace.

The Internet of Things, a concept dating back to 1999 (Ashton, 2009), captures the extent and promise of these machines. Originally centered on radio-frequency identification (RFID) tags, as seen in Figure 6-5, and the associated readers that were being introduced for supply chain monitoring in that time period, the Internet of Things is now much broader. It ranges from ever-smaller and more powerful RFID tags (30 billion in use today) to wireless sensor networks (WSN) monitoring environmental, industrial and even personal health measures. It covers utilities' use of smart metering to remotely monitor electricity and water usage. Also included are smartphones, vehicles, and kitchen appliances, all individually connected to and addressable on the Internet, creating a virtual world of information about events and measures in the real world. Although now much hyped and thus poorly bounded, the following is a reasonable definition: *"the future Internet of Things links uniquely identifiable things to their virtual representations in the Internet containing or linking to additional information on their identity, status, location or any other business, social or privately relevant information at a ...pay-off that exceeds the efforts of information provisioning and offers information access to non-predefined participants. The provided accurate and appropriate information may be accessed in the right quantity and condition, at the right time and place at the right price."* (Uckelmann, et al., 2011).

The business use of such data falls into three broad categories. First is the simple tracking of the physical characteristics measured by the sensors—including the time of measurement and location of the object, in many cases—and using the data gathered to automate basic operational processes. Smart meters replace human electricity meter readers, for example. Second is the opportunity to predict and influence ongoing consumer behavior around the specific objects as the data is gathered at more frequent intervals. Ongoing tracking of electricity use by households allows more accurate predictions of demand, and also the opportunity to encourage consumers to spread or reduce usage. Third, extrapolating from single-purpose physical measures—often from a combination of sensors of different characteristics—allows more generic or social behaviors to be predicted or influenced, as described in Chapter 2 in the case of pay-as-you-drive insurance. This machine-generated sensor data is still expanding rapidly today, as sensors become cheaper and more widely available. It is expected that it will become one of the largest and most important areas of big data, as the Internet of Things becomes a pervasive reality.

The lure of the web logs

Among our most complex machines today are computers, which also record much data about what goes on inside them and in their network connections. Originally collected for maintenance and security purposes, such computer-generated data was recognized to be more-widely useful as browser-based Internet use emerged. The web server log, which records information about web pages and objects requested and served to the browser, is the most important of these log files, from a big data viewpoint. The information it contains includes client IP address, request date/time, resource requested, HTTP return code, bytes served, browser /

Data exhaust

The digital byproduct human or machine activity on the Internet that is reused for other purposes, unrelated to the original reason for which it was collected.

Also known as ambient data, digital exhaust, and digital footprint, this data provides the foundation for much of the mining and analytics of big data. The potential for discovering novel information about human behavior is the reason for much of the excitement about big data. However, given that it may be saved unwittingly, gathered silently and used and combined inappropriately, it also raises significant privacy and security concerns for many people.

operating system, and referrer. On its own, this information allows limited analysis of how anonymous users arrive at a website—where they come from and the search information they use—and the pages/resources on the website they access. Query strings, added to uniform resource locators (URLs) during website development, are used extensively to track user actions on the site. With the further addition of tracking cookies (small text files downloaded to the browser) or page tags (also called web bugs, these are objects embedded in a webpage that request additional data from a server), more complete information can be compiled about user sessions and information saved across sessions from the same client device.

Extensive analysis of the above information—clickstream analysis, or more expressively, mining the data exhaust—enables marketers to track and predict user behavior on the website. What items are often bought together? Does viewing one item lead to purchase of another? Data mining can segment behaviors and the website can be optimized dynamically to engage the viewer more effectively, increase the propensity to buy something, cross-sell or up-sell, and so on. With a logon to the site, the session becomes personally identifiable and behavior analysis becomes more useful and extensive. Web retailers such as Amazon and eBay, both founded in the mid-1990s in the first bloom of the Web, were among the first to recognize the value of analysis by these and similar methods. Their effective use contributed greatly to these retailers' success and growth, both before and after the dot-com bubble collapse of 2000. When web log analysis and cookies are combined with third-party information from a broad enough set of sources—registrations, credit card purchases, legal records, demographics, and so on—analysis of behavior at an individual and personally identifiable level becomes possible. This has led to considerable concerns about privacy and security on the Web, a topic we return to in Chapter 8. Furthermore, the completeness and accuracy of the information gathered by any and all of the above approaches is questionable, as savvy users adopt approaches such as refusing cookies and disabling browser functions to protect their privacy or simply to speed up web performance.

Quick...follow that link

By 1996, the World Wide Web resembled the World Wild West to its burgeoning user community. Released five years earlier on the Internet—which, itself, dates back to 1975—on an unsuspecting public by the now knighted Tim Berners-Lee from CERN (the European Organization for Nuclear Research) on the French-Swiss border, W3 had grown by leaps and bounds. Matthew Gray of the Massachusetts Institute of Technology compiled a count in the early years that showed a growth from 130 web sites in June, 1993, including two with .com domain names, to some 650,000 (over 60% .com) by the end of 1996 (Gray, 1996). Unfortunately, finding the information available on the Web had become a serious problem by then. The early search engines, web directories and portal sites such as Go.com, Lycos, AltaVista and Yahoo! were struggling manfully—or spiderfully, in some cases—to find relevant information for a growing audience of users equipped with early web browsers. With such a growth rate in the number of websites, manual cataloging was already impractical and automated crawlers were returning an ever-increasing number of sites with little or no indication of their relative usefulness, accuracy or popularity.

The best answer found to these problems (at least until now) was actually hiding in full view in the structure of the web pages themselves, in the hypertext markup language (HTML) used to define the pages and, in particular, in the links and URLs used to navigate from page to page. By the mid-1990s, the Web consisted of an estimated 10 million documents, with an unknown number of links between them. In March, 1996, Larry Page and Sergey Brin, Ph.D. students at Stanford University, began a research project exploring the properties of the Web, focusing in particular on the problem of discovering links on web pages back to a given page. Page and Brin surmised that the number, location and nature of these *backlinks* gave a measure of the importance as-

Figure 6-6:
The first web server ran on Tim Berner-Lee's NeXtcube at CERN, 1991

signed by Web authors to the referenced page, and thus its likely broader relevance to users, in general. Thus was born the renowned PageRank algorithm and the foundation that supports Google (Batelle, 2005).

By the year 2000, the value and effort of scouring an ever-expanding Web, assigning a measure of relevance to a particular page in specific circumstances, and providing fast, appropriate search results to users was becoming both clear and enormous. With more than a billion URLs on the Web, Google was providing access to 560 million full-text indexed web pages through some 30 million searches per day (Google, 2000). New and additional measures and algorithms were (and continue to be) developed and applied to improve relevance and reliability. Which is just as well, because in 2008, Google announced that the Web had grown to 1 trillion unique URLs (Google, 2008). How well this measure represents how much real information is on the Web is unclear—and Google has not reported such numbers since. It is likely that the Web has rapidly grown into a highly linked, statistically significant representation of the information stored and how it is used by humanity at large. It is among the biggest of big data, and understanding and analyzing its significance requires big effort.

Link data is a special class of information that was relatively unimportant in traditional business computing. It has come into its own on the Web as a result of the enormous network of connections that have sprung up between the humans, machines, and processes that act as sources of information. It displays particular characteristics in terms of storage and computing that have led, in large measure to the creation of the highly scalable, parallel processing environments such as MapReduce and NoSQL data stores discussed in Section 6.4.

Face…the final frontier[2]

Much of the excitement about big data in today's market is generated by *social media*—a term almost as ill-defined as big data itself, but which roughly equates in this context to user-generated digital

---

[2] Wiliiam Shatner's oft-quoted voice-over introduction during the opening credits of the original *Star Trek* series, 1966-69

content collected and shared via the Web. Think everything from Twitter to YouTube, Facebook to LinkedIn, WordPress to World of Warcraft. The source of endless information about the opinions and potential behaviors of consumers, marketing types see in it their opportunity *"...to boldly go where no man has gone before"*[2].

Big data's beginnings as sensor data and the later inclusion of social media data point to a second characteristic of big data beyond its size: its variety. In a more general sense, variety refers to an admixture of two rather different characteristics of data: structure and sourcing, discussed in Chapters 3 and 4 respectively. Social media data begins with text typed by humans into blogs, comments and Tweets, and even old-fashioned emails, bulletin boards, and Usenet newsgroups. It includes the relationships between creator and consumers, even to the extent of social interaction and role play. And it expands to images, audio and video content. It is loosely and variously structured. Its purpose and meaning is (assumedly) clear to those who created it, perhaps less so to those who consume it, and opaque and difficult to extract—to varying degrees, depending of the type of medium involved—by computers and software algorithms. In the context of big data, let's examine social media as a data source in terms of its size, range of structures and quality.

Although email and newsgroups were early forms of social media, this category of data really only emerged in the early 2000s as individuals began to interact and create extensive content as Web 2.0 techniques became available. As of May, 2013, Wikipedia listed over 50 social networking sites with over 5 million registered users each, with the top ranking six—Facebook, Twitter, Google+, Qzone, Sina Weibo, and Habbo—each with more than a quarter of a billion (Wikipedia, 2013). Facebook announced 1.11 billion monthly active users in March, 2013, an increase of 23% year-on-year, although numbers are reportedly dropping in the US and Europe (Garside & Rushe, 2013). As of June, 2012, Twitter hit 400 million Tweets per day, an increase of nearly 18% in a month (Farber, 2012). YouTube reported 72 hours of video uploaded every minute and 3 billion hours of video watched by over 800 million unique users every month (YouTube, 2012). Note also that social behavior information is not confined to social media sites. Search engines such as Google and Yahoo!, and online retailers like eBay and Amazon glean extensive information about consumers through their social interactions. For example, Amazon's use of purchase information, recommendations and customer book reviews shows the power of social information in a non-social media site.

In terms of structure, social media consists of a mixture of hard and soft information. The major component is externally-sourced content, entirely dictated by the whims of individuals. This soft information includes 140-character text Tweets, text blogs, as well as other documents, images, and audio and video, both stored and streamed. This content is probably as close as you can get to being unstructured without becoming noise. (Some claim this boundary has already been crossed.) Social media also contains harder information, such as titles, user IDs, IP addresses, dates and times, technical metadata, and so on, which forms a key part of any statistical analysis. Today, most interest revolves around the textual content—including that derived from voice-recognition systems—and its associated descriptors. However, analysis of image and video content is rapidly gaining traction. Spanning all of this, the relational aspect of this information—not in the sense of the relational model, but who is connected to or influences whom—is of much interest to marketers. The bottom line is that the volumes of social media information are immense and capable of yielding information with high statistical significance. Furthermore, the content is rapidly changing, much of it with a fleeting lifespan, requiring near-instantaneous collection and analysis. With such statistically significant volumes of users and real-time information, such sites are the subject of extensive interest in marketing as a means of tracking, understanding and predicting customer behavior, identifying and tracking influencers and their networks, and so on. Today, the use of such information is often confined to marketing groups or still at an early stage of assimilation by most traditional IT departments.

In July, 2012, Rory Cellan-Jones, technology correspondent for the BBC reported: *"For the past week, I've been running a very successful small business via Facebook. It is called VirtualBagel and more than 3,000 people from around the world have decided they 'like' it—despite the fact that it does, well, absolutely nothing"* (Cellan-Jones, 2012). The revelations drew a rapid and dismissive response from Facebook and the methodology attracted criticism from marketing experts. However, the experiment graphically illustrated some of the key quality issues that arise with social media data. At the most basic level, are the people real? Are they who they say they are? What are their motives for saying what they say? Facebook admits that some 7-8% of accounts are fake (Edwards, 2013). eMarketer reports that some 10% of accounts are not human, but pets, objects or brands (Kleinman, 2013). The problem, of course, is not confined to Facebook. The outcomes range from fraud and spam to wasted marketing budgets. For BI practitioners, the challenge is to change their thinking about data quality. Being used to receiving data mainly from business operational systems, their normal assumptions are that poor data quality is the exception and can be tackled through process change at the source. With social media data, both assumptions fail, perhaps dramatically. The further challenge is that poor quality social media data may contaminate internally-generated and intentionally-governed data when the two are combined, leading to misplaced confidence in analysis results. Sometimes, breathing the data exhaust can damage your health!

Business imperative or social implosion

McKinsey has estimated that big data could generate $300 billion of value in US healthcare and $250 billion in EU public sector administration (Manyika, et al., 2011). Significant business opportunities clearly exist, and early movers are taking advantage. The types of big data we've seen—from sensors to clicks and Tweets to Web pages—combine to provide a 360°, 24/7 view of every event of interest to any company. The technology exists to gather and store such information, enabling business to create new *systems of engagement* that mirror and feed the traditional systems of record we met in Chapter 4. Systems of engagement capture customer and prospect actions that offer clues about their behaviors or intentions far earlier in the process than operational systems that see only transactions. Jane Doe, standing on High Street outside the shuttered competitor Classy Dresses at 6 p.m. (via FourSquare) is lusting after a scarlet ball gown (via its QR Code), which correlates with her earlier online search for stilettos. This prompts a message that our store is still open only two blocks away and can offer a 10% discount on the last scarlet dress and matching shoes, in Jane's sizes, that are in stock now. For business, such immediate big data

Big data

Given its diverse characteristics and sundry sources, the difficulty in defining big data is understandable. Its comprehensive overshadowing of traditional data it terms of volume suggests that big data is, in reality, now all data. However, focusing on its use offers a better handle.

Big data consists of hard and soft information—measures, events and messages—continuously captured by machines and used statistically to correlate observations and predict outcomes and, particularly, human behaviors.

"Small data", the logical opposite of big data, is, therefore, the formal transactions and derived information captured by operational systems to reliably run and manage committed business.

offers new and vital analytic and predictive opportunities enabling them to significantly outperform their competitors. Clearly, marketers anticipate their arrival in the Promised Land of real-time, pinpoint-targeted offers, of which buyers can simply and instantly take advantage (Dahlström & Edelman, 2013).

However, all is not rosy in the garden. Rather like climate change, where the sheer number of individual decisions and contributions of individuals adds up to the possibility of equilibrium-tipping conditions, the collection and use of big data has the potential to induce significant social and economic change. Google's collection and deep analysis of all search terms, for example, the proximate goal of which is to offer more accurate results and, of course, enable more targeted advertising, has the unintended side-effect that what any particular user sees of the world is becoming increasingly circumscribed by the sum of his previous searches. Eli Pariser in *The Filter Bubble* describes how two apparently very similar—educated, white, left-leaning women living in the Northeast US—friends of the author received starkly opposite results in a search for "BP" during the 2010 Deepwater Horizon oil spill: one got the news of the disaster, the other saw nothing but investment information (Pariser, 2011). If you only watch what Netflix calculates you'll like based on a history of teenage comedies watched by you, your friends, and those judged by Facebook to be similar to you, how will you ever see that Art house film that would inspire you to volunteer? Mark Zukerberg's comment that *"a squirrel dying in front of your house may be more relevant to your interests right now than people dying in Africa"* is worrying in light of the fact that over one third of Americans get their news from Facebook and much of what they see derives from their friends' "Likes". How many people think to "like" pictures of a starving child? This type of focusing of news and results leads to ever-more lopsided impressions and positions and a general decrease in openness and tolerance for alternate viewpoints. The more that big firms use big data to "simplify" our lives by reducing what we see, the more we don't even know what we are missing.

At a more mundane level, despite the enthusiasm of vendors and analysts, many businesses struggle to realize their big data visions. Among Gartner's predictions for 2012 and beyond was this: *"Through 2015, more than 85 percent of Fortune 500 organizations will fail to effectively exploit big data for competitive advantage"* because of their inability to deal with the technical and management challenges associated with big data (Gartner Inc., 2011).

Big data—however you define it precisely—is one of the most important trends in information management since the advent of business intelligence. Its adoption and consequences, however, will follow a very different path. In contrast to BI, big data immediately demands that operational and informational processes are combined. Business users see greater opportunities in big data, but they require significant process change. And big data may impact society at large in ways that BI never envisaged.

ThoughtPoint

6.3   INTERNAL REALITY MIRRORS THE EXTERNAL

We've largely focused, until now, on big data that comes from beyond the enterprise, simply because that's where much of it originates and has been the source of much of the recent buzz. However, big data in its most simplistic sense— data too big for commonly available tools—has been a reality for many large businesses since the earliest days of computing. More to the point, there is nothing technologically unique about data originating beyond the enterprise; the only difference, as we saw in Chapter 4, is that external data is less well controlled in sourcing and ongoing management than its internal cousin, and thus less trustworthy. So, let's briefly reexamine the types of information described above as they occur within the enterprise.

The Internet of Things is echoed in sensor-generated data originating within the enterprise in the form of call detail records, ATM messages, and more. Web logs and other computer-generated logs are found equally inside and outside the enterprise walls, so a complete set of machine-generated data also exists within the enterprise. HTML-linked documents and URLs are also found within the enterprise; as are personal relationship links, albeit to a much lesser extent than on the Web. Social media information has come to our attention because of its prevalence on the Web and its attraction for marketers. But, similar information also appears within the business as textual, image, audio and video information created everywhere from simple office productivity processes to call center logs and on to sophisticated design and marketing materials. In fact, only one category of information is uniquely created within enterprises: operational data, including transactions and reference data generated by automated business processes.

As we've seen, much of the big data movement derives from Internet-based businesses where large data volumes sourced from the Internet are an integral and significant component of their internal data resources. In contrast, many traditional companies still generate most of their information needs internally, and it seldom reaches anywhere near the volumes seen on the Internet. For businesses with large volumes of sensor-generated data, such as telecommunications companies with call detail records or retailers with till receipt data, this is data of which they've had long experience and existing processes before the advent of big data. Any of these categories—especially sensor-generated data and certain transactions—can grow within the enterprise to substantial volumes and are increasingly included in big data. However, both the concepts and technologies of big data are increasingly relevant to more traditional businesses, simply because the boundary between internal and external data is becoming blurred as the Web becomes pervasive. Where and how depends on industry and company business models, both current and emerging. Five clear use cases have emerged from existing practices and in the evolution of the biz-tech ecosystem; it is likely that more will follow:

1. In businesses such as retail and consumer packaged goods, where there is direct or indirect interaction with large consumer markets, segmentation, target marketing, and so on, have

been the norm. The use of social media information, both content and relationship, has moved analysis from sampling to full datasets, from demographic segments to markets-of-one, and from longer-term trending of historical data to near real-time reaction to emerging events and prediction of behavior.

2. Detecting fraud and other irregularities in financial transaction data has expanded to include larger volumes of often smaller-value transactions on ever-shorter timescales. Big data analysis techniques on data on the network—before or without storing it on disk—are now mandatory for financial institutions.

3. As utilities, from water and electricity supply to telecommunications, move from measuring consumption on a macro- to a micro-scale using pervasive sensor technology, the volumes and frequency of data grows rapidly beyond the traditional processes and technologies for handling it. The value of analyzing it in depth also increases steeply as consumption peaks and troughs can be predicted and, in some cases, smoothed by influencing consumer behavior.

4. Similarly, manufacturers, producers and distributors of physical goods of any sort—from food items to household appliances, from parcel post to container shipping—find increasing needs or opportunities to track each item from manufacture through distribution, use and even disposal. Big data methods and technologies are required to manage the data flows and optimize business processes or improve customer experiences.

5. Sensor-generated data offers opportunities to reinvent or restructure specific businesses or entire industries. Automobile insurance, as already mentioned, can set premiums based on actual behavior, rather than statistically averaged risk. The availability of individual genomic data and electronic medical records presents the medical and health insurance industries with significant opportunities, not to mention ethical dilemmas. Such changes are predicated on big data tools and techniques.

It is thus increasingly clear that big data has a big role in all types of business, whether Web-driven or traditional.

Big data is not about size. Nor is it necessarily about structure or speed. In particular, it's not about external Web sourcing. It's about looking at the activities that precede transactions or formal interactions with people. Such information can and does originate internally, in some cases. Starting with that internal information may be a safer, easier and, perhaps, more valuable approach than taking aim at Twitter or foraging on Facebook.

6.4 A PRIMER ON BIG DATA TECHNOLOGY

While the real interest in big data is the business value we can extract from it, much of the early discussion focused on the new technologies it demands. This section provides an overview of these new technological directions. Chapters 3 and 5 described the relational model and relational databases, as well as the analytical appliances that emerged in the early 2000s. This is the technology on which the majority of today's operational and informational business applications run. However, also in the early years of the new millennium, the volumes, velocities and varieties (to repeat the old big data saw) of data appearing on the Web posed serious challenges for the large Internet businesses then blooming. The largest of them believed that existing relational databases could not handle the volumes of data or flexibility to change required. Furthermore, even if they could, the costs would be prohibitive. Staffed with experienced, Internet-savvy software engineers, they began to design and develop new solutions.

What's all the Hadoop-la about, anyway?

It's well-nigh impossible to discuss big data without mentioning Hadoop. There *are* other tools and techniques, but first, let's deal with the elephant in the room. In fact, an elephant that's far beyond the room and trampling the entire data management landscape...

So what is Hadoop? In the early 2000s, Google began to design and build a highly scalable, parallel processing environment that could run on large clusters of commodity hardware. The result was *MapReduce*, a programming framework and implementation, shown

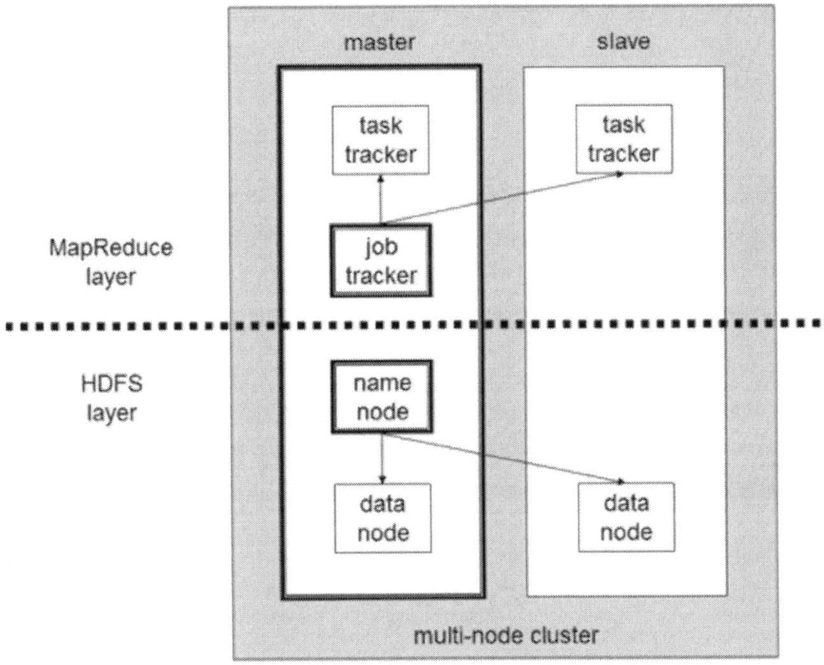

Figure 6-7:
Hadoop structure

in Figure 6-7 and ideal for processing large data sets (Dean & Ghemawat, 2004). Other web companies followed suit, and Yahoo!, in 2006, undertook the development of an Open Source implementation of MapReduce technology, that was soon to be named *Hadoop*—after a yellow, stuffed elephant owned by the young son of lead designer, Doug Cutting. By 2008, Yahoo! was running a 10,000 processor-core Hadoop cluster to power its search engine, and Hadoop became a top-level Apache project and the new darling of Silicon Valley (White, 2009).

Hadoop is often called an ecosystem for storing and processing large volumes of data in a distributed, commodity hardware environment. And given the plethora of oddly named, independently developed but related components, it certainly is an ecosystem. But, in a very simplistic view, the Hadoop ecosystem consists of a diverse set of fairly basic *utilities* to support programmers who need to write distributed applications. These utilities began with the Hadoop distributed file system (HDFS) and a framework and controllers (MapReduce) to distribute application code (Map) to multiple servers and to collect and recombine the results (Reduce). It is frequently overlooked that in comparison to the functionality of a relational database system, particularly an MPP version, Hadoop is a naked, batch programming environment. It is simply a system that manages the distribution of large files of data and the code to process them over thousands of servers, runs the code in parallel, and combines the answers into a final result. Its success stems from its speed and, especially, its flexibility. It is, after all, a programming environment and is not limited to the constraints of any database model—relational or otherwise. For those of us involved in data management, databases and data warehousing over many years, a couple of key considerations leap immediately to mind. Yes, given enough clever programmers and extensive arrays of cheap hardware, you can run serious analytic and data-munging applications that were previously too slow, too large, or a combination of both, to be viable. And given the hyper-exponential growth of data from the Internet and the devices attached to it, there are real needs to be met and significant potential benefits to be gained. But no, this is not an environment where data management issues like governance, quality, consistency and integrity will be easily handled. For that, you need databases, metadata stores, context-setting information, and the like.

Figure 6-8:
Elephant with howdah
Source: Pearson Scott Foresman

That is both the strength and the weakness of Hadoop. Good data management requires many of the functions that have been built into relational databases over their more than 30-year history. And so the Hadoop community has been adding a herd of smaller elephants like HBase to support random read/write, the Avro metadata schema, Oozie for workflow processing, and Sqoop to manage populating HDFS files with data. Open Source developers have spawned an entire menagerie of utilities with often exotic names like Pig Latin, Zookeeper and Mahoot to create a useful ecosystem. As the environment has become more widely used, especially by less skilled programmers and applications more operational in nature, the need for a more SQL-like environment has grown. Hive offers a Hadoop-based "data warehouse" with SQL-like queries translated into MapReduce jobs. And a number of distributions of pre-integrated components, from specialized companies like Hortonworks and Cloudera, as well as long-established data management vendors such as IBM, Microsoft and more have emerged to ease selection and implementation. In 2012, Cloudera Impala joined the Hadoop circus, providing a distributed query engine that bypassed MapReduce to support real-time, SQL-like queries against suitably structured data. By 2013, the howdah[3] has become very overcrowded, as every data management vendor and expert has jumped on board.

Don't get me wrong; there are enormous business incentives to jump on the Hadoop howdah, as discussed in the previous section. But, there's also an enormous hype machine that seems to suggest that some magic is happening with Hadoop. There isn't. It's nothing more than a very successful programming environment for writing applications to process large quantities of data in parallel. Its strengths include low cost, scalability and, perhaps most important-ly, flexibility to handle the wide range of ever-changing data struc-tures characteristic of the emerging big data environment. Its weaknesses include a rapidly evolving and incoherent tool set, a highly programmatic and largely batch environment, and a severe lack of attention to data management issues. This last point has been the downfall of many a business intelligence initiative. I see no reason why Hadoop should be an exception; in fact, given the data volumes and velocities involved, even bigger issues are likely in store for the elephant.

NoSQL—one small step for a coder, one giant *bleep* for data management[4]

A March 2009 InfoWorld article entitled *NoSQL Databases Break All the Old Rules* (Wayner, 2009) described a set of data storage and access tech-nologies that had been developed by Web giants like Google and Amazon and were been being rapidly taken up by the open-source software community. Since then, the term *NoSQL database* has become something of a battle-cry, a marketing meme, and a label attached to

Figure 6-9:
Neil Armstrong,
stepping onto the
Moon at 02:56 UTC,
July 21, 1969

more than a hundred products, some of which pre-date the label by many years (Edlich, 2012). Anything that defines itself by what it's not is literally unbounded, so it's unsurprising that even the mean-ing of the term—No SQL or Not only SQL—is also morphing. Stefan Edlich provides the following definition: *"Next Generation Databases mostly addressing some of the points: being (1) non-relational, (2) dis-*

---

[3] A carriage which is positioned on the back of an elephant
[4] Neil Armstrong: *"That's one small step for [a] man, one giant leap for mankind"*.

tributed, (3) open-source and (4) horizontally scalable. The original intention has been modern web-scale databases. The movement began early 2009 and is growing rapidly. Often more characteristics apply such as: (5) schema-free, (6) easy replication support, (7) simple API, (8) eventually consistent / BASE (not ACID), (9) a huge amount of data and more" (my enumeration).

The rationale behind eight of the nine characteristics in the previous quote relates directly to big data. (The exception—open-source—is driven more by financial concerns and development philosophy.) In fact, these seven characteristics are technical responses to the volumes, distribution, structure and processing needs of Web data. They miss entirely two of the arguably most important aspects of a database as defined in the 1970s by Codd (Codd, 1970) and Chen (Chen, 1976): separation of logical design from physical storage concerns and the modeling of business entities and relationships. The seminal paper (Chang, et al., 2006) on Google Bigtable—the source from which most subsequent work grew—admits as much: *"In many ways, Bigtable resembles a database"* (my emphasis).

Furthermore, although the authors acknowledge that the design does not support a full relational model, they go on to use terms such as table, row and column that are at the heart of relational databases to describe very different components of the system. These terms are carried into many subsequent developments and are the source of much confusion for many traditional practitioners. To see why NoSQL is so different from the relational model and to understand the implications for information storage and management, we need to take a look under the covers.

When is a table not a table?

All NoSQL implementations are based on the concept of a map, also known as associative array, dictionary or hash table. A map is very simply a set of data stored as `key : value` pairs, such that each possible key occurs no more than once. Data pairs are created, deleted and read by their key, which is sorted and/or indexed for rapid retrieval. The value in each pair is essentially opaque to this process—it is a string of bytes, and any internal structure or significance is unknown and unknowable to the map and its read and write mechanism. The business meaning of the key and value are thus known only to the program using them, unlike a relational database, which stores such information in its table and column metadata. As a result, these systems are usually called *data stores* rather than databases. The absence of a predefined schema confers great flexibility to change the content of the store in any fashion at any time without having to unload and reload the data, as is the case for some more primitive relational databases—a process that is near impossible for Web data volumes.

We might have a people map, for example, where the key is the email address and the value is all the information we want to store about that person, as shown in Figure 6-10. The quantity and type of information stored in the value about a person is determined only by the application using the map and can be changed at will. We might start with first name and surname. (We are very simplistic developers!) At a later stage, we decide to add a landline number, cell phone number, and date of birth without necessarily having to update earlier entries, also shown in Figure 6-10. Note that no metadata exists here; the fact that the key is an email address and what attributes are stored in the value field are known only to the programmer and the application responsible for reading and writing the data. Compare this to a relational table containing

Initial design

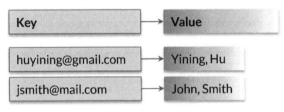

Redesign

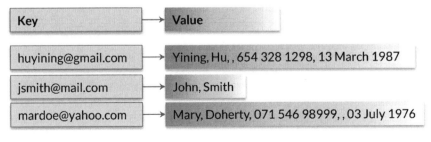

Figure 6-10:
A simple key:value store, with redesign

such information. The original design has three columns: email, first name and surname. If we want to add additional data, we need to add columns to the schema, which adds null entries to all existing rows and may necessitate a reload of the table. This is expensive in terms of processing and storage when dealing with big data and is one of the reasons why large Web companies began to experiment with non-relational approaches. In Web data, where different information is stored about each entity, there thus exist many unfilled values or null entries. Such sparse data is expensive in terms of storage. On the other hand, in a relational database, the metadata of the column names (and potentially, descriptions) is available to all programmers and applications that might want to use the table.

The map just described is one-dimensional, driven by a single set of keys describing some physical phenomenon. Among the commonly quoted examples of such data stores are Membase, Amazon Dynamo, and Apache Voldemort. Most applications require more than one key to their data, leading to the concept of a multi-dimensional map. There are two forms in common use in the NoSQL world: column-oriented and document-oriented.

When is a column not a column?

For those of us who cut our teeth on relational databases, the column-oriented (also known as columnar or wide column) NoSQL store is a very confusing concept because not only is it not a table, but it doesn't really have rows or columns, either! However, the original authors of the Bigtable paper (Chang, et al., 2006) chose, in their wisdom, to use all three terms to describe aspects of their approach. This is essentially an extension of the key-value store where the "primary" key is called a row and the "secondary" keys are called columns. Figure 6-11 shows a somewhat simplified view of the data model.

Here we see that each value is pointed to via a pair of keys, leading directly to the concept of a row and column pointing to a cell in a table. However, the column construct is rather special, consisting of two parts: column family and column. Note that it is the "column family:column" *name* that is indexed, not the content. Column families are defined in advance, but columns within a family can be added at any time. Efficient storage of sparse data is maintained, as is

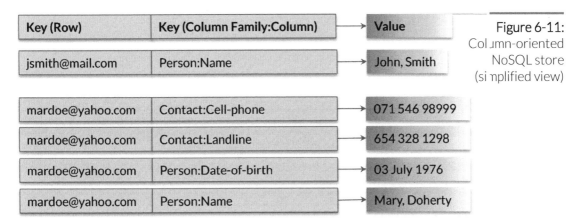

Figure 6-11: Column-oriented NoSQL store (simplified view)

the flexibility to add additional data fields as required. We do have additional metadata here in the form of the column families and column names in the store; however, the only way to discover all the columns in a store is by scanning the entire collection. The full implementation uses three keys, rather than the two shown. The third key is a timestamp enabling versioning of value contents, leading to a structure more akin to a cube than a table. This structure, used in the original Google Bigtable, is particularly useful for processing Web pages, links to or from them, or clicks on them. Other examples are Amazon SimpleDB, Apache Hbase, and Cassandra.

When is a document not a document?

The Bigtable model above, with three indexed keys for one value, is a rather specialized structure. A more general approach is to support multiple indexed keys, each with its associated value. This is the approach taken in document-oriented databases. But first, note that *document-oriented* has little to do with typical textual documents! *Document*, in this case, refers to *JavaScript Object Notation (JSON)* documents. JSON is a text-based open standard, that has become popular since the mid-2000s, which can represent simple data structures such as, among other things, `key : value` pairs. JSON documents offer the possibility of building schema-free databases that keep "related" data about an object together rather than spreading the data over joined tables.

Figure 6-12 shows the main characteristics. The objects are `key : value` pairs that can be nested, as shown in the name entry. We also can have arrays and other constructs. The structure is a rather

JSON {(Key : Value), (Key : Value), ...}

{ E-mail : jsmith@mail.com
Name : { First name : John ,
Surname : Smith } }

{ E-mail : mardoe@yahoo.com
Name : { First name : Mary ,
Surname : Doherty } ,
Date of birth : 03 July 1976 ,
Cell-phone : 071 546 98999 ,
Landline : 654 328 1298 }

Figure 6-12:
A document-oriented store, in JSON format

inefficient storage mechanism in that every document stores the name of every value, as well as the value itself. On the positive side, the fact that no storage is allocated for fields that do not exist in a particular document means that in very sparse data sets, there are significant savings in storage in comparison to relational databases. All of the data about each person is in a single structure, stored together, and we can envisage extending the structure indefinitely with address details, blog posts written, or any other information we need. Relational database experts will immediately note that this is potentially a highly denormalized structure and be tempted to normalize it to keep logically associated information together, linking between them using foreign keys. However, a good database designer will also recognize the tradeoffs between these two approaches: put simply, storage vs. processing and structure vs. agility. Keeping all related data together in a single structure is attractive for big data volumes spread across multiple, dispersed servers. Distributed update, with all its overheads to maintain data consistency, is avoided. Reading the data occurs in one place, avoiding relational joins. Structuring the data in JSON makes it possible to index on any of the key : value pairs or on any combination of them. As with all indexing, the tradeoff is write vs. search performance. CouchDB and MongoDB are examples of document-oriented databases.

Another document-oriented approach goes back further. *EXtensible markup language (XML)* is a W3C specification dating back to 1996 that defines a set of rules for encoding documents such that they are both human- and machine-readable. Documents are composed of content—fields containing arbitrary strings—delimited and described by markup tags. XML is used extensively on the Web to exchange documents, and a number of database representations have been devised to store these documents. Most relational databases have specialized data types for storing and processing XML. There are also native XML databases, such as BaseX and

MarkLogic, which are optimized to support large document stores with varying content. Because of its important role in the definition and use of soft information, we return to XML in Section 8.5.

For a few models more[5]

NoSQL is often used in a literal sense for anything that is not relational, thus including Hadoop, old hierarchical databases, and all the other database and data store approaches mentioned here. I will not cover the older hierarchical and network database models, as they are, like relational databases, reasonably widely known.

Graph databases use mathematical graphs—nodes, edges and the properties of both—to represent and store information. They focus on the associations between objects and are optimized for applications such as social networks, recommendation and route planning systems and so on. In fact, even the Web itself is ultimately a graph. Mostly, applications need to traverse the graph to find shortest routes, nearest neighbors, and similar measures, all of which can be expensive in relational databases, especially as the number of nodes grows large. Specialized graph databases, such as Neo4J and Infinite Graph, are much more efficient. Triple stores are specialized graph databases for processing triples—data entities composed of subject-predicate-object structures, such as "Dave – lives in – Cape Town" or "Cape Town – is – a city". Triples are the basic components of the Resource Description Framework (RDF), a family of W3C specifications originally designed as a metadata data model back in 1999 but now more widely used for the conceptual description or modeling of web resources, using various syntaxes. AllegroGraph and Bigdata are examples of triple stores.

NoSQL data stores offer speed and agility that may be vital in some new business areas or highly changeable markets. They are particularly useful in operational systems and also in data marts in such cases. However, they are unsuitable for use in EDWs or CBIRs, because they lack full support for context-setting information (metadata).

ThoughtPoint

---

[5] *For a Few Dollars More*, Sergio Leone's 1965 spaghetti western film

6.5   INFORMATION—THE TRI-DOMAIN LOGICAL MODEL

The exploration of big data in terms of its uses, structuring and technological demands over the previous sections should make it clear that big data comes in a wide variety of shapes and sizes. In fact, the exceedingly loose definition of big data means that it can be placed at almost every point in the information space defined by the three dimensions of the IDEAL architecture described in earlier chapters. Therefore, to come to a better architectural understanding of big data, we need to look through a different lens. A closer examination of the structure/context and timeliness/consistency axes leads us to consider the different sources of big data and, indeed, all business information, in a generic sense. We see three distinct types of information, or *information domains*, which provide a formal classification and a basis for the tri-domain logical information model, comprising human-sourced information, machine-generated data, and process-mediated data.

Figure 6-13 plots information/data sourcing against the timeliness/consistency and structure/context axes. (The reliance/usage dimension is omitted for clarity; here we deal with information in the local and enterprise classes.) While the boundaries are soft and there is overlap, three distinct domains of information/data emerge. Real-world events and measures are captured in machine-generated data in the lower left of the diagram. At some later stage, this data may be transformed by business processes into process-mediated data. Similarly, human perceptions or decisions create human-sourced information, which may also feed into business processes to generate process-mediated data. The dashed arrow on the left reminds us that behind any machine-generated data is a human design or action that causes such data to be captured.

An example from the banking world will clarify the power of this simple graphic. Way back in the 1960s, Allied Banking Corporation (ABC) computerized their processes for making simple deposit and withdrawal transactions on customer accounts. They modeled the data needed to track transactions and built applications to manage that data. In essence, they created a set of process-mediated data that reflected customer activities. Back then, the only way to capture these customer activities was through clerks in branches en-

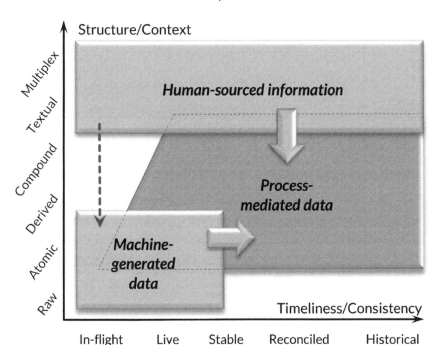

Figure 6-13:
The tri-domain
model of information

tering data on green screens. Even then, the bank had begun to store human-sourced information—images of handwritten checks stored in early content stores, called microfiche—although they could do very little beyond storing it and retrieving it when needed.

By the mid-1980s, ABC was ready to join the ATM revolution, giving customers the freedom to make their own transactions in the rain and (fortuitously) allowing the bank to reduce its costs. ATMs, designed by human engineers and operated by human customers, are simply machines that translate a complex series of events, such as typing on the keypad and counting bills into machine-generated data. These events are translated to account transactions by the banking processes and end up in the process-mediated data. ABC, being a forward-looking bank, was ready in the mid-2000s to begin reaping value from human-sourced information, analyzing customer emails and call center records to understand its customers better and (luckily) improve its profits. While this human-sourced information still remained separate from its process-mediated transaction data, some key metrics and triggers do cross the boundary to drive actions in marketing and customer retention.

Let's leave ABC to planning the next step in information use (and money making) and look at the three domains in more detail.

Human-sourced information

Philosophically, without people there would be no information. At the extreme, it is said that all reality exists in our minds; that model is unlikely to help us in practice. Indeed, one could argue that all information we use is human-sourced, but in the context of this work, human-sourced information is defined as our often highly subjective record of our personal experiences. Previously recorded in written documents, books and works of art, and later in photographs, audio and video recordings, this information is now largely digitized and electronically stored.

From the point of view of its structural and processing characteristics, we can further divide this soft information, or content, into two types based on the current ability of technology to store and process it, as we've seen already in Chapter 3 at the conceptual IDEAL level. First is textual information entered directly by people into computer systems or information easily converted to text, such as audio recordings or images suitable for optical character recognition (OCR) processing. Second, multiplex information comprises digital images and video recordings of any subject matter, factual and fictional material, artistic and computer generated. Today, our ability to analyze and process this second type is still more limited than the first, but is rapidly improving. Human-sourced information is typically found in content stores, discussed in Section 8.5, within the enterprise or the Cloud. However, its original storage is in an ever-growing multitude of files and formats on personal devices, from wearable computers and smartphones to PCs and servers, demanding close consideration of the reliance/usage axis.

Another way to look at this information is in terms of the purpose it serves for those who create or use it. This leads to three subclasses[6]:

- *Interpretative information:* all reflective and analytical thinking produces opinions about what has occurred in the *past* and why; such recorded opinions are interpretative information

- *Indicative information:* taking some immediate, *present-moment* action is indicated by this information; in the business context,

---

[6] Additional work is needed to relate this to pragmatics and speech act theory.

examples of this subclass lead to business transactions such as signing a contract, purchasing a product and so on

- *Inspirational information:* while including all fiction, of course, inspirational information also records the *future-directed*, innovative thinking that precedes and drives novel action in life and in business by presenting a view of what might or could be

As described, human-sourced information may or may not be a reliable representation of any commonly accepted version of reality. Structuring and standardization, for example, modeling, is required to define a relationship to some version of reality. In a business environment, systems of record convert human-sourced information to hard information in a variety of processes, the most basic of which is data entry, increasing its reliability and creating process-mediated data, discussed below.

Machine-generated data

Machine-generated data is the largely hard information output by sensors, processors, computers and machines of all types. As a civilization, we have become increasingly dependent on machines to measure and record the events and situations we experience physically. As hard information, it is considered to be a rather reliable representation of reality, when corrected for sensor errors, invalid and missing readings, etc. It excludes the language-based and visual content mentioned above. We divide it into three subclasses:

- *Sensor-generated data:* the discrete, largely numeric measurements recorded by mechanical and electronic sensors, together with its physical interpretation (units, variance, etc.)

- *Computer-generated data:* logging the events that occur in a computer, this is a more complex form of sensor data, containing textual information and more variability in structure

- *Geotemporal data:* describing date/time and physical location, this data is a fundamental component of all measurements and representations of reality

Machine-generated data is an increasingly important component of the information stored and processed by businesses of all sorts. Its volumes are growing rapidly as sensors proliferate and its well-defined and structured nature makes it highly suitable for computer processing. This data can be stored, processed and analyzed through the relational model, although increasing volumes may pose performance problems for traditional relational databases, demanding newer, more highly performing analytic relational databases, NoSQL tools, and, at the limit of extreme performance, complex event processing or streaming technologies. Web log data is another common form of machine-generated data structured in a standard text format that can be parsed into a relational or other database for analysis and reporting. Large volumes may require other technologies such as columnar relational databases, Hadoop or NoSQL stores.

Process-mediated data

For every enterprise, whether private business or public institution, an accurate, ongoing and recorded representation of what is happing within it is vital. These activities are the processes—both formal and informal—of the organization and the record is process-mediated data. Of course, in physical terms, it originates either from people or machines, but the formal processing it undergoes, from modeling in the design phase to cleansing in operation, is aimed at the creation of a reliable record of reality. We divide it into four subclasses:

- *Transactional data:* the formal record of all events of significance that occur within the business—hiring and firing employees, signing contracts, manufacturing products, sales, and so on—that affect the legal, financial and organizational structure of the enterprise

- *Foundational data:* standard, base data created internally or obtained from external authorities upon which all operations depend—including standard definitions, reference tables, and status records—and are regarded as facts or givens at a point in time or over some extended period of time

- *Derivative data:* data that is created through combination, calculation or other logical or mathematical procedures from one or more of the preceding subclasses of process-mediated data

- *Associative data:* defining relationships that have been declared or discovered between people, places, events and so on, associative data provides the "verbs" by which all actions occur in and around the enterprise

The first three subclasses are the data that IT has focused on almost exclusively since the early days of business computerization. They can be clearly seen in the atomic and derived classes of the conceptual architecture. They include both business data and metadata as they are traditionally named; metadata (or CSI) being the output of the process of understanding and structuring the activities and measurements that make up the business. This data is generally stored and managed in relational databases.

The last subclass, associative data, was relatively unimportant in traditional computing but has come into its own on the Web, as a result of the extensive network of connections that have sprung up between the humans, machines, and processes that act as sources of information. It displays particular characteristics in terms of storage and computing, and as it has exploded, the analysis required has rapidly exceeded the power of traditional databases. So, although relational in meaning and very much hard information, it is often processed in NoSQL data stores, and specifically in graph databases and triple stores, when it grows to any size.

Positioning the tri-domain model

The relative size and perceived importance of these three information domains has shifted over the past fifteen years and is likely to shift further in the coming decade. Up until the end of the last millennium, process-mediated data was dominant; what human-sourced information and machine-generated data existed was relatively small and thought unimportant. The past decade has seen an explosion of both digitally recorded, human-sourced information and machine-generated data; the former, in the form of social media data, has captured the limelight. The rapid growth of the Internet of Things will propel machine-generated data to enormous volumes and the heights of importance in the next ten years.

However, as seen in the tri-domain model in Figure 6-13, human-sourced information and machine-generated data are the underlying sources of the process-mediated data on which we have traditionally focused, although only a small and well-defined subset moves through the business process layer that intervenes. These sources are both more flexible and/or timelier than traditional process-mediated data. In fact, the business processes that create process-mediated data are, to some extent, designed to reduce flexibility and timeliness in the underlying information and data in order to ensure the quality and consistency of the resulting process-mediated data. This is most clearly seen in the processes that populate the (EDW) but also occurs in the data entry and validation processes of operational systems.

The tri-domain model recognizes that the prime mover for all activity is human thought and intention and that human-sourced information is the first place any thought is recorded. Machine-generated data derives from human-sourced information, both in its content when people operate machines and in its concept, as a means of capturing events or measures in the environment as defined by and of interest to people. The practical implications of this three-fold information model are significant and wide-ranging for our thinking about big data in particular. Big data processing, whatever the technology used, depends on traditional data to create context and consistency. In addition, the results of big data processing must be fed back into traditional business processes to enable change and evolution of the business. As a result, a fully coherent environment, including an integrated platform and enterprise-scale organization, are necessary for successful implementation of big data initiatives beyond pilot or prototype projects. In a broader context, we see that process-mediated data, although the traditional information lifeblood of business, is no longer enough to run a modern business in the biz-tech ecosystem. Furthermore, our design decision to split it into operational and informational categories is useful or even necessary for the integration and consolidation of core business information only in this domain, as we saw in the first delineation of the REAL architecture in Section 5.8.

6.6 REAL ARCHITECTURE (2): PILLARS REPLACE LAYERS

The plethora of technology choices available and/or necessary for big data implementations undermines a central tenet of the original data warehouse approach. Relational technology is no longer the only or necessarily the best technology for informational business needs in the biz-tech ecosystem. Of course, other data storage and access technologies, such as MOLAP and even spreadsheets, have also been used at the data mart level. However, while not purely relational, they still conform to a loose model of rows and columns of hard information. Hadoop, NoSQL and more, as well as the content stores we discuss in Section 8.5, all point to a new reality: there exist multiple and very different technologies to deliver information most efficiently or easily to users. Any modern logical architecture must respect that premise.

With such a multiplicity of varied technologies, the layered architecture of the data warehouse, where all data is fed through the EDW into dependent data marts, shown in Figure 5-4 (page 124), is further undercut. The amount of storage needed grows enormously as a result of storing multiple copies of data, and the intensive transformations required would bog down even the fastest and biggest servers. And to what purpose? Those of us—myself included—who taught that dependent data marts were the best or only approach to delivering users' informational needs are proven wrong in the biz-tech ecosystem. Layering is not the only answer. The alternative is pillars, the foundation of which is the tri-domain information model. Each domain becomes a pillar of the information platform in Figure 6-14.

These additional pillars stand beside the core business information pillar—already introduced in Section 5.8 in our first look at the logical architecture—and can now be identified as process-mediated data. While these pillars emerge because of the different technologies required, their *raison d'être* is more fundamental: they relate to three very different types of input to the biz-tech ecosystem. Measures and events, as detected by machine sensors, represent simple states and changes of state of the physical environment of interest to the business. Messages are the thoughts, impressions and actions of people captured as text, image or video. Transac-

Figure 6-14:
The REAL logical
model of information

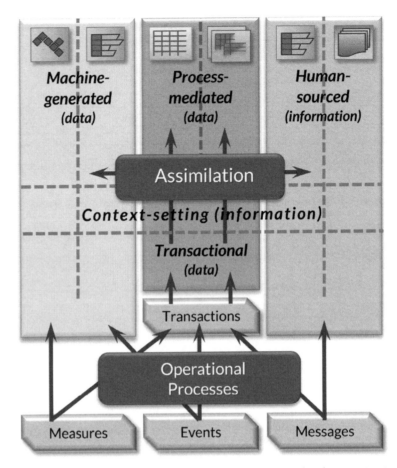

tions, the legally defined and binding interactions in the context of the business, are created by operational systems from measures, events and/or messages and receive special treatment because of their importance.

Within each of these pillars, we see there are often more than one business need to be met and more than one technological base. In machine-generated data, we have, for example, *in-flight analytics*, requiring the fastest (often sub-second) response times in areas such as fraud detection in financial transactions. Here, the data does not even land on disk; the analytics are performed on streaming data in *complex event processing (CEP)* tools. We also have *operational analytics*, performed on live transactional data. Depending on the speed of response and the level of database flexibility required, this need can be met by relational databases or NoSQL tools. The logical sub-components of process-mediated data were described in Section 5.8. Within human-sourced information, we may also have operational analytics as well as *predictive analytics*, the deep analysis of large, often loosely structured data sets performed in Hadoop or in high-speed relational analytical appliances.

Context-setting information or metadata, as noted in Section 3.8, is an integral part of all information and is shown explicitly in each pillar, rather than the separate component of traditional architectures. It is also placed in close proximity to the assimilation process, which intimately depends upon it. Assimilation, although clearly process rather than information, is shown here because of its key role in creating and maintaining the relationships between and within the three pillars. This involves both transforming and copying information, as well as the creation and maintenance of links between different elements. We will deal with assimilation as a process component in more depth in Section 7.7.

6.7 IN PRACTICE—BRINGING BIG DATA ON BOARD

Big data tooling, such as Hadoop and NoSQL data stores, originated from leading-edge, Internet-age companies with sophisticated software engineering skills and an emphasis on Web technology. As a result, these tools and the thinking underlying them are often very different than more traditional enterprise software, especially database technology, with its focus on data management, reliability, usability and so on. Some experts often recommend, for these and other reasons, that big data initiatives should be established apart from the BI environment and organization. This approach is, in my view, a recipe for disaster. Data—big or small, hard or soft—must all be treated the same way, and managed by professionals with experience of enterprise information management, using tools that offer appropriate levels of governance. The following steps are, therefore, suggested for introducing big data successfully:

✓ Include big data initiatives within the remit of the BI organization. Although a "skunk works" is fine for initial testing and determination of likely business value, the production use of big data needs particularly careful management and oversight. The programmatic approach of Hadoop and the technical characteristics of big data tools can easily lead to chaotic data management, akin to spreadsheets on steroids, with multiple, poorly controlled copies of data mismanaged by programmers with no knowledge of or interest in good data governance practices. The BI team *must* be put in control to avoid a possible disaster.

✓ Nonetheless, manage big data more lightly than process-mediated data; it is often peripheral to core processes and less critical, especially in the early stages. However, as it becomes more central to the business and mixed in with more critical data, proper data governance measures are mandatory.

✓ Create links with core business information. Where internal data exists that relates to newly gathered big data, ensure that the two are linked across the relational/non-relational divide. As far as possible, use novel big data technology in conjunction with your existing relational environment.

✓ Start with internally sourced big data, where available. It is more easily obtained and understood than its external counterpart.

✓ Address machine-generated data and human-sourced information separately. They have very different characteristics and often demand different technologies. In particular, check the possibility of using your already well-understood relational environment for machine-generated data. Hadoop is likely to be overkill and NoSQL may offer only limited advantages, given the skill shortages and steep learning curve for existing staff.

✓ Focus on the analytic value to be gained from big data. Bill Franks provides an extensive overview of the analytic approaches to using big data, including a GREAT acronym—guided, relevant, explainable, actionable and timely—to make an impact (Franks, 2012).

✓ Beware the hype about data scientists. While there are areas where more specialized analytical skills may be required, existing power users with real knowledge of your business may be better equipped to extract value from big data with appropriate training in statistical tools and methods.

✓ Self-service analytics can damage your business health. Statistics is a black art, where it is very easy for the unwary to draw wildly incorrect conclusions. Advanced analytical tools should be introduced to the wider business only with the greatest of care, with significant expert support, and later in the roll-out when the data involved is better characterized.

✓ Be aware that most big data technology is open source and in the early stages of development. Pay special attention to the typical software issues raised by these characteristics, including version incompatibility, uncertain support for defects, limited testing and so on.

6.8   CONCLUSIONS

First, scientific data collection and, later, commercialization of the Web drove the emergence of big data, initially as a feared concept and then as a set of innovative technologies. Big data, in turn, has driven the emergence of new markets, business opportunities and processes. This is the biz-tech ecosystem operating in full swing. Technology begets applications; applications fertilize technology.

While we most often hear of the breath-taking numbers and the breathless growth rates, the real news is in the increasing centrality of information in our lives and in business and our growing dependence on it. Increasingly, we must get it right: store it safely, understand it fully, process it accurately, and use it wisely.

Big data, despite—or, perhaps, because of—its all-encompassing but essentially meaningless definition, has also given us the opportunity to come to a deeper understanding of the true nature and ultimate source of information: people, sometimes directly, and at other times, via machines. IT has long focused on the transaction data created in and needed by business processes. Big data, in its incarnation as social media, reestablishes the relationship between people's intentions and interests and the transactions that the business records. Big data, as reams of sensor-generated events or measures, reconnects the increasing automation and instrumentation of the physical world with the process of running a business.

Big data thus gifts us with the breadth of vision to redraw the logical architecture depicting the information needs of the biz-tech ecosystem. It drives us to adopt a pillared orientation rather than the more traditional layered approach. Like all choices, this one has its pros and cons. The speed and flexibility it affords must be balanced by the care needed to ensure the various levels of consistency required in different processes. Perhaps the most important aspect of the REAL logical architecture for information is its emphasis on the relationship between transactions, the daily bread of business, and the physical measures and events and human messages that are the grain and yeast from which this bread is made.

"Information technology is part of what makes us human, and its story is our own" according to information architect, Louis Rosenfeld, in a jacket quote from *Glut: Mastering Information Through the Ages* (Wright, 2007). Written before big data burst fully into the mass consciousness, both Wright and Rosenfeld captured the depth to which information is rooted in our minds and in the structures we have created to store and use it over the ages. The information explosion is something of a big bang in the creation of a new information universe.

ROADMAP

→ *Sense and respond:* The level of uncertainty and rate of change in the modern world is such that traditional planning must be superseded by more adaptive approaches

→ *The MEDA model:* The monitor – evaluate – decide – act cycle applies sense and respond to decision making at strategic, tactical and operational levels

→ *Service oriented architecture:* SOA provides the best possibility to support adaptive, business-directed processes throughout the organization, for operational, informational and even collaborative activities

→ *SOA solves metadata:* The real-time, live metadata required to run an SOA environment is the answer to the lack of metadata so often encountered in BI projects

→ *Three axes of the process layer:* business effect, active scope and time span describe key process characteristics that enable linking people to information needs

→ *Process re-envisioning:* Process function covers three broad infrastructure areas: choreography of activities, information handling (instantiation, assimilation and reification) and overall organization and management

CHAPTER 7
How applications became apps
and other process peculiarities

"There's nothing more useless than executing a task efficiently, when it actually never should have been executed at all."	Peter Drucker
"It is not enough to understand, or to see clearly. The future will be shaped in the arena of human activity, by those willing to commit their minds and their bodies to the task."	Robert Kennedy

Much of this book observes the world and business through the lens of information and, so far, the data-based subset used to support today's decision making. But how is such data created and used? It's time to move to a more action-oriented view. After all, the world is driven by actions taken rather than data analyzed. Speak to any well-dressed business person—her emphasis is on results and on how to achieve them. We must consider the process of getting from A to B, from plan conceived to goal achieved—process, in a broad sense of the word: *a series of actions or steps taken in order to achieve a particular end*[1].

In the suit-and-tie business world, processes are predefined, standardized and refined over time, driving ongoing productivity gains in operational activities based on strategic planning for a predictable future. However, increasingly unexpected change has been the norm since at least the 1990s. To address this, the sense and respond model proposes that changes be recognized as they emerge and flexibly addressed on the fly. This favors innovation and responsiveness—characteristics that fly in the face of the pinstripe-suited process. The business-casual concept of an adaptive process with highly flexible tasks and event-driven workflows thus emerges, where decision making becomes a process in its own right.

---

[1] From *The New Oxford Dictionary of English*

In parallel, IT had to face its own makeover in the world of application development where it has long reigned supreme, tailoring business requirements into elegant code constructs written in arcane programming languages named by descriptive acronyms and flavors of coffee. In-house applications, written specifically for a particular process in one company, were replaced by commercial off-the-shelf systems, covering entire business areas and industries, reducing IT costs and, as a side effect, diminishing potential competitive advantage based on IT. But as complexity exploded, so too did the cost of maintenance and the difficulty in responding to new needs. Another new style, service oriented architecture (SOA), introduced renewed agility into application development. This allowed business users to define their processes, breaking down the barriers between IT-developed and user-created applications, as well as between applications and infrastructure. But now the fashions are changing again. It's jeans and t-shirts, as we briefly leave the earth-bound world and take to the Cloud and blue-sky mobile apps, to see this next regression from bespoke, innovative application development to commodity, one-size-fits-all solutions.

Our goal is to understand how process clothes information and how application development must work in the biz-tech ecosystem. To define the conceptual and logical architectures that supports the conflicting demands of speed and stability, agility and consistency, overview and detail. And to cut the cloth of application development evolution to the measure of new demands by business users, customers and prospects to create, manage and utilize all information.

7.1   HUNTER-GATHERERS, FARMERS AND INDUSTRIALISTS

On an imaginary expedition to the Late Pleistocene, we encounter Krog and his clan, recently awakened around the embers of a dying fire. Strategic planning is a concept many millennia in the future, but the children are hungry and action is needed. The business of the day for the menfolk is hunting; the women foraging. Information abounds as input for the activities to come. The spoor on the grassland. A scent in the air. The ochre leaves of a plant that bears a sweet tuber below. But, ask Krog and his family and they will surely mention little of this. Their thoughts circle on the outcome and the very first steps they must take, the direction to follow to where an earlier cry suggested a kill by saber-toothed cats and possible scavenging. A process, primitive and at first partially formed, evolves step by step, action after reconsidered action. In truth, thinking not far removed from that of a 20th century salesperson.

Figure 7-1: *The cave boy of the age of stone,* Margaret A. McIntyre, Harrap, London, 1900

Fast forward several thousand years, and Krog's descendants are growing early strains of wheat in ancient Egypt. Planning is still far from strategic but is now part of daily life. Knowing the motion of the sun and moon against the backdrop of the stars is a survival skill. The heliacal rising of Sirius signals the annual flood of the Nile River and a time to prepare the land for planting. Knowing when to plant and how long before the next harvest will refill the grain stores may mean the difference between life and death. But planning is still but a small part of the game of life. The daily chores, the process of planting and harvesting, storing and baking are the hub of people's lives. The process has become largely repeatable, predictable. Reminiscent, perhaps, of the life of a modern insurance clerk, although surely harder work in the fields.

A process-oriented century

Henry Ford was probably not a direct descendant of Krog, but he is credited with taking process thinking to new levels on his automobile assembly line in 1913, capable of producing a Model T in 93 minutes through the use of interchangeable parts and the adoption of a highly repeatable and sequential process. Ford may be the popular poster-child, but it was Fredrick Winslow Taylor who hewed the bedrock of theory and practical implementation for this advance. Arguably much of the management foundation of the Industrial Era throughout the 20th century builds on his approach of scientific management (Taylor, 1911) published just four years before his death. Entirely driven by the need for efficiency in business, Taylor's approach forms the basis for everything, from typical management hierarchies and time and motion studies to process automation and Six Sigma programs—much of the management theory still prevalent throughout business today. However, the modern approaches to innovation through teamwork we'll see in

Figure 7-2:
Ford, Taylor and
the Model T
assembly line

Chapter 9, not to mention the basic precepts of human equality, find little resonance with some of Taylor's underlying thought: *"in almost all of the mechanic arts, the science which underlies each workman's act is so great and amounts to so much that the workman who is best suited actually to do the work is incapable (either through lack of education or through insufficient mental capacity) of understanding this science."*

Application development emerged in the 1960s, against this background, and was largely based on the model of automating well-defined, repeatable processes comparable to those seen in assembly lines. Applications were designed and delivered as tightly integrated, functionally comprehensive "black boxes" to automate the specific needs of a business department or area for use by clerks who were *"incapable of understanding this science"*. Within that scope, applications delivered a consistent set of activities and functionality, creating and managing an increasingly reliable and dependable base of business information. That scope was limited to the department or area that had commissioned the application, and the function determined by their business needs at the time of the commissioning. Building applications within functional boundaries severely restricted the ability of the business to exchange information reliably between departments. But wider scopes were beyond the capabilities of IT of the day, and remain so to a large extent. Subsequent changes in application function often proved technically difficult and were often resisted, perhaps as a consequence of Taylor's thinking that processes should be largely fixed and unchanging once they were "properly" defined.

A more formal approach to running and managing a business according to a process—from a non-IT view—was developed in the 1990s with the precept that processes span the organization and that business activities and their relationships could be optimized through *business process reengineering (BPR)*. *Process Innovation* (Davenport, 1992) has provided the basis for much of the subsequent work, describing a process as: *"a structured, measured set of activities designed to produce a specific output for a particular customer or market. It implies a strong emphasis on how work is done within an organization, in contrast to a product focus's emphasis on what. A process is thus a specific ordering of work activities across time and space, with a beginning and an end, and clearly defined inputs and outputs: a structure for action."* In this, and other 1990s definitions of business process orientation, the emphasis is on action towards a known goal, activities arranged in a well-defined and repeatable order, and a smooth flow of work from input to output. In the industrialized world of the 19th and 20th centuries, efficiency of production was paramount. It was later combined with the goal of effectiveness in satisfying customer demand, provided that demand was reasonably predictable (typically driven by advertising and managed by marketing). But even as the BPR movement was taking shape, the possibility of driving and managing customer expectations—and, more to the point, the planning and perfection of production processes— was receding. The biz-tech ecosystem, with its focus on new levels of flexibility to respond to increasingly unpredictable market forces, had already begun to emerge.

An emergent manifesto

In 1992, Peter Drucker declared, *"No new theories on which a big business can be built have emerged. But the old ones are no longer dependable"* (Drucker, 1992). He was describing the organizational issues faced by business at the time, as different technologies became more embedded and interlinked, disrupting management structures and limiting the level of innovation any one company could deploy from internal resources. At its core, his message was of the emergence of uncertainty in planning and the limitations of the process approach. Without using the phrase, he was delineating the early stages of the biz-tech ecosystem.

Chapter 3 reimaged data and information as demanded by the biz-tech ecosystem. Process requires a similar re-thinking. The allegorical progression above from Stone Age to Information Age sets the scene. Business, in some sense, is simply an evolution of hunting-gathering and farming, through tool-making and bartering, to industrialized manufacture and commerce. Supply and demand, and the actions required to drive them. These actions certainly require ordering and an overarching direction. However, the hardening—

perhaps even fossilization—of such characteristics into largely im-mutable processes and IT-provided applications to support them is a legacy of Taylor's original thinking that sought to optimize each action and its relationships to those surrounding it. Widespread availability of information shifts the industrial-era imbalance of power from the producer towards a more equitable equilibrium between producer and consumer. The benefits of mass-production give way to mass-customization and, where the product is virtual rather than physical, to mass-individuation, where products are uniquely matched to the needs of a particular customer. Process becomes intelligent, adaptive, changing in real time as people and sensors provide input into emerging systems of engagement. Each hunt is unique, depending on the game found, land and weather conditions, and the distinctive skills of both stalker and quarry.

In this new world, there still exists process and the tools to auto-mate and operate it. But the basic characteristics have changed:

- *Agility:* where process once stood for stability and the search for perfection in actions and their relationships, today's pro-cesses must be adaptable, easy to create, and open to change

- *Universality:* the old approach where a process is applied to a single department and its needs must give way to processes that can span all players in the chain—suppliers, manufacturers and consumers—including the entire scope of all activities and their interactions, as needed for all participants

- *Modularity:* black-box applications developed for a single party or stage of the process are supplanted by independent, config-urable, and loosely interconnected "apps" that cooperate in creating, initiating, participating in, managing and responding to all aspects of a process

- *Equality:* automation of process actions and work flows is no longer confined to producers nor their IT departments, but equally available to suppliers, producers and consumers—and fully democratized across both IT and user communities

- *Discretion:* while in the past, participation in a defined process was mandatory, the level of innovation needed in the modern process world requires the option of breaking out of a previously defined process—at least in certain instances—and be capable of handling such an opt-out gracefully and effectively

With such characteristics, the processes of the biz-tech ecosystem can finally serve the needs of all participants equally and enable the people layer of the new architecture to create, manage and use all the information needed to the full breadth of the business possibilities imaginable. Section 7.4 describes the IT foundation for delivering on these characteristics. But first, we must briefly explore a modern approach to business management that moves away from Taylor's highly prescriptive foundation, shifting the focus from planning to action and enabling the level of innovation demanded by business and expected of people in the 21st century.

7.2   FROM MAKE AND SELL TO SENSE AND RESPOND

As the biz-tech ecosystem emerged in the 1990s and began to flourish in the following decade, planning and managing a business using only the traditional, industrial era approach based on Taylor's scientific management principles became increasingly difficult. Scientific management—sometimes called forecast-make-sell or simply *make and sell*—is a managerial framework that depends on a reasonable level of certainty about the future and the ability to predict that future with some degree of assurance based on the past. It is not an ideal framework when faced with the ongoing and unpredictable change created by the biz-tech ecosystem. An alternative, adaptive approach—*sense and respond*—emerged towards the turn of the century (Haeckel, 1999). Applying systems theory to social and business environments (Ackoff, 1994), sense and respond provided a new managerial framework by which a modern, post-industrial business might operate and succeed.

At the simplest level, sense and respond makes intuitive sense. A post-industrial business, like a well-integrated person, displays three behaviors: it *senses* events in its environment, both internal and external, uses its *intelligence* to evaluate the implications and possible outcomes, and *responds* to the situation in the most appropriate manner. I continue to use the word *intelligence* here for the moment, although in an all-inclusive sense, containing knowledge, understanding, intuition and so on. As we shall see in Chapter 9,

Figure 7-3:
Sense and respond
model

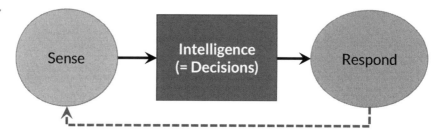

insight might be a more appropriate word. However named, these three aspects together enable an organism, be it animal, person or organization, to be adaptive to its world. So far, none of this is particularly new: it maps directly to BI as previously described. The first novel thought is that a response—intelligent or otherwise—causes changes in the environment, which should be further sensed, leading to a classic feedback loop. The simple model shown in Figure 7-3 represents this.

As in the animal world, not all sensory inputs require rational intelligence to generate an appropriate response. If you're hungry, you eat; thirst invokes drinking. These are instinctual reactions. In a business, if someone wants to buy a product, you sell it. At the most simplistic level, it is such instinctual responses that have traditionally been incorporated into operational applications. However, most sensory inputs demand a choice as to what is an appropriate response. In the face of a physical threat, an animal chooses between fight and flight based on an evaluation of the possible outcomes and its instinctual urgings. In business, a customer enquiry may lead to a choice about which particular product most closely satisfies the need. In the past, such basic decision making was also codified into operational applications or operational BI systems. However, in today's biz-tech ecosystem, the answer is more complex. Optimizing every decision on an individual basis—using operational analytics, as described in Chapter 5—is becoming common.

We can readily recognize the applicability of sense and respond in the scope and timeframes of operational and tactical BI. It simply makes sense, especially as the world changes in ever faster and less predictable ways. Its application to the longer timeframe of strategic decision making is less obvious. The word *strategy*, coming from the Greek στρατηγός (**stratēgos**, army general), refers to the military environment, where generals plan winning outcomes despite enemy opposition. Strategic planning in business has long had a similar flavor: the executive leaders set the direction and the company follows. However, Haeckel is adamant: if unpredictability prevails at a detailed level throughout the environment, traditional strategic planning will fail. The premise of *The Adaptive Enterprise* is that sense and respond must, and will, supplant the older approach. Furthermore, organizational structures and management approaches must change accordingly. Command and control is, according to Haeckel, replaced by context and coordination.

Sense and respond demands a significant paradigm shift in the business. Changing personal and organizational behavior to this degree is slow and painful. This may account for the limited uptake of the methodology a decade and a half later. Nonetheless, the problems posed by the speed and unpredictability of change have not diminished; they are more pressing than they have ever been. Even the current focus on predictive analytics—with its assertion that given enough data to play with, future outcomes can be foreseen—is to some extent an admission that the old certainties that underlay planning are no longer dependable. There is little doubt in my mind that sense and respond is the only viable approach to dealing with the current level of change and uncertainty, but there will still exist significant aspects of business where traditional strategic planning will continue to apply. As Steve Jobs showed with the "iPieces", sometimes you need to lead the market rather than follow—sense and respond to—the crowd. At other times, an investment is too large or too long-term to allow fully adaptive behavior. Businesses, as human constructs, are also driven by goal-setting.

More recently, a new concept—*listen and anticipate*—has been proposed (IBM Center for Applied Insights, 2012). *Listen* and *sense* are essentially equivalent. However, the implication of anticipating as opposed to responding is clear. Anticipation puts you ahead of the crowd, who can but respond after the fact. According to the authors, anticipation requires predictive analytics; it is impossible without it. However, on deeper consideration, we see that anticipation is another form of forecasting, a key aspect of the traditional approach that is overlooked when we shorten the term to make and sell. What this shows is that make and sell is actually a rather specialized case of sense and respond, where a lower level of uncertainty or a greater desire to lead the market prevails.

In the final chapter of his book, Haeckel talks of the need to change the corporate DNA to implement sense and respond and recounts a parable of the demise of the dinosaurs. At the time of that writing, it was not widely accepted that the dinosaurs' reign came to an end in an extinction event, externally imposed. It's likely, in my view, that something similar will be needed to destroy the hegemony of make and sell planning that still exists—perhaps the collapse of the financial system as we know it. That is speculation beyond the scope of this book. And, like the dinosaurs, make and sell will not totally disappear; rather, it will become more nimble and maneuverable, as are dinosaurs' avian descendants. We will thus use the sense and respond model as the basis for exploring and structuring the processes underlying business and the full breadth of its decision making, recognizing that the forecasting and planning at the heart of the traditional make and sell approach is still with us.

The Adaptive Enterprise centers on organizational and cultural change in business management and planning. The biz-tech ecosystem makes similar demands. However, the restructuring and refocusing of an existing BI environment towards a process orientation, as proposed here, offers a worthwhile and approachable first step towards implementing the sense and respond approach.

7.3   PROCESS IS AT THE HEART OF DECISION MAKING

It is a common belief among BI professionals—business and IT alike—that decision making is a process-free zone. The myth arises largely from the focus that both parties put on the desktop BI tools in use, and on the part of the activity that involves playing with data or visualizations using such tools. The truth is that this is but a small part of the total activity of decision making. From gathering and preparing the information all the way to driving action as an output, process abounds. IT runs processes to build and operate databases and ETL. Business runs the processes of the business. In truth, the real myth is that decision making can occur without process; decisions *always* encompass process. However, the process involved may be loosely defined, poorly documented, and highly changeable. Or, to use a more inspiring term, the process of decision making is often highly adaptive.

Figure 7-4 shows decision making in the context of the adaptive model and the IDEAL three-layer people, process and information view. Traditional BI is a vertical slice, emphasizing people and information and the interaction between them without reference to the process layer at the center. However, looking at the whole picture, it becomes clear that BI is simply a part of a larger process by which the business interacts with and responds to reality. Whenever something happens in the environment, internal or external, the event is—ideally—noted. Approaching that ideal of sensing every (relevant) event is a large part of the appeal of big data. In order to decide what to do about an event, intelligence is needed, the ultimate source of which is business users. This process knowledge may be invoked directly, for example through a call center agent or a business analyst using a BI tool, or through computer algorithms based on knowledge previously captured in application development. Information stores provide the basis for the decision, which then drives whatever response or action is needed. A few simple thought experiments show that whatever the event and action—from a pure operational action to a major strategic change—this model applies equally. The differences are only ones of degree: shorter or longer timeframe, more or less information, the level of direct or indirect involvement of business people and so on.

Figure 7-4:
Decision making in the sense and respond model

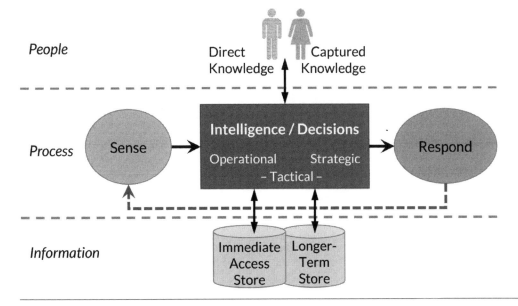

This picture clearly demonstrates that no valid business distinction can be made between operational and informational activities; this divide is an artifact of IT. They are simply part of a single continuum of sense and respond business processes. This should come as no surprise to anyone who has struggled with the emergence and positioning of operational BI in the 1990s, and later, of operational analytics. The issues we saw in Chapter 5 from an information viewpoint were that loading the BI environment via ETL was too slow, and running BI against operational data was too risky. While both of these issues have been progressively addressed over the years, the process view shows a more fundamental problem: business activities *cannot* be categorized into operational and informational buckets. Users simply see a seamless flow of actions in a process that must "get out of the way" and let them achieve their goal(s). The traditionally poorly-integrated operational and informational environments certainly do get in the way of that flow. The fundamental requirement in the biz-tech ecosystem is for an integrated, adaptive process support system that spans all types of business activities—those we traditionally call operational, informational, and indeed, as we shall see in Chapter 9, collaborative.

To further complicate matters, in traditional IT business-support environments, the feedback loop shown in Figure 7-4 can be rather tenuous. Responses and actions do, of course, cause changes to be made in existing business procedures in most businesses. However, even in the best-managed organizations, the follow-up questions— did we get the result we expected and can we prove cause and effect?—that would formally close the loop are seldom asked. This may be due to a variety of factors, such as decisions and outcomes widely separated in time or organizational space, interference from other unconsidered actions, and issues of span of control. Unfortunately, this inability to follow through is a bit like the wildebeest failing to make the association from year to year between the carnage in the Mara River crossing and the hordes of Nile crocodiles lurking in wait! While the corporate waters may not flow red, the cost of failed initiatives and missed opportunities are substantial. In today's biz-tech ecosystem, this feedback loop is a vital component in modulating behavior to environmental change.

A move to process-oriented BI thinking first occurs with operational BI, which, like pure operational activities, is process centric. As a result, operational BI must take on at least some process characteristics. This offers a good starting point, with incremental steps and potentially rapid results. However, it would be a missed opportunity to stop there. Tactical and even strategic BI can also be profitably addressed through a process approach.

Decision management

Sense and respond is closely aligned to the discipline of decision management. However, the focus in decision management is on repeatable, operational decisions impacting individual transaction or interactions, particularly with customers. The premise is that organizations make enormous volumes of such decisions and that, while each individual decision may be of miniscule value, in aggregate, they add up to a significant opportunity for optimization—through cost avoidance, revenue generation, or a combination of both (Taylor & Raden, 2007), (Taylor, 2011). While operational BI and analytics spring from informational thinking, decision management originates more from a process viewpoint. However, they end up at the same destination: maximizing agility and adaptivity of operational actions through embedded analytic function.

In line with their process view, decision management systems focus on the definition and management of specific rules or logic describing how a decision should be made by business users. The operation of these rules is supported by predictive analytic and modeling services. Monitoring enables continuous improvement in the process. Implementation may involve replacing existing operational environments with decision management systems. Operational BI and analytics focus more on the data-related aspects rather than the management and use of the logic and rules for decision making. The focus is thus likely to involve moving existing BI systems closer to real-time operation. However, although seldom explicitly mentioned, changes in operational systems and processes will probably be required to close the sense and respond loop. The two approaches are broadly complementary, and the biz-tech ecosystem in its full extent will demand functionality from both disciplines.

MEDA—monitor, evaluate, decide and act

A deeper dive into sense and respond brings us to the MEDA model, shown in Figure 7-5, which shows the cycle as four linked stages, described first in terms of traditional, tactical/strategic BI, in support of human decision making:

- *Monitor:* An ongoing process of observing what is happening in the environment, both within and without the enterprise, via enquiries, probes and triggers. Traditional operational systems are a key source of such information, but external, big data sources play an increasing role

- *Evaluate:* When any change, for good or ill, is observed, the implications are assessed, consequences gauged, and possible actions evaluated. This is the realm of traditional informational systems and BI tools

- *Decide:* Based on the outcome of the evaluation, decision makers compare and discuss recommended courses of action and choose the most appropriate. Face-to-face meetings and the use of collaborative tools characterize this phase

- *Act:* The decision is communicated via collaborative tools to the enterprise and acted upon. The action may involve changes in behaviors, measures or entire processes, affecting operational and even informational systems.

Figure 7-5:
MEDA model and traditional classes of applications

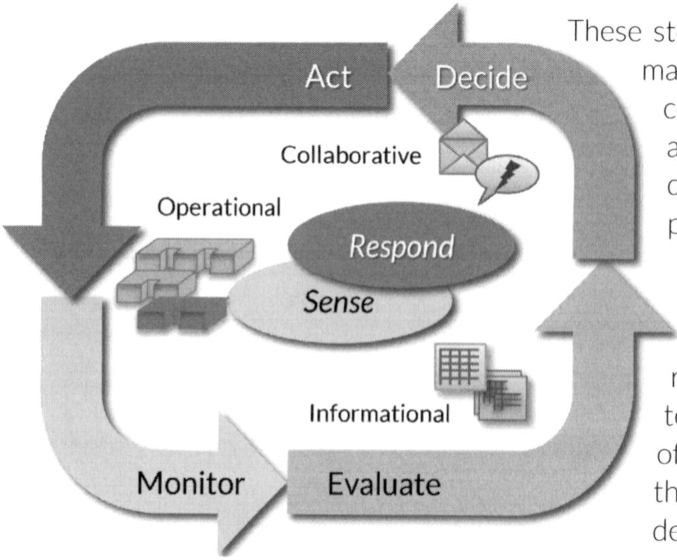

These steps apply equally to a fully automated *decision-making process* and all combinations of human-mediated and automated. In evaluate and decide, human involvement is replaced by analytical models and algorithms, while the act step involves computer-generated updates. For example, on a retail website, user input is monitored and evaluated in the context of purchases on previous visits by this and other similar shoppers. A decision is then taken on offers, upsells or cross-sells, and the next page is built accordingly, all in a fully automated manner. The rough distribution of operational, informational and collaborative systems around the cycle shown in Figure 7-5, as well as the traditionally different users of these systems in human decision processes, has engendered a belief that these three environments can be separately built, managed and owned. However, the tight handoffs between the four MEDA phases in the biz-tech ecosystem invalidate this belief.

> **Decision-making process**
>
> *The application to decision making of an adaptive, closed-loop approach, defined according to the MEDA model, leads to fully process-oriented decision making.*
>
> *A decision-making process is necessarily more flexible than traditional operational processes, but is fully aligned with SOA.*

We can further apply MEDA to what would traditionally be considered as purely operational processes. Monitor corresponds to recording and conditioning data, evaluate and decide are collapsed into traditional operational processing, and act becomes the commit phase of the agreement or transaction. At a personal level, the MEDA model also describes the steps in such a decision. For example, in a decision about what business expenses to claim, the model offers the insight that, contrary to many implementations, the process is a closed loop, where the monitor step allows claims to be reviewed and revisited by all involved parties. The cycles are equivalent, although the weighting of the stages differs, and the language varies depending on the nature of the activity.

If we accept MEDA as a basic closed-loop model and recognize that decision making is deeply process oriented, we come to a novel conclusion: that the prior approach of IT and vendors to the design and development of software systems to support business operations is completely inadequate. This realization was already becoming prevalent in the 1990s, as organizations struggled to innovate and react to market changes with the speed and flexibility they desperately needed. The large monolithic applications of the time could take months or more to upgrade. IT was denigrated as a bottleneck, slow to react and slower to deliver. The fault lay more in the architecture of application design and development than in the alleged bloody-mindedness of IT. A new approach to application design was required, and this first emerged under the banner of *service oriented architecture (SOA)* in 1996 in a Gartner Report (Natis & Schulte, 1996), described as *"a software architecture that starts with an interface definition and builds the entire application topology as a topology of interfaces, interface implementations and interface calls."* This is our next port of call.

7.4   STABILITY OR AGILITY (ALSO KNOWN AS SOA)

If timeliness is a first priority of the biz-tech ecosystem, as we saw in Chapter 5, agility is surely a second. Timeliness and agility are, of course, closely related. Timeliness is a measure of the speed with which business can recognize changes in its environment. Agility describes the extent to which the business can change itself in response to a stimulus. Timeliness, we saw, is most often expressed through the early availability of information to decision makers about the business and the surrounding world. As business moves ever more quickly, decision makers must react faster, using ever closer to real-time information as input. However, to be effective, such reaction must involve some change in business behavior: the business process must change. Agility, therefore, is more an attribute of process than of information (Bloomberg, 2013).

As we have seen, everything—literally *everything*—that is done within a business is part of a process, however strictly, loosely or poorly the processes are defined. However, business processes have traditionally been implemented as stand-alone *applications* that focus on the strictly defined and regimented set of steps required to automate some business area. In application development, the steps are analyzed in depth and defined in advance, implemented in fixed sequences—workflows—which users follow exactly. A high degree of stability, efficiency, productivity and reliability is thus achieved for a particular process. Over the years, many processes were automated in a growing number of stand-alone applications. Of course, the applications had to be linked together to automatically exchange information. They needed to be upgraded or replaced, and the environment became increasingly heterogeneous as new technologies were added. Eventually, the overall systems became so complex and fragile that they became unmanageable. Stability had coagulated into stasis; agility was fully forsaken.

To understand how agility can be supported, we note that process workflows contain *decision points* where the workflow splits on the basis of a decision. In "pure" operational workflows, these decisions are usually relatively straightforward and often automated through simple if-then-else logic, lookup tables, case statements, and more. In such applications, the logic of the decision points and the various actions invoked are pre-defined and pre-implemented in application code. This becomes a significant limitation in an environment where substantial and dramatic change is the norm, as is the case in the biz-tech ecosystem.

> ### Service oriented architecture
>
> *A flexible, extensible, business-oriented approach—including conceptual architecture, implementation and governance methodology—that allows well-bounded, heterogeneous, business-level software entities (called services) with well-defined communication interfaces to be assembled and easily rearranged in process flows that adaptively support wide-ranging and integrated business needs across disparate organizations.*

Any change in the logic flow or to an individual action demands instigation of an application development procedure where the business engages with IT, requirements are documented, code is developed and tested, reworked and, finally (yawn), the change goes live. This may take months or more in the traditional, waterfall development approach common in large enterprises. Even where agile development techniques have been adopted for development and maintenance of stand-alone applications, the task may still take too long for an adaptive business.

Reducing the delays in application change and maintenance was one of the main objectives of service oriented architecture when it was mooted in the mid-1990s. Very little practical progress was made, however, until the turn of the century when Web Services emerged. For SOA, Web Services were both a blessing and a curse. The blessing was that Web Services offered some foundational technology in a sexy field from which an SOA could be implemented, at least in part. The curse was that because the word *service* appeared in both, many people hopelessly confused the two.

So, what is SOA?

Beyond its regular conflation with Web Services, SOA suffers from another debility: there exist more definitions "than you can shake a stick at" of what it is. One expert on the topic lists five from a varie-

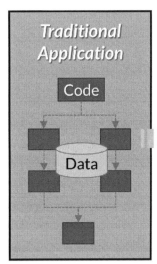

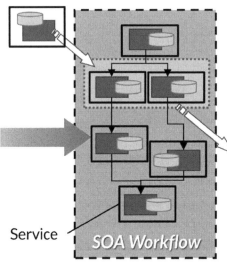

Figure 7-6:
Traditional
Application vs.
SOA Approach

ty of sources as a starting point before giving his own (Josuttis, 2007). Each contributes something of value, but none is complete, in my view. For our purposes, I offer one more.

In essence, what SOA proposes is that all business activity consists of highly flexible processes composed of business-oriented services loosely coupled in well-described and easily-understood workflows. Note the number of times the word *business* appears; bridging the business-IT gap is a central driver. Perhaps the easiest way to explore SOA is in comparison with the traditional application structure as shown in Figure 7-6. A traditional application is developed as a single, integrated structure with well-defined boundaries that enclose a set of code artifacts—a main program that defines the overall flow of execution, and procedures (subroutines) that execute individual tasks—and a store containing the data used by the entire application. The application is specifically developed for a known set of users at the behest of a business owner, whose unit pays the piper and calls the tune on all function originally included, as well as any later upgrades. This approach, replicated many times across the organization, leads to an application environment that is at once highly inflexible—technically and organizationally—and exceptionally fragile.

SOA defines a very different structure, starting from the premise that the organization as a whole requires a flexible, robust and easily changeable system comprised of multiple heterogeneous components. A workflow, defined in a high-level language—usually *business process execution language (BPEL)*—describes the overall business process in an extensible and loosely bounded way. This workflow is—in principle, at least—simple enough to be understood by business people and changed by them, as required. Services—the relatively small pieces of code that execute specific business tasks—are described in terms of the business actions they perform, have well-defined end points—input and output interfaces—and communicate with one another using messages, usually via an *enterprise service bus (ESB)*. Services are atomic in nature—self-contained, coarse-grained, discoverable, reusable and composable. The language in which they are coded is irrelevant, and their internal logic is unknown to the workflow at large.

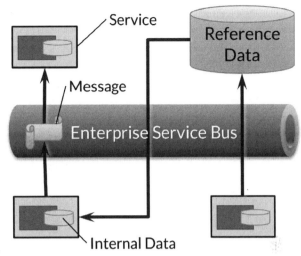

Figure 7-7: Data types in a service oriented architecture

As shown by the solid lines enclosing them, services logically include the internal transactional data over which they have full control within the boundary of the service, although the data is usually physically stored in a relational database. Such internal data is not the only data in SOA. The messages exchanged between services contain data, often in XML format. In addition, data—usually called *reference data*—is shared between services or made generally available. This includes foundational data such as customer numbers or product catalogs, derivative data such as data marts or monthly bank statements, and even larger collections of shared data. Each set of reference data is created, published and distributed by a dedicated service and available for use by all services, as shown in Figure 7-7. Workflows in a classic SOA are interpreted, executed and monitored through a workflow management component or business process manager that controls which services are started and when. In the most flexible approach, sometimes called *event-driven SOA*, services and workflows can also be initiated by specific events or combinations of events that occur in the environment. For example, a stock level dropping below some predetermined level in a warehouse could cause a stock replenishment service to be started to avoid an out-of-stock situation.

When a business task must be changed, the service implementing it can be easily replaced by simply removing the obsolete service or services from the process flow and inserting the required new function—provided it has the same inputs and outputs—at the same point in the workflow, as depicted in Figure 7-6. Ideally, a wide range of services are already described in a catalog, are easily discoverable, and are readily available, so that the business can straightforwardly add new or replace existing services in workflows with reduced IT involvement. This supports the goal of speedy and flexible process change in response to business needs. It offers a further and potentially dramatic increase in agility: giving business people the ability to directly modify process flows essentially removes IT as a bottleneck to the achievement of an adaptive business. While services themselves are most often designed and built by IT staff to ensure their internal validity, we can envisage that business people could also create—or more likely, modify—services. In some instances, certain "power users" might step up to such a task, as is the case in informational systems where such skilled users create analytic and reporting functions first for themselves and then for wider distribution.

This technical infrastructure is only part of the story, of course. Surrounding and supporting it must be a methodology and organizational structure that is very different to that found in traditional application development shops. These aspects, and indeed, the breadth and depth of the topic as a whole, are beyond what can be covered in a few pages. In depth information is available in a number of books— (Erl, 2005) and (Brown, 2008), for example—and in the online *SOA Source Book* (The Open Group, 2009).

But will it work?

SOA sets itself ambitious goals, and progress toward them has been slow. In the form of implementable but evolving technology, SOA has been available for a little over a decade. A wide range of commercial and open-source platforms now exist. Looking at examples of implementation, the underlying direction is to allow the business to take on more responsibility for changes and upgrades to business processes; first, the simpler ones, and then increasingly complex changes. Some experts doubt that the larger promise of SOA can be achieved, likening it to the challenge of changing the engines on a 747...in flight. However, no viable alternative has yet been proposed that could provide the business with the level of agility that the biz-tech ecosystem demands.

Beyond the obvious implications for operational development, SOA offers benefits and challenges to BI, as shown in Figure 7-8. Traditional BI is a stand-alone system fed by ETL from the operational databases. In SOA, we could retain the stand-alone BI and use ETL to feed it in a reference data approach. The number of feeds increases along with the number of services (for clarity, only two are shown). In addition, switching services and changing workflows on demand in SOA impacts ETL projects, which often struggle to keep up even with slow waterfall development speeds. On the other hand, SOA offers the ability to directly embed BI services in workflows, a key requirement of the biz-tech ecosystem. However, populating the BI service directly via ETL—either from multiple other services or from the stand-alone BI system—contravenes service orientation principles and may cause consistency problems. Using the messaging approach—either directly between services or by picking up broadcast messages on the bus—offers real-time updates for the BI environment, although again impact data consistency. SOA also promises to solve the conundrum of source metadata that has long plagued BI. With well-defined business services and interfaces, SOA demands clean and complete metadata. In fact, because SOA lives or dies on the quality of its real-time metadata management, it can offer to BI levels of metadata quality and quantity that have long been the Nirvana for BI developers.

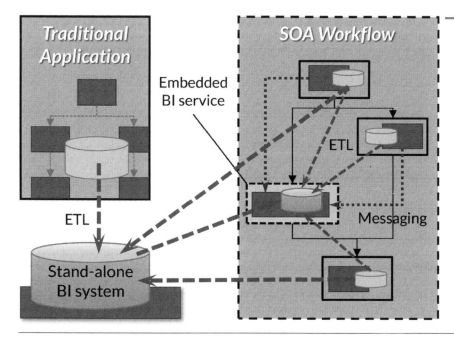

Figure 7-8:
BI options in a service oriented architecture

The change of perspective offered by SOA has two far-reaching and perhaps unintended consequences. First, it removes the distinction between operational, informational and, indeed, collaborative systems. A process such as customer registration on a website, for example, may involve services in each category—operational data entry and validation, informational analysis of the customer's likely preferences and collaborative email to confirm their identity. Business users and, more importantly, customers cannot see the difference between these types of service and cannot be expected to follow different integration rules, go to diverse IT support groups and so on. Second, it blurs the boundary between business and IT. IT is no longer the only source of computer functionality (applications, services, and workflows) for the business. Business users also play a role. This challenges current organizational thinking, which makes a clear distinction between business processes that run the business and IT processes that build and manage data and applications. SOA drives the elimination of this divergence, which is also key to the emergence of a true biz-tech ecosystem.

Application vs. infrastructure services

SOA challenges another distinction made in IT: that between applications and infrastructure components. Applications, such as the order entry or customer registration applications, are described as supporting business functions. Infrastructure components, on the other hand, perform more generic functions, often focused on data manipulation or other tasks that are more interest to IT than the business. Examples include the ETL function used widely in data warehousing, database management systems (DBMS), and transaction processing monitors used in operational environments.

In SOA, every piece of function exists as a callable service. As defined in the *SOA Source Book* (The Open Group, 2009), a service is *"a logical representation of a repeatable* business activity *that has a specified outcome"* (my emphasis). This would seem to exclude infrastructure components as SOA services. Two questions arise, however, around this definition. First, what is a business activity, and second, why the sole focus on business activities? One could argue that anything a business does—including that done by its IT department—is, by definition, a business activity. An ETL job populating a data mart is performed as a result of good business requirements, after all. I believe that the emphasis on business activity is actually an attempt to avoid the definition of highly granular programming tasks—subroutines, in older terminology—as services. Incrementing a counter or updating a generic field in a database record, for example, could certainly be implemented as services but would not count as tasks that would be recognized by a business person as achieving a business goal. This, undoubtedly, is a vague and fuzzy boundary. However, as the concept of the biz-tech ecosystem makes clear, the old wall between business and IT has become a hindrance to a more intimate relationship. Figure 7-8 thus shows services that traditionally would be positioned on different sides of that ancient wall but can now all partake in an integrated flow of tasks within any required process.

7.5   KEEPING UP WITH THE FASHIONISTAS

From the foregoing discussion, it should be clear that I consider SOA, despite its detractors and slow progress, as the foundation for the process layer required to support the needs of the biz-tech ecosystem. However, it seems to have largely disappeared from current thinking in IT, replaced by Cloud computing on one side and consumer-driven evolution of mobile devices and apps on the other. So, what are the implications of these trends?

Cloud—just fog seen from a distance?

Joni Mitchell sang[2], *"I've looked at clouds from both sides now / From up and down, and still somehow / It's cloud illusions I recall."* Cloud, in computing terms, also comes with many sides and illusions, promoted by vendors and vested interests. The breadth of the topic permits a multitude of arguments, pro and con: cost avoidance on a number of fronts, agility, privacy and security, governance, competitive differentiation, scalability and more. Most are beyond the scope of this short section, which has as its goal to explore how Cloud affects the biz-tech ecosystem and, in particular, the two key foundations, BI and SOA.

Figure 7-9:
Venus von Willendorf,
c. 25,000 years old,
Naturhistorisches
Museum,
Vienna, Austria

---

[2] Joni Mitchell's *Both Sides, Now* (1967) was first recorded by her on the 1969 album, *Clouds* and was originally a hit for Judy Collins in 1968.

A relatively well-respected and independent set of definitions was published by the U.S. National Institute of Standards and Technology in 2011 (Mell & Grance, 2011). The essential characteristics are listed as on-demand self-service, broad network access, resource pooling, rapid elasticity, and measured service. Public, private, community and hybrid Cloud are identified as the main deployment modes. Infrastructure-, platform-, software-as-a-service (XaaS) are the identified service models; data-as-a-service and other models proposed by other players also fall under the shadow of Cloud. While the phrase *something-as-a-service* would seem to imply a close alignment between Cloud and SOA, the services referenced in Cloud are much more generic and broadly defined than those of SOA. Nonetheless, Cloud can be as suitable for SOA deployment as internally run and managed traditional IT environments. In fact, an IT environment that has been logically structured into business-oriented services makes an ideal (although not mandatory) starting point for a Cloud migration, because existing, individual, well-bounded services can be evaluated and migrated separately from one environment to the other. However, questions remain as to how far a Cloud provider's environment is SOA enabled. In the case of infrastructure- and platform-as-a-service, the choice is yours—you decide to install or include an SOA backbone. For software-as-a-service, individual Cloud provider implementations vary and must be individually evaluated.

BI has often been targeted as a good match for Cloud computing. Its large and variable data volumes seem ideally suited to Cloud's elasticity. Although highly valued by CEOs—at least in recent years—as a competitive differentiator, BI is also perceived to be very expensive to implement and maintain; another tick for Cloud. Amazon's Redshift BI Cloud environment, a fully managed, petabyte-scale data warehouse service, announced in late 2012, offers very significant cost savings over in-house deployments, with pricing as low as $1,000 per terabyte per year (Amazon, 2012). As operational applications move to the Cloud—Salesforce.com is still the poster child—it seems reasonable that BI must follow. And yet, as of mid-2013, Cloud BI has been slow to take off. Much of the reason for the delay seems to revolve around the infrastructural aspects of replicating data from internal operational systems to the Cloud, combined with concerns about privacy and limitations on competitive advantage. For now, the jury is still out on Cloud BI. In the context of the biz-tech ecosystem and the conceptual and logical architectures being developed in this book, the bottom line is that we are discussing IT and business architectures here; these precede and are largely independent of the deployment decision that any Cloud implementation actually represents.

Surviving the mobile app-valanche

The mobile app-valanche has a much broader potential impact than that of Cloud. There are four broad areas:

- *Geotemporal data:* Mobile devices and apps are a major source of spatial and temporal data and present significant business opportunities. The topic is discussed in Section 6.5.

- *Privacy and security:* Data residing on mobile devices and in transit to and from them is subject to a greater danger of loss, corruption and abuse than centrally stored information, as discussed in Section 4.7.

- *Deployment aspects:* Mobile devices and apps raise a number of issues regarding deployment. These are particularly prevalent in bring your own device (BYOD) implementations. As for Cloud, deployment is below the architectural level of this book.

- *Application architecture:* The concept and structure of apps as deployed on mobile devices is a valid architectural topic and is the focus of this section.

App took the prize for the word of the year for 2010 (American Dialect Society, 2011), as the term was most trendy and growing in popularity. Of course, in one sense, it's just abbreviated slang for application. And while often used for an application that runs in a browser (a Web app), the apps of interest here are those that run on smartphones—as in *"There's an app for that!"* The key technical characteristics of apps are that they must work under a set of constraints perhaps reminiscent of the earliest days of client-server. Physical constraints include small screen size, limited memory, and available electrical power. Network limitations to be considered are bandwidth speed and cost, as well as frequent and unpredictable disconnection. Security issues include the loss or unauthorized use of sensitive data through theft or loss of the device, as well as hack-

Figure 7-10:
Mobile use of
smartphones in
business processes

ing of communication channels. These constraints drive app design towards simple, restricted function sets in a strictly stand-alone context. For consumer apps, this is an accepted and currently workable state of affairs; most apps provide one (or fewer!) useful functions and operate in a strictly independent mode.

However, our interest here is more in business-oriented apps, whether aimed at consumers or business personnel. Here, the need is for a more complex and nuanced level of interaction in discrete tasks, spanning these activities with some level of a connecting process within a defined context. The parallel with SOA services as independent business tasks within a workflow is obvious. Current thinking in the SOA community is that SOA can provide the architecture and a practical basis for this process orientation within an enterprise architecture, given the impracticality of orchestrating the workflow on the device. Debates at a technical level—REST vs. SOAP, for example—aside, this seems a reasonable assumption. However, there are some important contextual aspects to consider. Most important is whether mobile technology changes the way that business people work and, as a consequence, how their process and workflow should be supported.

There are significant differences in behavior between a user sitting at a desk and following a workflow on a PC and one addressing a similar business need on the move. The static user, tethered to her PC and the server behind it, is focused on the process and tasks in hand. She has probably gathered the required information in advance walking the shop floor, for example, and is now fully engaged in what is, essentially, a data entry phase. Interruptions can be managed and limited in impact. Compare this with the salesman on the road, calling on potential and existing customers, engaging with the sales support and order entry process via a mobile app. Interruptions, both personal and technical, are constant. His focus is on interacting with the customers and the physical world; interactions with the back-end process may only consist of snatched moments visiting Starbucks or stopped at traffic signals. The meaning of task and workflow in the user's eyes may thus differ considerably between the two situations. The level of flexibility and adaptability of the SOA implementation required in the mobile situation is considerably higher. In principle, the process management for the static user should also include the possibility for interruption, diversion and so on; in practice, the implementation may have cut these seldom-encountered corners.

As we are still in the early days of rolling out mobile enterprise-wide app environments, firm conclusions would probably be premature. However, the probable spread of mobile apps suggests we must take them into consideration at an architectural level. The likely consequences are in extending the adaptability and temporal flexibility of SOA-supported processes.

> The future is both dispersed and peripatetic. Cloud and mobile implementation are technically interrelated and inevitable aspects of the biz-tech ecosystem. However, they operate at different levels of architectural thought. Mobile addresses people and their behaviors; Cloud appears at the technological level. Therefore, mobile drives Cloud (as well as other technological issues). A first step is an in-depth exploration of the needs and implications of mobile BI.

ThoughtPoint

7.6 IDEAL ARCHITECTURE (4), PROCESS

Over previous chapters, we've explored the information space of the IDEAL conceptual architecture. It's time to turn to the process space. Here we also find three dimensions or axes of interest, as shown in Figure 7-11, against which we can position *tasks* or types of activities in order to better understand their key characteristics. As in the case of the information space, the classes on each axis should be viewed as a continuum, merging from one to the next, rather than discrete divisions. The process space is somewhat simpler than its information counterpart; each axis here represents a single, simple characteristic.

Active Scope

The most obvious process dimension is *Active Scope (AS)*, which starts with SOA and expands beyond the business-level concepts

Figure 7-11:
Dimensions of the
process layer

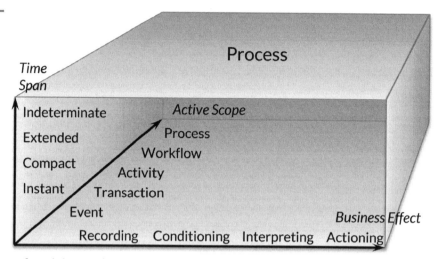

of activity and workflow defined there to also include more technical scopes. The lowest level is an *event*, the act of making an observation of the real world. This might be a machine sensor measurement of a state, such as external temperature or velocity, or of a change in state, such as a sudden drop in temperature or a deceleration. In a more complex machine, it might be a calculated value based on more basic measures. An observation in the real world also includes noting communications of information by people, such as a Tweet or an email. Events exist beyond and before the context of the business. Individual events, or more likely, combinations of events arriving in the business, constitute raw information, as described in Section 3.6, of interpretative value. Legally significant events or combinations thereof take on special significance and become *transactions* through cleansing and validation. Transactions are IT defined and implemented, and their recording conforms to the *atomicity, consistency, isolation and durability (ACID)* constraints long seen as mandatory in operational systems. Live, atomic data is the main output of transactions.

An *activity*, also called a service in SOA, is the smallest unit of function that makes sense to a business user, usually consisting of a number of related transactions and events. Activities may be nested within one another to form more complex services. They are defined by the business, in business terms, but generally implemented by IT in order to maintain the internal consistency of the actions and data involved.

A *workflow* involves the flexible linking of activities into an easily created and changed sequence of activities using logical operators, as we saw in Section 7.4. Workflows are defined by the business, and depending on their complexity and the skill level of business users, may be implemented or changed by them. Workflows may also be nested, all the way up to a *process*, which is the highest level of workflow corresponding to a value-generating set of interdependent activities and workflows identified and controlled entirely by the business and supporting the business vision.

Business Effect

The second dimension, *Business Effect (BE)*, describes how any action taken relates to the underlying business information, based on the observation that in the biz-tech ecosystem, all business function uses information—hard and/or soft—in some way. In the past, IT focused only on transactions and data in databases, so the prior view of this characteristic would have been mainly confined to CRUD—create, read, update and delete. This view is both too technical and too limited in scope for our needs. We need to consider the softer information of big data and content, as well as in-flight information that may never be permanently stored at all.

Recording is the act of capturing raw/atomic data or textual/multiplex information from any source. Traditionally, capturing would equate to storing it permanently or semi-permanently in a database on a spinning disk within the enterprise. This is no longer the only possibility. In-flight data may never be stored at all. Multiplex information on the Web might be accessed remotely, being too voluminous or legally forbidden to copy. In these cases, *noticing* might be a better word than recording. In some cases, such as transactional data or legally binding documents, a permanent record is necessary. Because metadata (context-setting information) is defined as a sub-class of information (see Section 3.7), recording the information structures and context is also included here.

Having recorded the information, the next step is *conditioning* it. This covers all subsequent changes to, calculations about, derivations and deletions of the recorded information and CSI. Clearly, conditioning can loop back to recording in order to capture the derived, compound and other information classes thus created. In the biz-tech ecosystem, we are continuously faced with decisions about the permanence of recording and conditioning, both information/CSI stored and the methods used. The old data warehousing answer—store everything forever—is no longer viable; the volumes and velocities of big data and streaming data preclude it. However, business needs and legal requirements mandating that certain information and process definitions be kept for periods varying from months to years must be considered when defining what is kept and for how long.

With information recorded and conditioned, the "real business" can begin. *Interpreting* is the process of applying intelligence to the information to understand its business implications in a sense and respond system, as shown in Figure 7-4. Interpreting is thus a function found in both operational and informational systems as traditionally implemented. Transactional data recorded in an order entry application must be interpreted before any action is taken. In the simplest sense, interpretation involves no more than validating and understanding the data entered. As we saw earlier, it may also involve operational analytics that allows the business to offer the customers other options beyond simply buying what they selected.

Interpreting may thus lead back to further conditioning, and even recording or forward to *actioning*, which involves reaching a decision on what to do and taking the appropriate action. In the sense and respond paradigm, this closes the loop all the way back to recording the information that the decision and action entails.

The categories on the Business Effect axis are generalizations of the four stages in the MEDA model of decision making, described in Section 7.3, in their use of information. Recording and conditioning are the fundamental actions required to *monitor* the environment, interpreting aligns with *evaluate* and *decide*, while actioning and *act* are the same activity. There is one further point to note. As mentioned, CSI, as a sub-class of information, is subject to these process stages. Furthermore, SOA offers business users the opportunity to become involved in process creation and manipulation. Mashups and similar Web 2.0 tools, as well as BI tools, also allow users to manipulate processes. Such process manipulation involves structuring information—creating new fields or tables, redefining existing columns, and so on. Traditional thinking assigned such work to IT; this is no longer true. New or changed information structures (concepts and relationships) and context-setting information—such as entities, attributes, table and column names/descriptions, and much more—thus follow information usage on the Business Effect dimension.

Time Span

The final dimension is *Time Span (TS)*, representing the period of time over which a process element is active or open. Developers of operational systems are familiar with this characteristic as the period between the first and last updates of data related to a business transaction, at the end of which the transaction is deemed committed. In the interim period, any information involved is in an uncertain state, likely to be internally and externally inconsistent and subject to unilateral revocation. Within this scope, the concept and consequences of this time span are reasonably well-understood. However, the shorter and, in particular, longer time spans demanded by informational, collaborative and big data systems are less well-defined and their consequences seldom considered. This dimension addresses these questions.

The *instant* time span, associated only with events and the simplest of transactions on the Active Scope axis, refers to the shortest measurable timing, of the order of a few computer clock cycles. Such events and transactions are essentially atomic; they cannot be further decomposed, and each deals with a single, integral piece of information. Examples include measuring an engine's revolutions per minute or the creation of a Tweet.

The typical operational transactions mentioned above occur in a *compact* time span, a period of time within which a person might place an order for an item of medium complexity—an airline ticket, for example. This definition is, of course, vague and varies with cultural norms. However, we can see that there are real-world conditions—seats at the required price may sell out—and technical constraints—a number of data records must be updated consistently—that limit the time span involved.

The *extended* time span recognizes that some activities can spread over hours, days or more because of temporal dependencies either in the real world or in the technical environment. Developers of ETL jobs to populate a data warehouse are familiar with multi-hour time spans, as various data sets only become available in a particular order and over a period of hours as various processing constraints and data interdependencies are resolved. In the real world, agreeing on a complex contract—to buy a house, for example—may take weeks to close for similar information-related reasons and also because of the human interactions required. In fact, any tasks requiring a degree of human interaction, communication and decision making are likely to need an extended time span. This time span is characteristic of some activities and most workflows on the Activity Scope axis. And although we may not be able to predict their exact duration, we do have a plan or expectation for their completion. This is the difference between the extended and *indeterminate* time spans. The latter applies to processes that could possibly go on forever and where no end condition can be defined. Business processes at the highest level have this characteristic.

The foregoing discussion illustrates that the Time Span and Active Scope axes are not truly independent or orthogonal. This is one of the clearest interdependencies between dimensions. Other, more subtle relationships exist between dimensions, both within the process and information spaces and between them. In a topic as complex as the conceptual IT architecture for the biz-tech ecosystem, this is to be expected, illustrating the design trade-offs that building such supporting infrastructure demands.

7.7   REAL ARCHITECTURE (3), THE SIX PROCESS–ATIONS

At the conceptual architecture level, we've treated applications and infrastructure—as described in Section 7.4—as equal partners in process. As we move to the logical, REAL view, the focus is firmly on infrastructure and the six key functional areas required in the biz-tech ecosystem shown in Figure 7-12. The nomenclature is, perhaps, unusual—the names have been chosen to convey the function involved, but also to avoid confusion with widely used terminology in the BI field. Where appropriate, I point out the relationship between common terms and individual functional components.

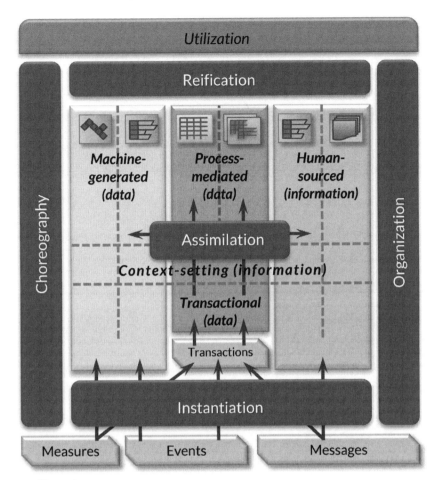

Figure 7-12:
Process support in
the REAL logical
architecture

Utilization

Business applications, or SOA workflows, with their business focus and wide variety of goals and actions, are gathered together in a single component, *utilization*, referring to the notion that such business-oriented services use all underlying function and information as required. Significant application architecture and design work is, of course, required within these services and workflows, but is clearly beyond the scope of this book.

Choreography

The adoption of the SOA process- and services-based approach to delivering the biz-tech ecosystem requires an underlying *choreography* infrastructure, which coordinates the actions of all participating elements to produce the desired outcome. For the purposes of this discussion, we treat this in two parts: workflow management and message bus support. This treatment is, by necessity, summary in nature; this topic of process enablement deserves—and, indeed, has driven—entire books describing its various parts and approaches.

Adaptive Workflow Management

Workflow management supports the creation, management, execution and monitoring of a system of workflows or processes consisting of independent, disparate services and activities. It is also referred to as *Business Process Management (BPM)* by tool vendors, although this may lead to confusion with the higher level methodology for managing business using a process approach (Ko, 2009). The exact meaning and scope of such systems or suites differs by vendor and by industry. BPM has traditionally focused on well-understood, predefined workflows, common in highly structured production environments—insurance claims handling, for example. The emphasis is on improving worker productivity through accurate and comprehensive process support at the detailed level of individual activities, and traceable links between them. A further, important aim is in the refinement and optimization of processes—also known as *Business Process Reengineering (BPR)*. The biz-tech ecosystem, on the other hand, is a far more variable and innovative environment that additionally requires more sophisticated and flexible processes and thus, adaptive management. This combination of needs has been described over the past few years as the convergence of BPM and BI (Fischer, 2010) and provides the starting point for a definition of *adaptive workflow management*.

We therefore define this component in the most inclusive sense, spanning both computer and human tasks, as well as emphasizing that the workflows to be managed include both predefined and highly variable cases. At the core of adaptive workflow management, as

Figure 7-13:
Adaptive workflow management logical architecture

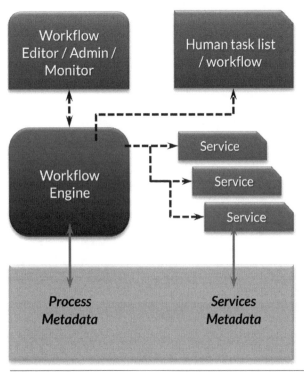

shown in Figure 7-13, is a workflow engine, which provides execution-time support for all aspects of the workflow, including initiating services in the active workflow, exception handling, performance monitoring, and so on. It is also responsible for generating and managing human task lists / workflows. Workflow models, definitions and rules are created in the workflow editor and stored as process metadata/CSI. The editor also provides workflow administration and monitoring functions. Definitions of services and their interfaces are also part of the CSI stored in the information layer. This CSI-based, rule-driven approach allows business users to define and modify workflows and provides a highly adaptive environment. A number of standards for workflow CSI/metadata exist, including *XML Process Definition Language (XPDL)*, a format standardized by the Workflow Management Coalition (WfMC); *Business Process Model and Notation (BPMN)*, maintained by the Object Management Group; and *Business Process Execution Language (BPEL)*, an OASIS standard executable language for specifying actions within business processes with web services (Chang, 2006). The *Workflow Reference Model* (Hollingsworth, 1995) forms the basis for most workflow software systems and provides a starting point for understanding much of the terminology. Decision management clearly fits here, too.

Extensible Message Bus

SOA describes the communications between services as via messages. The services are well-defined in the literature, although often misinterpreted in practice, as we saw in Section 7.4. Messages, on the other hand, are less clear. With its origins in operational environments, SOA has generally emphasized messaging that is designed to support action taking. In this environment, messages tend to be succinct, the focus is on making sure they are transmitted reliably and quickly. An enterprise service bus is often seen as the foundation for messaging. While early message definitions were based exclusively on Web Services (WS-*) standards, particularly *SOAP* (no longer an acronym for Simple Object Access Protocol), many other protocols are possible, with more recent focus being placed on the *RESTful (Representational State Transfer)* implementations favored by Web 2.0 proponents (Erl, et al., 2012).

With the merging of operational and informational systems demanded by the biz-tech ecosystem, the more common file-based communications approaches used in ETL as efficient bulk-transfer mechanisms must be explicitly included as first class citizens. A general definition of SOA message types (Chatterjee, 2004) includes a document type that can include any content of any size. Many—although not all—descriptions of vendor-provided ESBs also include file based transfer protocols. With these considerations in mind, we use the term *extensible message bus* to indicate the required generality and flexibility of this REAL component..

Organization

The *organization* component of REAL covers all design, management and governance activities relating to both processes and information. It is through this component that services are catalogued and workflows defined and changed, information modeled and managed. Rather than try to provide a fully inclusive list of all such function, I emphasize two aspects that span all such functionality in the biz-tech ecosystem: *immediacy* and *breadth*. Immediacy relates to the fact the biz-tech ecosystem is always active and changing. A design function such as modeling, for example, can no longer be seen as something that is done only up-front, in advance of implementation. In the case of modeling, process-mediated data can and must be modeled in advance of its use to ensure valid and consistent structure and contents. On the other hand, a large proportion of human-sourced information, such as emails, must be "modeled" on the fly to determine their meaning. Such modeling, rather than being performed manually, is done in text analytics tools as the information is processed. Breadth refers to the fact that the boundaries between business and IT become blurred in the biz-tech ecosystem. Business people create and modify workflows in SOA and mashup applications in Web 2.0 tools, as discussed in Chapter 9. IT staff are intimately involved in business design and governance activities where technology is a gating factor. Many of these considerations appear only at the physical level of the architecture and during the implementation phase of development, and are thus beyond the scope of this book.

Information processing

Information processing is spread over three components through-out the information pillars of the REAL architecture, focusing on gathering, consolidating and accessing distributed information.

Instantiation

The first of these components is *instantiation*, the means by which measures, events and messages are represented as or by instances of information within the enterprise environment. While a common implementation might be as simple as reading a file and storing it in an internal data store, instantiation implies much more subtlety. In particular, the demands for timely information delivery in today's business may be such that reading a file or landing data on disk may be too slow. Information collection thus ranges from streaming events, also known as complex event processing (CEP), to bulk file handling. The following cases and more must be considered:

- The simplest case involves events, messages, etc. copied into the internal environment. Included here, and in subsequent cases, is collecting the CSI for use in decoding, processing and interpreting the received information.

- Making copies of some information may be impossible for reasons of volume or legal constraints, a situation we encounter most often with messages composed by people. In this case, instantiation reduces to reading—or streaming—an external information source within whatever other processing is required.

- We may want only to collect changes—new events or updated communications—since the last time we accessed the data because of the size of the source. Only a subset of the information may be of interest. Instantiation thus requires functionality to select data according to a variety of sub-setting conditions, such as change data capture or replication.

- We may want to instantiate transactions. This is the most complex case. Events, measures and messages exist in their own right in the real world. Transactions are created in the context of the business operations. As shown in Figure 7-12, instantiation combines real-world measures, events and messages into such transactions, and in many such cases, is implemented as traditional operational systems taking input from human operators, both internal and on the Web, with all of the necessary validation and data consistency functionality built in. Other cases may involve reading event data from sensors or messages from people, validating them, ensuring consistency and affording them the legal status of transactions.

In all cases, the result is information stored or streamed for use within the enterprise. This information is understood within a known scope and context, reliance, etc., defined by its associated context-setting information. It may or may not be consistent across its breadth; in fact, it is most likely to be at least partially inconsistent. Ensuring the required level of consistency in storage or use is the task of the information processing components that we come to next.

Assimilation

To anyone involved in building data warehouse or business intelligence solutions, *assimilation* will probably feel like home ground. Its primary function is the creation of reconciled and consistent information sets, as has long been done with ETL tools. In the case of process-mediated data like the core business information repository and core analytic and reporting stores, the approach is to populate these informational assets largely from existing transactional data in operational systems within the process-mediated data, as well as from event or message information, if appropriate. Across the information pillars, the most likely approach is to create referential links to key values and similar approaches, rather than copying human-sourced or machine-generated information into the process-mediated core environment. As a result, while ETL (sometimes called *data integration*) tooling is a key source of such function, *data virtualization* functionality may also play a role in building these linkages.

Assimilation is carried out before users have access to the information. This pre-planned and pre-executed approach is vital in cases where temporal inconsistency is a feature of different sources. In the past, this has often led to significant delays in making information available, ranging from overnight to weekly or monthly processing. This is increasingly unacceptable, although some delays are inevitable. The point to recognize, however, is that assimilation is specifically aimed at driving a basic level of information consistency that would be difficult to achieve in real time. This requirement also leads to the positioning of the component as shown in close association with context-setting information, both in using it to drive the process and in creating it as part of the process. As we saw earlier, the initial creation of some of this CSI, such as data models, occurs in the organization component..

Reification

Above the information stores in Figure 7-12, we see the final information processing component, *reification*, defined as the process of making something abstract more concrete or real[3]. Sitting between all business application functions and the information itself, this component provides a consistent, cross-pillar view of information according to an overarching model and access to it in real-time. In terms of current technology, the corresponding tools are variously called *data virtualization*, *data federation*, and *enterprise information integration (EII)*; the exact scope and meaning of these terms often differs from vendor to vendor.

Within the BI community, this function has long been a cause of controversy, as we saw in Chapter 5. However, the pillared information architecture necessitates reification for three distinct reasons. First, with information residing in multiple storage technologies, a variety of access methods are required that retrieve data and convert it to a common language, often SQL. Second, where information must be joined for particular business needs from these multiple storage technologies, a mediating layer is required to do semantic interpretation and matching, schema translation, and so on. Third, particularly in the process-mediated case, real-time information may not be available in the core information stores, necessitating online joins between these stores and the underlying operational systems real-time data.

Of course, context-setting information is also key to reification (despite its distant positioning in the diagram). In fact, reification

---

[3] From *The New Oxford Dictionary of English*

and assimilation are also closely interdependent through the CSI they use and generate. Design decisions in assimilation—how customer keys are related, for example—must be echoed and available in reification to ensure consistency of processing. There is a strong argument from this viewpoint for a single, integrated set of tooling addressing both assimilation and reification functionality...

7.8   IN PRACTICE—IMPLEMENTING PROCESS FLEXIBILITY

In many IT organizations, process and data management knowledge and responsibility reside in two largely separate silos. In the biz-tech ecosystem, this is no longer a possibility. In fact, as we've seen, decision management and operational BI both already cross this boundary from opposite directions. We are led to consider the following steps toward bridging the gap and moving toward an adaptive process and information environment:

✓ Create a steering committee at executive management level to drive adoption of integrative practices needed for the biz-tech ecosystem. Even more than data warehousing, this initiative requires commitment and direction from the very top of the organization. The CEO must sponsor and all executives completely support this approach.

✓ Restructure the IT organization to matrix-manage across business functions and IT technologies. In the operational environment, IT is usually aligned to functional boundaries such as finance, fulfillment, etc. while in the informational world, a more cross-functional approach at the EDW level is often combined with functional alignment for data marts. Extending this latter approach across both operational and informational areas will be beneficial.

✓ Cross-pollinate operational and information departments in IT. Skills exchange, secondments and similar programs at both management and technical levels between different parts of IT drive collaboration. In many cases, the beginnings of such cooperation have emerged in BI implementations and have been embedded in BI Centers of Excellence.

✓ Instigate (if not already started) or prioritize decision management and operational BI projects. If both types exist, combine them. For operational systems, they show how flexibility is important and possible; for BI they introduce process thinking.

✓ Ensure any SOA projects incorporate adaptive, sense and respond thinking in their design scope. While some processes in the early stages of SOA roll-out may require little or no flexibility, adding such design thinking at a later stage can prove difficult in the extreme.

✓ Put structures in place to drive close cooperation between SOA projects or program and the data warehouse Center of Excellence. This is required to ensure that (i) SOA does not disrupt ETL for the warehouse, but rather enables more real-time messaging, (ii) operational BI or decision management is properly incorporated in SOA, linked back to the data warehouse and (iii) metadata approaches are shared between the two environments, in particular so that the data warehouse gains maximum benefit from SOA metadata.

✓ Experiment (at least) with data virtualization tools. With data and information increasingly distributed, access strategies must include virtualization. Start with hard information, first with relational data on different systems, then including other forms of well-structured databases. Expand to all information types. As Davis and Eve show in ten real business examples, there exists a wide variety of potential areas of use of the technology, both within and beyond BI, so choosing an area that proves the technology and delivers value at an acceptable level of risk should prove relatively easy (Davis & Eve, 2011).

✓ Incorporate closed-loop thinking in all BI projects and in the overall BI program. Design projects where the outcome of decisions and subsequent actions can be tracked, and outcomes compared to those expected.

7.9   CONCLUSIONS

A single chapter on the process aspects of the biz-tech eco-system is necessarily limited in the depth to which it can cover this vast topic. And as someone whose primary career focus has been on information, I must depend on others to explore this subject matter to its full extent. This chapter sketches the broad outlines and focuses mainly on the interface between process and information. And in this, I believe it serves its purpose.

Modern business and the emerging biz-tech ecosystem demand ever faster turnaround times, both in processing regular operational activities and in reacting to unexpected changes in the environment. Such speeds of reaction and agility have placed all processes of the business—organizational and technological—under enormous stress. The concept and practice of sense and respond is a reaction to this stress at a business organization level. Its impact can be traced all the way down to the decision-making processes at operational, tactical and strategic levels. Furthermore, we can see the deep implications for application and infrastructure design across all areas of IT support. Applications become increasingly modularized and processes ever more adaptive. Service oriented architecture, recently resurgent, offers the most likely solution to these demands. Further work will be required to evolve SOA as Cloud and mobile directions become more prevalent.

Conceptually, process is the functional layer through which people within and without the business create and use information. And in the biz-tech ecosystem, if it's not in the information layer, it doesn't exist! Process, as has always been the case, is vital to the creation and management of information. Now we see that it is also central to all of its use, particularly in decision making. From a logical view, process encapsulates all three pillars of information. It is responsible for the instantiation of events in the real world into meaningful information, and its further assimilation and reification into (sufficiently) consistent information that is useful to the business. Increasingly, process facilitates the intelligent and adaptive use of information—well-defined and highly managed, as well as loosely structured and ephemeral. And in this integrative and adaptive role,

process provides the underlying platform for the business transition from data-based to well-informed decision making.

ROADMAP

→ *Soft information (content) tells the full story:* Significantly more contextual information is found in content than in data; it is thus more meaningful to people

→ *Copyright and privacy:* Concerns about these issues have far reaching impacts and should be a top consideration for collection and use of soft information

→ *Soft information tools are different:* Content management, search and other tools provide insight through inspection rather than querying

→ *Insight from combining data and content:* In the evaluation phase of MEDA, most analysts employ both data (explicitly) and content (implicitly)

→ *More modeling required:* Modeling tools and techniques remain largely inadequate to deal with the complexity, variability and changeability of soft information

→ *Knowledge management also needs new thinking:* As a solely and fully a mental construct and, whether tacit or explicit, knowledge cannot be managed in the manner suggested in traditional knowledge management

"As a general rule, the most successful man in life is the man who has the best information."	Benjamin Disraeli
"All our knowledge brings us nearer to our ignorance... Where is the wisdom we have lost in knowledge? Where is the knowledge we have lost in information?"	T. S. Eliot

Information begets data, as we've seen. The opposite view, that data is the father of information, led to the evolution of data-based decision making support described in Chapter 5. When we accept that information—the recorded and stored symbols and signs we use to describe the world and our thoughts about it, and to communicate with each other—is the fundamental base matter of decision making, our view of the process begins to subtly morph. The statistical and analytic magic possible only with data loses some of its recently acquired glamour, although that particular genie strenuously refuses to be put back in his bottle. Information lends itself to less formal analysis but more nuanced interpretation.

As we shift our attention from data to information, we need to explore a new landscape of thinking from the 1930s to 1960s focused on books and documents, library and information science far from the bits and bytes of data and databases. These early explorers were hamstrung by the technology of their time to a far greater extent than today's data scientists and geeks. Beyond their contribution to information science, these explorers also created much of the modern infrastructure of desktop computing and its ambassador, the humble mouse. Their footprints map much of the territory that became the Internet and World Wide Web.

Furthermore, a range of considerations around ownership, copyright, and privacy come into sharp focus. Data, because of how it is created and managed, lends itself to much clearer answers to these issues. Information often leaves such questions unanswered as it is increasingly collected, recorded and stored for posterity. Today, it is put to uses—particularly in decision making—of which its creators were unaware and to which its human subjects may object.

In IT, information has followed a very different evolutionary path than data, managed in different tools and by other departments. We explore these foreign (to BI experts) lands of content creation and management, document administration and search to position this soft information in the emerging architecture of the biz-tech ecosystem. Of particular interest is the context of big data, within which such information is a large component. We discover that soft information resists the classification and categorization approach used in defining the meaning and scope of its hard counterpart. And so, self-classification via XML or similar approaches is required—information containing explanation of its context. We revisit modeling in search of new ways to understand the context of information, whatever its location or structure, and its relationship to the human knowledge it captures. And so, we are led to knowledge and our attempts to civilize and manage it. Knowledge forces us to step back from the IT obsession with data and recognize that the purpose of information and all we do to capture, store and manage it is simply to grasp knowledge, to preserve it for posterity, to increase its realizable value to people and organizations.

8.1   BI (THE FIRST TIME)[1]

Although it's not widely known—at least among the BI community—the first definition of the term *business intelligence* appeared over fifty years ago in an article by Hans Peter Luhn, entitled *A Business Intelligence System* (Luhn, 1958). In it, he proposes a system not for data-based decision making, but one that operates in the context of information retrieval and document management. The paper describes a system using computers *"for auto-abstracting and auto-encoding of documents and for creating interest profiles for each of the 'action points' in an organization."* Luhn starts from the premise that *"efficient communication is a key to pro-*

---

[1] *Summer (The First Time)*, the 1973 hit for Bobby Goldsboro, where he reminisces about a boy's first sexual experience.

gress in all fields of human endeavor" and that the then-prevalent communication methods used in organizations were totally inadequate to handle the increasing pace of information generation and utilization, presaging today's pervasive big data refrain. We are clearly in the territory of Dan Power's document- and communications-driven DSS (Power, 2009). While much of the technology shown in Figure 8-1 clearly dates from a bygone era, Luhn provides three significant initial insights into the scope and context of what we call *insightful* or *well-informed decision making*. First, he recognized that the largely free-form documents produced and used by humans contain useful information that can be condensed and categorized into more compact and useful forms for later retrieval based on their content. In his system, incoming and internally generated documents are subject to (what we would call today) rather primitive text analytics to automatically create abstracts and encoded categorizations.

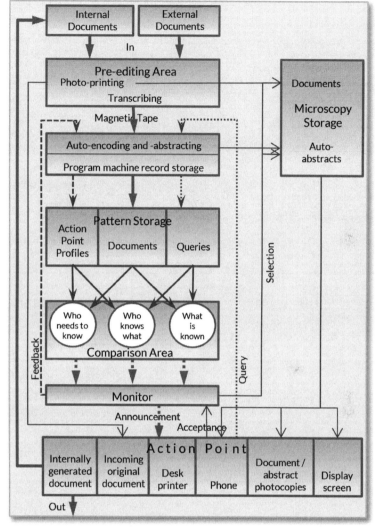

Figure 8-1:
A Business Intelligence System, based on Luhn, *IBM Journal, 2 (4) Oct 1958, p 317*

Second, Luhn proposed that communication could be significantly improved by automatically disseminating relevant documents to "action points"—the individuals, groups or departments—that act on them. These same people or departments self-describe the action points in documents, which are analyzed in a similar manner to business documents to create profiles. These profiles are automatically compared to the encoded categorizations of business documents as they arrive in the organization, allowing the documents to be sent to the appropriate local printer. The system monitors acceptance or rejection of documents by action points and progressively expands their profiles, behaving as a learning system. This linking of information delivery to action taken is a key concept in closing the decision-action loop that data-based decision making support systems have been slow to recognize as important.

Third, because information retrieval is often initiated by action points, rather than being triggered by external events, the system provides a query function. This operates in a similar profile-driven manner as the dissemination function above, although Luhn envisaged that a human librarian might often be required to support this process. Further, the system can also use action point profiles to determine who in the organization may be knowledgeable about a particular subject and thus able to link people together.

Luhn's thinking was well beyond the realizable technologies of his day; he died in 1964 without seeing his business intelligence system built. But his contributions to library science, selective dissemination of information (SDI), and his invention of machine-generated keyword-in-context (KWIC) indexes for technical literature formed a solid foundation for manual and later electronic library systems over the succeeding decades (Soy, 1996). Luhn's definition of business intelligence is an appropriate place to whet the appetite of BI-savvy readers, but we must travel a little further back in time to understand why using information for decision making requires a completely different mindset to that still common in the prevalent data-based approach.

8.2   INFORMATION—SOME RECENT HISTORY

We have already tripped back to the dawn of mankind and seen the fundamental role of information in the emergence of civilization. To span the intervening millennia and chart the emergence of thinking about information would require a book to itself. Fortunately, that book has been written— *Glut: Mastering Information through the Ages* (Wright, 2007)—so we can concentrate on some key developments in the last hundred years or so and the question of how information (as distinct from data) can be understood and most effectively retrieved and used.

Hierarchical hypotheses

Since the earliest libraries were collected, scholars have striven to put order on the books stored in them, to categorize the information therein, or mundanely, to simply know where to place or locate a particular book in miles of shelving. From Aristotle's *Categories* of the 4th century BC to the Dewey Decimal Classification first devised in 1876, familiar in public libraries worldwide, all of the systems are hierarchical in nature. The Universal Decimal Classification system, first published by Belgian bibliographers Paul Otlet and Henri La Fontaine in 1905 (Otlet & La Fontaine, 1905), and popular in non-English speaking countries, is the most extensive hierarchical, faceted library classification system available today.

By the early 20th century, it was becoming obvious that information storage was not limited to books; photographs, movies and audio recordings also needed to be classified. Furthermore, stopping classification at the level of a physical artifact, such as a book, missed the fact that a book could contain valuable information about many concepts beyond those classifying the book as a whole. Classifying this book, for example, under the topic of BI, fails to point to the topics of psychology and neurobiology in Chapter 9. By 1934, in his *Traité de Documentation* (Otlet, 1934), Otlet was envisaging a system that could document the interrelationships, or links, between information elements at the most detailed level in a great *réseau* or web of human knowledge. Of course, the technology of the time was unequal to the task, and the advent of World War II would see most of Otlet's classification system on some 15 million index cards destroyed. But his concept of a web was prescient.

As we may think

On the other side of the Atlantic during the closing months of the same war, Vannevar Bush, director of the Office of Scientific Research and Development, which coordinated the work of some 6,000 American scientists in support of the war effort, began to consider how science might be applied to the management of the inherited knowledge of the ages. *As We May Think*, first written in

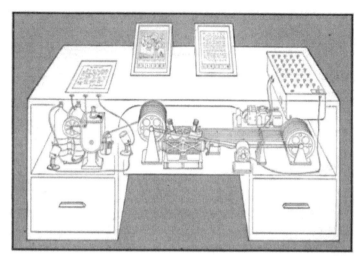

Figure 8-2:
Bush's "memex" by
Alfred D. Cimi,
*LIFE, 19 (11), Sept
1945, p 123*

1939, but only published six years later in *The Atlantic Monthly* magazine (Bush, 1945), provides an early view of how technology could be applied to the storage and, in particular, retrieval and association of information. Bush's concern was that *"the summation of human experience is being expanded at a prodigious rate, and the means we use for threading through the consequent maze to the momentarily important item is the same as was used in the days of square-rigged ships."* At the time, and until this century, such information existed only in printed form—in journals and books—stored in physical libraries. Of course, that summation is now many orders of magnitude larger and stored electronically, as we noted in Chapter 6, and many would argue that we still face enormous difficulties in finding what we need and relating ideas together.

As a researcher himself, Bush knew the time and effort required to find information in a library via the classes and sub-classes of manually generated index systems, following often complex rules and classifications. Bush postulated an electro-mechanical document storage and retrieval system in the shape of an office desk, which he dubbed "memex", where documents—both publicly sourced and generated by the user—were stored on microfilm and projected as needed on two desktop screens, as shown in Figure 8-2. The technological concept caught the public imagination, but of perhaps more lasting importance was the idea that the user could create associations between documents and trails, modeled on the way the human brain works, that could be easily followed afterwards.

Of mice and men[2]

The hierarchical structure of information, seen everywhere from the table of contents of this book to the nested folders and sub-

---

[2] *Of Mice and Men*, John Steinbeck's 1937 novel is the tragic story of two displaced migrant ranch workers during the US Great Depression.

folders on your PC, is pervasive. It also works as a way of finding and understanding information—mostly. Unless the volume of information is too large, the hierarchy too deep, or the topics too diverse. Or if you need to see the information in a different way from that defined in their hierarchy by the author or librarian.

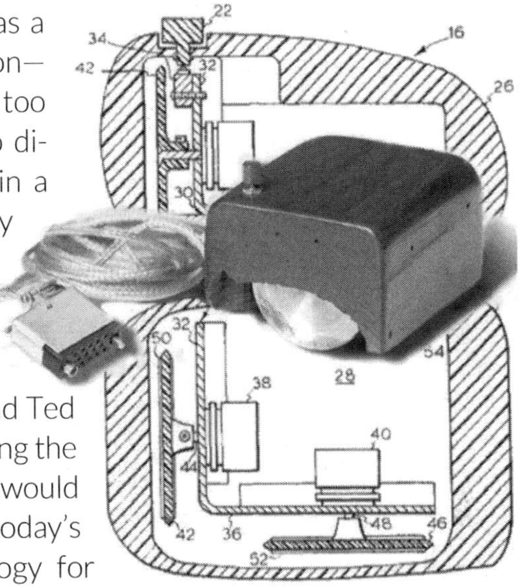

By the early to mid-1960s, some of the recognizable names in the field of information science, such as Gene Garfield, Doug Engelbart, and Ted Nelson, were exploring new ideas for representing the value and interrelationships of information that would eventually lead to the familiar constructs of today's Internet. Garfield's citation ranking methodology for scientific papers would be later adapted by Larry Page and Sergey Brin to create Google's Pagerank algorithm (Brin & Page, 1998). Engelbart, who died as I finished this book, is best remembered for the invention of the mouse in the mid-1960s (Figure 8-3 may interest users of today's sleek, 5-button, laser devices), but his 1962 report *Augmenting Human Intellect: A Conceptual Framework* (Engelbart, 1962) and subsequent work at the Augmentation Research Center (ARC) he founded in 1959 at the Stanford Research Institute is relevant to our current discussion of information and its evolution, as well as providing a foundation for the *adaptive decision cycle* in Section 9.4. In this document, Engelbart proposes a general framework wherein computers can be used to enhance all daily professional work activities—office automation, as it would be called today. This conceptual framework was required because until that time, computers were generally viewed—as their name implies—as useful only for calculating and computing tasks. Engelbart envisaged human activities as composed of multiple, nested hierarchies of processes: for example, the process of making pen strokes is used both to write alphabet letters and to draw pictures; the process of making letters is used in writing a document, which is part of making a business plan; and so on. Augmenting these processes at all levels with computer support was a means to the goal of improved personal creativity and productivity. The report also provides a fictional exposition of how such a system would be used, from document creation and editing—with techniques that would

Figure 8-3:
First prototype mouse and patent art, by Bill English and Doug Engelbart, mid-1960s

only become possible with WYSIWYG (what you see is what you get) word processors on PCs in the 1980s—to elaborate tagging and semantic manipulation of information, which remains largely untested and unused today.

Engelbart describes how *"a given concept structure can be represented with a symbol structure..., with all sorts of characteristics and relationships given explicit identifications that the user may never directly see. In fact, this structuring has immensely greater potential for accurately mapping a complex concept structure than does a structure an individual would find it practical to construct or use on paper. Thus, inside the computer there is an internal-image, computer-symbol structure whose convolutions and multi-dimensionality...represent[ing] to hitherto unattainable accuracy the concept structure we might be building or working with. This internal structure may have a form that is nearly incomprehensible to the direct inspection of a human (except in minute chunks). But let the human specify his particular conceptual need of the moment, [and]...the computer will effectively stretch, bend, fold, extract, and cut as it may need in order to assemble...its response. With the set of standard translation rules appropriate to the situation, it portrays to the human via its display a symbol structure designed for his quick and accurate perception and comprehension of the conceptual matter pertinent to this internally composed substructure.*

"No longer does the human work on stiff and limited symbol structures, where much of the conceptual content can only be implicitly designated in an indirect and distributed fashion. These new ways of working are basically available with today's technology—we have but to free ourselves from some of our limiting views and begin experimenting with compatible sets of structure forms and processes for human concepts, human symbols, and machine symbols."

In this framework, we can dimly see the shape of tags and hyperlinks, XML markups, ontologies and semantic structures, some implemented and some still awaited in the World Wide Web today. Engelbart continues to build on the thoughts and concepts formulated in the 1960s, proposing *dynamic knowledge repositories* in support of a vision of augmenting society's "Collective IQ" to tackle *"the complexity and urgency of the problems faced by us earth-bound humans [that] are increasing much faster than are our aggregate capabilities for understanding and coping with them"* (Engelbart, 2004).

From Xanadu to the World Wide Web

In or around 1965, Ted Nelson began using the words *hypertext* and *hypermedia* to describe information that is generalized and non-linear rather than serially structured (Wedeles, 1965). Information would no longer be confined between the covers of books or bound in the pages of reports; rather, it could exist as independent, individual chunks of useful knowledge, interlinked and contextualized, and capable of being gathered and combined as required by anyone in any manner required. The title alone of his seminal paper, *A File Structure for the Complex, the Changing and the Indeterminate* (Nelson, 1965), says it all: the computer could—and should—step beyond the dry and defined world of numbers and data and come play with literature, sociology and all the other loosely constructed universes of information.

Figure 8-4:
Xanadu,
Patten Wilson, 1898

By 1974, Nelson had begun to construct Xanadu[3], a system he conceived as a world-wide network containing the world's stored writings, graphics and data in a universal data structure, *"permitting promiscuous linkage and windowing among all materials; with special features for alternative versions, historical backtrack and arbitrary collaging"* (Nelson, 1974). In Xanadu, we can see the influence of early information scientists such as Otlet, visionaries like Luhn and Bush, and the practical advances of Engelbart in his *oN-Line System (NLS)* of the 1960s. This soaring vision of a system was never completed but is acknowledged by Tim Berners-Lee (Wright, 2007) as a direct inspiration for the now pervasive World Wide Web that finally, in 1989, birthed an arguably small subset of the type of information cataloguing, cross-referencing, deconstruction, and retrieval that has been the golden thread of this history. With associations and trails, Bush inspired some of the modern giants of information retrieval, although both, as he defined them, await complete implementation. Ironically perhaps, the WWW has also forever destroyed the possibility of creating a complete encyclopedic catalog of the knowledge of humankind. There is simply too much of it. It is growing too fast. And it has finally broken the concept of there

---

[3] *Xanadu*, the opium-inspired poem by Samuel Taylor Coleridge describing Kublai Khan's stately, and wholly imaginary, pleasure dome.

being authoritative voices whose wisdom could be universally accepted as providing the "right answers" in many areas of knowledge (Weinberger, 2012). Truth no longer exists in a single version.

The view from Xanadu

From Luhn's very business-oriented Business Intelligence System—written, after all, for International *Business* Machines (IBM)—our historical wandering has, of necessity, led us into library and information sciences, and even into the land of liberal arts. Information is not easily bounded. But how does this apply to the biz-tech ecosystem? Is Xanadu forever fated to be but a dream?

Dresner's 1990s reintroduction of the term *business intelligence* and its subsequent use were heavily, even entirely, data-centric, as we saw in Chapter 5. In the interim, data has been managed and modeled—some might say to death—to wring the maximum meaning and value from it. IT people see it as home ground. Even business users have grown comfortable with its familiar spreadsheet guise. But data is insufficient for the next phase. As we saw in Section 6.1, data already accounts for less than 1% of the digital footprint of humanity, and continues to shrink. Soft information has become the new frontier. In order to discover how to use it effectively in business, we need to understand its shape and its potential. Today, both IT and business are still immersed in the serial and sequential view of information. Beyond the use of simple, unidirectional links on websites, we still think in terms of documents, presentations, books and the other macro-instances of information. This history suggests that there is a finer-grained structure to be mined. We must take a more comprehensive view than that afforded by search engines and content management systems to extract information's inherent and extensive value. The message of this history is fourfold:

1. Thinking about information is very different from thinking about data: finding detailed, relevant information in context and creating, using, and managing associations and further context around it are central to its effective use.

2. The challenges to and opportunities for effective information use date back to the earliest creation of reproducible information and were already becoming critical by the mid-20th cen-

tury; there is much that can be learned from work done in the fields of information science since then.

3. The use of information in business intelligence today and in the emerging biz-tech ecosystem is fundamentally nascent.

4. The current explosion of digitized information, given its wide variety of content and form, offers both the biggest challenge and the best opportunity for using information in business.

But before we narrow the scope of our interest to business, we must briefly explore the broader topics of information ownership and privacy, both of which emerge as particular issues for information in a much more extreme form than they do for data, and are significantly exacerbated by the Internet.

For many BI professionals, the extent of thinking about information, as opposed to data, outside the business arena may come as a surprise. The complexity of managing such information, understanding its content and relationships, and extracting value are also news to many in BI. Defining and implementing solutions in the combined scope of data and information is a high priority goal for BI to support decision making in the biz-tech ecosystem.

ThoughtPoint

8.3   Copyright or copywrong

The ever-growing deluge of information on the Internet, the ease with which it can created, stored, copied, combined and updated, and the difficulty in tracing or, in many cases attributing, ownership to information creates a serious dilemma for society at large and, by extension, for the biz-tech ecosystem. We are generating zettabytes of digital information every year. Projects are ongoing to digitize all previously created paper documents, artwork, and so on that have survived the ravages of time. For example, as of 2010, Google Books had scanned some 20 million of an estimated 130 million unique books in the world (Taycher, 2010).

One might ask: what has driven—and continues to drive—us to create so much information? We may sensibly point to the innate

(261)

Anno Octavo

Annæ Reginæ.

An Act for the Encouragement of Learning, by Vest-ing the Copies of Printed Books in the Authors or Purchasers of such Copies, during the Times therein mentioned.

Whereas Printers, Booksellers, and other Persons have of late frequently taken the Liberty of Printing, Reprinting, and Publishing, or causing to be Print-ed, Reprinted, and Published Books, and other Writings, without the Con-sent of the Authors or Proprietors of such Books and Writings, to their very great Detriment, and too often to the Ruin of them and their Fami-lies : For Preventing therefore such Practices for the future, and for the Encouragement of Learned Men to Compose and Write use-ful Books ; May it please Your Majesty, that it may be En-acted, and be it Enacted by the Queens most Excellent Majesty, by and with the Advice and Consent of the Lords Spiritual and Temporal, and Commons in this present Parliament Assembled, and by the Authority of the same, That from and after the

Figure 8-5:
The First Copyright Act, 1710

creativity of the human psyche that led artists to starve in garrets and motivates bloggers to produce over 100 million sel-dom-read accounts of their daily experi-ence (Lisha, 2012). In many cases, however, this creativity craves recognition, often through some form of economic reward—if only to keep body and soul together. This human urge to benefit financially, and in other ways, from the products of one's creativity and effort, in this, as in any field, has led to barter, trade and all forms of economic activity, together with ethical and legal frameworks to define rights, respon-sibilities and regulations. However, much of this approach was developed when these products were entirely physically instanti-ated. As more and more of the products of our creativity and effort become digital, the relevance and applicability of these frame-works is increasingly questionable.

Consider as an example the concept of copyright. First introduced in British law in 1710, the Statute of Anne (Figure 8-5) was entitled *An Act for the Encouragement of Learning, by Vesting the Copies of Printed Books in the Authors or Purchasers of such Copies...* Beyond the laudable aim of the opening phrase, the main purpose of the act was to regulate the printing industry, which in the preceding two centuries had enabled mass production of books—and the publica-tion of copies of books without the agreement of the writers or original publishers. Since then, the technology for creating copies has advanced from an expensive, industrial process with physical output to a very inexpensive, personal and digital process that pos-es fundamental questions about what constitutes a copy, how these copies can tracked and how the initial creative effort can sufficiently benefit its author. Additionally, extensive hyperlinking enables the possibility—indeed, the valuable opportunity—that any number of subsets of information copies from disparate sources can be knitted together by a third party; how is the value thus gen-erated disbursed back to the aggregator and the numerous sources? As in other commoditized spheres, the raw material—chunks of content without context—loses its value (IBM, 2007). But, by which criteria can such a chunk be deemed valueless?

On the other side of the equation, blogging and social media have opened the world of content creation to just about anyone who wants to expose literally anything. The ease with which any information can be "published", the lack of any editing or curation, and the absence of any verifiable expertise on the part of the author, can be seen as a welcome democratization of knowledge or a devaluing of the entire knowledge ecosystem. For every piece of information, there exists a whole spectrum of contradictory positions (Weinberger, 2012). And not only contradictory, but perhaps deliberately biased or misleading, as seen in the growing debate around content on Wikipedia on controversial topics (Blue, 2013). Information stored in databases and other electronic content stores thus presents an enormous challenge in terms of defining the boundaries of what content might need to be legally protected, what rights could be asserted and protected, what authority it claims, and indeed, how ownership of individual components of the information might be assigned. Only the European Union has enacted database rights legislation, beginning in 1996, and that is little more than a minimal reworking of existing copyright law.

In this broad context, without fundamental, internationally agreed philosophical, political and legal work, it is difficult to see how the vast and undoubtedly valuable information resource that the Web already is and will become, can be equitably harnessed, regulated and monetized. In a business context, this is a problem of increasing importance, given that web-sourced information (and data) represents a growing proportion of both raw materials and products for more and more businesses. This challenge filters down into the internal use of information. Within the biz-tech ecosystem, there is an unquestioned belief that information is highly valuable. As we've seen in the preceding chapters, businesses are investing heavily in gathering, creating and sharing timely information, in storing and analyzing vast and growing quantities of data, both centrally and in distributed environments. BI and business analytics programs continue to be expanded to identify context and distill insight from content by storing and manipulating it electronically. This process will certainly continue. In the absence of legal remedies, individual practitioners and organizations must invent and ensure an ethical and equitable framework in which value is created and shared..

8.4   I SPY WITH MY LITTLE EYE SOMETHING BEGINNING...

Media that spies on and data-mines the public is destroying freedom of thought, and only this generation, the last to grow up remembering the 'old way', is positioned to save this, humanity's most precious freedom," says Eben Moglen, professor of law and legal history at Columbia University and Chairman of the Software Freedom Law Center at re:publica Berlin in May, 2012 (Moglen, 2012).

"The Senate [passed] legislation...granting the public the right to auto-matically display on their Facebook feeds what they're watching on Netflix...However, they [lawmakers] cut from the legislative package language requiring the authorities to get a warrant to read your e-mail or other data stored in the cloud", David Kravets, in Wired, Decem-ber, 2012 (Kravets, 2012).

In the flatland of data, security is the key. In an interconnected cosmos of information, privacy matters...but probably less than you might imagine or wish. In the transition from data-based to well-informed decision making, one of the most subtle but far-reaching changes is in matters of security and privacy. The two quotes above illustrate some very significant issues that need careful considera-tion as we make this transition. The arguments are many-faceted and range from high level ethical and business considerations to deep technological and algorithmic opportunities and problems; this is the biz-tech ecosystem at its most challenging.

Data security

The traditional approach to business computing that generates process-mediated data, as we saw in Chapter 6, is characterized by a policy of collecting and storing only the data needed, of separat-ing and structuring data across diverse business functions and data stores, and of limiting access to them. The business value of such data is long and well understood, from the costs of creating and storing it, through the return on that investment, to the damage of losing it or allowing a competitor to access it.

Since the earliest days of data warehousing, it has been recognized that this business value and associated risk increases as the business' data is made more understandable in the EDW or data marts, is summarized and interpreted in BI tools and distributed, and made more widely accessible on PCs and networks. Hence, data security as an area of investment, with typical tools such as data encryption, table-, row- and column-based access restrictions, and more. Such security—and similar information security for internally produced documents, etc.—is clearly in the interest of the business to implement. I introduce it mainly to distinguish it from (i) privacy and (ii) "societal security", which is often labeled simply as *security* and set in contrast to privacy. When data comprised the vast majority of what resided in computers, data security was the primary concern. But, even in the early days of data warehousing, particularly among data mining projects, issues of privacy were raising their ugly heads. Because even if it's only data, and you generate it from your business processes, you can, at least in theory, ultimately identify specific individuals and find information or make inferences about them that they may otherwise not be intending or willing to share. With the rapid and ongoing shift from a data- to an information-centric decision-making process, issues of privacy come to the fore, both within the enterprise and especially in the cornucopia of information on the Web. Emotionally laden comments, like those at the beginning of this section, raise fears—well-founded or otherwise. To move the discussion forward, let's set some foundations.

What do we mean by information privacy

Wikipedia defines privacy as *"the ability of an individual or group to seclude themselves or information about themselves and thereby reveal themselves selectively"* (Wikipedia, 2012), noting that what is considered private differs among individuals and cultures, and relating it to anonymity—the ability to remain unidentified in the public realm. Article 12 of the 1948 *Universal Declaration of Human Rights* protects privacy among other rights: *"No one shall be subjected to arbitrary interference with his privacy, family, home or correspondence, nor to attacks upon his honour and reputation"*, as does article 17 of

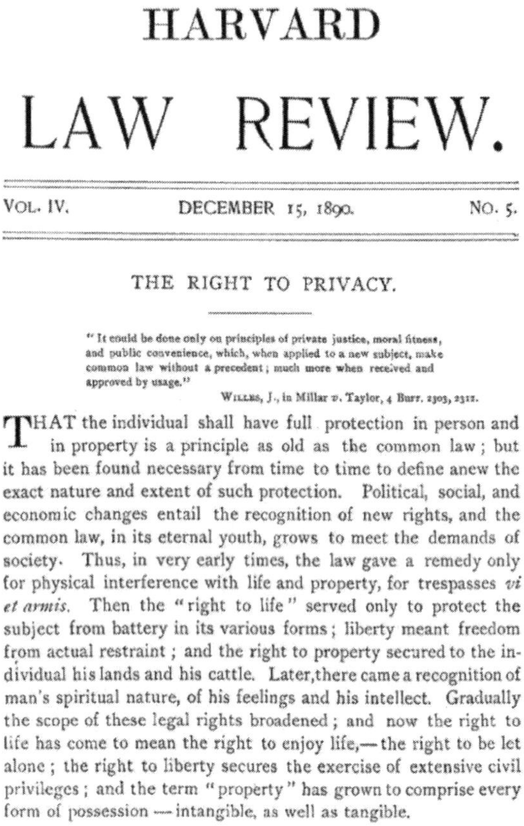

HARVARD
LAW REVIEW.

| VOL. IV. | DECEMBER 15, 1890. | NO. 5. |

THE RIGHT TO PRIVACY.

"It could be done only on principles of private justice, moral fitness, and public convenience, which, when applied to a new subject, make common law without a precedent; much more when received and approved by usage."

WILLES, J., in Millar v. Taylor, 4 Burr. 2303, 2312.

THAT the individual shall have full protection in person and in property is a principle as old as the common law; but it has been found necessary from time to time to define anew the exact nature and extent of such protection. Political, social, and economic changes entail the recognition of new rights, and the common law, in its eternal youth, grows to meet the demands of society. Thus, in very early times, the law gave a remedy only for physical interference with life and property, for trespasses *vi et armis*. Then the "right to life" served only to protect the subject from battery in its various forms; liberty meant freedom from actual restraint; and the right to property secured to the individual his lands and his cattle. Later, there came a recognition of man's spiritual nature, of his feelings and his intellect. Gradually the scope of these legal rights broadened; and now the right to life has come to mean the right to enjoy life,—the right to be let alone; the right to liberty secures the exercise of extensive civil privileges; and the term "property" has grown to comprise every form of possession — intangible, as well as tangible.

Figure 8-6:
Brandeis and Warren's seminal article on privacy

the 1966 International Covenant on Civil and Political Rights. Privacy is thus widely held to be a human right, standing at the heart freedom and civil liberty. It is among the first to die in authoritarian regimes. Even in democracies, it is immediately and easily circumscribed when danger threatens. And business, particularly when it comes to advertising, feels free to drive a coach-and-four through it. It seems we are on shaky ground, even before we mention information or technology.

Information technology—in its broadest sense of everything that can record, store and disseminate information, from the first cameras and telephones to the Internet—impinges, by necessity, on the concept of privacy, according to Louis Brandeis and Samuel Warren as far back as 1890 (Figure 8-6): *"Instantaneous photographs and newspaper enterprise have invaded the sacred precincts of private and domestic life; and numerous mechanical devices threaten to make good the prediction that 'what is whispered in the closet shall be proclaimed from the house-tops'"* (Warren & Brandeis, 1890). Brandeis went even further in 1928 in his US Supreme Court dissenting opinion in a case concerning wiretapping: *"Discovery and invention have made it possible for the Government, by means far more effective than stretching upon the rack, to obtain disclosure in court of what is whispered in the closet"* (U.S. Supreme Court, 1928).

The sentiments expressed by Brandeis some hundred years ago find echoes in the opening quotes of this section. Information technology has "growed like Topsy"[4] since; progress in ethical and legal thinking has been somewhat patchier. Recent—and largely unsurprising to many observers—revelations (Gellman & Poitras, 2013) about how democratic, Western governments have used technology to compromise people's right to privacy to protect society from terrorist threats give rise to serious privacy concerns. John Naugh-

---

[4] From *Uncle Tom's Cabin; or, Life Among the Lowly*, Harriet Beecher Stowe (1852).

ton, Emeritus Professor of the Public Understanding of Technology at the British Open University, summarizes the emerging situation thus: *"the government excuses we are hearing from both the US and UK are Kafkaesque. They say we need to be protected from things they can't tell us about, using systems they can't tell us about, and have stopped incidents they can't tell us about. All of this with (sometime) oversight from courts, governing bodies or individuals that by law cannot reveal what they know or, in many cases, even that they know anything at all"* (Lillington, 2013). It would appear that the state view is that information privacy is irrelevant.

Information privacy—the current business status

The foundation for information privacy in the computer world dates from 1980, when the Council of the Organisation for Economic Co-operation and Development (OECD) adopted its Guidelines on Trans-border Data Flows and the Protection of Privacy. As an organization whose focus is economics, protection of privacy may seem a stretch, but the document still provides a widely espoused starting point for current and future thinking after thirty years (Kirby, 2011). Today's great mother lode of information is, of course, the Internet. But, three foundational and emerging characteristics, previously referenced, have combined to create conditions reminiscent of the California Gold Rush of 1848-55:

Figure 8-7:
Crystalline gold specimen from the California Mother Lode

1. *Structure:* hyperlinking of web pages, as well as other metadata associated with information on the Web, has created a vast network of cross-referenced and interlinked information. While nowhere near as powerful as the schemes envisaged by Nelson and others (see Section 8.2), this network is well-suited to automated searching and categorization.

2. *Processing:* driven by the inability of humans to find what they were seeking on the Web, cheap, sophisticated and powerful search and recommendation engines based on commodity hardware and software were developed by companies such as Yahoo! and Google, as discussed in Chapter 6.

3. *Personal information:* social networking sites, such as Facebook and YouTube, encourage users to post a

Information privacy

With the pervasive and ongoing digitization of communication and information, its widespread storage, sharing, combination and analysis, personal privacy, and, with it, individual freedom, is under growing pressure. We need, at least to start, a definition of information privacy.

Information privacy is the right to define a domain of information about us, which includes identity, thoughts, feelings, secrets, activities, and more; to choose which parts in this domain can be accessed by others; and to control the extent, manner and timing of the use of the information we choose to disclose.

deluge of personal information—from demographics to photos of their lunches. Users thus create a vast store of personal information and unwittingly trade privacy for limited personal gain, such as connections to old friends or minor discounts on purchases.

The combination has unleashed a feeding frenzy among retail and marketing organizations to micro-segment consumers all the way to the ultimate segment-of-one, predict most likely behaviors, and automate recommendations and next best actions on an individual basis. It is probably no exaggeration to say that privacy concerns were way down on the list of priorities for the development teams. And indeed, businesses collect data for one purpose and find new uses through combination with other sources or through mergers or acquisitions. Wal-Mart's March 2012 acquisition of the Social Calendar Facebook app, for example, allows personal information entered solely for private use to be used for marketing purposes. Users can opt out, of course, but the loss of calendar data previously entered may prove a lock-in, even if the users know about or consider the possibility (Krotoski, 2012). Add to the mix the geolocational and behavioral information generated minute by minute by the billions of smartphones we carry, and the marketing opportunity becomes truly mind-boggling. And the impact on privacy is mind-numbing to anyone who cares to think about it.

But it still remains a difficult trade-off—progress vs. privacy—in areas of greater value to humankind than marketing. Two articles published in the *New York Times* in the same week in January, 2013 illustrate the point. The first describes how patient records—transcribed and digitized from scrawled (why do they always scribble?) doctors' notes, anonymized and stored on the Web—can be statistically mined to discover previously unknown side-effects of and interactions between prescribed drugs (Jaret, 2013). Clearly useful and valuable work. The second article, three days later, revealed how easily a genetics researcher was able to identify five individuals and their extended families by combining publicly available information from the anonymized 1000 Genome Project database, a commercial genealogy Web site, and Google (Kolata, 2013). The underlying genetic data is used in medical research to good effect, of course, but what are the possible consequences for those individuals thus identified as insurance companies, governments or other interested parties make potentially negative assessments based on their once private genomes?

The underpinning ethical and legal principles on which the current guidelines and laws are based include (i) that the collectors of personal data declare the purposes to which it will be put, (ii) that access to it will be regulated, and (iii) that the providers of such data give informed and ongoing consent to its use. In today's Web, none of these principles can be clearly or unambiguously applied. The Wal-Mart / Social Calendar example is a simple and obvious case. The automated tagging of images with the identities of friends on Facebook involves no declaration of purpose on the part of the poster, so the informed consent of the person depicted is questionable at best (despite Facebook's introduction of a tagging approval process in 2011). Google's defense in a class action lawsuit in June, 2013 of its right to mine Gmail content is on the basis of a 1979 US Court ruling that *"a person has no legitimate expectation of privacy in information he voluntarily turns over to third parties"* (Goyette, 2013). The ruling, itself, raises questions and concerns for privacy advocates. Google's use of it might not come as a surprise, given the company's dependence on the process to drive advertising income and CEO Eric Schmidt's 2009 statement that *"if you have something that you don't want anyone to know, maybe you shouldn't be doing it in the first place"* (Lennard, 2013). Corporate and legal understanding of the meaning of privacy seems to be sadly simplistic.

A further and more dangerous threat to privacy, however, is the ever growing mixing and matching of data from multiple data stores by marketers, financial institutions, governmental agencies, and—given the commoditization of data mining on the Cloud—just about anyone who wants to do so. This process allows conclusions to be drawn that are totally orthogonal to the original purposes for which the data was gathered and virtually guarantee that any anonymization techniques can be broken (Warden, 2011) . Thus, privacy *per se* turns out to be the least of our concerns. Of even greater impact is what organizations—from the original gatherers, through partners and acquisitions, all the way to governmental bodies—can or will do with the information. As an editorial in *International Data Privacy Law* remarked: *"Big data will also place data protection in a different context. We often talk about data being the 'currency' of the information age, but in a world in which data represent individuals in more and more transactions, and provide the basis for decision making, issues such as the accessibility, accuracy, and reliability of data may matter as much or maybe more than privacy"* (Kuner, et al., 2012).

That's not to say that at least some in government and industry aren't looking for technological solutions. Privacy by Design (P_bD), the notion of embedding privacy into the design of technology, was conceived by Ann Cavoukian, Information & Privacy Commissioner in Ontario, Canada in the mid-1990s (Cavoukian, 2009), and has led to the definition of a range of principles for privacy-enabled software. With the perspective that enhanced privacy is actually a benefit rather than something that has to be traded off against the business results of analytics, we can envisage software designed with privacy in mind from the beginning. Jeff Jonas of IBM, for example, describes a new analytic environment that includes seven privacy-enhancing features, two of which are seen as so important that they cannot be disabled: (i) full attribution, that every record is permanently tagged with its source and time of creation, and (ii) data tethering, where any changes in data sources must be applied in the downstream data immediately (Cavoukian & Jonas, 2012). Translucent databases embody concepts such as encryption, ignorance, minimization, misdirection, and more to protect data from everyone except its legitimate owner (Wayner, 2009). These features are, at heart, information management and database design principles that must be embedded in the infrastructure through which information is gathered, stored and used by the business.

Which finally closes the circle back to well-informed decision making. Information is used to make decisions that are increasingly divorced from the original reasons for creating or gathering it. If the sources are unknown or untrustworthy, if the intermediate processing is suspect, or if access in compromised, the resulting decisions may be flawed and the side-effects dangerous to the business, individuals or even to society at large. This basic premise is as old as information itself. Business owners have been reading newspapers since the first publication of *Lloyd's List* in the 1740s (Section 4.5) and making inferences on which to base business decisions. Success depends on knowing which information to act upon. Governments have been gathering hearsay on citizens since before the invention of the rack. Businesses have done the same, albeit with more subtlety. Whether used for the benefit of the rulers and owners or the protection of people depends on the wisdom of the society. None of this has changed.

What has changed is the scope of information available and the speed and automation of the inferences drawn. Such changes do impact the ethical and legal principles of information gathering and use; significant work is needed in these areas. They also affect the infrastructure and practices of information management; thus, we must return to the practice of well-informed decision making within the emerging context of the biz-tech ecosystem. We step from the broad canvas of information creation and management in the world at large, as seen in libraries and cataloguing systems, and in the later emergence of information science, to the narrower confines of information in business, known as *content management*, which is our next stop.

As business moves from data to information as the foundation for its support of decision making, issues of ownership and privacy take on a new and greatly expanded level of importance. We have largely ignored them even as they apply to data, as the poorly regulated and sometimes casual use of data mining, particularly in retail, demonstrates. Abuse of "information mining" is far more invasive and perfidious. Now is the time to define and place boundaries around what we are prepared to do in the name of business profit or state protection. If it is not already too late...

ThoughtPoint

8.5   THE CARE AND GROOMING OF CONTENT

*S*tar Trek fans may recall how Lieutenant Commander Data's lack of emotions led to mix-ups with his human colleagues[5]. In the world of business and IT, data and content have a similar, dysfunctional relationship. Data has long been the darling (and major investment) of IT—*data processing* was an early term for computing, of course—while content was left to fend for itself, relegated to largely academic work in the 1960s and '70s, and more recently on PCs. And yet, as noted again and again, data is but a form of information (or content), specially prized because it has been codified and structured most suitably for arithmetic and logical processing.

Business-oriented content

As we move from the books and journals of library and information science to **business-oriented content**—or simply content, a number of different characteristics of information become important:

- Content has a much wider variety of purposes and uses, often tied to different business processes, than is typically the case for published books

- This drives a desire or need to reuse specific chunks of content in larger documents and in differing contexts

- Content exists in larger quantities of smaller chunks, much of it in sizes each the equivalent of a few pages, from contracts to internal memos, from public website content to personal notes

- Multiple versions of the same base content may exist, which need to be tracked as part of work in progress, often among multiple authors

- The full set of processes of content creation, in addition to those for its use, must be supported

Advances in technology in the past century have allowed this content to be created, stored and managed in ever smaller chunks. As a

---

[5] *"Since I do not require sleep, I propose you take the... shelf, sir, I am content to stand,"* Data to Captain Jean-Luc Picard, *Star Trek, The Next Generation, Unification I,* (November, 1991)

consequence, while the considerations of library and information science certainly do apply, their application demands a greater degree of automation and computerization in business. As we've seen, visionaries such as Vannevar Bush in the 1930-40s and Hans Peter Luhn in the 1950-60s were certainly exploring the problems of and potential solutions to information management in the business environment. Bush suggested that business documents and even handwritten memos could be stored on microfilm for easier indexing and retrieval by means of an electrical switchboard to enter document identification codes. Luhn retained microfilm for bulk content storage but envisaged using a computer for analysis of scanned content to enable indexing and retrieval—document or content management as we call it today. In fact, microfilm was already in use in large banks to store cancelled check images by the mid-1920s (Heritage Archives, 2005). However, indexing and retrieval relied on largely mechanical means, with microfilm images mounted in punched cards being a common method for engineering drawings, for example (Wikipedia, 2013).

Figure 8-8:
Microfilm and microfiche is still used for document access and preservation

It was only in the late 1980s that technology had advanced sufficiently to enable viable electronic document management systems to be developed, which evolved into today's *enterprise content management (ECM)* products. These products capture content from many different formats; store and preserve the content; and manage a wide variety of aspects of its subsequent protection, delivery and use. The main challenge has long been to understand and describe the content sufficiently well—create metadata, or context-setting information—to help people find relevant content or to manage or deliver it automatically, as required. The initial approach was to create largely hierarchical categories as found in physical libraries. This type of categorization is still used, especially in the management of content produced as part of formal product deliverables, such as engineering reference material for aircraft maintenance, for example. When content is produced and remains under the control of a formal and centrally controlled process, this library-inspired approach can work—as long as volumes remain at manageable levels.

Unfortunately for ECM, these conditions largely ceased to exist around the same time as the first products emerged. By the late 1980s, many documents were being produced on PCs, usually with WYSIWYG word processors. As wonderful for personal creativity and productivity as such software is, it offers little support for and even less enforcement of the structural aspects of documentation that ECM categorization needs. Individual users are notoriously bad at following formal, hierarchical categorization schemas for documents, even when supported by the software. And, being WYSIWYG, the products encourage visual, manual formatting of text to achieve document structures that should be more correctly a representation of the logical meaning of the underlying information: many users simply set font characteristics such as size, weight and typeface to format section headings, for example, rather than use even the simple styles provided by the software. Furthermore, these styles fail to enforce the true hierarchical nature of the ensuing document; removing a heading, for example, should at least cause the software to enquire if the following paragraphs should also be deleted. The result is content that is structured and formatted for a particular purpose and presentation medium.

Of course, the emergence of the Internet as both a content target and, in particular, a content generation environment—websites, social media sites, and more particularly, the growing plethora of connected mobile devices—has multiplied the management and categorization problems many-fold. The sheer volumes of information generated, the diversity of types and sources, the spread of locations, and the anonymity of many sources leave ECM struggling. And it becomes well-nigh impossible to apply to big data. Consider the use of social media information sourced from Twitter and used by the enterprise to track brand awareness in the market. Its sources are multiple and largely unidentifiable. It is ephemeral. Nonetheless, it is used as the basis for significant decisions about product directions, marketing spend, and more. Management of this content is limited to internal copies, categorization is statistical, and declaration about authenticity, authority and fitness for purpose are largely based on personal knowledge.

With such content, a different approach to its management is required. Within the organization, we are limited to "health warnings"—descriptive metadata that defines the limits within which such information should be used, particularly as it relates to the regulatory processes of the business. Outside the organization, we are dependent on the creators of the content to document it and, of course, must rely on their integrity. Such descriptive metadata, often stored with the content itself, is often called a *markup*. The most common markup today is XML.

XML and the thorny script[6] family tree

Extensible Markup Language (XML) is a W3C standard first codified in 1996-98 for coding and distributing structured documents with simplicity, generality, and usability on the Web. It aims to be both human- and machine-readable, and is characterized by its use of angle-brackets to delimit the tags that describe the document content, as in `<name>Barry Devlin</name>`. It is derived from *Generalized Markup Language (GML)*, the true root of this genealogy.

In 1969, Dr. Charles Goldfarb and a small team at IBM's Cambridge Scientific Center in Boston began work on a system to apply computers in legal practices. From that was born GML, described as a set of codes *"to identify the structure and purpose of the parts of text...The composition program would identify the codes as calls to stored formats; the retrieval program would use them for classification."* GML was introduced at the 1970 Annual Meeting of the American Society for Information Science (Goldfarb, 1996) and used internally in IBM well into the 1990s (I still have a few old documents in that format!). It was distinguished from its successors by a lack of angle brackets—e.g. `<h1>` was then written as `:h1.`—and the absence of end-tags such as `</h1>`. This "thorny" notation was introduced in 1981 in the seminal *A Generalized Approach to Document Markup* (Goldfarb, 1981), which became the basis of *Standard Generalized Markup Language (SGML)* adopted as an ISO standard in 1986. SGML grew over succeeding decades *"inexorably...[into] an elegant grammar for creating and applying markup languages that, despite its elegance or perhaps because of it, proved insurmountably challenging for application developers to work with. Despite its complexities, SGML could be used to create simple markup languages that would, it turns out, achieve great success"* (Goller, 2009).

---

[6] Ted Nelson's descriptive name for XML **Invalid source specified.**

Figure 8-9:
XML Haiku
by Eve Maler, 2006

Thus, in 1991 came *HTML, Hypertext Markup Language,* the *lingua franca* of the Web, first described in an email exchange (Berners-Lee, 1991). It is essentially a gross simplification of SGML to allow formatting of web pages for rendering by browsers. I use the word *gross* because the fundamental semantics of the SGML structure was abandoned in favor of basic formatting—how the content should appear in a browser window. XML returned to that semantic heritage in 1996 but retained much of the simplicity of HTML. The strength of XML lies in that simplicity and in its eponymous extensible structure, which allows the creation of nested, hierarchical structures according to schemas specifically designed for a wide range of information definition and exchange purposes. XML is now widely used as the storage structure for documents—even Microsoft adopted it as the default format in Office 2007. It has also gained wide acceptance as a way of structuring content and defining the attributes of its elements. Thus, it is used extensively for the documentation of ontologies of business terminology in specific industry or subject-matter areas and then for the storage of information according to the model specified, including, for example, FIXML, the Financial Information eXchange protocol; Atom and RSS for news syndication; and the *Darwin Information Typing Architecture (DITA)* for document authoring.

XML is not without its detractors. Its verbose and complex structure increases storage volumes and slows processing and data transfer. It is allegedly human readable but is actually quite difficult to make sense of, as Eve Maler's haiku laments (Figure 8-9). In addition, its strictly hierarchical structure is inimical to the more multi-faceted approach to document structure and navigation that allows users to thread through documents along multiple lines of enquiry as envisaged by Xanadu (Nelson, 2011) and others. In recent years, we've seen the emergence of *intelligent content*, (Rockley, 2012) a concept that provides *"a persistent expression of meaning that has been encoded using an open standard and that can be efficiently processed by automated systems to facilitate its management, validation, discovery, and publication given the full range of uses to which that content may potentially be put"* (Gollner, 2010). This methodology expands on XML and DITA content structuring and proposes— once again—that a rationally-based, standards-oriented approach is the required foundation for valid content management. However, this seems overly optimistic; it depends on people "doing the right thing". In an outburst of frustration, Cory Doctorow defined *meta-crap* in 2001, citing seven reasons why metadata is a utopian dream, ranging from *"people lie"* to *"there's more than one way to describe something"* (Doctorow, 2001).

Search and content rescue

If there is one single word that comes to mind when we discuss content, it must be *search*. Way back in late 1998, a small start-up pioneered a minimalist user interface—an input box and two buttons—which has set the expectation for search among end-users since. This expectation is that a user can type in a string of words, click and be presented with a highly relevant list of hits. The idea of search was hardly new, but the company's success sprang fundamentally from the patented algorithms (Brin & Page, 1998) that consistently placed the items of most interest to the user at the top of the list. Web user's flocked to this *keyword search* approach in preference to the hierarchical, subject-oriented search engines that were then prevalent. We were well and truly Googled as the word became common parlance. It became both the bane and the Holy Grail of enterprise software developers, as business users demanded the elegant simplicity of this search interface and its almost uncanny ability to deliver the expected results.

What is not obvious to users (nor should it be) is that the approach is heavily dependent on the size of the corpus of content and the number of users searching it. These statistics work heavily in favor of an algorithmic approach to finding the likely best matches, while the cost of building and maintaining subject hierarchies grows rapidly, depending on the level of human curation required. In addition, these further challenges arise when translating the approach to enterprise content, an entirely different environment to Google's original design point:

1. *Size:* While the sheer size of the Internet can pose problems for any search engine, it also enhances the statistical significance of even very small percentages of relevant results

2. *Scope:* The variety and variability in even the largest enterprise's content is far less than that found on the Web, reducing the relevance of result sets in enterprise search

3. *Sentiment:* The numbers and variety of Internet users similarly provides a much larger range of sentiment contributing to result weighting due to popularity, and also allows statistically significant segmentation based on user attributes

4. *Structure:* Within the enterprise, a significant percentage of business information exists in a highly structured form, such as relational databases. The relationships expressed in this model contribute significantly to information understanding in a way that is uncommon on the Internet

Keyword search and, in particular, the text analytics and indexing technology that underlie it, offer a vital pathway to accessing the context and knowledge embedded in soft information. However, within the enterprise context, only a formal reconciliation of hard and soft information can provide access to the underlying knowledge and meaning residing in the complete information resource of the business.

8.6   A MARRIAGE OF CONVENIENCE

Why reunite soft and hard information, data and content? One reason is that the business neither understands nor accepts the difference. Users have accepted hard information but with some reluctance; they have to think and behave more like computers to use it. Information is placed in rigorously defined fields, with only certain values allowed. Searching data requires knowledge of where it is stored, via a precisely structured query, and the answer (if found) restructured into something meaningful. As often as not, IT has to be involved, creating a bottleneck to the solution. In short, a disjoint data/content environment lacks agility and accessibility for business. Web search has changed users' expectations radically. Google delivers answers instantly, with apparent relevance, offering a "human", accessible experience. The more fundamental reason is, however, that the biz-tech ecosystem demands fully integrated information. With this, search can guarantee the integrity of the content required in the business world. Data's pre-determined, *a priori* models of established relationships can then support a rapidly morphing world. Only such a marriage offers users the convenience of full information access and IT the confidence of information consistency and flexibility. Only in the union of data and information can insight be found.

The monitor and evaluate steps of MEDA (see Figure 7-5) are usually described in terms of traditional BI and/or spreadsheet functionality. In reality, top business analysts gather both hard and soft information as needed and use both types in analysis. The data analysis is explicit; content is included implicitly or obliquely. The two are visibly combined only at the end of the analysis when the results are presented to management, the content surfacing as notes, assumptions and similar annotations to the graphs. In these cases—and they are relatively common—the correct representation of the lower part of the MEDA cycle would show twin paths, one for data and the other for content. This is far from ideal.

The search for insight

Despite differing search/query tools and storage structures for hard and soft information, business thus increasingly needs a combined view where the context of the question—rather than the source or structure of the information—dictates correct answers and the relevant approaches to them. This requirement has been called *unified information access* (Evelson & Brown, 2008). Call centers, messaging systems from email to Twitter, social media, and more routinely collect vast quantities of soft information about customer desires, product problems, etc. Interpreting and linking such soft information to the data of sales, returns, etc., enables quick and appropriate reaction to emerging trends. Amazon's recommendation system, for example, combines data from purchases and page visits with the softer information in users' reviews to influence buying behaviors. The five-star rating system quantifying reviewer opinion allows Amazon to provide the soft content of reviewer opinion as a valued data point for buyers.

Full business use of information depends on real insight into its real meaning in the context of the people and activities involved. Such meaning is implicit; it must be made explicit to be useful in IT systems. However, extracting meaning from the putatively separate classes of data and content has long been a tale of two cities. One set of tools comes from the hard information space, starting with relational and other database management systems. Databases, relational and otherwise, emphasize hard information, from storage to querying and processing. They do provide places such as CLOBs and BLOBs (character/binary large objects) for free text and other softer information, with limited search and manipulation functions within these fields. Text analytics offers the further possibility to create and populate indexes and other metadata/CSI in the database itself. The CSI may be stored in relational or XML formats, with the text remaining in its original form. While these enhancements do support content in databases, there are pitfalls: retrieval is largely dependent on pre-defined models and IT-generated SQL queries. This limits support for changing content and decreases agility to respond to unpredicted user exploration needs. Database systems were never designed to maintain rich interaction with content that dynamically responds to users' needs.

The second set of tools starts from soft information, with search and content/document management as their technologies of choice. Predictably enough, content tools take an index-centric approach to addressing data. A typical index used for text search can be expanded to simply treat a row of relational data as a rather specialized "document", ingesting it as such into the indexing mechanism. Both the existing CSI, such as table and column names, and the actual data values in the database are included into the index. Text analytics is also used to understand meaning and identify textual relationships and patterns. But the cardinal relationship—the *raison d'être* of the relational system—is lost because with the search index, everything is flattened.

Conceptually, the database and index approaches are rather similar. The common basis is the analysis that models meaning and relationships within information, whether hard or soft. For hard information, modeling is performed at design time and permanently stored in the database structure and metadata. While this provides data quality and consistency as well as efficiency in use, it lacks agility to respond to unexpected queries. Softer information doesn't require a formal design-time model; the "modeling", in this case, occurs as a byproduct of ingestion. When a document arrives in the environment, its content is analyzed and indexed, often deploying various text analytics to add meaning, such as entity extraction, clustering, sentiment analysis, or classification. Both approaches generate context-setting information describing the semantics and syntactics of the information. This is stored in an index or within the database to enable business use of the information. The differences lie in the timing of the analysis and the permanence of the resulting CSI. Hard information has its structure hardened when the schema is created. Because, in practice, schema change is cumbersome, all information must conform to the model. Soft information, in contrast, is defined on the fly. In other words, the CSI is generated as each piece of content is indexed, creating potentially unique context-setting information for each document. The downside is the difficulty in recognizing relationships spanning multiple documents and in creating and maintaining consistency of meaning across document stores.

The lure of the "mashup"

Mashups of database and search technologies promise users the possibility of combining hard and soft information from multiple sources, despite doubts about the levels of integration and agility they deliver. Users want the "Google experience" integrated with the precision and analytics of their business intelligence, enhanced with the awareness of context and personalization, and applied across the entire information landscape. Application level mashups extend BI to embrace search-like user capabilities such as natural language querying, spelling correction, tag clouds, and more. In some cases, content is added to the data warehouse, creating a convenient single-source information store. However, the limitations of the relational architecture remain; the soft information is essentially made hard, and much relevancy and agility is lost in the process. More advanced mashups allow business users to request information from both database and content, using the appropriate querying model each time. Each portlet displays either hard or soft information (but never both), with bridging logic that links information across the portlets.

The difficulty with mashups is twofold. At the level of the underlying data and content stores, the inherent limitations in capturing meaning and relevancy of both approaches still exist. At the level of the mashup, the bridge between the two worlds is weak and limited. The insight and agility to dynamically interact with the information in response to the user's exploration of the information is lacking. Neither *"ad hoc* querying" promoted by business intelligence—the ability to ask new queries on demand based on the answers to the previous query—nor   Google-like intuitive search easily span the chasm to the opposite information class. The underlying meaning has not been sufficiently modeled or integrated to bridge the gap. Imagine a mashed-up customer profile dashboard for a wealth management provider. A Google-like search for a customer's name can produce data identifying the customer's investment history. Selecting one of the investments—a company name—can trigger a search of news articles mentioning the company, the most relevant articles first. But is this sufficient? Consider the queries: "What are our top-selling products that get good or better reviews?" Mashups struggle because each question contains both hard and soft components that cannot be easily broken down into independent hard and soft queries. The problem is that there is no true integration of hard and soft information in the information layer, and thus no way to relate them. The relationship is between the product data and news articles, the "join" occurring between the sales data's product column and product names in the news articles. To execute such a query requires:

1. *Fully integrated metadata* covering and interlinking hard and soft information equally

2. *Pre-defined models* in key areas of the information (especially hard information) to assure the quality and integrity of the data

3. *Post-defined models,* created at the time of document ingestion, of key concepts, phrases and relationships within the soft information and across to existing hard information

4. *Post-discovery relationship creation* (Albala, 2009) applied on demand at query time and defined by the context of the query

This analysis of mashups and the requirements listed here and earlier lead us to take a deeper look at context-setting information—metadata—within the information layer of the IDEAL architecture and, in particular, its positioning on the structure/context and timeliness/consistency axes. In some sense, what we're pursuing are knowledge and meaning, defined in the upper layers of the m^3 model. For now, we seek the insight business users need to judge the context and relevance of the information they're considering. Figure 8-10 aligns the structure/context axis to the concepts of hard to soft information. In data, we know precisely what a particular item stands for—because that is what it has been defined to mean. Its relationships are also predefined, so we understand it in a very specific context. However, other meanings and relationships are lost. The limited needs and insights that motivated the original modeling ignore its broader context and relevance, especially at the time when the information is explored and analyzed. We cannot know everything beforehand. Soft information, on the other hand, often contains tacit knowledge about context and relevance of information that *a priori* modeling was not looking for and therefore overlooked. Compound information bridges the two worlds through context-setting information, providing a highly practical link between hard and soft information, between data and content. In terms of insight, compound information provides the best of both worlds.

Figure 8-10:
Context-setting and
core business
information

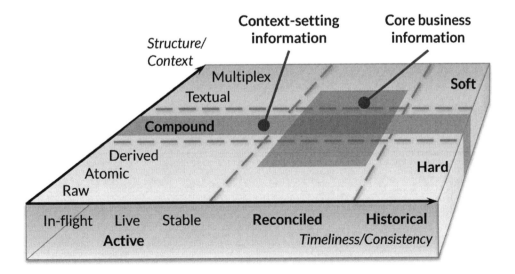

Analytics based on core business information and CSI

Context-setting information is at the heart of the information architecture. Whether we approach the convergence of data and content from the hard or soft information side, we immediately encounter the need to create extensive indexes, pointers, descriptors, and so on—CSI—to enable later use of the information. Whether it's created in the database design phase for hard information or at document indexing for use in soft information, this is still CSI. And whether derived from predefined structural elements in documents or folksonomies built on data warehouses, it is all still part of the compound information class. From left to right along the compound row of the grid, the active cell contains the shorter-term, changing CSI needed for the agile, on-the-fly analysis of information characteristic of post-discovery intelligence. The reconciled and historical cells represent more stable CSI, predefined via traditional modeling, distilled by text mining, or gathered through usage analysis. Longer-term CSI is key to data quality; it defines basic meanings and relationships, which, if changed or ignored can render business information incorrect or meaningless. In its entirety, CSI underpins context and relevance of all information—hard and soft.

All insight begins from the CSI or metadata. In content, from basic search to advanced post-discovery work, almost the entire analytic process occurs in this CSI component, using value-based or inverted indexes, document vector maps, and so on. Traditional BI pays lip-service to metadata; beyond using it to identify tables and columns, it is largely ignored. Analysis is presumed to happen in the data, but a large part of the analysis actually occurs in the indexes, as evidenced by the increase in query speed as indexes are added. These indexes are key-based and predefined at database creation, and lack the agility, context and relevance of the content approach. Extending inverted indexes to the data, a relatively simple technical step, is vital. When this is done, all analytic work—for both hard and soft information—occurs almost exclusively in the CSI. With data and content re-united, users can immediately benefit from the combined strengths of the search and query paradigms—the agility and context of soft information and the accuracy and relationships of hard information. Core business information, which we met in Section 5.8, is also central and of particular importance in ensuring the long-term quality and consistency of information understanding. This information is modeled and defined early in the design phase and its content and structure subject to rigorous change management. While other information may undergo changes in definition or relationships over time, the core business information must remain very stable. Often termed *master data*, it is widely understood that such data requires special controls, because it is at the heart of much of the data relationships that make up the business. Among softer information, there also exist key documents, such as legal agreements, that also require special control to ensure that the business is what it says it is.

> ### Unified information store
>
> *An information store that offers users a consistent, consolidated view of and access to related data and content.*
>
> *Under the covers, the environment is likely to consist of multiple stores optimized for hard and soft information and both query and search access methods.*

Recent progress in hybrid search technology has extended its use for combined soft and hard information (Devlin, 2010) and in a fully relational environment (Devlin, 2011). This emphasizes again the demand of the biz-tech ecosystem: business users do not—and should not have to—distinguish between different types of information in their exploration of business reality. When one considers the large and growing ratio of soft information to data, now likely to be approaching 99:1 (see Chapter 6), the inverse ratio of market sizes of content management to BI—$4.3 billion (Gartner, 2012) vs. $32 billion in 2011 (IDC, 2012a)—would be surprising if we hadn't explored IT's continuing focus on hard information.

When it comes to truly useful and meaningful business insight, the missing link for data is context-setting information and the connection to soft information. In content, the reverse is the case: data holds the key. Bringing these two long-separated partners together in a realistic and practical marriage is mandatory in the biz-tech ecosystem. Some vendors have begun the process, but it's up to IT and the business to walk up the aisle to the altar.

ThoughtPoint

8.7   KNOWLEDGE MANAGEMENT IS THE ANSWER;
NOW, WHAT WAS THE QUESTION?

Business and IT professionals can usually recognize and define information management when they see it. A definition of knowledge management, a practice dating back to the early 1990s, can be trickier. Tom Davenport and Larry Prusak start with a definition of knowledge as: *"a fluid mix of framed experience, values, contextual information and expert insight that provides a framework for evaluating and incorporating new experiences and information. It originates and is applied in the minds of knowers. In organizations, it often becomes embedded not only in documents or repositories but also in the organizational routines, processes, practices and norms"* (Davenport & Prusak, 1998). This is a very useful definition of a complex phenomenon, especially the first sentence. Our definition in Chapter 3 springs from it. However, as we reach the concept of organizational knowledge and the phrase *"embedded…in documents and repositories"*, we stumble on the basic problem—is this not information? By our definition, documents and repositories are information. The authors, like many who define knowledge in the business/IT world, promote knowledge management, which seeks to create, identify, distribute, and enable adoption of the insights and experiences of knowledgeable people throughout an organization. In order to do this, one has to think about how to store knowledge—and the inevitable answer today is in databases or content repositories on computers. Oops, we're back to information again! The other store of knowledge mentioned—*"routines, processes, practices and norms"*—also smacks of information, at least in so far as they are documented, and even in their implementation in computer systems.

A frequently cited definition (Duhon, 1998) of knowledge management, itself, illustrates the conundrum: *"Knowledge management is a discipline that promotes an integrated approach to identifying, capturing, evaluating, retrieving, and sharing all of an enterprise's information assets. These assets may include databases, documents, policies, procedures, and previously un-captured expertise and experience in individual workers"* (my emphasis). Michael Koenig categorizes knowledge management activities in the 21st century in four broad areas: (i) enterprise content management, (ii) lessons learned databases, (iii) expertise location and (iv) communities of practice (Koenig, 2012). This list—with its progression from soft information, formal and informal, to collaborative work tools and techniques—confirms that confusion reigns.

Where does this leave the discipline of knowledge management? As an aim and requirement, it is certainly vital in all organizations as a way of measuring and promoting knowledge and its value, particularly as a source of innovation. However, the lack of distinction between knowledge and information in most treatments leads to much confusion in the practices and processes needed to achieve its aims. In a practical sense, only information can be physically managed, stored and shared. Knowledge, residing only in the human mind, can and should be nurtured. Knowledge can be shared and exchanged directly between people; particularly for the tacit variety, mentoring and apprenticing remain key methods for doing so. With this distinction in mind, knowledge management can be seen to consist of knowledge nurturance, information management (in the broadest sense of the term), and support for the processes of transforming knowledge to and from information.

While knowledge can be recorded and stored as information, and information can certainly increase personal knowledge, the m^3 model discussed in Section 3.4 disavows the widely held notion that information is a subset of knowledge. They are distinct entities that can be inter-converted; moving between them in either direction is both necessary and useful as we create a human image of the real world. Understanding the difference and relationship between the two is vital to positioning knowledge management.

Knowledge, residing as it does in the mental rather than physical world, marks a limit to the domain of computers, at least in terms of its storage and management. We can thus define and implement processes that nurture people in knowledge creation and transfer. But when it comes to recording or storing it, we must recognize that it has then become information, pure and simple. There is no need for separate stores or databases; in fact, they cannot exist.

ThoughtPoint

8.8 MODELS, ONTOLOGIES AND THE SEMANTIC WEB

It was way back in Chapter 3 that we met our first data models as they took to the catwalk in the then-emerging world of relational databases. By the end of the 1970s, the three levels of data model—conceptual, logical and physical representing the scope, business and technological views of data—were already well established (ANSI, 1975). Driven by the need to create commonly understood data definitions in databases that could be shared across applications, the logical and, to a larger extent, conceptual levels moved to describe a cross-enterprise view of data in the Zachman Framework (Zachman, 1987) and, later, in approaches such as the IBM Information Framework (Evernden, 1996). Since then, data models have arguably evolved very little indeed. Perhaps this is in part due to their origin in database technology and, particularly, relational databases, which impedes their development. Their focus is exclusively on process-mediated data—hard information forward-engineered from business needs for implementation in highly structured databases. But what of information? There exist three clear impediments to the evolution of data/information modeling to fully support the biz-tech ecosystem. First, data models are technical in origin; how can they be made attractive to business? Second, data is only one aspect of information; how can we make models intelligent enough to cover all types of information? Third, models are nothing more than simplified maps of much more complicated phenomena; how can they ever adequately represent the real world? We attempt to answer these questions with another look at the world of the models, starting at the enterprise level.

Industrial models

Predefined enterprise/industry models have been available since at least the early 1990s (Evernden & Evernden, 2003). The very reasonable premise is that, in most instances, the businesses in an industry have very common processes and information for the vast majority of what they do, driven by both the fundamentals of the industry and regulations governing running and reporting the business. Figure 8-11 shows a typical structure of such a model based on IBM's Industry Models (Devlin, 1997). At the top, the *scope and architecture* provides a highly consolidated view of the business. It identifies a small number, fewer than 20, of business concepts that are the primary subject areas about which the business must maintain information. The *business data classifications* further define the concepts and categorize them according to business rules, allowing different parts of the organization to verify the business concepts. This links from a hierarchical structure to the *generic entity-relationship model (ERM)*, which is the pivotal layer of the model, structured as a classical entity-relationship diagram. The model is still enterprise-wide in scope, consisting of 200 to 300 entities. It provides a first view of the organizational divisions of the company. The generic ERM identifies and describes in detail all entities, attributes, and relationships used throughout the business.

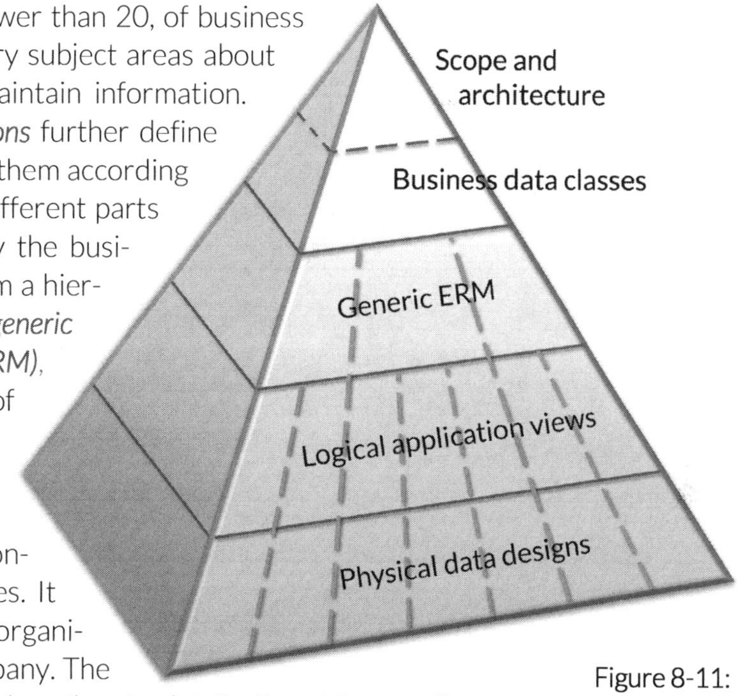

Figure 8-11: Enterprise data model—a typical structure

Next are the *logical application views*, based on the generic ERM but partitioned as the basis for specific applications. A single generic ERM entity can appear in many views, with its attributes subsetted in different ways for different business applications. The final layer of the model, the *physical data design*, applies the physical implementation constraints, such as performance, data sourcing, physical distribution of the data between a number of locations, etc. These constraints are applied separately from the business usage considerations to ensure that technology changes can be accommodated without impacting the logical model. For further details on enterprise data models and information architecture, see (Graham, 2010) and (Godinez, et al., 2010).

Attractive models

If IT hadn't come up with data models—with their formal terminology, mathematical rigor and data integration focus—in the 1970s, what would we use today to carry the conversation with business on how it works and what it needs to record? If we hadn't started from database theory, where would we have begun? Arguably, giv-

Figure 8-12:
Nascita di Venere,
(1486), detail,
Sandro Botticelli,
Uffizi, Firenze

en the aim to create a cognitive map of the business and figure out how to improve it, we might have turned to educational psychology. Prof. Joseph D. Novak was creating *concept maps* as early as 1972 at Cornell University while researching how children assimilate new concepts in science and mathematics (Novak & Canas, 2006). Novak's approach has been widely and successfully applied since in areas ranging from learning psychology, work system design, and human-machine collaboration to knowledge discovery. In this approach, a concept is defined as a perceived regularity in objects or events, or records thereof, designated by a label. Concepts are then connected by linking words or phrases to create meaningful propositions, which can be represented graphically as a concept map, shown in Figure 8-13.

Data modelers may wonder just how different this is from a conceptual data model, beyond its simplicity of representation. In fact, it is its simplicity that makes it attractive to the business people who are the rightful creators and owners of this information. The purpose of the concept map is to assist the business in thinking about their processes and information needs, whereas a data model, even by its very name, tends to focus thinking towards data and away from process. It is the latter that is typically of much higher interest to business users. More formal and detailed data and process models will, of course, be required to begin in-depth design and implementation work.

A concept map is thus a tool to support understanding of the as-is business and to enable thinking about and discussing the desired to-be situation. It provides a basis for a design thinking approach to designing innovative technology solutions for a wide variety of business opportunities, from traditional business intelligence to big data (Frisendal, 2012). We will return to design thinking in Section 9.6, but for now, note that it is characterized by a combination of analytic and intuitive thinking approaches to problem solving, balancing the goals of reliability—to produce consistent and repeatable outcomes—and validity—to produce outcomes that meet objectives (Martin, 2010). The simplicity and elegance of the concept map is likely to enable business people to more easily envisage future states of the business in comparison to traditional data modeling, where the emphasis on formal, systematic analysis of information meaning and use can lead to too much focus on defining and characterizing the past. And the structure lends itself to easy translation to any of the more traditional data model structures favored by modelers.

Intelligent models

You may conclude from the foregoing that attractive models are simple. This should not be construed as a non-PC statement. As a concept map is a simplification of basic entity-relationship modeling to enable business people to describe a limited and well-defined process, so the ontologies and object role modeling we come to next aim to provide a complete and correct representation of a more complex reality. As can be inferred from this chapter, constructing a general and useful model of information in the wild is not a task for the average business person. Highly intelligent models are required, and they are seldom noted for their easy-going nature. They demand the attention of information specialists, library scientists, logicians and even philosophers. And yet, we have been engaged over the past two decades in amassing the largest collection of information ever known—the World Wide Web. It is also, arguably, the most disorganized, disparate and disjointed collection ever known. It was to address these issues that Tim Berners-Lee returned to the fray in 2001 with the Semantic Web (Berners-Lee, et al., 2001) as *"a new form of Web content that is meaningful to computers will unleash a revolution of new possibilities"*. Berners-Lee envisaged extending the messy, poorly structured human-sourced information of the Web with context-setting information (to use our terminology), describing in machine-readable terms the semantics or meaning of the content and inference rules that allowed software agents to make

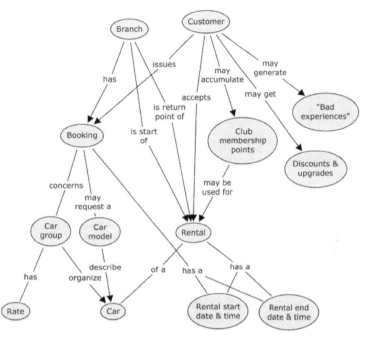

Figure 8-13: Concept map of car rental business, courtesy Thomas Frisendal. (Frisendal, 2012)

logical deductions about how to link and use the content. He further proposed that these rules and contextual information could only be created and evolve as the Web itself had done, as distributed, independently named and loosely cooperative definitions, website by website and interest area by interest area. Which leads us to ontologies.

An *ontology* (simply) represents the knowledge about concepts within a domain and the relationships between those concepts. It's a model, albeit a complex one in a form perhaps unfamiliar to a data modeler. In a genealogical database, for example, an ontology would consist of a taxonomy of all the possible roles of people—husband, wife, daughter, son, brother, sister, etc.—and the relationships between them—a son is a brother of a daughter if both are offspring of the same husband and wife, except when... A little thought reveals that even within such a limited domain, the rules rapidly become very complex and cumbersome as they attempt to account for all the possible combinations and exceptions that human life produces. Fortunately, the various players on the Web have mostly agreed to use a common language, *Web Ontology Language (OWL)*, now at version 2 (W3C, 2012), a family of knowledge representation languages based on formal semantics represented in the *Resource Description Framework (RDF)* and XML-based serializations (Allemang & Hendler, 2011). A wide variety of tools and approaches exists for building ontologies. However, one that best illustrates the link to traditional data modeling is *object role modeling (ORM)*, also known as fact-oriented modeling. It dates back to the 1970s (Halpin, 2009), when the more common entity-relationship model also emerged, from which it differs mainly by treating all facts as relationships and thus avoiding the use of attributes. Terry Halpin, its main proponent, offers a wealth of description at the site www.orm.net, where the model's ability to represent and query complex aspects of reality with precision and depth is apparent. Its claim of ready use by non-technical

Figure 8-14:
An Object-Role-Model diagram, Jakob Voss, 2010

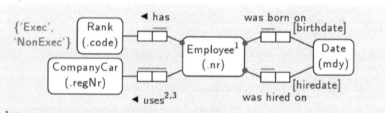

[1] **For each** Employee, birthdate < hiredate.
[2] **Each** Employee **who** has Rank 'NonExec' uses **at most one** CompanyCar.
[3] **Each** Employee **who** has Rank 'Exec' uses **some** CompanyCar.

users is doubtful, however, as a quick look at the notation for the very limited and simple example in Figure 8-14 will attest.

The Object Management Group (OMG) has adopted *Semantics of Business Vocabulary and Business Rules (SBVR)*, based in part on object role modeling, as a component of the *Model Driven Architecture (MDA)*. It forms the basis for formal and detailed natural language declarative descriptions of a business. It is intended to formalize complex rules, such as operational rules for an enterprise, security policy, standard compliance, or regulatory compliance rules.

So, twelve years after Berners-Lee introduced his vision of the Semantic Web to the world, how much progress has been made? Particular scientific disciplines, such as genomics, medicine, chemistry and more, have made significant strides in creating useful ontologies. Social media, health care, retail and telecommunications, to name but a few, have created sufficient semantic data to noticeably enrich Web interactions. Apple's Siri and Google's Voice Search are beginning to display some of the characteristics of the software agents of the original Semantic Web description (Berners-Lee, et al., 2001). But, in the eternal words of the bored child in the back seat, *"are we there yet?"* Soon...maybe.

Real-world models

Steve Hoberman points out (Kent & Hoberman, 2012) that we are moving from a world where modeling was primarily aimed at eliciting the data structures needed to support emerging business requirements—forward engineering—to one where extracting models from existing systems—reverse engineering—is more prevalent. Reverse engineering applies not only to existing internal systems, but, perhaps more importantly, to the information we increasingly source from the web. Not only is such information often loosely defined, but both its owners and users have a penchant for changing it "whenever". We've already mentioned the role of text analytics in these circumstances. More fundamentally, however, the role of the data modeler must be recast—from defining data structures for business use to inferring business uses from data structures and contents.

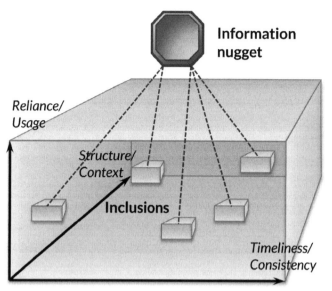

Information nugget

Reliance/ Usage

Structure/ Context

Inclusions

Timeliness/ Consistency

Figure 8-15:
Information nugget and inclusions

Furthermore, the data and information we use for any business process no longer resides in a single database, nor even in one type of store. Rather, it is distributed and possibly duplicated throughout the information space defined by the IDEAL architecture. We need a new way of modeling information in these circumstances. Previously (Devlin, 2009), I have defined an *information nugget* as the smallest set of related information that is of value to a business user in a particular context. It is the modeling equivalent of an SOA service, which is also defined in terms of the smallest piece of business function *from a user viewpoint*. An information nugget can thus be as small as a single record, when dealing with individual transactions, or as large as multiple, complete datasets describing the business status at a particular time. As with SOA services, information nuggets may be composed of smaller nuggets, as well as be part of many larger nuggets. They are thus granular, reusable, modular, composable, and interoperable, and may span traditional information types. As modeled, an information nugget would exist only once in the information space, but would consist of multiple *information inclusions*, perhaps widely dispersed along the three axes. The purpose of this new modeling concept is to provide a modeling construct that ensures that information, as seen by business users, is uniquely and directly related to its use, while describing the related information in multiple locations. So far, no data modeling practice has pursued this thinking.

The challenge we face today is that modeling remains largely focused on the design of databases of hard information. While some progress has been made in expanding the view from applications to the enterprise, little or no account has been taken of the broader question of the multiple and diverse sources we encounter in the biz-tech ecosystem. Furthermore, as Bill Kent points out in his seminal (and recently reissued) *Data and Reality* from 1978: *"There is probably no adequate formal modeling system. Information in its 'real' essence is probably too amorphous, too ambiguous, too subjective, too slippery and elusive, to ever be pinned down precisely by the objective and deterministic processes embodied in a computer."* (Kent & Hoberman, 2012). This assertion remains true some 35 years later. In a keynote at the 11th International Semantic Web Conference, 2012, Mark A. Musen remarks that the old challenges of artificial intelligence still exist, unresolved in the Semantic Web: *"the cognitive challenges in debugging and maintaining complex systems, the drift in the meanings ascribed to symbols, the situated nature of knowledge, the fundamental difficulty of creating robust models. These challenges are still with us; we cannot wish them away with appeals to the open-world assumption or to the law of large numbers"* (Musen, 2012).

> ## Well-informed decision making
>
> *Decision making based on all relevant hard and soft information, with a full understanding of the explicit meanings and relationships expressed within.*
>
> *Well-informed decision making requires a logically unified information store and extensive context setting information. Advances in information modeling to take account of highly changeable soft information, poorly defined and regulated external information, and more are needed to create the contextual richness required in such an environment.*

Clearly, more work is needed here. We need to get to the value and use of information and knowledge. It seems that depending on people to formally define and document the meaning(s) of the information they create and use does not necessarily lead to the depth of insight or the breadth of innovation we desire. We need to revisit the modern meaning model, m^3 that we built in Section 3.4 and note that the meaning layer is mental and the knowledge layer interpersonal. We need to get inside people's heads and understand how they work, individually and collectively.

ThoughtPoint

Data modeling has long been a foundation for BI. However, its practitioners have perhaps been too focused on the processes of data creation rather than on information use. As business redirects its interest from data to information, the time is ripe for a new and broader focus on modeling information in all its forms across diverse and distributed environments. Of particular importance will be the development of new methods of real-time, reverse engineering of models from textual and multiplex information.

8.9   IN PRACTICE—FINALLY MOVING BEYOND DATA

Most businesses invest far more time, effort and money in data than in information, in BI than in content management, in query than in search. This allocation of resources demands reconsideration. Of course, data—hard information—by its very nature, is more valuable byte for byte than soft information. After all, data has been carefully defined and captured in the core processes of the business; it has been refined and managed, governed and cared for. Data is the astronaut's nutrition pill to the hunter-gatherer's savannah of information. Phrased in such terms, it can be difficult to see where to start with managing soft information and extracting value from it, other than the big data uses discussed in Chapter 6. But, there also exists soft information within the business that offers opportunities to begin:

✓ Extend information governance to internal content as described in Section 3.9.

✓ Investigate intelligent content as a means of capturing the meaning of important documents in a standard and reusable form. Legal and contractual documents that frame business activities provide a good starting point when considering the support required for decision making. Formal inter-company communications and agreements are also of interest.

✓ Investigate a *unified information store* approach (Devlin, 2010). A number of products offer the possibility to search and query against a combination of data and content residing in separate, diverse data stores. An initial proof of concept, focusing on the business value to be gained in a specific area, should be followed by a broader program that evaluates the approach across the business and with business partners.

✓ Evaluate Web 2.0 and Enterprise 2.0 tools and techniques for sharing and cooperating around soft information.

✓ Rejuvenate enterprise modeling for soft information. Investigate ontologies and emerging aspects of the Semantic Web for application to internal information resources in the business.

✓ Revisit and repurpose knowledge management programs. In our terminology, they are actually about information rather than knowledge. Nonetheless, if they were broadly-based and well-run, they offer a wealth of information about the information that exists in the business and a quick roadmap to where value may be gained through better management and broader use.

8.10   CONCLUSIONS

Having explored information and its use in decision making in some depth, it should be clear why IT's long-standing affair with data leaves business less than satisfied. Data—hard information—tells only a small part of the story. Yes, it is closest to the "facts" of a situation and amenable to mathematical and statistical analysis. Even IT's recent infatuation with big data and analytics, although it may provide a better predictive basis for action in some cases, will be found lacking in the longer term, as it increasingly fails to answer that uniquely human question, *Why?* Only soft information, or content, provides the big picture, the nuances of the context within which facts must be interpreted, predictions and decisions made, and actions taken.

As we've seen from the evolution of information science and content management, this is no simple task. Managing soft information—in general, in business and especially as it has exploded in social media—is an engineering challenge. Even our modern, Web-based software solutions fall short of the functionality envisaged by early pioneers like Engelbart and Nelson. In addition, the conceptual model for information, similar to the relational model for data, is still incomplete and limited in its acceptance. Nonetheless, the need and the direction are clear, the theory and tools are emerging. Some of the most challenging issues, however, are not technical but relate to privacy and security, which require consideration of changing societal patterns and demand rethinking of legal approaches to copyright and consent to use.

But it is also clear from the work of information science that information in itself is not the solution to the dilemma of decision makers. Business-oriented content, whether sourced internally or externally, adds a further layer of complexity to understanding the basis for insightful decision making. We discover that data, although formally derived from information, must be recombined with it in context-setting information and the other contents of compound information. Data modeling, in its current form, takes us only a part of the way and must reinvent itself to encompass all the information used and needed in the biz-tech ecosystem. It is only when data and content are remarried that true insight at a business level emerges. Information—hard or soft—is but the scaffolding that supports the creation and collection, emergence and enhancement of knowledge.

Our brief exploration of knowledge management as practiced today serves only to emphasize that here, too, something is missing. Knowledge cannot be managed because it exists only in the mind of the knower. And, as we search for the magic ingredient of decision making, we need to move beyond knowledge as an abstract concept. We must move to the human and social levels where knowledge informs decision making, where meaning drives behavior, and where personal intent, as well as collaborative and social interactions, drive action. It is there we must journey next to complete the three-layer model of information, process and people.

N

ROADMAP

→ *Meaning:* The stories we tell ourselves about what information means, based on all we know and have experienced in business and in life

→ *Rationality is overrated:* Contrary to established theories, facts and rational thinking play only a (sometimes small) part in decision making; modern thinking about sense-making and information foraging make some more sense

→ *Heuristics and integrative thinking:* Instant impressions and right-brain thinking may be as reliable as rational (left-brain) processes in some circumstances, but are faster and often more compelling

→ *Emotions are important:* Motivation and intent, which come from the emotional mind, can be socially and personally constructive or destructive; they cannot be ignored in modeling real decision making

→ *Adaptive decision cycle:* In hierarchical decisions, this cycle combines center-out (BI) and edge-on (spreadsheet-like) support across personal, team and corporate levels

→ *iSight:* Innovative team decision making is supported through collaborative Enterprise 2.0 tools and informal information

→ *Three axes of the people layer:* Motivation, attitude and role describe behavior; software is not the answer

CHAPTER 9

INNOVATION IN THE HUMAN AND SOCIAL REALM

"A person is a person through other persons. We would not know how to think, or walk, or speak, or behave as human beings unless we learned it from other human beings. We need other human beings in order to be human. I am because other people are." | Desmond Tutu

"The heart has its reasons of which reason knows nothing." | Blaise Pascal

A philosophy major reading this book might wonder why it has taken until now to focus on people and their role in decision making, although we have mentioned them often in passing. Indeed, this student may ask why the title implies that innovation can even occur in the absence of human or social aspects. Sadly, there are too few philosophy majors today and even fewer who venture into the world of business. As for the IT experts who have traditionally defined this topic...well, this is a world renowned for its geeks, more at home with technology than people. Purveyors of process, imperators of information. And yet, as we acknowledged back in Chapter 1, people are the top layer of the decision making model. In truth, only people can make decisions (although they may delegate well-defined instances to algorithms) and it is only for people—ultimately—that innovation is meaningful.

And so, we must venture from the world of hard technology to the softer sciences of psychology and sociology. In order to understand the functioning of the biz-tech ecosystem and to induce the level of innovation required for success, we must explore information and process from a human viewpoint. How do people use and share information? What motivates us as human beings? By what processes, personal and social, do we come to decisions? And transmute decisions to useful actions? Beyond the hardware and software, how does this work...or not? And how should it?

We have traversed the plains of information, and clambered up the foothills of knowledge. Finally, we scale the heights of the stories we tell ourselves—the beginnings, middles and endings—through which we seek meaning and explanation. Dressed in intellect, veiled in intuition, we infer cause and effect to make sense of what has happened, to describe our current situation, and to attempt to predict the future. Information is a starting point, knowledge a waypost. Through meaning, we co-create and share a context for our decisions with our peers, superiors and subordinates.

Ultimately, decisions are a human process of the mind. A belief in rational decision making has dominated Western culture since the Age of Enlightenment, and especially since the emergence of computers. However, even rational thought admits that real decision making is far from rational; heuristics, gut feel, emotions and ethics all play a role. We thus delve into the depths of the mind and the brain to understand the role of insight and what truly makes us tick as individuals. At a collective level, it is collaboration—in the broadest sense of the word—that is at the heart of all business decision making and action taking. It is the lifeblood of innovation. True collaboration goes far beyond current features and thinking in today's BI tools. Enterprise 2.0 is a further step forward, but more is needed to support and benefit from collaboration to the fullest.

From personal insight and within social collaboration emerges the motivation to understand possibilities, solve problems, make judgments, and take action for the good of the business, personal gain, or even revenge. This process we call MEDA, a part of an adaptive, sense and respond, command and control environment through which decisions are made, actions taken, and results reviewed. However, we must dig deeper if we are to support fully the diverse inhabitants of the biz-tech ecosystem. In a team environment, we do this through iSight, a proposed combination of process choreography, information orchestration, and a personal innovation platform. These components lead us to detail the final people layer of the IDEAL conceptual architecture.

9.1 MEANING—AND THE STORIES WE TELL OURSELVES

It was back in Chapter 3 that we first introduced the concept of meaning and its interpersonal locus. Meaning, as we defined it, leads us far beyond BI, requiring us to include the personal, inner landscape in which every decision occurs, to look at human motivation and intent, both individually and in the social, relational world that we inhabit. To reiterate, meaning is the many different and often diametrically opposed stories we make up and tell ourselves about what we know, what we don't and, more importantly, what we can or should do about it. It's complex, many times messy but ultimately, it is the source of insight and innovation in decision making—and in every aspect of our business and our lives.

Figure 9-1:
Thomas Malthus and his *Essay on the Principle of Population*
Jesus College, Cambridge, UK

Truth or dare

A key point to bear in mind as we contemplate meaning is that we are moving away from the concept that there are only facts—data—to be considered. Facts are becoming devalued as a basis for decision making. The growing volume and use of soft information from social media makes the point clearly. An event occurs in the physical world. Instantly, the Twitter stream twinkles into activity, and hundreds of Tweets describe, opine and debate the issue. Which, if any, are facts? As we mine the Twitterverse for sentiment and predict consumer behavior based on aggregated information from social media, click streams and transactions logs, how much of what we use is factual?

In fact (the pun is intended), the use of "facts" as a basis for decision making dates back only to the early- to mid-1800s, as outlined in *Too Big to Know* (Weinberger, 2012). Prior to that, expert, interested or considered opinion was sufficient to argue any case. Malthus' 1798 warning of over-population and mass starvation is based, not on any assembly of facts and figures about population growth or crop yields, but rather starts from "postulata" that he assumes as granted, which lead to an inevitable, self-evident conclusion (Malthus, 1798). In his opinion. Much of the book was actually devoted to explaining why various populations seemed to remain in balance. Some thirty years later, the sixth edition (Malthus, 1826) was, in contrast, richly annotated with studies and statistics to support his thesis. According to Weinberger, facts had become fashionable by then, especially among English social reformers who could use them to argue against the interests of the upper classes. But what are facts?

In physical science, the facts appear at first to be indisputable. The use of facts in the scientific method dates to Francis Bacon's *Novum Organum* in 1620. The length of a beam at 24.67cm is a fact; as long as we all agree to measure in centimeters of an agreed size. Only the most contrarian might argue. The sodium lamp popular in street lights emits light of wavelengths of 589.0 and 589.6nm. This basic, measured fact is indisputable—the experiment has been repeated often enough and produced the same result. But, the method for measuring wavelengths of light requires a good knowledge of physics. So, to accept this unquestionably as a fact, we must trust the physicists. As science extrapolates from simple measurements to theories about past occurrences (the asteroid impact of 65 million years ago caused the extinction of the dinosaurs) and predictions of the future (average global temperatures will rise by 4 degrees by 2030), it moves from relatively agreed facts to more debatable opinions. The acceptance of such factually based opinions depends less on the underlying facts than on the authority of those who devise and support the theories. Such authority, Weinberger eloquently argues, emerges from the long-standing method of peer-reviewed scientific publishing designed for a world where publication was expensive and thus rare. The Web has changed that dramatically: no opinion is too unusual or too unsupported to publish. The identity or affiliation of the writer may be unknown, hidden or even falsified. So how does one establish or judge the authority of the author? Opinions and facts are increasingly hard to distinguish in common usage in this Internet Age.

Universally accepted facts or truths are becoming a smaller proportion of the expanding world of big data we explored in Chapter 6. Today's business people, who grew up with Google and Wikipedia, are less bound by facts and more open to opinions than previous generations. Whether this is "good" or "bad" is also only an opinion, but our decision making systems must surely take this into consideration. Data-based decision making belongs to a business world where facts are facts, not to be disputed. And even here, it's a lot less clear than we might like to believe. The figure called profit in the financial month-end report is a fact that we can compare with that of the previous month with a smile or a frown. However, we have long known that there is more than one way to calculate the number. So which is the fact? Even at the level of a basic transaction in the order entry database—this computer was sold to Acme Inc. on 27th June—may be less a reflection of reality and more a salesman's wishful thinking that the deal will close by quarter end. As we calculate and extrapolate ever further, facts become increasingly uncertain. Information-based—rather than data-based—decision making adds further human variability and complexity.

The meaning of meaning

"Εὕρηκα!" ("Eureka!", "I've found it!"), shouted Archimedes as he ran naked (allegedly) through the streets of Syracuse after taking a bath, where he discovered the simple principle that a submerged object displaces a volume of fluid equal to its own. Eureqa, from the Cornell Creative Machines Lab, is an evolutionary computing *"software tool for detecting equations and hidden mathematical relationships in your data. Its goal is to identify the simplest mathematical formulas which could describe the underlying mechanisms that produced the data"*[1]. It has been used to model physical systems such as harmonic oscillators and single and double pendulums (Schmidt & Lipson, 2009), spore formation in bacteria (Kuchina, et al., 2011), and more. In science, knowledge is often expressed in the form of mathematical equations—both form and content. Newton's three laws of motion express the knowledge that enables classical mechanics to predict positions and motions of solid bodies. This is relatively simple mathematics; many high school physics students can explain the *meaning* of these laws. Generally, however, as systems become more complex, so do the mathematics, leaving college physics students and professors to

Figure 9-2: Archimedes' eureka moment, 16th century print

---

[1] See http://creativemachines.cornell.edu/eureqa

struggle to capture and express their meanings. Einstein's $E=mc^2$ is probably the most famous exception to this generalization about complexity, but it also shows that it is the meaning—simplistically, matter and energy are equivalent—that allows us to make sense of the world we live in. Eureqa poses a problem of meaning. It can generate and evolve large numbers of mathematical equations, check them for fit to the data, and eliminate trivial solutions quickly and automatically. However, if the scientist cannot, at the end, explain the reason why the equation works or what the variables or constants mean, the overall result lacks meaning, and the predictive value of the knowledge becomes less secure in the face of unanticipated future circumstances.

Although the bacteria experiment above is the only one widely referenced, the suggestion is that Eureqa will begin to churn out new "laws of nature" at a rate far greater than scientists' capacity to understand them (Mullins, 2011). Gürol Süel, the biologist responsible for that finding, maintains that scientists must have a role in framing the questions, selecting data and evolutionary starting points, as well as attributing meaning to the results. This leads us back to the correlation vs. causation debate in Section 5.3, although from a somewhat different angle. Science has as a grand purpose to explain the meaning of the universe; causation is central to that. Business, on the other hand, is more interested in what works. Using big data and predictive analytics provides correlations that have clear business value—more sales, less churn, etc.—but that do not lead to a better grasp of the reality of the situation. We are on the cusp of losing a sense of meaning for customer behavior in the interest of improving the bottom line. Contrary to the largely utopian view presented by big data advocates in *Big Data: A Revolution That Will Transform How We Live, Work and Think* (Mayer-Schonberger & Cukier, 2013), among others, I believe this human loss of meaning will ultimately be a significant detriment to decision making.

Meaning in the context of m^3

Forward looking decision support and other IT systems in the biz tech-ecosystem must mirror the complexity and variability of humans being and interacting in the interpersonal world. While data-based (fact-based) and insightful (information-based) systems can and must continue to play important roles, we must now extend our model to include meaning. If we accept that meaning and knowledge can only be represented and stored in IT systems as information created by people or machines and processed by applications, we can see a need for a new level of representational wealth and subtlety to effectively capture meaning and enable its broad use throughout the entire organization and beyond. The modern meaning model provides this representation.

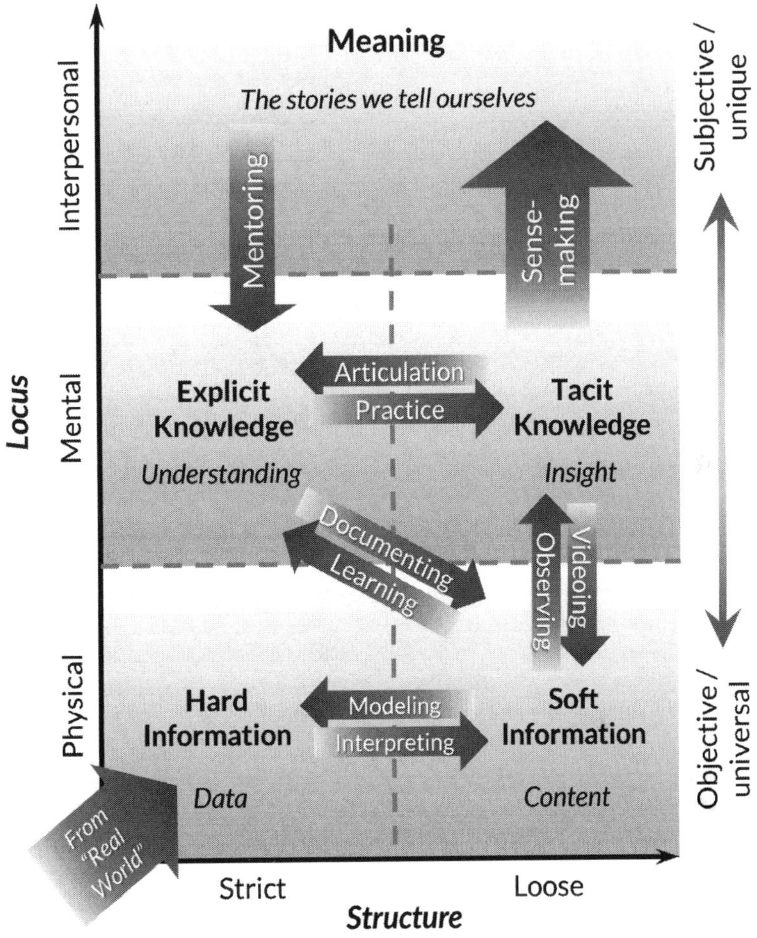

Moving through the levels of m^3, we create the internal narratives that make events and results meaningful. These stories we tell ourselves spring from our life histories and internal landscapes as much as they do from the "real world". We slip easily between the objective and universal view captured in information and the subjective, unique meaning we create as humans in our heads. Indeed, philosophers have long debated whether the world is real or a construct of our minds.

Figure 9-3
The complete m^3 modern meaning model

But this is far from a philosophical debate. Just as physics has evolved from Newtonian certainty to Einstein's relativity and uncertainty, as biology has progressed from classifying species to exploring intra-cellular communications and energy exchange, so too has business advanced from recording transactions and legal entities—the macroscopic day-to-day running of the business—in systems of record to observing customer comments and imagining their consequences—attempting to predict future trends and even events—in systems of engagement. Big data moves us from probably well-agreed facts to changeable and perhaps unpredictable opinions. From a very practical vantage point, the biz-tech ecosystem is real and becoming more so daily. The implications are that we must start to pay attention to the sciences of the mind, from psychology to neurobiology.

9.2   RATIONAL DECISION MAKING, ALLEGEDLY

*B*ut I am an economist...I just see [everyday things] in a different light. Economists are always looking for the hidden logic behind life, the way it is shaped by countless unseen rational decisions.*" Perhaps it's just me, but I find this quote from the introduction of *The Logic of Life* (Harford, 2008) just a little scary. But that makes my point—something a little irrational or emotional in my thinking, perhaps. Harford espouses a view based on neoclassical economics where money is not the only subject of a profit and loss account; health, time, pleasure, pain and more, both current and future, are all supposedly subjected to rational, albeit often unconscious, benefit vs. damage calculations in daily decision making. Economists like Harford claim that *rational choice theory* can provide unexpected and powerful insights into the majority of human decisions. Our minds apparently spend inordinate amounts of time and energy in defining objectives, making long lists of pros and cons, adding measures of utility, multiplying by probability, and coming to rational conclusions. Or they must operate as if they process as just described...because there is no other rational possibility. Harford even states that *"there is nothing irrational about love"*. Now that stretches my understanding of rationality, defined by Herbert Simon as behavior well-adapted to its goals (Simon, 1993). And we might also be tempted to doubt the rational, well-adapted behavior of world economics—in governmental and financial institutions—that resulted in the financial meltdown of the past five years.

The concepts of bounded rationality (based on a limited set of alternatives or consequences considered), satisficing (choosing an alternative that exceeds some criterion),

Figure 9-4
Le Penseur,
Auguste Rodin,
1902,
Les Invalides,
Paris

and rule following have long been used to describe the mechanism underlying decision making at a personal level, largely in a business context (March, 1994). Lack of information is typically considered as an important constraint, together with decision makers' limitations in attention, memory, comprehension and communication. Within these constraints, the basic assumption is that decision makers strive to be rational. Much work has been undertaken in psychology to understand how individuals deal with the conflict between these constraints and their intention to be rational— framing, simplifying and editing problem spaces; decomposing problems into parts; using heuristics (Gladwell, 2005) and so on. This thinking is the foundation of all data-based decision making and drives the focus of data warehousing and BI toward gathering ever more numerical and statistical data—simplified models of the real world—and attempting to summarize and visualize it in increasingly sophisticated ways. While these approaches purport to discern truths—in some rational sense—about reality, most real-world decision makers are very aware that numbers are massaged and conclusions subverted for a variety of reasons, some of which stretch any definition of rationality to breaking point.

Dan Ariely, professor of psychology and behavioral economics at Duke University and founder of the Center for Advanced Hindsight, offers a rather contrarian view in *Predictably Irrational* (Ariely, 2008). Behavioral economics explicitly studies the effects of a range of social, cognitive, and emotional factors on individuals' and institutions' decisions. It further posits that controlled experiments can uncover and predictably explain behaviors that fall far from the tree of rational choice theory. Over thirteen chapters, Ariely provides a plethora of examples of irrational decisions, based on factors ranging from social and market norms, self-control and procrastination, the use of the label *Free!* in promotions, and all the way to the level of sexual arousal of the decision makers. This latter case is, of course, seldom encountered in business decisions, but Ariely contents that other strong emotions, such as anger or frustration, can have similar effects. From here, it's but a short step to attempting to influence behaviors through libertarian paternalism—"*that make[s] it easier for people to choose what is best for themselves, their families, and their society*"—as advocated in *Nudge* (Thaler & Sunstein, 2008), a book that is influencing political thinking in the US and UK. You may now argue that we've strayed far from decision making and BI—until you recall that the suggestions offered on retail websites based on predictive analytics falls fairly in the center of the biz-tech ecosystem.

Whether we focus on the supposed rationality or irrationality of these behaviors and decisions, the approaches outlined above focus on an internal and largely fixed mental reasoning that performs independently of the social and cultural world in which decisions are made. Psychologists identify simple, low-level mental heuristics—rules of thumb—that are widely used and effective in many circumstances. Although accepting that heuristics often serve us well, behavioral economists, social scientists, and others use simple logic to explore how these rules of thumb explain or predict specific and rather limited experimental or real-world situations for good or—mostly—for ill. The outcome is the identification of a set of "mental deficits" that include:

- *Anchoring:* the mind puts too much emphasis on the first information received

- *Confirming evidence:* the mind subconsciously decides on a course of action and tends to favor evidence in its support

- *Framing:* how a problem or question is stated can affect the outcome of a mental choice of answer

Of course, such deficits must be diligently compensated for or avoided. In *The Hidden Traps in Decision Making* (Hammond, et al., 1998), the authors claim that *"sometimes the fault lies not in the decision-making process but rather in the mind of the decision maker. The way the human brain works can sabotage our decisions."* Their solution? Gather more evidence, examine more alternatives, include more people in the process, and so on. Forewarned, they say, is forearmed. Which is, obviously, something of a rule of thumb. But, an unquestioning search for and trust in human rationality as a recipe for good decision making seems to increase our addiction to collecting ever more data and to cause us to distrust the ability of our own minds.

Does sense-making make sense?

A more pragmatic approach emerged in the early 1990s in the form of *sense-making* (also written as sensemaking) initially from the thinking by Brenda Dervin, now a professor of communication at Ohio State University, on how we communicate with one another in an environment where people always see the world through their own eyes—and will continue to do so. From there, the focus shifted to the process of seeking knowledge and meaning, and how we make and unmake sense of reality through gathering and processing information (Dervin, et al., 2003). In this view, knowledge cannot exist apart from human behavior; its value arises in its creation and use of meaning by one or more persons at specific points in time. These people are seen by Dervin as simultaneously both rational/orderly and non-rational/chaotic, individually shaped by their personal histories, beliefs, cultures and more. The nature of knowing is thus sometimes absolute and at other times interpretative; knowledge is at once both objective and subjective. The human need—individual, and defying simple categorization—is to create meaning through sense-making in this dichotomous reality. Systems that offer only a strictly defined and unchanging view of information to the people who use it thus cannot hope to succeed.

Sense-making has been applied in a number of areas, of which the most relevant here are organizational theory (Weick, 1995) and human-computer interaction, particularly that related to information retrieval and use called information foraging (Pirolli, 2009). Both areas contribute in different ways to defining the people layer of the conceptual architecture. Organizational sense-making proposes that understanding or framing situations that require decisions in business is a collaborative process. This framing emerges from the differing perspectives and experiences of the people involved. In fact, it claims that people *enact* their environments; as they communicate and build narratives to apprehend their situations, they actually direct and control the outcomes in an ongoing feedback loop of change and growth. The consequences of such thinking are far-reaching. Business organization should be modeled in a *multi-ontology* framework (Snowden, 2005) that ranges from traditional process engineering based on Taylor's scientific management, through sense and respond, as discussed in Chapter 7, to social complexity that takes account of chaos theory, emergence and the belief that human systems cannot be understood solely from the perspective of physics or biology. *"Thus, organizations are talked into existence locally and are read from the language produced there"* (Weick, 2009) and the relationship between what is said—varying and diverse views of reality—and what is written as the authoritative view of what "really happened" is a fundamental question that traditional BI seldom, if ever, addresses.

To support that 10,000 foot view, sense-making plunges into the interior motivation of people and groups to avow that people favor plausibility over accuracy. Andrew Brown, professor of Organization Studies at the School of Management at Bath University, analyzes the authoritative and supposedly impartial report into the collapse of Barings Bank in 1995 from a sense-making perspective, to conclude that it is *"a monologue that closes down competing ideas, explanations, and plots, discouraging sceptical questioning, thus cementing and unifying ideological structures"* (Brown, 2005). His comment in the same paper that *"accounting and auditing activities are fundamentally exercises in the manipulation of meaning, and that the memoranda and reports which they generate are power effects"* also deserves deeper investigation by proponents of BI as a "single version of the truth". The bottom line here is that although IT may be tasked to deliver accurate and consistent information through BI, we must increasingly recognize that how that information is used afterwards in the very human process of sense-making may be more significant.

This brings us neatly back to information foraging and the question of the real role of information in decision making. Sense-making and information gathering were brought together in human-computer interface thinking at the 1993 InterCHI Conference with a presentation from four Xerox PARC researchers entitled *The Cost Structure of Sensemaking* (Russell, et al., 1993). The paper explores the process of sense-making as applied to information-centric tasks such as course development, research and business intelligence. Among the conclusions was an observation that information gathering—finding the relevant documents, selecting the information, and transforming the information into canonical form—was the most costly step in the process, leading to Pirolli and Card's subsequent focus on *information foraging* as a way to model the process by which people make sense of information and maximize their success in terms of time expended vs. value attained (Pirolli & Card, 1995). In the biz-tech ecosystem, with enormous and exponentially growing volumes of information, the value of such thinking is obvious. As a result, this theory has elicited interest in diverse areas including Web navigation, content search and analysis, and BI.

Information foraging is based on a biological *optimal foraging theory*, which models how animals and hunter-gatherers optimize energy consumption by balancing two behaviors: stay in an area where once-plentiful food is diminishing or look for a new area with more food. It has also been used in a variety of anthropological studies of hunter-gatherer societies. Its application to information stems from the idea that humans are "informavores" whose adaptive success in the world depends on our success in finding, understanding and using relevant information. An analysis of the behavior of intelligence analysts, for example, shows a highly iterative approach divided into two key loops—foraging and sense-making—and suggests focus areas for technology support and improvement (Pirolli & Card, 2005). Information foraging sees behavior as highly rational (or, at least, capable of being usefully described in rational terms), directed toward goals, and chosen through trade-offs between effort expended and results potentially achieved.

The data-frame theory is yet another attempt to make sense of sense-making (Klein, et al., 2007), starting from the premise that the frame—story, script, map or plan—we use to structure our interpretation of reality and the data that informs it are closely intertwined and interdependent. (Klein uses *data* here in the meaning of cues from the environment, rather than our definition in Chapter 3.) Sense-making is fitting data into a frame and fitting a frame around the data. In this view, data is not a perfect representation of reality; it is an abstraction influenced by the frame through which it is viewed and, indeed, created. Such frames are inferred from at most three or four key data points or anchors. Often, a single anchor will suffice, and abductive reasoning (loosely put, guessing), which is useful in an uncertain world, is used as well as logical deduction. Plausibility and pragmatics are often more important than accuracy in sense-making under this hypothesis. This leads to a more functional understanding—what to do about a situation—as

Figure 9-5
Optimal foraging giraffe,
Barry Devlin, 2011

opposed to an abstract understanding of why something has occurred. Furthermore, many decisions seem to rely on just-in-time mental models, even in cases where there is little or no time pressure, because most situations are evaluated from a position of incomplete or fragmentary knowledge and data. The authors define a cycle of sense-making that includes both altering the frame to fit the data and altering the data to fit the frame.

In effect, we have now closed the loop from the information processing view of Pirolli back to Snowden's proposal of a socially complex decision-making environment. The danger is to suppose that only one type of process is going on here. Human decision making is a multifaceted affair that likely involves everything from unconscious influences, through simple heuristics, all the way to formal logic. However, it would seem that we place far too much weight on that last component, especially in the world of business and economics where the biz-tech ecosystem is emerging.

Thinking machines

In my view, this attraction to rationality and logic as a way to understand and improve human decision making stems, at least in part, from their central role in computer design, both in hardware and software. The well-known Turing Test, dating back to 1950, to distinguish between a person and a computer, as well as the development of *artificial intelligence (AI)* as a research field in the mid-1950s, both contributed to the perception that thinking in computers and humans could be treated in the same manner. While impressive results, by the standards of the time, were achieved in the 1960s, twenty years later the systems were still struggling to move beyond solving the simplest representational problems. The limited computational power of the time was certainly a factor in the so-called *AI winters* of the 1970s and 1980s. As computers became more powerful and the focus moved to more specific and practical problems, by the late 1990s features once considered advanced AI were becoming widespread in different guises. However, although computers were solving problems and performing tasks once considered the preserve of the human mind, what was seldom recognized was that ours and their ways of working are quite different.

In May, 1997, IBM's Deep Blue became the first chess program to defeat a reigning world grandmaster, Garry Kasparov, in a match under tournament conditions. Because chess is a fully deterministic game—the rules are known, all information is in full view, and luck has no role—all possible moves can, in theory, be calculated and evaluated from any position for any number of future plays. Unfortunately, the number is so large that even today no computer can do it. Nor, of course, can humans. Both computers and humans depend on heuristics to play, albeit rather different ones because of differing strengths. A computer can calculate moves far more quickly than humans—200 million vs. Kasparov's three positions per second, according to IBM at the time—and can also evaluate board positions statistically based on huge databases of previous games. Even so, computers must use heuristics to pare down the decision tree to manageable proportions, and the human mind's more strategic use of such heuristics can sometimes balance out the difference in computing power. Humans rely on visual pattern recognition and imagination. By 1997, computers had progressed to the stage where their combination of brute force and heuristics enabled Deep Blue to pose a reasonable challenge to Kasparov's skills. As Nate Silver describes it in *The Signal and the Noise: The Art and Science of Prediction*, the outcome of the match rested on a simple coding error in the program, which Kasparov misinterpreted to mean Deep Blue was more powerful than he thought, causing Kasparov to lose confidence and the match (Silver, 2012).

In February, 2011, IBM Watson defeated *Jeopardy!* champions Ken Jennings and Brad Rutter. A general knowledge TV game, where contestants must guess the correct question for a given answer, *Jeopardy!* poses an intelligence problem of an entirely different class to that of chess. In essence, Watson is a question answering system using sophisticated search and analysis approaches to access to vast quantities of hard and soft information—in the game show it had access to 200 million pages of content on 4TB of disk. After the show, IBM announced a project to apply the technology in the medical diagnostics to support staff in selecting optimal treatments, with other applications to follow. Watson can truly be labeled a business intelligence system, focused on soft information rather than hard data. It plays to the information processing and storage strengths of computers to provide current and relevant

The concept of rational decision making is appropriate for computers—at least as they exist today. Its use in the human sphere may be a desirable outcome in terms of Enlightenment Era thinking. But even a limited review of human behavior leads to the conclusion that rationality is honored far more in aspiration than in reality. In this respect, we can see why business intelligence, decision support systems and knowledge management have far less impact on decision making than we would like to believe.

information to supplement human skills in decision making. Computer-like logic and rationality makes perfect sense here, in Dan Power's terms as a knowledge-driven DSS (Power, 2009). But surely we cannot insist that people think like computers.

9.3   INSIGHT—ENGAGING THE EVOLVED MIND

Figure 9-6:
The Kiss,
Auguste Rodin,
1889,
Musée Rodin,
Paris

Perhaps a better starting point is to accept that our mental functioning has evolved, and continues to do so, along with our environment, in line with the theory of *survival of the fittest for purpose,* and that what we have is probably best adapted to the current world where we cooperate in society and in business toward partially shared goals. And rather than focusing on intelligence in its old rational sense, we must include emotional, ethical, social and other types of intelligence now recognized as important contributors to successful behaviors and decisions. Gerd Gigerenzer, a director at the Max Planck Institute for Human Development, proposes in *Gut Feelings: The Intelligence of the Unconscious* that the mind should be seen as an *adaptive toolbox* that has developed a wide range of rules of thumb to best deal with a highly uncertain environment, characterized by ill-defined problems and opportunities, with loose and changeable rules and variable definitions of success (Gigerenzer, 2007). This actual, real world in which we live is computationally intractable; any real decision of business interest cannot be solved conclusively with any conceivable amount of information and processing power. Gigerenzer describes decision making in terms of this adaptive toolbox of heuristics, which often reach conclusions more quickly and directly than logic. Such rationality remains, of course, valid, valuable and often necessary, but has been promoted to the exclusion of all other approaches since the Age of Enlightenment in the 17th and 18th centuries. A broader and more inclusive model, which we may call *insight*, includes intuition and the more classical intelligence. Human intuition—which, of necessity, ignores some available information—may be more likely to reach good conclusions based on the largest number of *relevant* factors than human intelligence, which may seek too much information and try to balance all possible outcomes. Furthermore, people often prefer to include a certain amount of ambiguity in their formulation of problems and solutions; they tend to bet on reciprocity in their dealings with others to co-create the best solutions to shared opportunities and challenges.

Such modern psychological thought implies that, at the very least, business intelligence programs and tools must expand their focus to support and encourage such intuitive thinking. Accepting that there may exist many valid solutions to any problem or opportunity, they must enable multiple approaches to be recorded and pursued, allowing space for human ambiguity throughout the process. And they must focus attention on the phases of this process where discussion and negotiation of meaning occur, most especially on the closing stages where agreements and conclusions emerge. Furthermore, the limitations of big data—particularly where it is used in attempts to confirm or support specific conclusions—must be recognized and made clear when using it.

Mind, meet brain; body, this is mind

Accepting that formal logic is but a part—and probably a small part, at that—of human decision making, and the mind has evolved a wide range of adaptive behaviors to facilitate decision making in its broadest sense, we should also consider the role of other mental constructs. In particular, should we also posit a role for aspects such as emotions and ethics in a full exploration of support for decision making? Traditional approaches avoid such topics like the proverbial plague. And yet, even common sense shows us that everyday decision making is influenced and, to some extent, directed by our emotional states and ethical positions. Surely, so too

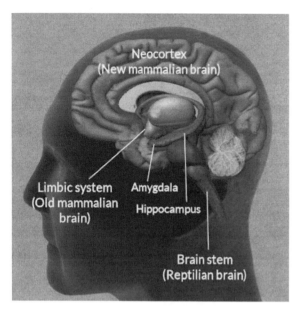

Neocortex
(New mammalian brain)

Limbic system
(Old mammalian
brain)

Amygdala

Hippocampus

Brain stem
(Reptilian brain)

Figure 9-7:
The triune brain
(simplified)
After McLean

is business decision making, given that the mental faculties are the selfsame ones employed since we began the long ascent to civilization, with the co-evolution of the human body and brain as adaptations to survive and thrive in the physical world. Recent work in the field of neurobiology confirms that our mental, neurological and chemical processes are deeply inter-connected and must be treated as a complex system with emergent properties.

The triune brain, first proposed in the 1960s by Paul D. McLean (McLean, 1990), has proven a highly useful, if somewhat simplified, evolutionary model of the human—and mammalian—brain. Our brain consists of three regions: the brain stem (reptilian brain), the limbic area (old mammalian brain), and the cortex (new mammalian brain). These areas are thought to have developed in layers over the course of evolution, and take shape from the bottom up as we develop in the womb. The brain stem matures first. By the time we are born, the limbic areas are partially developed, but the neurons of the cortex lack extensive connections to one another.

The reptilian brain receives input from the body and regulates basic functioning of our heart, lungs, etc. It also shapes the energy levels of the limbic and the cortical regions above it. The brain stem controls our states of arousal, including hunger, sexual desire, etc., and is engaged in the *motivational systems* that satisfy our basic need for food, shelter, safety and reproduction. A compulsion or deep, urgent need to behave in a certain way likely implies that your brain stem is working with the limbic area to galvanize you into action. Clusters of neurons in the brain stem fire in the *fight-flight-freeze* response to danger, which today may be triggered across the oak boardroom table or by opening an email that announces a company down-sizing. This instinctual response to threats—gathering our energy to fight, flee or collapse in the face of an overwhelming situation—makes it well-nigh impossible to be open and receptive to others or to make rational decisions in such situations.

The limbic area, deep within the brain, works closely with the brain stem and the body to create our basic drives and emotions. The emotional hardwiring to be in relationship with one another also resides here, a part of our mammalian heritage. The limbic brain evaluates our current situation: if "good", we seek it out; if "bad", we withdraw from it. Thus, we react in response to the meaning we assign to the news that our company is down-sizing, or that we have exceeded our sales target. The limbic area also plays a regulatory role through the endocrine system, which sends and receives hormones throughout the body. When we are stuck in traffic and miss our flight to Boston, we release cortisol, which mobilizes energy by putting our entire metabolism on high alert to meet the challenge. In the short term, this is a great adaptation to challenging situations. But in the long term, cortisol is toxic to the growing brain and can interfere with the growth and function of neural tissue, leading to chronic stress and emotional reactivity. The limbic area also plays a key role in different forms of memory—facts, specific experiences, and, importantly, the emotions that give color and texture to our experiences. Two areas of the brain have been extensively studied in this regard: the amygdala and the hippocampus. It is in the amygdala that our emotional states are created without consciousness, and we act upon them without awareness, doing things that may save our lives or perhaps later regret. The hippocampus is central to linking such raw emotions into sequences that later allow us to become aware of the feelings inside us and to consciously attend to and understand them in the neocortex.

The neocortex expanded greatly as primates became more successful. It creates more intricate firing patterns that represent the three-dimensional world beyond the bodily functions and survival reactions mediated by the lower subcortical regions. In humans, the more elaborate frontal portion of the cortex allows us to have ideas and concepts. To think about thinking, to imagine, to recombine facts and experiences, and to create. It is here that we create representations of concepts like moral judgment, insight, and empathy. This is the hub, the engine room, containing the functional pathways that connect us to every part of our own brain and to the social world of other brains. Moral reasoning requires the integrative capacity of the middle prefrontal cortex. When the mind works well together, we are integrated and our relationships thrive. Our deci-

Insightful decision making

Decision making that is well-informed but, in addition, is cognizant of the mental landscape of the decision maker.

Insightful decision making seamlessly combines left and right brain, and takes account of intuitive and emotional responses to reach an integrated and well-rounded position on the decision in hand.

sion making is sound. We attune to others, allowing our own internal state to shift; we resonate and align with the inner world of another. This resonance is at the heart of empathy. Intuition gives us access to the wisdom of the body—that gut-feel of the "right decision"—coming from the interior of the body, our viscera, and our heartfelt sense of what to do. In *Mindsight: The New Science of Personal Transformation*, Daniel Siegel, professor of psychiatry at the UCLA School of Medicine, contends that *"this integrative function illuminates how reasoning, once thought to be a 'purely logical' mode of thinking, is in fact dependent on the non-rational processing of our bodies. Such intuition helps us make wise decisions, not just logical ones"* (Siegel, 2010). Insight and empathy help us connect the past to the present and the anticipated future.

The neocortex is divided into left and right brain, with their complementary but largely separate functions. The right brain, which develops earlier in life, deals in imagery, nonverbal language, symbolism and autobiographical memory; it is the seat of *integrative thinking*. It is also more directly connected to the limbic and brain stem areas than the left hemisphere, giving a more direct link to the inner world of body and emotions. The left brain, a slower developer, handles logical and literal thinking, as well as spoken and written language. Unfortunately, in basic education or management training, it is the left brain that gets most attention. Our culture values science over arts, grammar over storytelling, figures over meaning. While the right brain is often said to be the seat of creativity, it is only through the integration of both sides, through the *corpus callosum*, that true *insight* and, eventually, *innovation* emerge. Integrating the brain involves linking the activity of all these regions vertically and bilaterally. And this is a process that will take our entire lives if we are willing to self-reflect and refine our skills with compassion and deeper understanding of our vulnerability and humanness. We sense the emotional meaning in a certain situation, override impulses to respond reactively, and move beyond our primitive survival needs. We are then able to envision a larger interconnected whole. Siegel draws the analogy of the camera lens. When it is stabilized, he says, the details come into focus: *"We see with more depth and precision. From this stabilization we gain all the gifts of acuity: keenness, insight, perception, and, ultimately, wisdom."*

9.4   WORKING 9 TO 5^2...AT THE MIS MILL

Anybody who has worked with data-based, BI decision making environments in a corporate setting will be very aware that there are two opposing modes through which such support is delivered to business users (Devlin, 2009): the center-out and edge-on decision cycles. The former is highly favored and promoted by BI departments; the latter often resorted to by business analysts to get something—anything—done. Both approaches have their strengths and weaknesses. Neither, on its own, is sufficient in the biz-tech ecosystem. An amalgam is required, which I call the *adaptive decision cycle*.

The *center-out decision cycle*, named for the flow of data out from a central source, is shown in Figure 9-8(a). It has a long history and is often a valid and viable way of working, especially in large and highly structured or regulated businesses. In some cases, and with particular types of information, it is well-nigh mandatory. For example, information about financial results can and should be defined and controlled in the accounting department and, once posted, should be immutable except under very limited conditions. The center-out model posits four steps:

---

[2] *"9 to 5"* was written and performed by Dolly Parton for the eponymous 1980 comedy movie.

Figure 9-8:
Center-out and
edge-on decision
cycles

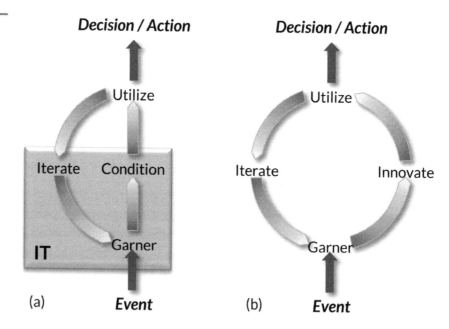

1. *Garner:* the raw and atomic data about business events and their status is collected and stored

2. *Condition:* derived data is generated by cleansing, combining, filtering and enriching the raw and atomic data. Together this creates a complete and consistent base for decision making

3. *Utilize:* the recorded and conditioned data is then used by managers, business analysts, etc., to make decisions and take action

4. *Iterate:* learning from the use made of the data and any issues encountered, any changes to the data needed by the process are applied to the cycle

Implicit in this model is the assumption that there exists a central authority—usually IT—that knows users' needs and asserts control over the data content and how it is manipulated in steps 1,2 and 4. The center-out model is clearly the basis of the traditional data warehouse architecture, and IT perceives this model as key to achieving and maintaining data quality and auditability. Steps 1 and 2 form the design and delivery process of the data warehouse or marts. Also implicit is the belief in a largely unidirectional progression from raw data to final use; the iterate step 4 typically occurs during development of a later version of the mart or warehouse

The *edge-on decision cycle*, shown in Figure 9-8(b), is named for the way in which data originates and circulates on the edge of the organization. This cycle focuses is on immediate problem solving and operates in a shorter timeframe. It originates with business analysts. The utilize step is the same as before, while garner and iterate differ only in who does them and when they occur. Business analysts garner data when they need it from any and every available source, from the data warehouse to spreadsheets created by whomever yesterday. Similarly, they iterate rapidly, within each decision-making cycle. Finally, business analysts seldom worry about conditioning data; instead they:

5. *Innovate:* create, combine and modify data as needed to solve the problem or address the opportunity in hand

In terms of processing, condition and innovate are rather similar; they differ mainly in intent and location. In the former, IT processes the data to improve the quality of its content, while in the latter, the business processes it to improve its usefulness in decision making. These aims and actions are complementary, as are the two cycles themselves. As Table 9-1 shows, both approaches have their ad-

Table 9-1: Center-out vs. edge-on models

Characteristic	Center-out	Edge-on
Data provenance	Correct, centrally controlled single version of truth exists	Multiple and possibly conflicting versions of truth can exist
Data flow	From central store to users	Directly from user to user
Data manipulation by users	Basic data is read-only; users control derived data	Users have full control over all data
Process focus	Reporting and *ad hoc* performance analysis	Creative exploration of data and business scenarios
Typical tools	BI reporting and query tools	Spreadsheets and similar tools
Data quality & auditability	Can be closely controlled and managed	Open to rapid degradation
Work approach	Hierarchical and standardized	Emergent prototyping and innovation

vantages and disadvantages. Unfortunately, as we've seen before, the two processes are often set against one another as mortal enemies (Eckerson, 2003). Center-out favors control, consistency and stability; edge-on supports innovation and change. IT prefers the former; business analysts favor the latter. Neither provides real support for the insightful decision making described in the previous chapter. So, how can these two approaches be fully integrated into a single process for decision making that supports both innovation and control, hard and soft information?

People roles and the adaptive decision cycle

The fundamental reason why neither of the above decision support cycles fully works is because they fail to recognize the different roles that people play in the preparation and use of information in the organization. There are many ways to define personal roles, but a simple scheme consisting of three roles suffices here:

1. *Personal:* a person working alone, using personal skills, knowledge and incentives to manipulate and utilize information in support of a business (or private) goal

2. *Team:* a group of people of similar abilities and status, including those in immediate reporting relationships, working toward agreed goals in the use of information

3. *Corporate:* a diverse set of people using information to work toward over-arching corporate goals spanning multiple business functions

In the center-out model, IT—in a corporate role—undertakes to globally create and preserve data quality and consistency, leaving data utilization at the individual level, as shown by the enclosed IT box in Figure 9-8(a). However, in this model, IT fails to recognize that individuals require access to some aspects of the remaining three activities to perform their tasks. Similarly, in the opposite edge-on case, business users go about their tasks without regard for the corporate need for data quality and IT's role in overseeing it.

The *adaptive decision cycle*, shown in Figure 9-9, clearly separates the three people roles in information creation and use, allowing the different responsibilities to be supported through differing tools and techniques. The personal (P) role operates largely as in the edge-on case, but with additional controls on garnering data to limit the impact of using non-certified sources. Innovation, utilization and iteration thus cycle on the individual level using spreadsheet and/or BI tools until the business analyst comes to some conclusion with which she is satisfied. In most cases, this conclusion is promoted to the team (T) level for further validation and conformation. This starts with discussions and result sharing with colleagues in the same or other departments, benefiting from the collective wisdom, knowledge and diversity of the group. Today, results are shared and discussed extensively via presentations and emails. Although decision context and information relevancy are important determinants of what is shared among peers, personal relationships and trust tend to have even greater relevance in decisions to share knowledge (Pirolli & Card, 1999), (Pirolli, 2009). The result is that emerging collaborative and social networking tools are the basis for support of the team level in general and, in particular, the peer-to-peer interactions that lead to the promotion of personal analyses to group usage. It continues with the formal involvement of line management and later leads to the emergence of cooperative development within and across groups. In the adaptive decision cycle here, however, only the iterate step is collaborative. (We'll see how the entire cycle can be collaborative in Section 9.6.)

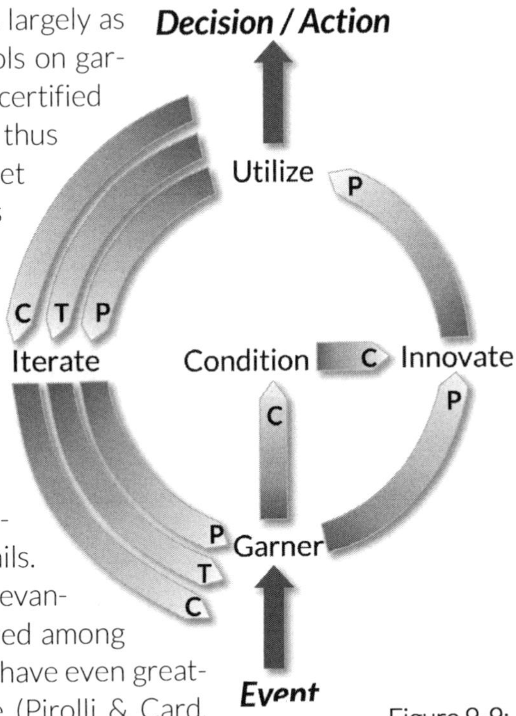

Now, imagine that the analyst and her team have come up with a procedure that could be of value to the organization as a whole. For the most part, even today, such analyses do get shared informally. The results of a worthwhile spreadsheet developed by one analyst are used as the basis for another spreadsheet solution by a second analyst. In some cases, chains of spreadsheet use and reuse may develop, with attendant quality issues. So, how does that procedure get incorporated safely and securely in the production environment? Today, it depends at best on an entirely manual development process, with IT reaching out to the analyst; at worst—and most likely—it will never happen. A formal process for promoting proce-

Figure 9-9:
The adaptive decision cycle

dures and associated data that have been proven at the group level to the corporate (C) level, the outer loop in Figure 9-9, is thus the next logical step. The support and tool function needed to enable this comes in part from social networking and collaborative tools, especially those in the area of Enterprise 2.0—the application of such tooling in business. Again, the iterate step is where linkage between the levels logically occurs. Between the personal and group levels, the mechanism is essentially a push where the user who creates an analysis declares the value and availability of a particular function to his peers.

Facilitating peer-to-peer interaction and sharing is key to easy and speedy movement of knowledge and analyses from the individual to the peer group level. Going from peer to corporate level, the mechanism is more likely to be a pull, with the IT function proactively seeking suitable procedures on a regular basis from those shared at the group level. Both aspects of such promotion of function are discussed from a collaborative viewpoint in Section 9.5. This approach is also instrumental in the emergence of a better process for creating and managing the core quality data needed by the enterprise. In Figure 9-9, the external change is minimal: the creation of a loop process between garner and innovate via the conditioning step. But the underlying meaning is that IT facilitates users in the "playing" with the data, an aspect already supported via *sandboxes* and similar exploratory environments in the data warehouse environment. However, we can already see this approach going much further in the truly collaborative environments spanning business and IT now beginning to emerge.

Collaborative tooling is also at the core of expanding the focus of the adaptive decision cycle beyond data to the broader aspects of soft information discussed in Chapter 8. This is very different from the so-called "collaborative enabling" of BI tools, which basically means allowing online commenting by colleagues on the ongoing work of a business analyst on some data-oriented BI tool. Rather, documents, emails, web pages and more become first-class citizens in the decision-making process. Soft information must also be analyzed in the context of a business problem or opportunity, although the analysis largely excludes mathematical tools or visualizations beyond keys and tags that have been extracted or added. Documents must be summarized and presentations interpreted. All this must be linked together and with more traditional data-based decision making. Advances in search, text mining and related technologies are making inroads, but more needs to be done.

Return to MEDA[3]

In the biz-tech ecosystem, business analysts work at the sharp information edge of the organization, close to the real business and to its customers and suppliers. They are hunter-gatherers who forage throughout the business and beyond for a rich and diverse bounty of timely and sometimes transient data. They are open to including soft information in the scope of their work, knowing full well that not everything can be reduced to numbers when business managers require innovative decisions and solutions. Rather than trying to change this behavior, we must encourage them to first come to the supermarket to obtain pre-processed data to start their hunt for novelty with quality and consistency. The biz-tech

ecosystem needs all the innovation it can get; both behaviors must be encouraged and harnessed. In reality, depending on the data in question, there may exist one or multiple versions of the truth, and the BI environment must support both possibilities.

Figure 9-10:
The adaptive
decision cycle within
the MEDA model

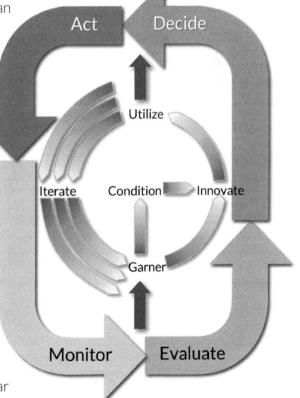

More importantly, it must recognize that the early steps of any new way of analyzing and understanding emerging patterns is a process of *emergent prototyping*, where multiple visions of the truth are explored. Hypotheses are built and discarded iteratively and repeatedly. Information from diverse sources is combined and filtered. Analyses build upon and modify existing work. This exploratory process is the key innovative stage in the evolution of new solutions. The process may appear

---

[3] *Return to Eden* was a 1983 Australian TV miniseries.

disruptive to BI professionals who have focused long and hard on the quality and consistency inherent in the center-out approach. Without emergent prototyping, analysis degenerates to static reporting. With emergent prototyping in play, reporting becomes dynamic and exploration starts from known lands before pushing the limits. This is nothing less than sense and respond thinking applied directly to decision making—MEDA—as we discussed in Section 7.3. The adaptive decision cycle is overlaid on MEDA in Figure 9-10, where the relationship to monitor, evaluate, decide and act is self-evident. The act-to-monitor loop, which was previously identified as the weakest link in most organizations, is clearly related to and emphasized by the multiple paths through the iterate step here. Collaborative and social networking tooling and techniques are at the heart of this step, and to these we now briefly turn our attention.

ThoughtPoint

Decision making today demands a combination of flexibility and control that emerges only by combining the prior BI and spreadsheet approaches. Most BI vendors already embrace the use of spreadsheets. Spreadsheets—Excel in particular—must integrate formal and mandatory (in enterprise environments) control mechanisms for sharing work, tracking usage and change, and back-linking to the enterprise BI environment. Without this, internal IT groups and smaller vendors have to create workarounds or alternative spreadsheet-like tools to support the adaptive decision cycle and truly integrate the innovation of business analysts and the data governance and information management required.

9.5   ENTER PRIZE TWO DOT ZERO

As little as ten years ago, mentioning *social networking* during work hours to your manager might have elicited an enquiry about liquid lunches at the local. Recall that Facebook was only founded in 2004, but let's (not) forget the earlier Friendster, MySpace and others long or more recently departed. The year 2004 also saw the birth of *Web 2.0* at the first conference in San Francisco, an event that ran annually as the Web 2.0 Summit with much hype for seven years. It's interesting to note that Tim O'Reilly continued to attempt an actual definition of Web 2.0 over the following two years (O'Reilly, 2005), (O'Reilly, 2006). *Collaboration* has been better accepted as a work practice, although one doesn't have to go too far back in European history to find that a collaborator was treated with the opprobrium reserved for a terrorist today. In 1997, Warren Bennis remarked that although *"the myth of the triumphant individual is deeply ingrained in the American psyche...we all know that cooperation and collaboration grow more important every day"* (Bennis & Biederman, 1997). Within the business context, social networking, Web 2.0, and collaboration, in particular, provide the foundations for *Enterprise 2.0*, which Andrew McAfee defines as *"the use of emergent social software platforms by organizations in pursuit of their goals"* (McAfee, 2009). This covers a multitude of sins, so let's try to be a bit more specific.

Enterprise 2.0 and the call of the Cs

While big data seems to value Vs above all else, Enterprise 2.0 has been lured by the siren call of the Cs. Communication, collabora-

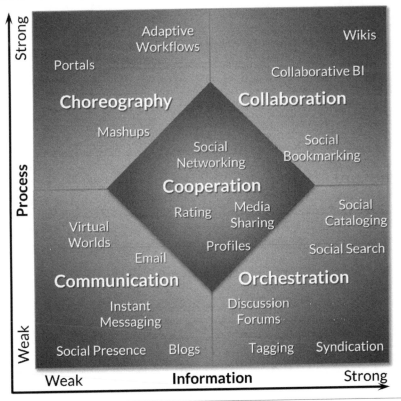

Figure 9-11:
Enterprise 2.0
function mapped
against process and
information

tion and coordination, later called the 3C framework, were identified as central to groupware in the early 1990s (Ellis, et al., 1991). Niall Cook defined a 4C model in 2008, dropping coordination but adding connection and cooperation (Cook, 2008). By 2011, we had an 8C framework—although I saw ten Cs in the definitions—consisting of four inner core activities/technologies—combination of content, coordination, collaboration/cooperation, and communication, as well as four broader aims/outcomes—compliance, contribution (value), change and content management (Williams & Schubert, 2011). Confused? Me, too. And I can add at least one more C of interest here: community. In terms of understanding Enterprise 2.0 functionality, the four broader categories are less interesting, as is community. We need a simpler view. Given that all Enterprise 2.0 functionality, almost by definition, involves people, the most useful way to catalog it, as shown in Figure 9-11, is with reference to the remaining two layers of the IDEAL architecture—process and information. We end up with five clear groupings of function which align reasonably well with those of both Cook and Williams & Schubert, taking into account their overlapping and somewhat contradictory definitions. Unfortunately, one of them doesn't begin with a C. Note that the boundaries are much vaguer than the figure implies. The categories are:

- *Communication:* platforms that allow people to talk, chat, or converse with one another by text, image, voice or video, with minimal limitation on the content or expected outcome. Process orientation is largely absent and information needs limited.

- *Orchestration:* systems connecting people strongly to information, where they create well-defined meaning around information and share it with others. Process remains embryonic.

- *Choreography:* systems that focus on enabling and structuring the processes of people interacting with one another, with limited attention to the information being shared.

- *Cooperation:* platforms enabling people to share reasonably well-defined information with one another with an evolving level of process support.

- *Collaboration:* goal-oriented systems focused on creating and sharing well-defined information within understood and managed processes. In this area, the biz-tech ecosystem stands to gain maximum benefit from Enterprise 2.0.

The vast majority of the functions and tools are well-known by now, and more details can be found in Cook's book, if required. For now, we note that communication and cooperation are the foundational categories of Enterprise 2.0; many of the functions there are now in widespread use within leading-edge companies. The three categories that extend toward more extensive and integrated process and information functionality, particularly collaboration, are still emerging. Although defined in the larger context of all the processes of a business, these concepts and components are central to innovative decision making in the biz-tech ecosystem.

This is made clear in the phrase *decision sourcing*—a play on crowd sourcing—introduced recently by Dale Roberts (Roberts & Pakkiri, 2013). His journey begins from the world of social networking and the ideas brought forth in *The Cluetrain Manifesto* (Weinberger, et al., 2000) and *The Wisdom of Crowds* (Surowiecki, 2004) but ends up in a very similar place to me. Decision making is not what we thought of in BI as a solitary exploration of internal data. It is forever changed by ambient data—a phrase used by IDC in their second Digital Universe forecast (IDC, 2008)—the human-sourced and machine-generated data that pervades the Web. And by the growing acceptance of collaborative approaches and tools by the so-called Millennial Generation coming into the workplace. As Roberts opines: *"Better decisions could be made by groups. They can be smarter. They can generate a diverse range of decision alternatives, guard against personal bias and introduce diversity."* Let's see how such an idea can support innovative decision making and define the structures and tools that could support it in practice.

9.6   PEOPLE WHO NEED PEOPLE...[4]

A simplified view of a business or business unit through a sociological lens reveals it to be a group of people cooperating together to achieve an agreed set of goals according to

---

[4] "*...are the luckiest people in the world*" from the musical *Funny Girl* (1964), by Jule Styne and Bob Merrill, as performed by Barbara Streisand.

an agreed set of rules. The steps they take—both proactive and reactive—to achieve those goals are defined through day-to-day decision making. At a higher level, agreements on goals and rules also emerge through decision making. Individuals within the organization have their own goals and rules, which align to varying degrees with those of the organization. These individuals also bring information, knowledge and meaning to the decisions in which they participate. Decisions made lead to actions taken; the organization thus progresses towards its goals. In the traditional approach, a hierarchy emerges (or is imposed) and processes put in place. A more fluid and emergent strategy is described by *design thinking*, which dates to the 1980s, with Prof. Peter Rowe's book of the same name bringing the term to general awareness (Rowe, 1987). In business management, the term has been promoted by Prof. Roger Martin since the early 2000s (Martin, 2009). As he describes it, design thinking requires a dynamic interplay of structured, analytical, as well as creative and intuitive thinking that is at its most productive in a team environment. The use of the approach in BI, particularly in the design and modeling stage, has also been proposed by Thomas Frisendal, who comments that designing BI solutions falls squarely in the class of *wicked problems* often invoked by proponents of design thinking (Frisendal, 2012). However, we can also consider any team decision making that requires true innovation as a suitable candidate for the application of design thinking.

Figure 9-12 provides a graphical representation of innovative decisions made according to this model. A team—which may or may not appear in the formal organization chart—of people come together to deal with a situation that requires new thinking and a decision about what to do next. Some or all of the participants bring existing

Figure 9-12:
Typical, informal decision making model in today's business

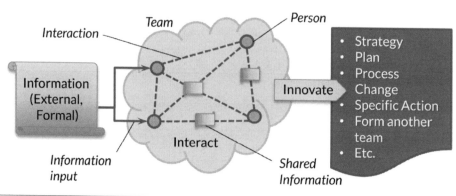

information or documents to the team from the formal information that exists in the larger context. The team members interact with one another through meetings, emails and phone calls, creating and exchanging further information. Finally, an innovative decision emerges and is put into action.

There is little with which to overtly disagree in this description. And yet, the real world shows little enough evidence to suggest that we are trying to support such a model. BI tools, as well as focusing on the data and nothing but the data, take a strictly individualistic approach to decision making support. Other than a few notable exceptions, BI vendors have added only a thin veneer of collaborative functions to existing individual-centric tools. Enterprise-oriented collaborative tools support team building and management, as well as the use of shared documents, but provide no specific support for decision making. The informality of the process and the lack of tool support mean that we lose much of importance that goes on within the work of the team, including:

1. *Context:* The business environment and background to the decision, team members involved and the activities involved in initiating and closing the decision-making process

2. *Consequences:* Non-closure of the loop between expectations set in the decision and what actually happened in reality

3. *Interactions:* All informal communications among team members and with parties external to the team, including meetings (face-to-face and electronic), phone calls, instant messages, Tweets, and email, other than that managed centrally

4. *History:* The unfolding of thought processes leading to options considered and discarded, performance of team members, when events happened and information was requested/received, and a formal record of how innovation occurred

We have encountered point solutions to these issues previously. Points 1 and 2 require the extension of process-oriented thinking to decision-making processes, as discussed in the MEDA model in Sections 7.3 and 9.4. Points 3 and, to a lesser extent, 4 are addressed by the concept of informal information introduced in Section 3.4. In order to bring these aspects together in a complete solution, we must first examine two distinct but interrelated levels of activity involved: what happens within individual activities and

Figure 9-13:
The iSight team
decision making
model

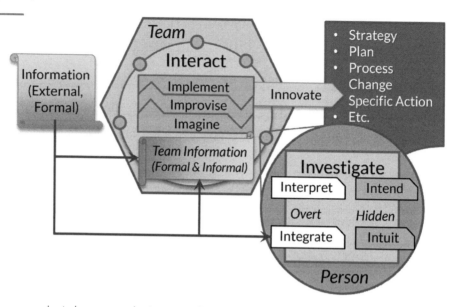

Figure 9-13:
The iSight team
decision making
model

what happens between the participants in the team. Together, these two aspects create the insight required. This underlying goal and the fact that all of the components begin with the letter "I" leads us to the term *iSight model* (Devlin, 2012), shown in Figure 9-13, for innovative team-based decision making.

The iSight[5] team decision making model

In comparison with Figure 9-12, we see a number of changes. First, the individuals in the team are defined in terms of their primary role—investigation. Second, the activities of the team are brought together and managed in a functional block—interaction. Third, the information resources—both formal and informal—of the team are integrated in a single, logical store.

Personal iSight: Investigation

When a person acts as an individual within a team decision context, her primary role is to *investigate* the information already available in the organization, largely in the formal documents and databases, but also the informal information gained through the team. In the process, she gains personal insights into the context, significance and implications of this information. This is the creation of meaning as discussed in Section 9.1. There are four constituent functions:

---

[5] Some of this material is reprinted from my article (Devlin, 2012a) in the Business Intelligence Journal with permission of 1105 Media, Inc.

1. *Integrate:* Collecting formal information from the business, the world at large, and other team members, the user creates new and combined information artifacts in the personal realm.

2. *Interpret:* Human interpretation supplies meaning and judgment to information received. It often requires detailed analysis and integration of further extended sources of information to provide a sufficient understanding of the situation and possible causes. Interpretation is rational, the typical analytical behavior supported by today's BI and office productivity tools.

3. *Intuit:* Internalized (or tacit) information and knowledge become the basis by which a user has flashes of inspiration about what is really going on, previously unseen correlations, possible solutions, and so on. This intuitive spark, for which minimal software support is possible, is driven by personal intention but, perhaps even more importantly, quickened through live discussion between co-workers as part of interaction below.

   Interpretation keeps us in the rationalistic, cause-and-effect world of Newtonian physics—the land of the left brain. Novel thought arises in intuition, in the realm of the right brain.

4. *Intend:* In another highly personal and internal behavior with minimal software support, the user is motivated by business, team and personal goals to gather and analyze information, make conclusions in a particular direction, and play a role in decision making.

   Interpretation and intuition have no direction *per se.* For that, we need to set intention. Intention drives thought and behavior. At its simplest and purest, intention drives the business analyst in search of complete, relevant information. More broadly, it drives decision-making towards a business goal, such as maximizing profit or reducing customer churn. More deeply, intention drives the interpretation in a particular direction, to prove or disprove hypotheses that emerge from intuitive or interpretive thinking. More hidden, perhaps, intention includes personal goals, which may be overt and aligned to the business or even covert for personal gain—or downright illegal.

In terms of software support, integration and interpretation have been the focus of most attention in the evolution of BI tools, with a continuing, almost exclusive concentration on numerical data that remains a concern, given the explosion of human-sourced information and the value to be found there, as we discussed in Chapters 6 and 8. The concepts of well-informed decision making are vital to personal iSight. Intention and intuition are hidden aspects of the personal sphere; they cannot easily be supported by software tools. However, we envisage that software will offer some peripheral support. For example, it could detect and record intention through pattern analysis and data mining. The most obvious reason for this is to track and prevent illegal and inappropriate decisions. Such analytics could also discover behavior patterns characteristic of users who consistently make "better" or more useful decisions for the business, enabling development of appropriate training, motivation and reward programs. Another, broader, reason would be to facilitate distinguishing between intended and collateral effects of decisions taken, feeding into adaptive business methods.

Team iSight: Interaction

As already noted, the interaction function is the link between the behaviors of individuals and the actions of the team as a whole. Interaction is the engine that drives the team together and towards the goal of making a decision. From a team view, interaction focuses on the ongoing orchestration of the individual interactions of team members and the information they use and create. Interaction thus monitors all team conversations and acts as gatekeeper for all inbound and outbound information. For the individual, to interact means to step up to the whiteboard, grab a marker, and begin drawing boxes and arrows, all the while talking animatedly. For the team environment, interaction is capturing the drawings and the conversation, extracting information from them, relating the content to other information artifacts and storing it all for future use. Think team room software—on steroids. We now have the technology to digitally record many or all of these informal interactions. As more of the conversation is recorded, more informal information can be captured, analyzed and reused. Of course, the issues of privacy and personal freedom must be addressed.

With this, we've reached the nub of innovation. We humans are social animals. And business is a highly social affair. Personal intention, intuition and interpretation are enhanced through social interaction. Social networking refines our interpretations, expands our intuition, and tests our intentions. Decision making in business is largely a collective process, whether openly in democratic companies or hidden and denied—but still widespread—in an autocratic environment. Interaction with colleagues and competitors, customers and contacts, is both the lifeblood of the business and the wellspring of innovation. In a world where businesses are increasingly international and geographically dispersed, where people are increasingly comfortable conducting social intercourse online, an ever-larger set of information is exchanged electronically, discussions are digital, and conclusions reached in the ether. And, more than ever, all of this can be stored, tracked, interpreted and reused. We have reached a tipping point where social networking and collaboration tools can provide the framework for decision making and enhance the process itself, so that decision makers can obtain real benefits. These include reuse of prior experience and artifacts, savings in time and costs and, most importantly, improvements in the quality, effectiveness and tracking of decision making.

Within the team environment are three further functions that support interaction and enable team innovation:

5. *Implement:* This process creates the collaborative team. People added and removed, meetings arranged, and documents shared. Implementation covers the drudgery we forget until we're asked to create a team to solve some problem and struggle to gather phone numbers and email addresses, book meeting rooms, and so on. Without the mundane activities of implementation, the magic of imagination and improvisation never materialize.

6. *Imagine:* Imagine is the team-level counterpart of personal intuition. In an effective team, ideas arise through the interaction of the team members. Conversation and challenge inspire individuals to new thinking; individuals feed new thoughts into the conversation, which in turn generates new ideas for the team. Conceptual combination—the synthesis and merging of previously separate, individual concepts—gives rise to new ideas.

    Brainstorming, group ideation, decision templating, feedback and co-editing, mind-mapping, and whiteboarding are among a wide variety of techniques used in team imagining. Some have been developed for physically collocated teams where much of the interaction is face-to-face. Some have been extended for electronic use or specifically created for virtual teams using Web 2.0 techniques to support electronic communication.

7. *Improvise:* While the drive in imagining is to expand the set of possible ideas and solutions, improvisation focuses on what is actually possible in the given situation, taking account of physical constraints such as budget, current physical and staffing limitations, competition, etc. As Figure 9-13 shows, imagining, improvisation and implementation coexist in a tight symbiotic loop; an effective team moves fluidly back and forth among the three. The discipline of improvisation balances the creative energy of imagination; the team's focus and view contracts or expands accordingly.

Consensus building, voting and obtaining buy-in from team members and external stakeholders are all part of the social processes of improvisation. Many of the techniques of imagining can also be used here—such as co-editing, decision templating and mind-mapping—to aid in the development and documentation of a solution that is likely to gain wider support and lead to a politically acceptable and implementable change in the business.

Capturing the decision context

Human interaction has, since time immemorial, been face-to-face. Such communication is highly effective and information rich. This information has typically been ephemeral—mostly lost as soon as it is created or dependent on highly unreliable human memory for subsequent use. The invention of writing over 5,000 years ago enabled interaction at a distance and provided a permanent record of the information conveyed. However, in comparison to face-to-face communication, writing is information poor. Until recently, our choices in interaction were proximate rich information vs. incomplete long-distance information and fleeting comprehensive information vs. permanent incomplete information. Electronic communication and digitization have dramatically shifted the balance between information density, proximity and permanence. We can optimize all three in the business environment—provided we store and manage the informal information currently lost in traditional, poorly tooled team decision making. Ungoverned or poorly managed information is always in danger of being lost; therefore, in the team-based decision making approach, we must carefully manage such information. The central role of the interaction component both within the team and as the linkage point between individuals and the team allows it to moderate and manage all information input to and output from the team information store.

Today's social networking and team room tools support the capture and management of all text-based interactions and file sharing between team members. However, such interaction is slow and relatively information poor. Voice messaging is also now common, offering the potential for storing both audio content and text captured via voice recognition. Advances in processing power and bandwidth could enable storage and use of visual interaction. As we move towards this more interactive approach, we can envisage a more attractive environment for team members. Participation and trust levels increase. Meetings can be replayed to check what was actually said. Decisions can be more easily reviewed and revisited to understand how a particular decision evolved and, if necessary, take action to avoid future problems developing.

At the heart of every decision is a *decision context* consisting of people, their behaviors, and the information used. In a highly predictable business environment, the people and information involved in a particular decision context are largely stable; whenever a particular type of decision is required, the same actors and information are involved, creating and using tacit knowledge. In the biz-tech ecosystem, *ad hoc*, multidisciplinary teams are assembled to deal with specific situations. In this case, only limited tacit knowledge can be carried forward, so the explicit capture and storage of informal—as well as formal—information becomes mandatory. In fact, the capture and storage of the decision context is a primary driver for the interact function. Simply facilitating interaction between team members—offered by many BI tools—is hardly

> ## Innovative decision making
>
> *Decision making that is well-informed and insightful but is also fully cognizant of the external environment—an ever-changing physical and interpersonal landscape—in which the decision occurs.*
>
> *Innovative decision making is the ultimate goal and, in reality, the only possibility for making effective decisions in the biz-tech ecosystem.*

novel today and does little to encourage user involvement and teaming. Faithfully recording the decision context provides the incentive for team members to participate and enables decisions to be reviewed for the following:

- *Coherence:* Closing the loop on the decision. Did we achieve the desired outcome? Could any unintended consequences have been identified in the decision-making process?

- *Reuse:* Can the team knowledge be captured and reused in whole or in part for future decisions? Can we speed up similar decisions in the future? And if so, how?

- *Participation:* Were there team members who were central to the decision? Were they overly influential? Were there under-contributing members? Were personal agendas or motivations at play in the decision, and if so, were they ethical and legal?

iSight: a logical architecture

The pathways and processes described above exist today. Unfortunately, they're largely unnoticed. Significant parts of them are implemented only manually. Some, as we've seen, even have basic software support in Enterprise 2.0 tools. We can thus envisage an architectural platform to integrate and enhance the investigation and interaction pathways as seen in Figure 9-14, showing three high-level groupings of the most important functions needed. Further details can be found in my 2012 white paper[6] (Devlin, 2012). As of mid-2013, none of these components have been developed.

Interaction Choreographer

The interaction choreographer (IC), which is part of the choreography function of the REAL architecture, is the heart of the iSight platform. It coordinates and tracks all digital interactions that occur between the individual members of the team. Its role begins with the creation of the team, gathering profile information about the team members. If individuals have been involved in previous team efforts, relevant contribution information may also be included. As the team evolves, changes in team membership are also recorded.

---

[6] Thanks to Scott Davis, CEO Lyzasoft for his invaluable contribution to this paper.

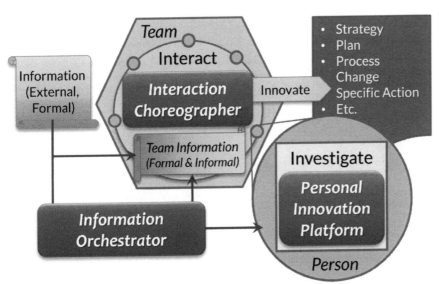

Figure 9-14:
An initial iSight
architecture

The main role of the IC is to keep a record of all digital interactions of the team members. This is a background function that requires no additional work for team members. Its value-add for the team is the ability to easily find and use the history of the team's work. Who knows about this topic? Who proposed that? Why did we choose that option over the other? What happened in that meeting I missed? The IC does *not* define or direct the flow of the decision-making process; rather it records it, creating the links between individuals and their interactions, between individuals and information, and between information and interactions. This record persists after the team has disbanded, allowing reuse of the process flow and information resources in future, similar projects and supporting evaluation of individuals' contributions to the decision process and deliverables. The IC depends on the information orchestrator for all links to stored information.

Information Orchestrator

The information orchestrator (IO) is simply a distributed content management system and store, which is part of the assimilation function of the REAL architecture. As we've already seen, the vast majority of the formal information used in decision making already exists and is thus stored in existing databases and content stores. The IO provides virtualized access to these stores. Formal information is also created during decision making but is often stored locally and poorly managed. For such information, the IO provides a shared content store, virtualized access, or a combination of both. Informal information, on the other hand, is largely unrecorded or discarded after use. The role of the IO is vital here in providing permanent storage for such information.

Personal Innovation Platform

The personal innovation platform (the friendly PIP?) is the individual user's interface to the working environment of the team. Its goal is to be invisible to the users, seamlessly extending their use of existing collaboration and BI tools. So, rather than being a brand-new user interface, it is a virtualized mashup of the existing tool interfaces used by the individual in their day-to-day work.

ThoughtPoint

In the biz-tech ecosystem, a business will live or die based on the level of innovation underlying its decisions. Such innovation is best achieved through collaborative teamwork that maximizes the use of the formal and informal information resources of the enterprise. Building an iSight system should be well within the reach of a skilled IT department, although an integrating product from a vendor spanning the BI and collaborative spaces would be optimal.

9.7   IDEAL ARCHITECTURE (5): PEOPLE

So, finally, we come to the top layer of the IDEAL conceptual architecture, representing the human aspects of this environment. Here, again, we find three dimensions or axes of interest, as shown in Figure 9-15, against which we can position aspects of human behavior in order to better understand their key characteristics. As in the case of the information and process layers, the classes on each axis should be viewed as a continuum, merging from one to the next, rather than discrete divisions. Like the process layer, the people layer is somewhat simpler than its information counterpart, with each axis here representing a single, simple characteristic. An intersection point of these three dimensions represents a *human pursuit*—the mental concept of what a person seeks to achieve.

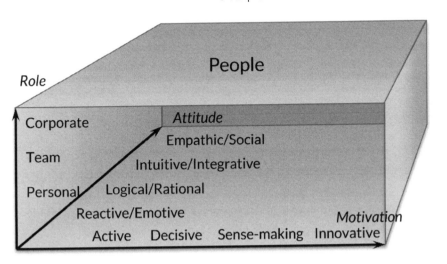

Figure 9-15:
Dimensions of the
people layer

The dimension of attitude

Exploring human insight and the characteristics of the evolved mind in Section 9.3 led to the conclusion that all human behavior operates at a number of levels, which we'll call attitudes for simplicity. This conclusion applies equally to decision making by individuals in the business setting. While many of us have been taught to value rational thinking above all else, modern psychology and neurobiology shows otherwise. The *attitude* people axis therefore aligns to the current, widely accepted mental model. At the lowest level, we see *reactive/emotive* impulses. In its more problematic manifestation, these are driven by unconscious woundings, underpinning antisocial actions that are not in the best interests of the business or the person. In a more positive sense, feelings—ranging from fear to joy, determination to love, and more—are found here, providing the impetus and energy to do or think about something. The goal here is not to eliminate the reactive/emotive; rather, we seek to integrate the negative and positive characteristics to create a more holistic foundation for higher mental functioning.

Logical/rational attitude—the lord of the left brain—needs no further explanation here. It is so deeply embedded in Western culture that we default to imagining it as both the most desirable and most prevalent mode of thinking. We've seen that this is a myth. While vital for many tasks, logic alone can miss the bigger picture and come to distinctly inhuman conclusions.

The realm of the right brain—*intuitive/integrative* attitude—is all about seeing the forest for the trees and finding the ah-ha insights. This is the source of creativity and the mother of invention. Alone, it is artistic and conceptual, but working together with the structured and rational left brain, the outcome is the seed of innovation that the biz-tech ecosystem seeks.

The final class on the mental axis is *empathic/social* attitude. In evolutionary terms, the most recently emerged and most developed part of the brain, this is the foundation of relating at the personal, group and societal levels. Collaboration springs from here, and with it, our best opportunities for innovation.

The axis of role

Section 9.4 and the adaptive decision cycle introduced three roles in human behavior, which map to the *role* axis. The *personal* level involves solitary work. The in-depth research and exploration supported by today's BI tools and information foraging operate here.

Team working emerges from empathic/social attitude and is supported mainly by collaborative tools. This team role should not be confused with the traditional team approach of a manager who orders and evaluates workers, or even with the leader who must inspire them. This is much more about teams of equals, collaborating towards a shared goal, contributing their diverse skills, and acting according to their unique, evolved personas.

At the *corporate* level, we see the hierarchical and process-oriented thought most familiar in traditional enterprise structures. Human behavior in the 21st century cannot be constrained by the hive mentality of corporate thought at its most extreme, although it will continue to be required in some circumstances. Businesses that thrive in the biz-tech ecosystem will need the personal motivation and team innovation characteristics of the other classes on this axis in increasing quantity and quality.

The facet of motivation

The *motivation* axis brings together considerations from throughout this book as to why people act as they do in the context of business information and process. As such, it provides the primary linkage from the people layer to the layers below it. In particular, it relates to the business effect axis of the process layer.

Active motivation is perhaps the simplest and most common motivation in business, especially in day-to-day operations and in time-constrained or highly driven activities. The operative phrase is often JFDI[7]. This is the human behavior that operates in the pure act phase of MEDA and is most widely and fully supported by IT today through operational applications. These typically apply very rigid processes and controls to ensure governance, which, unfortunately, limit flexibility to change or grow. While SOA offers additional flexibility here, the likelihood is that less will change here for users than in the support for the other classes of motivation. Operational analytics / decision management will take over some of the decision making that occurs on today's operational-informational boundary.

The *decisive* class of motivation operates at the top of the MEDA cycle in both the decision phase and the transition to act. It is seen most obviously in people to whom an organization grants the right to make decisions of some level of significance: managers and executives. However, everybody in the organization is responsible for some decisions of value. Cleaning staff who notice a leaking toilet valve face a decision on whether to take time from a highly regimented and measured schedule to report it—a tradeoff between saving the company money on water charges and the possibility of criticism by a supervisor.

As we move to the lower part of the MEDA cycle, we encounter the *sense-making* motivation prevalent in monitor and evaluate. This leads to the behavior of seeking a story to explain some phenomenon and what to do about it. In the more traditional, rational view, this is where BI tools—and spreadsheets—operate. However, as we've seen, much more is at play here in the way the mind works. The right brain plays an integrative and intuitive role. Team working, with its social and empathic skills, is required. Significant expansion and improvements in IT support are needed here, driven by the explosion of information types available but also, perhaps

---

[7] If you don't know the meaning of JFDI, check it out at
http://www.urbandictionary.com/define.php?term=JFDI

more importantly, by the recognition that human behavior is far more complex and nuanced than business typically imagines.

This leads us to *innovative* motivation that can and should occur throughout the MEDA cycle. It is most prevalent at the junction points of the four phases—the ah-ha moments that move us from one phase to the next, from one level of behavior to another. This motivation leads to the creation of novelty, the spark for new products or processes. It is the least understood, most poorly supported and least managed of all four motivations. In the biz-tech ecosystem, it is arguably the source of the most important behaviors and requires substantial business and IT focus in the future.

The space of pursuit

For IT readers, the people layer usually presents the greatest challenge. There is a tendency to consider the software tools that people use directly—BI tools, collaboration software, tools supporting creative thinking, and so on—and fit them into this space. While understandable, this is misleading. Software tools are intrinsically elements of process that use information in the layer beneath that. IT designs and delivers, supports and governs in these lower layers. Business, a social and organizational construct composed of, run by, and aimed at people, lives and breathes in the people layer. Behavior resides in people and their *pursuits*, as defined by the intersection of their attitudes, motivations and organizational roles.

Despite the absence of software tools here, IT ignores this layer at its peril. In fact, much of the traditional disconnect between IT and business springs from IT's disregard for the subtleties of the human condition. Truth to tell, business dysfunction stems from the same source. The work in understanding and defining this layer of the architecture lies with the softest of sciences from psychology to sociology, from behavioral to organizational science. This work has only just begun.

9.8   IN PRACTICE—INTRODUCING COLLABORATIVE DECISION MAKING

Much of the discussion about decision making revolves around software support and technology—the mechanics of what BI tools can do. This chapter moves the conversation to the personal level, to what happens in the human mind. However, this topic requires both fundamental research and a significant shift in thinking by the majority of the business community. In practical terms, a starting point for immediate action is in the area of collaboration and its application to BI. This is far beyond adding notes and sharing screens as offered by most BI tools today. It's about reinventing team collaboration, as discussed in Sections 9.4 and 9.6. We can begin with the following steps in three distinct areas:

A new approach to spreadsheets

✓ Break the spreadsheet roundabout. A major part of the problem with spreadsheets lies in their viral distribution and infection of the organization, rather than in the innovative work that analysts perform within the tool itself. Encouraging the use of basic collaborative tools for peer review and improvement of spreadsheets can reduce the spread of errors and interrupt the reuse-and-adapt process among peers within and across departments.

✓ Control spreadsheet promotion. Collaborative tools such as scoring and voting approaches can be used to support a new process by which useful and successful spreadsheets can be identified by IT and production-ready BI tools with certified data introduced to replace them. The goal in this point, and the previous one, is certainly not to reduce or eliminate spreadsheet; rather it is to focus their use on innovative tasks where they excel (pun intended) and use BI tools for production tasks where control and management is vital.

Innovation for the sake of innovation

✓ Based on the investigation into and storing of informal information described in Section 3.9, prototype innovative team decision making by adding Enterprise 2.0 collaborative and team building/working tools. This should be done in an area of the business where novel thinking and teamwork are vital, such as product design or marketing campaign planning. In particular, explore the personal and social implications of the approach, rather than just the product outcomes or technical issues.

Novel support for strategic executive decision making

✓ Tackle strategic decision making (one last time!) with a novel proof of concept. Executive-level decision making has very different information needs and working processes than the much more common tactical level that is the target of most BI efforts. The information needed is broader and softer, external and internal. Judgment, experience and gut feel play greater roles. Collaboration is central. Outcomes are longer term and wider in impact and consequences.

✓ Apply Enterprise 2.0 tools and techniques to support collaboration, teamwork and information use. BI tools and the data warehouse are far down the agenda here. So, focus on understanding the decision-making process. What can be automated? Where must it be adaptive? How can information be gathered, managed, made readily available?

✓ Investigate the MEDA model, especially the link between act and monitor. How can we understand if the expected outcomes of the decision actually occurred? Over what time frame? Were there other events that influenced success or failure? Could they have been anticipated? This investigation, and the previous two bullets, offer the opportunity to explore decision making in its broadest scope and as far from traditional BI as is possible. In that respect, it might be the most useful exploration of decision making possible.

9.9   CONCLUSIONS

*A*ll innovation is social innovation. Innovation does not happen 'out there' in the world of objects, but in society and in...the minds of the users, which are intrinsically integrated with [their] activities" (Tuomi, 2003). To find innovation—indeed, to truly discover insight—we must try to understand people.

In the biz-tech ecosystem, we can sometimes get too focused on the tech to the exclusion of the biz. Discovering innovation, demands that we must delve deeply into the people whose business this is and ask: How do they perceive the world? This begins with the substrate of individual, deeply personal meanings we assign to information. The notion of a single version of the truth does not exist at the personal level, nor even very much in the team view; it is an artifact of the enterprise, and circumscribed portions of the enterprise at that. And if we allow personal meaning, the theory of rational—however bounded—decision making is seen to stand on shaky ground.

We have looked deeper into the psyche and explored how the brain-mind complex is now becoming understood by neuroscientists. The roles that emotion and intuition, as well as the integration of the personality play in how we see the world, assign significance to, and reason—in the broadest sense of the word—about it. The modern psychology of sense-making describes a very different internal world than that assumed by most BI software as it ostensibly offers decision support. The outlines of a new approach to data and information are emerging. And just in time, as information is exploding in our faces and we need new models to cope.

At the social level, Web and Enterprise 2.0 have moved us somewhat further along the path towards a new model of innovative team working. We can envisage some of the tools and techniques we need to preserve the context in which decisions are made, the better to trace the emergence of insight, to identify the moments of innovation, and to discover the underlying motivations that enabled or denied progress. In this social milieu, we can see how we might monitor personal behavior, whether we choose to use it for good or for ill. The model of iSight offers an integrated and adaptive approach to real collaborative work within the enterprise.

Having reached, at last, the topmost, people layer of the conceptual, IDEAL architecture, we find ourselves standing above software and data, attempting to map the human mind in some simplistic, three-dimensional space. Of course, we can only fail: the mind is multidimensional, complex beyond such representation. But the value of the model is that it gives us a starting point, especially those of us with a more technical bent, to begin to explore what makes people tick, what they pursue and how they create and rec-reate the business, and what information and process support they need. From the concept of IT supporting the business, we move to the thought of IT supporting *all* the people who *are* the business.

ROADMAP

→ *IDEAL architecture to link business and IT:* The three layer enterprise architecture provides the basis for business and IT to create the biz-tech ecosystem together; scenarios cut across information, process and data

→ *REAL implementation scenarios:* (i) Migration from the enterprise data warehouse, (ii) rejoining operational and informational systems and (iii) introducing collaborative, innovative team decision making

→ *The threat and promise of Business unIntelligence:* Understanding and engaging Human unIntelligence for a view of the problems we create and those we could solve.

"Usually, when we hear or read something new, we just compare it to our own ideas. If it is the same, we accept it and say that it is correct. If it is not, we say it is incorrect. In either case, we learn nothing." — Thich Nhat Hanh

"Vocations that we wanted to pursue, but didn't, bleed, like colors, on the whole of our existence." — Honoré de Balzac

In choosing the title *Business unIntelligence*, my aim was to create cognitive dissonance, particularly for readers who hail from the world of BI and data warehousing. Bram Stoker used the term *undead* to describe Dracula[1], meaning neither dead nor alive, but something entirely different that is difficult to define and harder to encompass its full import. In journeying with me this far, I trust that you have discovered the subtlety of unIntelligence. That it is now clear that Business unIntelligence is both BI and more than BI, both its negation and its opposite. That in this particular *"hearing or reading of something new"*, you have learned something.

That, I hear you say, is all very well, but what shall we do with it?

In the telling of the then-novel story of data warehousing in the mid-1980s, I learned that evangelizing a new architectural idea is not enough. Businesses need clear and relatively safe roadmaps to move from where they are to implement something of their new learning. They need to see where the benefits may lie; it is easier for most to do nothing until it is no longer safe to do so. Vendors too need encouragement to build the new tools and techniques and promote them, enabling and encouraging a new approach. Much of this chapter is about creating that momentum. We look again at the

---

[1] My thanks to David Snowden (Snowden, 2005) for reminding me of the undead.

IDEAL conceptual architecture holistically to see how it can bridge the business-IT gap and offer a common language for progress. We examine how businesses today can start to implement pieces of the REAL logical architecture from a variety of starting points.

That is the practical answer. And then, I will finally and firmly close with, of course, a call to action.

10.1 IDEAL ARCHITECTURE (6): SUMMARY

Figure 10-1:
Salk Institute of Biological Studies, La Jolla, CA, 1959
Lois Kahn, architect

Of conceptual architecture, Louis Kahn, the Estonian-born and Philadelphia-based architect (of buildings), said: *"It doesn't work, it doesn't have to work. [Frank Lloyd] Wright had the shape conceived long before he knew what was going into it"* (Frampton, 2007). The same could be said for the IDEAL conceptual architecture. The three layers are not novel. And many other layered architectures include additional or alternative levels; technology is often favored. The initial driver for this image was to emphasize the unity of information as an integrated resource of the biz-tech ecosystem, in contrast to the layered scheme of the data warehouse. A similar driver for process soon emerged: the necessary unification of business and IT processes driven by both business need and technological possibility. That people should be a technology-free layer took longer to conceive. But the human mind that drives both business and technology exists independent of business and precedes technology. The purpose of the IDEAL architecture is thus to enable and drive a different way of thinking about the relationships between information, process and people; a novel approach to the conversation between business and IT, whose symbiosis is a necessity for the biz-tech ecosystem.

Five key characteristics of the conceptual architecture are included in its acronym:

- *Integrated:* within each layer and across all three, a unity of thought and purpose drives the approach; all aspects of this environment must link seamlessly together

- *Distributed:* each layer of this architecture consists of a concept space with diverse attributes of equal importance, individual independence, and mutual dependence; there is no single, central control point

- *Emergent:* this is a mathematically and socially chaotic/complex environment, the characteristics of which cannot all be predicted or calculated in advance; order materializes from the disordered to drive coherent structure and behavior

- *Adaptive:* as business needs and technological possibilities change, the architecture is sufficiently agile to adjust to and take advantage of them without re-architecting

- *Latent:* being latent, or hidden, the conceptual architecture is not in a form that can be directly implemented; it is a guide for business and IT thought and conversation about what is desired and possible

The remaining four characteristics are equally important, but didn't make it into the acronym:

- *Complete:* although impossible to prove and perhaps immodest to claim, the architecture aims to fully describe all aspects of the biz-tech ecosystem that drive thinking about how it can be designed and delivered

- *Elegantly simple:* the picture is simple enough to be understood by both business and IT and elegant enough to enable coherent discussion of the possible consequences of actions and designs under consideration

- *Enterprise-wide:* the architecture is most effective—and perhaps can only be effective at all—when applied across the entire scope of the activities of the enterprise

- *Open-system:* in contrast to the closed system thinking of many IT architectures, the IDEAL architecture crosses the enterprise boundaries to include the external world within which the business operates, by which it is influenced, and it intends to influence in turn

Enterprise Architecture

The characteristics above place IDEAL in the rather ill-defined category of enterprise architecture explored in *recrEAtion* (Potts, 2010). The Enterprise Architecture Research Forum (EARF) defines enterprise architecture as *"the continuous practice of describing the essential elements of a socio-technical organization, their relationships to each other and to the environment, in order to understand complexity and manage change"* (Van der Merwe, et al., 2009), a definition that has been submitted to the Open Group. The Zachman Framework provides perhaps the most complete and well-engineered view of the concepts and relationships of an enterprise architecture. The six-column information systems architecture framework, introduced in 1992 (Sowa & Zachman, 1992), has evolved to the Zachman Framework Version 3.0 (Zachman, 2011). The IDEAL architecture addresses a subset of that scope and provides a simpler view of that more limited scope. Broadly speaking, the three layers map to the columns—what, how, where, who, when, why—of the Zachman Framework. Information and process map directly to *what* and *how*. People maps to *who* and *why*. *When* appears partially as axes in both the information and process layers. *Where* does not appear (as yet) in the IDEAL architecture, because the concept of physical location of the three key characteristics of information, process and people has diminished to some extent with the emergence of Cloud and mobile. All three layers of the IDEAL architecture exist in the two upper rows—contexts and concepts—of the Zachman Framework.

Modeling business activities across the layers

Taking a vertical view through the layers of the IDEAL architecture defines the relationship from personal/business pursuits, through processes—both fixed and adaptive—that implement the ideas to the information resources thus required or created. In a general sense, this vertical relationship describes a model of business activities from their initial conception to full implementation. We might call it IDEAL modeling. Unfortunately, to my knowledge no language or methodology exists that could be used to formally define the details of such a model. However, two examples can show how useful this model would be.

Financial performance analysis

A traditional, straight-forward BI scenario leads to a simple map of a business activity to the architecture, as shown in Figure 10-2. In the people layer, the pursuit of a financial analyst investigating some aspect of the company's performance is categorized as sense-making of a logical/rational mental approach in a personal or individual role. Moving to the process layer, this links to a single instance of function, classed as an activity in scope, over an extended timespan, with an interpreting business effect. This clearly maps to some BI tool. Linking to information, we find this function uses reconciled/historical, derived information at an enterprise level of reliance.

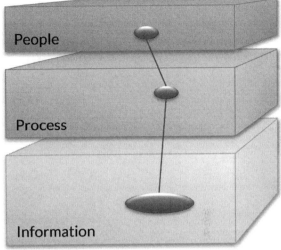

However, a more realistic view of how the financial analyst performs his work reveals the picture shown in Figure 10-3. In reality, along with the BI tool, the analyst uses a spreadsheet (the second ellipse in the process layer) to play with the data, which accesses information at the personal level of reliance/usage and stable timeliness/consistency. The issue identified here is well known. The use of this latter data, because it's at the personal reliance level, can and does introduce data consistency problems. The issue is often attributed to the lack of governance in spreadsheets, which is partially true, of course. However, we see here a more fundamental problem: the existence of two independent instances of process prevents formal recognition of any information inconsistency that exists in the lower layer. Reconciliation—if it occurs at all—falls to the analyst himself. The existence of data in the two areas of the information space is both reasonable and realistic; it makes perfect sense that the analyst should require some personal set of data to play with, record his hypotheses, check assumptions and so on. The real problem occurs in the process layer, where the two instances of function should be integrated by embedding spreadsheet functionality in the BI tool or providing more comprehensive data management and governance in the spreadsheet. Both these solutions actually depend on the tool vendors fixing their products. Imagining that IT can solve the problem in the information layer—the old call to simply eliminate "spreadmarts"—cannot work.

Figure 10-2:
Financial performance analysis in the IDEAL architecture (1)

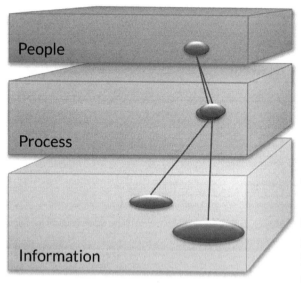

Figure 10-3:
Financial performance analysis in the IDEAL architecture (2)

This basic analysis points to a broad class of similar problems that can and do arise with the spread of big data. Much of this data, originating outside the enterprise, is classed as vague (at best) on the reliance/usage axis of the information layer. Some of it is not even stable in terms of its timeliness/consistency and it may fall in the raw class at one end of the spectrum or textual or multiplex at the other in its structure/context. Great care is required when combining such information with enterprise class, stable-to-historical data (the data used to manage and run the business). At the process layer, using Hadoop to handle one class and a relational database the other will inevitably lead to chaos in the longer term unless strict procedures are put in place in the process layer to handle the disparity and ensure that business users do not end up performing "unnatural acts" by combining data that was never reconciled. .

The marketing and sales support function

At the opposite extreme of process complexity, we consider how the marketing and sales support function might manage a campaign in Figure 10-4, focusing on two pursuits to limit pictorial complexity. We consider two related business needs in campaign management: enhancing aspects of the campaign and monitoring the impact of such changes during its course and reacting accordingly. This is the type of real-time, closed-loop business activity that characterizes a company operating in the biz-tech ecosystem—action enables invention, and invention must lead to action. In the people layer, we depict two distinct pursuits. To the right, campaign enhancement (A) proceeds from sense-making/innovative motivation, at a personal/team level using a range of logical and intuitive faculties. Monitoring and reaction (B) on the left shows active/decisive motivation on the part of a single individual using logical faculties.

Moving to the process layer, these human pursuits map in a somewhat simplified view to the following tasks:

- Website change (a) flows from campaign enhancement and encompasses the decision about what action to take and the definition/application of changes to the site. It is positioned as a workflow of extended timespan and actioning effect.

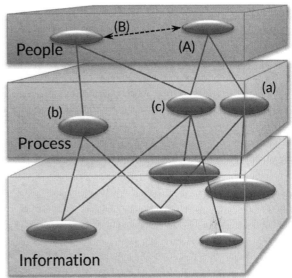

- Response monitoring (b) flows from monitoring and reaction above and occurs at the event/transaction scope in a compact timeframe with recording/conditioning effect.

- A/B testing (c) flows from both pursuits at the people level and is the task designed to test changes to the campaign by allocating incoming sessions to one of two buckets that receive different versions of the website. It is positioned as a workflow of extended timespan with interpreting/actioning effect.

Figure 10-4: Campaign management in the IDEAL architecture

- These positionings are vague and indicative because the process is only loosely defined here; in reality, many more tasks would be involved. In particular, we could envisage an overarching, coordinating task with multiple levels of subtasks in a full process definition. At the information layer, the complexity of the nuggets and inclusions (see Section 8.8) is beyond the scope of this simple picture to display, leading to the representation consisting of multiple information areas accessed by the three process tasks. In a deeper analysis, I would expect that a number of information nuggets would be identified roughly corresponding to the process tasks involved, with each nugget linking to a number of different types of information distributed throughout the information space.

This example demonstrates both the potential value and the crying need for a modeling tool spanning these three layers in order to map business needs to technological possibilities and *vice versa* in the biz-tech ecosystem.

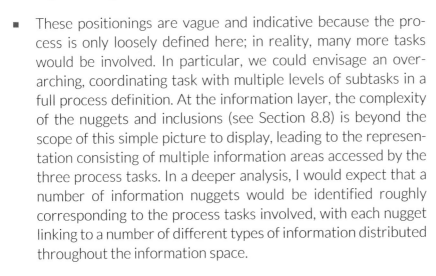

10.2   REAL ARCHITECTURE (4): IMPLEMENTATION

While the strength of the conceptual architecture lies in its ability to outline the story that links business thinking with the process and information required for implementing it, the REAL, logical architecture is aimed squarely at IT and providing the functionality needed. The characteristics of the architecture outlined in its acronym are:

- *Realistic:* implementing this architecture can begin today with existing technology and its full, foreseen extent is achievable with tools and techniques that can be expected within a few years

- *Extensible:* given the early stage of emergence of the biz-tech ecosystem, the functions and features are open to extension and expansion to allow technology evolution

- *Actionable:* the actions and approaches required of the business and IT are clearly identified at a high level and can easily be extrapolated to lower levels of detail

- *Labile:* the architecture is flexible enough to allow changes in business needs as the biz-tech ecosystem evolves

We explore at a high level three contrasting starting points and separate plans for implementing the REAL architecture. Of course, these plans could be pursued in parallel and, provided the organization can cope with the project complexity, could further benefit from a more integrated approach.

In the beginning was the data warehouse...

Many readers of this book will come from an information management or BI background, with substantial investments in existing supporting infrastructure. In addition, with the ongoing push to include big data in the information strategy of the business, it is likely that many organizations are undertaking new investment to address one or more big data characteristics expressed in the V-words of volume, velocity and variety. This presents a perfect opportunity to begin moving toward that REAL logical architecture—provided you avoid the temptation to create an independent big data environment and focus solely on predictive analytics or some highly specific business need. As we've seen, a considerable percentage of big data today is human-sourced information, characterized by poorly documented and changing context-setting information. Assigning an agreed base meaning can be a challenge. Furthermore, the programmatic Hadoop environment offers little to encourage any form of data governance or management. (For simplicity of discussion here, we equate Hadoop and the big data environments.) The clear and present danger of currently favored project approaches is longer-term information disintegration, even where the project delivers early business value.

What is required is an information-centric approach. One starting point lies in the pillar structure in the logical architecture, shown in Figure 10-5. The classic EDW, with its enterprise model and extensive metadata, is the obvious and necessary anchor point for big data. This is in no way to suggest that social media information, for example, should be loaded into the EDW. Rather, such human-sourced information is loaded into Hadoop as shown (a). This data and, in particular, the analytic results in Hadoop are linked to the EDW (b) via the assimilation function provided by a data virtualization tool. Product names identified in Hadoop, for example, should align to product IDs in the warehouse. Individuals in social media environments should be linked to customer IDs, where possible. This demands early and continuing focus in the big data environment where the tendency to "play" with the data often trumps the need to manage it. Contrary to some suggestions, the BI team must be intimately involved in the creation and ongoing use of the Hadoop environment, to provide the data

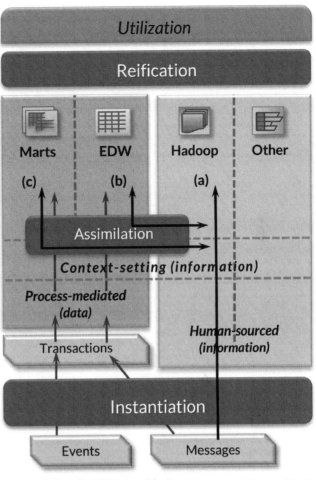

Figure 10-5: Implementing big data in the REAL architecture

management focus. Discoveries of interest in Hadoop must be "productionalized" as far as possible in the data warehouse and mart environments, (b) and (c) of the central pillar, especially if the outcomes are to be combined with internal data and financially significant or legally binding decisions based upon them. In essence, we are moving along the reliance/usage axis of the IDEAL architecture from unknown/vague to local/enterprise, which requires conscious investment of effort and money, as discussed in Chapter 4. Finally, data virtualization function in the reification box allows users to access data across the multiple pillars.

The REAL architecture provides a visual and explicit view of how to design a new big data environment in a way that supports the need of the biz-tech ecosystem for a well-integrated information resource that can be shared among all users as required.

Crossing the great operational-informational divide

Before big data became flavor *du jour*, my initial interest in the need for a new architecture to upgrade the data warehouse was driven by the increasing need of businesses for ever closer to real-time decisions. Today, this need is often rolled into big data under the banner of velocity. But that conflation is actually quite deceptive. In many cases, speeding up the decision cycle is completely unrelated to big data. The myth appears often in arguments around combined operational-informational environments, such as SAP HANA, in the form of "memory will always be more expensive than disk, so why or how should we put huge volumes of big data there?" This misses the point that the operational-informational divide is a characteristic of process-mediated data—the traditional data we always treasured, long before big data stole our hearts.

The structure of the central information pillar of the REAL architecture addresses the need for more timely decision making directly, as discussed already in Section 5.8, under the topic of core business information. In terms of early, practical implementation, we see a number of opportunities. The first, and most obvious, involves tackling the current widespread problem of data mart proliferation. This requires both organizational and technical approaches. Part of the problem arises from the rapid decrease in the price/performance ratio of servers, and indeed the emergence of

SaaS and PaaS BI solutions. In many instances, it is a low-cost or even no-cost option to create a new data mart when a new business need arises—allegedly. This, of course, is not a new problem. It is, however, becoming an ever bigger one because both the level of data duplication is increasing exponentially and the cost of fixing data inconsistency problems is rising even faster. In short, it may be cheaper to create a new copy of data initially, but in the longer term, it's a very bad deal. The solution is proper financial control of such expenditure—pure and simple. The technical approach to addressing data mart proliferation is to take advantage of the price/performance gains in the shared BI / data warehouse environment. Hardware and software optimized for BI are now powerful and cheap enough that many medium- to large-sized businesses could fruitfully consider a single machine solution where dependent data marts are replaced by views (as envisaged in the earliest data warehouse architecture shown in Figure 5-3) and specialized high-performance independent data marts are provided centrally by IT, if required. Data governance is maintained through metadata/CSI rather than ETL, leading to a more flexible and more easily maintained environment. Eliminating data mart proliferation is key to enabling operational-informational consolidation.

As noted, much of the current focus on such consolidation is driven by in-memory database technology. While this is understandable, we should also keep SOA firmly in the forefront of our thinking. Operational-informational consolidation demands much more than the processing power and database function to run read/write and read-only queries simultaneously on the same data. Understanding and supporting overlapping activities and workflows, as well as creating and managing the supporting CSI, are arguably more important. The adoption of an SOA approach and implementation of the corresponding infrastructure is thus an important and early aspect of implementing the REAL architecture. The equal involvement of IT architects and designers from both operational and informational sides of the house is mandatory. BI teams are not renowned for their understanding of process or the demands of high reliability and availability systems. Operational and web developers, in general, lack deep data management expertise. It was these considerations, among others, that led to the positioning of both the IDEAL and REAL architectures at the enterprise level—

including all operational, informational and collaborative systems—rather than as an upgrade only of BI and data warehousing.

We should be talking to one another

The Millennials are coming. The generation born during the approximately 20-year period from the early 1980s to 2000s have been in the workplace for a quite some time, but they are now moving into management and other positions of responsibility in ever greater numbers. While some of their alleged psychosocial characteristics—entitled, narcissistic and needing lots of direction are among the more common—may be open to question, there is no doubt that they are the most technologically literate, socialized and networked cohort ever to hit management (Alsop, 2008). These latter characteristics often drive mobile computing, bring your own device (BYOD), and other hardware technology programs. But, it is in the softer areas of social interaction and information use—Enterprise 2.0—that we will see the biggest impact. It may be a stereotype, but Millennials communicate electronically and continuously, get their information online, and are comfortable sharing information—even of a highly personal nature—on the network. Collaborative, technology-assisted decision making and innovation offers the potential for significant return on investment for leading edge companies in the biz-tech ecosystem.

Let's explore, using Figure 10-6, what aspects of the iSight model, introduced in Section 9.6, could be realized in the near term:

- *Personal Innovation Platform:* Enterprise 2.0 tools and techniques, together with collaborative software, provide social interaction between peers and groups, as well as information in support of specific goals. BI tooling, in its usual role and extended to informal and softer information, supports automated and rational approaches to personal decision making.

- *Information Orchestrator:* Content management systems, which store highly unstructured information, could be applied to collect, store and serve the informal information that underlies decision making.

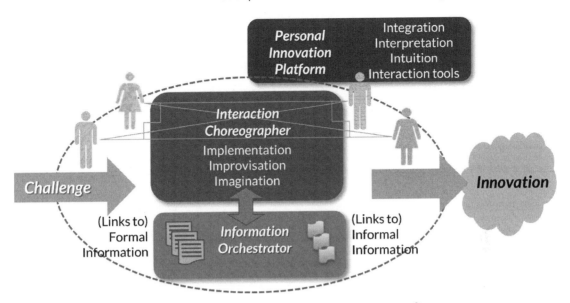

Figure 10-6:
Implementing iSight

- *Interaction Choreographer:* Workgroup and team support software provides some support for the more primitive aspects of this component, but significant extensions are needed.

We note that many BI tools have recently implemented "collaborative BI". This is a different and more limited concept than what we discuss here; it is likely to be a poor starting point for iSight. Collaborative BI starts from a model of BI where individuals do analysis, and then want to share it with others and work the analysis over with peers and managers. The focus is largely (and often entirely) on the results of BI analysis of formal, numerical information. The collaboration and content management described above start from an entirely different set of information and with a very different goal: supporting the process of decision making rather than the individual decisions themselves. Furthermore, as we examine the full scope of information used in decision making, we can clearly see that the remit of the BI team in most organizations is far too narrow to cover everything needed. The bottom line is that the iSight model must start with collaboration and the tools to support it broadly in the organization. This will require a rather different focus than traditional BI, although the skills and knowledge of the BI team around decision making will need to be applied. As electronically assisted collaboration becomes the norm in the organization, the concept of storing and using the informal information that supports that collaboration can be introduced—with due regard for privacy concerns and issues of control and transparency. Finally, BI tools can be applied to the stored content of the decision-making process in order to derive the full benefit of the iSight model.

10.3 PAST TENSE, FUTURE PERFECT

On September 15th, 2008, at 1:45 a.m., Lehman Brothers, the fourth largest investment bank in the US, filed for Chapter 11 bankruptcy protection. Over the following weeks, the global financial system ground to a halt. Liquidity drained from the system as short-term inter-bank lending all but stopped. There were multiple causes—proximate and far removed—of the crisis, but from one perspective, the majority of financial institutions just *stopped* making decisions. Despite running some of the most sophisticated BI systems and having access to hard and soft information in considerable volumes, decision making—immediate, tactical and even strategic, in some cases—simply seized up. The reason was equally simple: a complete loss of trust. If you were searching for irrationality in corporate decision making, few better examples can be found than in the rise and fall of the financial markets in the first decade of the new millennium. Other than the Dutch tulip mania of 1637... The behavior of financial institutions—from banks to investors and ratings agencies—in the development of a scheme based on sub-prime lending, mortgage-backed securities, credit default swaps, and a dependence on David X. Li's Gaussian copula function (Salmon, 2009) was driven more by emotions, from exuberance to hubris, than by rationality. Just as fear drove its eventual catastrophic implosion.

It is to complex, human situations such as the above that Business unIntelligence stretches. Traditional BI scratches the surface of the available and relevant information. It skirts issues of reliance that arise when information from multiple sources is integrated, and ignores meaning and motivation in a circumscribed belief that analyzing data alone will give useful answers. With Business unIntelligence, we look above the data trenches and simultaneously into the human mind to seek some semblance of sense. The composite landscape we encounter is both worrying and energizing—depending on how you ascribe meaning.

Dystopian dreams

A mere two and a half years ago, I wrote in Chapter 1 about Spread Networks' investment of $300 million to lay the shortest possible fiber optic cable and reduce the round trip for stock trades between Chicago and New York to approximately 13 milliseconds. By late 2012, McKay Brothers and Trade-worx were competing by microwave to reduce the time to 8.5-9 milliseconds. Similar and more extreme races are going on across the Atlantic and under the Arctic (Adler, 2012). All in the name of high frequency (HFT) or algorithmic trading, where milliseconds matter. Described as the logical extreme of the legendary use of a carrier pigeon by the Roth-schilds to trade on the outcome of the Battle of Waterloo in 1815, HFT is little more than highly mechanized, high-speed spread bet-ting, ideally with other people's money. In daily life, pushing argu-ments to logical extremes—more grandly *reductio ad absurdum* and less grandly, arguing with your teenage son—is generally acknowl-edged to be a good way of achieving nothing and losing face. The logical extreme of algorithmic trading has already set off loud alarms. The 600 point "flash crash" of the Dow Jones in five minutes on May 6th, 2010, followed by HFT Knight Capital's market disruption and loss of $440 million in 45 minutes on August 1st, 2012 are well known in the trade. Yet, as Andrew Haldane, execu-tive director for financial stability at the Bank of England, com-mented in 2012: *"What we have out there now is this complex array of multiple mutating interacting...algorithms...developing and travelling at ever higher velocities...And that's not an accident waiting to happen, that's an accident that has been happening with increasing frequency over the last few years"* (Harford, 2012). In fact, as I finalize this man-uscript, the news reports that a technology failure caused a three-hour crash of the Nasdaq stock market on August, 22nd, which fol-lowed a fortnight of notable outages of Google, Amazon, and more (Garside, 2013).

Figure 10-7:
Zeus Ammon associated with gambling, Museo Barracco, Roma

To the untrained eye of the non-economist, surely the real question is that beyond making profits for the owners of the servers in-volved and compromising market stability as an unintended conse-quence, how does HFT contribute to the *raison d'être* of the market mechanisms of funding development loans, reducing price uncer-tainty in trading, and so on? It seems that what we have here is another example of rational decision making gone mad—at two levels. First, the algorithms themselves, while mathematically rational, are combining in a chaotic system with unpredictable outcomes and are conceived by humans whose intent is, at best, wholly self-centered and, at worst, duplicitous. Second, the absence of any right-brain, integrative thought allows the development of systems with no vision of a real-world, sensible goal.

And, so as not to pick on financial services, similar monocular vision is prevalent among manufacturers, retailers and utilities in their rush to expand from print and other mass media to embrace micro-segmented, web-based, mobile-enabled pervasive advertising. Advertising decorates every corner of our lives and our world, illustrating the central role of decision making both in its consumption and creation. Advertising, after all, is designed to influence personal and social decision making—and not through rational evaluation of alternatives. From the Latin, *ad vertere*, "to turn toward", the purpose is unashamedly to create a desire for and to promote consumption of goods or services produced. And from there to return money to the producers to make more goods or services, which must in turn be sold in a depressing, positive feedback loop. As Sut Jhally, professor of Communication at the University of Massachusetts at Amherst, opines: *"the function of [the advertising industry is] to create a culture in which desire and identity would be fused with commodities to make the dead world of things come alive with human and social possibilities...And indeed there has never been a propaganda effort to match the effort of advertising in the 20th century. More thought, effort, creativity, time, and attention to detail has gone into the selling of the immense collection of commodities than any other campaign in human history to change public consciousness"* (Jhally, 2000). It is not for naught that people have been relabeled as *consumers*.

With Internet advertising set to equal or overtake that for broadcast TV at over $40 million in the US in 2013 the Web, especially in the mobile arena, is becoming the new attention battleground (PricewaterhouseCoopers, 2013). As the clamor for our limited time and attention increases, ads are more precisely targeted and each individual's view of the world further narrowed. We increasingly see only what the advertising industry and Google want us to see. Google Glass potentially extends that corralling to every waking moment; the glass becomes a one-way mirror reflecting the drive towards ever increasing consumption. The decision of each and every company to advertise on the Web and on mobile devices is exquisitely rational; in its sum total, an integrative mindset questions the outcomes—a cultural attention deficit disorder coupled with hyper-consumerism.

These and similar directions open—in Lord Denning's infamous 1980 words during an appeal by the subsequently acquitted Birmingham Six—*"such an appalling vista that every sensible person would say, 'It cannot be right that these actions should go any further'"*. And yet, no doubt, they will go further. Technology is a Jinni—the Anglicized *genie* sounds far too friendly—that once released, can seldom, if ever, be persuaded to return to its bottle. This is at once the challenge and opportunity for Business unIntelligence: to find the common ground between rationality and intuition, intelligence and insight, stability and innovation, business and IT.

Utopian vistas

The big data affair is coming to an end. The romance is over. Business is looking distraught in its silver Porsche, IT disheveled in the red Ferrari. Of course, it wasn't just the big data. It started long ago when IT couldn't deliver the data and business looked elsewhere to PCs and spreadsheets. It's time for business and IT to renew their vows and start working on renewing their marriage of convenience.

Figure 10-8:
Saturn Cutting off Cupid's Wings with a Scythe,
Ivan Akimov (1802),
Tretyakov Gallery, Moscow

When data warehousing was conceived in the 1980s, the goal was simple: understanding business results across multiple application systems. When BI was born in the 1990s, business needs were straightforward: report results speedily and accurately and allow business to explore possible alternatives. IT struggled to adapt. The 2000s brought demands for real-time freedom: the ability to embed BI in operations and *vice versa*. The current decade has opened the floodgates to other information, shared with partners and sourced on the Web. Divorce seemed imminent, IT outsourced.

But, almost invisibly, beyond the walls of this troubled marriage, a new world has emerged. A biz-tech ecosystem has evolved where business and IT must learn to practice intimate, ongoing symbiosis. Business visions meet technology limitations. IT possibilities clash with business budgets. And still, new opportunities emerge, realized only when business and IT cooperate in their creation—from conception to maturity. The possibilities seem boundless. But the new limits that do exist are beyond traditional capital and labor. The boundaries are imposed by the realities of life on this small blue planet afloat in an inky vacuum, with its limited and increasingly fragile resources and the tenuous ability of its people to survive and thrive in harmony with nature—within and without.

For the corporate world, Business unIntelligence will succeed when it brings insight into business workings, innovation into business advances, and integration into business and IT organizations. But in the broader context, in the real world in which we all must live, our success in the social enterprise that is business can be measured first and foremost in the survival of the cultures and communities of alleged intelligent man, *homo sapiens,* as well as all the other creatures of this tiny planet, and finally in our willingness to limit our growth and greediness and embrace the good inherent in each of us. It becomes incumbent on each and every one of us to integrate the rational and the intuitive, the individual and the empathic. To take stock of our personal decision making and reimage it in the vision of the world we want to bequeath to our children.

Beyond Business unIntelligence. Human unIntelligence.

Ackoff, R. L., 1967. Management misinformation systems. *Management Science*, December, 14(4), pp. B-147 - B-155.

Ackoff, R. L., 1989. From data to wisdom. *Journal of Applied Systems Analysis*, Volume 15, pp. 3-9.

Ackoff, R. L., 1994. *The Democratic Organization*. New York, NY: Oxford University Press.

Adler, J., 2012. *Raging Bulls: How Wall Street Got Addicted to Light-Speed Trading*. [Online]
Available at:
http://www.wired.com/business/2012/08/ff_wallstreet_trading
[Accessed 5 July 2013].

Albala, M., 2009. *Post-discovery intelligent applications: The next big thing*, Oakland, NJ: InfoSight Partners LLC.

Alexander, R., 2013. *Reinhart, Rogoff... and Herndon: The student who caught out the profs*. [Online]
Available at: http://www.bbc.co.uk/news/magazine-22223190
[Accessed 11 June 2013].

Allemang, D. & Hendler, J., 2011. *Semantic Web for the Working Ontologist, Second Edition: Effective Modeling in RDFS and OWL*. 2 ed. Waltham(MA): Morgan Kaufmann Publishers.

Alsop, R., 2008. The 'Trophy Kids' Go to Work. *The Wall Street Journal*, 21 October.

Alter, S., 1980. *Decision Support Systems: Current Practice and Continuing Challenge*. Reading, MA(Massachussets): Addison-Wesley.

Amazon, 2012. *Amazon Redshift*. [Online]
[Accessed 18 May 2013].

American Dialect Society, 2011. *"App" voted 2010 word of the year by the American Dialect Society (UPDATED)*. [Online]
Available at: http://www.americandialect.org/app-voted-2010-word-of-the-year-by-the-american-dialect-society-updated
[Accessed 18 May 2013].

Anderson, C., 2012. The End of Theory: The Data Deluge Makes the Scientific Method Obsolete. *Wired Magazine*, 16(07).

ANSI, 1975. ANSI/X3/SPARC Study Group on Data Base Management Systems; Interim Report. *FDT - Bulletin of ACM SIGMOD*, 8 February, 7(2), pp. 1-140.

Ariely, D., 2008. *Predictably Irrational: The Hidden Forces That Shape Our Decisions*. First ed. New York(NY): Harper Collins.

Ashton, K., 2009. That 'Internet of Things' Thing. *RFID Journal*, 22 July.

Bagley, P. R., 1968. *Extension of programming language concepts*, Philadelphia, PA: University City Science Center.

Batelle, J., 2005. The Birth of Google. *Wired*, August.13(8).

Bengson, J. & Moffett, M. A., 2012. *Knowing How: Essays on Knowledge, Mind, and Action*. New York(NY): Oxford University Press.

Bennis, W. & Biederman, P. W., 1997. *Organizing Genius: The Secrets of Creative Collaboration*. Reading(MA): Addison-Wesley, Inc..

Bergin, T. J. & Haigh, T., 2009. The Commercialization of Database Management Systems, 1969–1983. *IEEE Annals of the History of Computing*, October-December.pp. 26-41.

Berners-Lee, T., 1991. *Re: status. Re: X11 BROWSER for WWW*. [Online]
Available at: http://lists.w3.org/Archives/Public/www-talk/1991SepOct/0003.html
[Accessed 19 January 2013].

Berners-Lee, T., Hendler, J. & Lassila, O., 2001. The Semantic Web. *Scientidic American*, May.

Bloomberg, J., 2013. *The Agile Architecture Revolution: How Cloud Computing, REST-Based SOA, and Mobile Computing Are Changing Enterprise IT*. Hoboken(NJ): John Wiley & Sons, Inc.

Blue, V., 2013. *Big Oil's Wikipedia cleanup: A brand management experiment out of control*. [Online]
Available at: http://www.zdnet.com/big-oils-wikipedia-cleanup-a-brand-management-experiment-out-of-control-7000013160
[Accessed 30 March 2013].

Bogoshi, J., Naidoo, K. & Webb, J., 1987. The oldest mathematical artefact. *The Mathematical Gazette*, 71(294).

Box, G. E., 1979. Robustness in the strategy of scientific model building. In: *Robustness in Statistics*. New York, NY: Academic Press.

Bricklin, D., 2009. *Software Arts and Visicalc*. [Online]
Available at: www.bricklin.com/history/sai.htm
[Accessed 27 July 2010].

Brin, S. & Page, L., 1998. The Anatomy of a Large-Scale Hypertextual Web Search Engine. *Computer Networks and ISDN Systems*, Volume 30, pp. 107-117.

Brown, A. D., 2005. Making sense of the collapse of Barings Bank. *Human Relations*, 58(12), pp. 1579-1604.

Brown, P. C., 2008. *Implementing SOA: Total Architecture in Practice*. Upper Saddle River(NY): Prentice Hall.

Bush, V., 1945. As We May Think. *The Atlantic Monthly*, July, pp. 101-108.

Business Week, 1976. Corporate 'War Rooms' Plug into the Computer. *Business Week*, 23 August, p. 65.

Cameron, W. B., 1967. *Informal Sociology - A Casual Introduction to Sociological Thinking*. s.l.:Random House.

Cartwright, N., 1999. *The Dappled World: A Study of the Boundaries of Science*. Cambridge: Cambridge University Press.

Cavoukian, A., 2009. *Privacy by Design*, Ontario, Canada: Information and Privacy Commissioner of Ontario.

Cavoukian, A. & Jonas, J., 2012. *Privacy by Design in the Age of Big Data*, Ontario, Canada: Information and Privacy Commissioner, Ontario, Canada.

Cellan-Jones, R., 2012. *Who 'likes' my Virtual Bagels?*. [Online]
Available at: http://www.bbc.co.uk/news/technology-18819338
[Accessed 20 August 2012].

Chamberlin, D. D. & Boyce, R. F., 1974. SEQUEL: A Structured English Query Language. *Proceedings of the 1974 ACM SIGFIDET Workshop on Data Description, Access and Control*, pp. 249-64.

Chandrasekaran, S., 2013. *Becoming a Data Scientist - Curriculum via Metromap*. [Online]
Available at: http://nirvacana.com/thoughts/becoming-a-data-scientist/
[Accessed 12 August 2013].

Chang, F. et al., 2006. Bigtable: A Distributed Storage System for Structured Data. *Proceedings OSDI 06, Seventh Symposium on Operating System Design and Implementation*, November.

Chang, J. F., 2006. *Business Process Management Systems: Strategy and Implementation*. Boca Raton(FL): Auerbach Publications.

Chatterjee, S., 2004. Messaging Patterns in Service-Oriented Architecture, Part 1. *The Architecture Journal*, April.Issue 2.

Chen, P. P.-S., 1976. The Entity-Relationship Model—Toward a Unified View of Data. March, 1(1), pp. 9-36.

Christensen, C. M., 1997. *The Innovator's Dilemma - When New Technologies Cause Great Firms to Fail*. Boston, MA: Harvard Business School Press.

Codd, E., Codd, S. & Salley, C., 1993. *Providing OLAP (On-line Analytical Processing) to User-Analysts: An IT Mandate*, Sunnyvale, CA: Hyperion Solutions.

Codd, E. F., 1970. A Relational Model of Data for Large Shared Data Banks. *Communications of the ACM*, 13(6), pp. 377-387.

Cook, N., 2008. *Enterprise 2.0: How Social Software Will Change the Future of Work*. Aldershot: Gower Publishin Ltd.

Cooper, D., 2012. *IBM: 'We must build an Exascale computer before 2024'.* [Online]
Available at: http://www.engadget.com/2012/04/02/ibm-we-must-build-an-exascale-computer-before-2024-video/
[Accessed 30 June 2012].

Copeland, D. G., Mason, R. O. & McKenney, J. L., 1995. Sabre: The Development of Information-Based Competence and Execution of Information-Based Competition. *IEEE Annals of the History of Computing*, September, 17(3), pp. 30-57.

Croll, A., 2013. *The vanishing cost of guessing.* [Online]
Available at: http://radar.oreilly.com/2013/08/the-vanishing-cost-of-guessing.html
[Accessed 22 August 2013].

Dahlström, P. & Edelman, D., 2013. The coming era of 'on-demand' marketing. *McKinsey Quarterly*, April.

Date, C. J., Darwen, H. & Lorentzos, N. A., 2002. *Temporal Data & the Relational Model*. San Francisco(CA): Morgan Kaufmann.

Davenport, T. H., 1992. *Process Innovation: Reengineering work through information technology*. Boston, MA: Harvard Business School Press.

Davenport, T. H. & Harris, J. G., 2007. *Competing on Analytics: The New Science of Winning*. Boston, MA: Harvard Business School Press.

Davenport, T. H. & Prusak, L., 1998. *Working Knowledge: How organizations Manage What They Know*. 1 ed. Boston(MA): Harvard Business School Press.

Davis, J. R. & Eve, R., 2011. *Data Virtualization - Going Beyond Traditional Data Integration to Achieve Business Agility*. s.l.:Nine Five One Press.

Davis, J. R. & Eve, R., 2011. *Data Virtualization: Going Beyond Traditional Data Integration to Achieve Business Agility*. First ed. s.l.:Nine Five Zero.

de Heinzelin, J., 1962. Ishango. *Scientific American*, 206(6), pp. 105-116.

Dean, J. & Ghemawat, S., 2004. *MapReduce: Simplified Data Processing on Large Clusters*. San Francisco, s.n.

Dervin, B., Foreman-Wernet, L. & Lauterbach, E., 2003. *Sense-making Methodology Reader: Selected Writings of Brenda Dervin*. s.l.:Hampton Press.

Devlin, B., 1996. *Data Warehousing—From Architecture to Implementation*. Reading(MA): Addison-Wesley.

Devlin, B., 1997. *Data Warehousing: From Architecture to Implementation*. Reading(MA): Addison-Wesley.

Devlin, B., 2003. *Information integration - Extending the data warehouse*, San Jose, CA: IBM.

Devlin, B., 2009. *Business Integrated Insight BI2, Reinventing enterprise information management*. [Online]
Available at: http://www.9sight.com/bi2_white_paper.pdf
[Accessed 28 July 2010].

Devlin, B., 2009. *Collaborative Analytics: Sharing and Harvesting Analytic Insights across the Business*, Cape Town: 9sight Consulting.

Devlin, B., 2010. *Beyond the Data Warehouse: A Unified Information Store for Data and Content*, Cape Town, South Africa: 9sight Consulting.

Devlin, B., 2011. *Freedom from Facets - Discovering the data you really need*, Cape Town, South Africa: 9sight Consulting.

Devlin, B., 2011. *Will data warehousing survive the advent of big data?*. [Online]

Available at: http://strata.oreilly.com/2011/01/data-warehouse-big-data.html
[Accessed 3 May 2013].

Devlin, B., 2012a. Collaborative Business Intelligence: Socializing Team-based Decision Making. *Business Intelligence Journal*, September, 17(3), pp. 9-17.

Devlin, B., 2012. *iSight for Innovation: Breakthrough collaboration for decision making*, Cape Town: 9sight Consulting.

Devlin, B. A. & Murphy, P. T., 1988. An architecture for a business and information System. *IBM Systems Journal*, 27(1).

Devlin, B. A. & Murphy, P. T., 1988. An architecture for a business and information System. *IBM Systems Journal*, 27(1).

Doctorow, C., 2001. *Metacrap: Putting the torch to seven straw-men of the meta-utopia.* [Online]
Available at: http://www.well.com/~doctorow/metacrap.htm
[Accessed 16 January 2013].

Dolk, D. R. & Kirsch, R. A., 1987. A Relational Information Resource DIctionary System. *Communications of the ACM*, January.30(1).

Drucker, P., 1992. Planning for Uncertainty. *Wall Street Journal*, 22 July.

Drucker, P. F., 1992. *Managing for the Future.* Oxford, UK: Butterworth-Heinemann.

Duhigg, C., 2012a. *The Power of Habit: Why We Do What We Do in Life and Business.* New York, NY: Random House.

Duhigg, C., 2012. *How Companies Learn Your Secrets.* [Online]
Available at: http://www.nytimes.com/2012/02/19/magazine/shopping-habits.html?_r=3&ref=charlesduhigg
[Accessed 10 March 2012].

Duhon, B., 1998. It's All in our Heads. *Inform*, 12(8), pp. 8-13.

Eckerson, W., 2003. The Rise and Fall of Spreadmarts. *DM Review*, September.

Edjlali, R., Feinberg, D., Beyer, M. A. & Adrian, M., 2012. *The State of Data Warehousing in 2012*, Stamford, CT: Gartner Group.

Edlich, S., 2012. *The ultimate reference for NoSQL Databases.* [Online]
Available at: http://nosql-database.org/
[Accessed 7 April 2012].

Edwards, J., 2013. *Facebook Targets 76 Million Fake Users In War On Bogus Accounts.* [Online]
Available at: http://www.businessinsider.com/facebook-targets-76-million-fake-users-in-war-on-bogus-accounts-2013-2
[Accessed 3 June 2013].

Ellis, C. A., Gibbs, S. J. & Rein, G. L., 1991. Groupware - Some Issues and Experiences. *Communications of the ACM,* 34(1), pp. 38-58.

Engelbart, D. C., 1962. *Augmenting Human Intellect: A COnceptual Framework,* Menlo Park, CA: Stanford Research Institute.

Engelbart, D. C., 2004. *Augmenting Society's Collective IQ.* New York, NY, Association for Computer Machinery, Inc.

Erl, T., 2005. *Service-Oriented Architecture: Concepts, Technology, and Design.* Boston(MA): Prentice Hall.

Erl, T., Carlyle, B., Pautasso, C. & Balasubramanian, R., 2012. *SOA with REST: Principles, Patterns & Constraints for Building Enterprise Solutions with REST.* Upper Saddle River(NJ): Prentice Hall.

EuSpRIG, 2012. *EuSpRIG Horror Stories.* [Online]
Available at: http://www.eusprig.org/horror-stories.htm
[Accessed 26 June 2012].

Evelson, B. & Brown, M., 2008. *Search + BI = Unified Information Access,* Cambridge, MA: Forrerster Research, Inc..

Evernden, R., 1996. The Information FrameWork. *IBM Systems Journal,* 35(1), pp. 37-68.

Evernden, R., 1996. The Information FrameWork. *IBM Systems Journal,* 35(1), pp. 37-68.

Evernden, R. & Evernden, E., 2003. Third-generation Information Architecture. *Communications of the ACM,* 46(3), pp. 94-98.

Farber, D., 2012. *Twitter hits 400 million tweets per day, mostly mobile.* [Online]
Available at: http://news.cnet.com/8301-1023_3-57448388-93/twitter-hits-400-million-tweets-per-day-mostly-mobile/
[Accessed 7 July 2012].

Fayyad, U., Piatetsky-Shapiro, G. & Smyth, P., 1996. From Data Mining to Knowledge Discovery in Databases. *AI Magazine.*

Ferraro, C., 2010. Sacred Script: Ancient Marks from Old Europe. *Alphabet,* Summer.35(3).

Fischer, L., 2010. *2010 BPM and Workflow Handbook, Spotlight on Business Intelligence.* Lighthouse Point(FL): Future Strategies Inc..

Fishman, C., 2003. *The Wal-Mart You Don't Know.* [Online]
Available at: http://www.fastcompany.com/magazine/77/walmart.html
[Accessed 28 December 2011].

Frampton, K., 2007. *Modern Architecture: A Critical History.* 4th ed.
s.l.:Thames & Hudson.

Franks, B., 2012. *Taming The Big Data Tidal Wave: Finding Opportunities in Huge Data Streams with Advanced Analytics.* First ed. Hoboken(NJ): John Wiley and Sons.

Frické, M., 2009. The Knowledge Pyramid: A Critique of the DIKW Hierarchy. *Journal of Information Science*, April, 35(2), pp. 131-142.

Frisendal, T., 2012. *Design Thinking Business Analysis - Business Concept Mapping Applied.* Berlin Heidelberg: Springer-Verlag.

Garside, J., 2013. Nasdaq crash triggers fear of data meltdown. *The Guardian*, 23 August.

Garside, J. & Rushe, D., 2013. *Facebook profits rise despite drop in US visitors to its website.* [Online]
Available at:
http://www.guardian.co.uk/technology/2013/may/01/facebook-loses-10m-visitors-us
[Accessed 9 May 3013].

Gartner Inc., 2011. *Gartner Reveals Top Predictions for IT Organizations and Users for 2012 and Beyond*, s.l.: Gartner Inc..

Gartner, 2012. *Market Share Analysis: Enterprise Content Management Software, Worldwide, 2011*, Stamford, CT: Gartner, Inc.

Gellman, B. & Poitras, L., 2013. U.S., British intelligence mining data from nine U.S. Internet companies in broad secret program. *The Washington Post*, 6 June.

Gigerenzer, G., 2007. *Gut Feelings: The Intelligence of the Unconscious.* 1st ed. New York(NY): Viking Adult.

Gladwell, M., 2005. *BLINK: The Power of Thinking Without Thinking.* New York, NY: Little, Brown & Company.

Gladwell, M., 2005. *BLINK: The Power of Thinking Without Thinking.* New York, NY: Little, Brown & Company.

Godinez, M. et al., 2010. *The Art of Enterprise Information Architecture: A Systems-Based Approach for Unlocking Business Insight.* Armonk(NY): IBM Press.

Goldfarb, C. F., 1981. A Generalized Approach to Document Markup. *SIGPLAN Notices*, June, 16(6), pp. 63-73.

Goldfarb, C. F., 1996. *The Roots of SGML -- A Personal Recollection.* [Online] Available at: http://www.sgmlsource.com/history/roots.htm [Accessed 19 January 2013].

Goller, J., 2009. *The Emergence of Intelligent Content,* Ottawa, Ontario, Canada: Joe Goller.

Gollner, J., 2010. *The Emergence of Intelligent Content - The evolution of open content standards and their significance,* Manotick, Canada: Gnostyx Research.

Google, 2000. *Google Launches World's Largest Search Engine.* [Online] Available at: http://www.google.com/intl/en/press/pressrel/pressrelease26.html [Accessed 9 July 2012].

Google, 2008. *We knew the web was big....* [Online] Available at: http://googleblog.blogspot.com/2008/07/we-knew-web-was-big.html [Accessed 9 July 2012].

Goyette, B., 2013. *Google: Email Users Can't Legitimately Expect Privacy When Emailing Someone On Gmail (UPDATED).* [Online] Available at: http://www.huffingtonpost.com/2013/08/13/gmail-privacy_n_3751971.html [Accessed 20 August 2013].

Graham, A., 2010. *The Enterprise Data Model: A framework for enterprise data architecture.* s.l.:Koios Associates Ltd.

Gray, M., 1996. *Wanderer Results.* [Online] Available at: http://www.mit.edu/~mkgray/net/web-growth-summary.html [Accessed 8 July 2012].

Greenwald, G., 2013. NSA collecting phone records of millions of Verizon customers daily. *The Guardian*, 6 June.

Haas, L. M. et al., 2005. *Clio Grows Up: From Research Prototype to Industrial Tool.* New York, NY, ACM, pp. 805-810.

Haeckel, S. H., 1999. *Adaptive Enterprise: Creating and Leading Sense-and-Respond Organizations*. Boston(MA): Harvard Business School Press.

Halevy, A. Y. (. et al., 2005. Enterprise Information Integration: Successes, Challenges and Controversies. *SIGMOD '05, Proceedings of the 2005 ACM SIGMOD international conference on Management of data* , pp. 778-787.

Halpin, T., 2009. Object-Role Modeling version 2 (ORM 2). In: L. Liu & M. T. Özsu, eds. *Encyclopedia of Database Systems*. Heidelberg: Springer.

Hammond, J. S., Keeney, R. L. & Raiffa, H., 1998. The Hidden Traps in Decision Making. *Harvard Business Review*, Issue September-October 1998.

Harford, T., 2008. *The Logic of Life*. New York(NY): Random House.

Harford, T., 2012. *High-frequency trading and the $440m mistake*. [Online]
Available at: http://www.bbc.co.uk/news/magazine-19214294
[Accessed 10 July 2013].

Hayes, F., 2002. *The Story So Far*. [Online]
Available at:
www.computerworld.com/s/article/70102/The_Story_So_Far?taxonomyId=009
[Accessed 22 July 2010].

Heritage Archives, 2005. *Brief History of Microfilm*. [Online]
Available at: http://www.heritagearchives.org/history.aspx
[Accessed 14 January 2013].

Hoberman, S., 2009. *Data Modeling Made Simple*. Bradley Beach, NJ(New Jersey): Technics Publications LLC.

Hollingsworth, D., 1995. *The Workflow Reference Model*, Winchester, UK: Workflow Management Coalition.

Hopwood, P., 2008. Data Governance: One Size Does Not Fit All. *DM Review*, June.

IBM Center for Applied Insights, 2012. *Outperforming in a data-rich, hyper-connected world*, Armonk, NY: IBM Corporation.

IBM, 2003. *The birth of the IBM PC*. [Online]
Available at: www.ibm.com/ibm/history/exhibits/pc25/pc25_birth.html
[Accessed 24 July 2010].

IBM, 2007. *Global Innovation Outlook: Media & Content*. [Online]
Available at: www.ibm.com/ibm/gio/us/en/media.html
[Accessed 01 12 2010].

IDC, 2007. *The Expanding Digital Universe.* [Online]
Available at: http://www.emc.com/collateral/analyst-reports/expanding-digital-idc-white-paper.pdf
[Accessed 11 May 2011].

IDC, 2008. *The Diverse and Exploding Digital Universe*, Framingham, MA: IDC.

IDC, 2012a. *Worldwide Business Analytics Software 2012–2016 Forecast and 2011 Vendor Shares*, Framingham, MA: International Data Corporation.

IDC, 2012. *The Digital Universe in 2020: Big Data, Bigger Digital Shadows, and Biggest Growth in the Far East.* [Online]
Available at: http://www.emc.com/leadership/digital-universe/index.htm
[Accessed 14 July 2013].

IMF, 2013. *World Economic Outlook Database.* [Online]
Available at:
http://www.imf.org/external/pubs/ft/weo/2013/01/weodata/index.aspx
[Accessed 12 August 2013].

Inmon, W., 1992. *Building the Data Warehouse.* New York, NY(New York): Wiley & Sons.

Inmon, W., Imhoff, C. & Battas, G., 1996. *Building the Operational Data Store.* New York, NY(New York): John Wiley & Sons.

Iverson, K. E., 1962. *A Programming Language.* Hoboken(NJ): John Wiley & Sons.

Jaret, P., 2013. Mining Electronic Records for Revealing Health Data. *The New York Times*, 14 January.

Jhally, S., 2000. Advertising at the Edge of the Apocalypse. In: *Studies in Media Commercialism.* New York(NY): Oxford University Press, pp. 27-39.

Johnston, T., 2010. *Integrating Canonical Message Models and Enterprise Data Models.* [Online]
Available at: http://tdwi.org/Articles/2011/11/01/Integrating-Message-Models.aspx
[Accessed 31 July 2013].

Johnston, T. & Weis, R., 2010. *Managing Time in Relational Databases: How to Design, Update and Query Temporal Data.* 1st ed. Burlington(MA): Morgan Kaufmann.

Josuttis, N. M., 2007. *SOA in Practice: The Art of Distributed System Design.* Sebastopol(CA): O'Reilly Media.

Kaniclides, A. & Kimble, C., 1995. *A Development Framework for Executive Information Systems.* Groningen, NL, s.n., pp. 47-52.

Kent, W. & Hoberman, S., 2012. *Data and Reality.* 3rd ed. Westfield(NJ): Technics Publications.

Kirby, M., 2011. The history, achievement and future of the 1980 OECD guidelines on privacy. *International Data Privacy Law,* February, 1(1), pp. 6-14.

Klein, G., Phillips, J. K., Rall, E. L. & Peluso, D. A., 2007. *A Data-Frame Theory of Sensemaking.* New York, Lawrence Erlbaum Associates.

Kleinman, A., 2013. *Facebook User Numbers Are Off: 10 Percent Of Reported Users Are Not Human.* [Online]
Available at: ww.huffingtonpost.com/2013/05/17/facebook-user-numbers_n_3292316.html
[Accessed 3 June 2013].

Koenig, M. E. D., 2012. *What is KM? Knowledge Management Explained.* [Online]
Available at: http://www.kmworld.com/Articles/Editorial/What-Is-.../What-is-KM-Knowledge-Management-Explained-82405.aspx
[Accessed 21 July 2013].

Kolata, G., 2013. Web Hunt for DNA Sequences Leaves Privacy Compromised. *The New York Times,* 17 January.

Ko, R. K. L., 2009. A computer scientist's introductory guide to business process management (BPM). *ACM Crossroads,* 15(4).

Kravets, D., 2012. *Congress Defeats E-Mail Privacy Legislation — Again.* [Online]
Available at: http://www.wired.com/threatlevel/2012/12/congress-caves-privacy/
[Accessed 5 January 2013].

Krotoski, A., 2012. Big Data age puts privacy in question as information becomes currency. *The Guardian,* 22 April.

Kuchina, A., Espinar, L., Garcia-Ojalvo, J. & Süel, G. M., 2011. Reversible and Noisy Progression towards a Commitment Point Enables Adaptable and Reliable Cellular Decision-Making. *PLoS Computational Biology,* 7(11).

Kuner, C., Cate, F. H., Millard, C. & Svantesson, D. J. B., 2012. The challenge of 'big data' for data protection. *International Data Privacy Law,* May, 2(2), pp. 47-49.

Laney, D., 2001. *3-D Data Management: Controlling Data Volume, Velocity and Variety*, META Group: s.n.

Laney, D., 2012. Infonomics: The Practice of Information Economics. *Forbes*, 22 May.

LeHong, H. & Fenn, J., 2012. *Hype Cycle for Emerging Technologies, 2012*, s.l.: Gartner Inc..

Lennard, N., 2013. *The dangerous ethics behind Google's transparency claims.* [Online]
Available at:
http://www.salon.com/2013/06/11/the_dangerous_ethics_behind_google
s_transparency_claims/
[Accessed 05 July 2013].

Lillington, K., 2013. Rerouting data to avoid prying eyes. *The Irish Time*, 27 June.

Lisha, 2012. *Internet Usage, Web, and Blog Statistics.* [Online]
Available at: http://blogandretire.com/blog/2012/04/internet-usage-
web-and-blog-statistics-infographic.html
[Accessed 12 January 2013].

Luhn, H. P., 1958. A Business Intelligence System. *IBM Journal of Research and Development*, October, 2(4), pp. 314-319.

Malthus, T., 1798. *An Essay on the Principle of Population.* London: J. Johnson, in St. Paul's Church-yard.

Malthus, T., 1826. *An Essay on the Principle of Population.* Sixth ed. London: John Murray.

Manyika, J. et al., 2011. *Big data: The next frontier of innovation, competition and productivity*, s.l.: McKinsey Global Institute.

March, J. G., 1994. *A Primer on Decision Making: How Decisions Happen.* New York(NY): The Free Press.

Marco, D., 2000. *Building and Managing the Meta Data Repository: A Full Lifecycle Guide.* New York(NY): Wiley Computer Publishing.

Marco, D., 2000. *Building and Managing the Meta Data Repository: A Full Lifecycle Guide.* New York, NY: Wiley Computer Publishing.

Martin, R., 2009. *The Design of Business: Why Design Thinking is the Next Competitive Advantage.* 1st ed. Boston(MA): Harvard Business Press.

Martin, R., 2010. *The Design of Business - Why Design Thinking is the Next Competitive Advantage.* [Online]
Available at: http://www.slideshare.net/fred.zimny/slide-deck-by-roger-martin-the-design-of-business-presentation
[Accessed 2 June 2013].

Matthews, I., 2004. *The Amazing Commodore PET.* [Online]
Available at: www.commodore.ca/products/pet/commodore_pet.htm
[Accessed 26 July 2010].

Mayer-Schonberger, V. & Cukier, K., 2013. *Big Data: A Revolution That Will Transform How We Live, Work, and Think.* s.l.:Eamon Dolan/Houghton Mifflin Harcourt.

McAfee, A., 2009. *Enterprise 2.0: New Collaborative Tools for your Organization's Toughest Challenges".* Boston, MA: Harvard Business Press.

McAfee, A. & Brynjolfsson, E., 2008. Investing in the IT That Makes a Competitive Difference. *Harvard Business Review,* July.

McGee, W., 1981. Data Base Technology. *IBM Journal of Research and Devrlopment,* September, 25(5), pp. 505-519.

McLean, P. D., 1990. *The Triune Brain in Evolution: Role in Paleocerebral Functions.* s.l.:Springer.

McTaggart, L., 2001. *The Field: The Quest for the Secret Force of the Universe.* London: HarperCollins Publishers.

Mell, P. & Grance, T., 2011. *The NIST Definition of Cloud Computing, Recommendations of the National Institute of Standards and Technology,* Gaithersburg, MD: s.n.

Moglen, E., 2012. *Why Freedom of Thought Requires Free Media and Why Free Media Require Free Technology.* [Online]
Available at: http://archiv.re-publica.de/2012/05/04/why-freedom-of-thought-requires-free-media-and-why-free-media-require-free-technology/
[Accessed 5 January 2013].

Mullins, J., 2011. Move over, Einstein: Machines will take it from here. *New Scientist,* 22 March.Issue 2804.

Musen, M. A., 2012. *Tackling Climate Change: Unfinished Business from the Last "Winter".* Karlsruhe, Semantic Web Science Association.

NASA, 1999. *Mars Climate Orbiter Official Website.* [Online]
Available at: http://mars.jpl.nasa.gov/msp98/orbiter/
[Accessed 17 January 2013].

Natis, Y. V. & Schulte, W. R., 1996. *"Service Oriented" Architectures, Part 1*, Stamford, CT: Gartner Inc..

Nelson, T. H., 1965. A File Structure for the Complex, the Changing and the Indeterminate. *TBA*.

Nelson, T. H., 1974. *Computer Lib/Dream Machines*. Chicago(IL): Nelson.

Nelson, T. H., 2011. *The ZigZag Database and Visualization System*. [Online]
Available at: http://www.xanadu.com/zigzag/
[Accessed 14 January 2013].

Novak, J. D. & Canas, A. J., 2006. *The Theory Underlying Concept Maps and How to Construct and Use Them, Technical Report IHMC CmapTools 2006-01 Rev 01-2008*, Pensacola, FL: Florida Institute for Human and Machine Cognition (IHMC).

O'Reilly, T., 2006. *Web 2.0 Compact Definition: Trying Again*. [Online]
Available at: http://radar.oreilly.com/2006/12/web-20-compact-definition-tryi.html
[Accessed 11 December 2011].

O'Reilly, T., 2005. *What Is Web 2.0*. [Online]
Available at: http://oreilly.com/web2/archive/what-is-web-20.html
[Accessed 21 December 2013].

Otlet, P., 1934. *Traité de documentation: théorie et pratique*. Brussels: Mundaneum.

Otlet, P. & La Fontaine, H., 1905. *Manuel du Repertoire Bibliographique Universel*. Brussels: IIB.

Pariser, E., 2011. *The Filter Bubble: What the Internet Is Hiding from You*. New York(Ny): Penguin Press.

Pirolli, P., 2009. *Information Foraging Theory: Adaptive Interaction with Information*. New York(NY): Oxford University Press.

Pirolli, P. & Card, S., 1995. *Information Foraging in Information Access Environments*. New York, Association of Computing Machinery, pp. 51-58.

Pirolli, P. & Card, S., 2005. *The sensemaking process and leverage points for analyst technology as identified through cognitive task analysis*. s.l., s.n.

Pirolli, P. & Card, S. K., 1999. Information foraging. *Phychological Review*, 106(4), pp. 643-675.

Plattner, H., 2009. *A Common Database Approach for OLTP and OLAP Using an In-Memory Column Database*. New York, NY, ACM.

Polanyi, M., 1966. *The Tacit Dimension*. Chicago(IL): University of Chicago Press.

Potts, C., 2010. *recrEAtion*. Bradley Beach(NJ): Technics Publications LLC.

Power, D. J., 2009. *A Brief History of Decision Support Systems*. [Online] Available at: http://dssresources.com/history/dsshistory.html [Accessed 15 July 2010].

PricewaterhouseCoopers, 2013. *IAB internet advertising revenue report: 2012 full year results*, s.l.: PricewaterhouseCoopers.

Reimer, J., 2005. *Total share: 30 years of personal computer market share figures*. [Online] Available at: arstechnica.com/old/content/2005/12/total-share.ars/4 [Accessed 25 July 2010].

Reinhart, C. M. & Rogoff, K. S., 2010. *Growth in a Time of Debt*, Cambridge, MA: National Bureau of Economic Research.

Roberts, D. & Pakkiri, R., 2013. *Decision Sourcing: Decision Making for the Agile Social Enterprise*. Farnham(Surrey): Gower Publishing Ltd..

Rockart, J. F., 1979. Chief Executives Define Their Own Data Needs. *Harvard Business Review*, 67(2), pp. 81-93.

Rockart, J. F. & Treacy, M. E., 1982. The CEO Goes On-Line. *Harvard Business Review*, Issue January-February, pp. 82-88.

Rockley, A., 2012. *Managing Enterprise Content: A Unified Content Strategy (2nd Edition)*. Berkeley, CA: New Riders.

Rowe, P. G., 1987. *Design Thinking*. Cambridge(MA): The MIT Press.

Rowley, J., 2007. The wisdom hierarchy: representations of the DIKW hierarchy. *Journal of Information Science*, February, 33(2), pp. 163-180.

Russell, D. M., Stefik, M. J., Pirolli, P. & Card, S. K., 1993. *The Cost Structure of Sensemaking*. New York, Association of Computer Machinery, pp. 269-276.

Ryle, G., 1949. *The Concept of Mind*. London: Hutichinson's University Library.

Salmon, F., 2009. Recipe for Disaster: The Formula That Killed Wall Street. *Wired*, 2 February.

Schmandt-Besserat, D., 1996. *How Writing Came About*. Austin, TX: University of Texas Press.

Schmidt, M. & Lipson, H., 2009. Distilling Free-Form Natural Laws from Experimental Data. *Science*, Volume 324, pp. 81-85.

Scott Morton, M. S., 1967. *Computer-Driven Visual Display Devices -- Their Impact on the Management Decision-Making Process.* Boston(Massachusetts): Harvard Business School.

Siegel, D. J., 2010. *Mindsight: The New Science of Personal Transformation.* Oxford: Bantam Press.

Silver, N., 2012. *The Signal and the Noise: The Art and Science of Prediction.* NewYork(NY): Penguin Books.

Simon, H. A., 1971. Designing Organizations for an Information-Rich World. In: *Computers, Communications and the Public Interest.* Baltimore, MD: The Johns Hopkins University Press.

Simon, H. A., 1993. Decision Making: Rational, Nonrational, and Irrational. *Educational Administration Quarterly*, August, 29(3), pp. 392-411.

Simsion, G., 2007. *Data Modeling Theory and Practice.* Bradley Beach(New Jersey): Technics Publications.

Snowden, D. J., 2005. Multi-ontology sense making: a New Simplicity in Decision Making. In: R. Havenga, ed. *Management Today Yearbook 2005.* s.l.:s.n.

Sowa, J. F. & Zachman, J. A., 1992. Extending and formalizing the framework for information systems architecture. *IBM Systems Journal*, 31(3), pp. 590-616.

Soy, S. K., 1996. *Class Lecture Notes: H. P. Luhn and Automatic Indexing - References to the Early Years of Automatic Indexing and Information Retrieval.* [Online]
Available at: http://www.gslis.utexas.edu/~ssoy/organizing/l391d2c.htm
[Accessed 29 December 2012].

Steiner, C., 2010. Wall Street's Speed War. *Forbes*, 27 September.

Stonebraker, M. et al., 2008. *HStore: A High Performance, Distributed Main Memory Transaction Processing System.* New York, NY, ACM, p. 1496–1499.

Surowiecki, J., 2004. *The Wisdom of Crowds: Why the Many Are Smarter Than the Few and How Collective Wisdom Shapes Business, Economies, Societies and Nations.* 1st ed. s.l.:Doubleday.

Swoyer, S., 2012. *Experts Reconsider the Data Warehouse*, Renton, WA: The Data Warehouse Institute.

Sysop, 2003-2010. *Tandy Radio Shack TRS-80 model I computer.* [Online]
Available at: oldcomputers.net/trs80i.html
[Accessed 25 July 2010].

Taycher, L., 2010. *Books of the world, stand up and be counted! All
129,864,880 of you.* [Online]
Available at: http://booksearch.blogspot.com/2010/08/books-of-world-
stand-up-and-be-counted.html
[Accessed 12 January 2013].

Taylor, F. W., 1911. *The Principles of Scientific Management.* New York, NY
and London, UK: Harper and Brothers.

Taylor, J., 2011. *Decision Management Systems: A Practical Guide to Using
Business Rules and Predictive Analytics.* Armonk(NY): IBM Press.

Taylor, J. & Raden, N., 2007. *Smart Enough Systems: How to Deliver
Competitive Advantage by Automating Hidden Decisions.* Boston(MA):
Pearson Education.

Thaler, R. H. & Sunstein, C. R., 2008. *Nudge: Improving Decisions About
Health, Wealth, and Happiness.* New Haven(CT): Yale University Press.

The Open Group, 2009. *The SOA Source Book.* [Online]
Available at: http://www.opengroup.org/soa/source-
book/intro/index.htm
[Accessed 22 March 2013].

Thierauf, R. J., 1991. *Executive Information Systems: a guide for senior
management and MIS information.* NewYork: Prager.

Thimm, M. et al., 2012. *Linked Open Data: Are we Drowning in Information
and Starving for Know-How?.* Karlsruhe, Semantic Web Science Association.

Tuomi, I., 2003. *Networks of Innovation: Change and Meaning in the Age of
the Internet.* 1st ed. New York(NY): Oxford University Press.

U.S. Supreme Court, 1928. *Olmstead v. United States - 277 U.S. 438 (1928).*
[Online]
Available at:
https://supreme.justia.com/cases/federal/us/277/438/case.html
[Accessed 6 January 2013].

Uckelmann, D., Harrison, M. & Michahelles, F. (., 2011. *Architecting the
Internet of Things.* Berlin, Heidelberg: Springer-Verlag.

Van der Merwe, . et al., 2009. *Definition for EA as defined by EARF.* [Online]
Available at: http://earf.meraka.org.za/earfhome/our-projects-

1/completed-projects
[Accessed 8 July 2013].

W3C, 2012. *OWL 2 Web Ontology Language Document Overview (Second Edition).* [Online]
Available at: http://www.w3.org/TR/owl2-overview/
[Accessed 10 June 2013].

Warden, P., 2011. *Why you can't really anonymize your data.* [Online]
Available at: http://strata.oreilly.com/2011/05/anonymize-data-limits.html
[Accessed 7 January 2013].

Warren, S. D. & Brandeis, L. D., 1890. The Right to Privacy. *Harvard Law Review,* 15 December, 4(5), pp. 193-220.

Wayner, P., 2009. NoSQL databases break all the old rules. *InfoWorld,* 24 March.

Wayner, P., 2009. *Translucent Databases: Confusion, Misdirection, Randomness, Sharing, Authentication And Steganography To Defend Privacy.* 2nd ed. s.l.:CreateSpace Independent Publishing Platform.

Wedeles, L., 1965. Prof. Nelson Talk Analyzes P.R.I.D.E.. *Vassar Miscellany News,* 3 February.

Weick, K. E., 1995. *Sensemaking in Organizations.* 1st ed. s.l.:SAGE Publications, Inc.

Weick, K. E., 2009. *Making Sense of the Organization: Volume 2: The Impermanent Organization.* 1st ed. s.l.:Wiley and Sons.

Weinberger, D., 2012. *Too Big to Know: Rethinking Knowledge Now That the Facts Aren't the Facts, Experts Are Everywhere, and the Smartest Person in the Room Is the Room.* New York(NY): Basic Books.

Weinberger, D., 2012. *Too Big to Know: Rethinking Knowledge Now That the Facts Aren't the Facts, Experts Are Everywhere, and the Smartest Person in the Room Is the Room.* New York, NY: Basic Books.

Weinberger, D., Levine, R., Locke, C. & Searls, D., 2000. *The Cluetrain Manifesto.* Basic Books: s.n.

Weyhrich, S., 2010. *Apple II History.* [Online]
Available at: apple2history.org
[Accessed 26 July 2010].

White, C., 2004. In the Beginning: An RDBMS History. *Teradata Magazine,* September, pp. 32-39.

White, T., 2009. *Hadoop: The Definitive Guide*. Sebastopol, CA: O'Reilly Media, Inc..

Wikipedia, 2012. *Big data*. [Online]
[Accessed 10 March 2012].

Wikipedia, 2012. *Privacy*. [Online]
Available at:
http://en.wikipedia.org/w/index.php?title=Privacy&oldid=529963623
[Accessed 6 January 2013].

Wikipedia, 2013. *List of social networking websites*. [Online]
Available at: http://en.wikipedia.org/wiki/Social_networking_websites
[Accessed 9 May 2013].

Wikipedia, 2013. *Microform*. [Online]
Available at:
http://en.wikipedia.org/w/index.php?title=Microform&oldid=531102837
[Accessed 14 January 2013].

Williams, S. P. & Schubert, P., 2011. *An Empirical Study of Enterprise 2.0 in Context*. Bled, s.n.

Wright, A., 2007. *Glut - Mastering information through the ages*. Washington, DC: Joseph Henry Press.

YouTube, 2012. *YouTube Press Room*. [Online]
Available at: http://www.youtube.com/t/press_statistics
[Accessed 7 July 2012].

Zachman, J. A., 1987. A framework for information systems architecture. *IBM Systems Journal*, 26(3), pp. 276-292.

Zachman, J. P., 2011. *The Zachman Framework Evolution*. [Online]
Available at: http://zachman.com/ea-articles-reference/54-the-zachman-framework-evolution
[Accessed 7 July 2013].

Zins, C., 2007. Conceptual Approaches for Defining Data, Information and Knowledge. *Journal of the American Society for Information Science and Technology*, January, 58(4), pp. 479-493.

Zloof, M. M., 1975. Query by Example. *NCC (proceedings)*, May.Volume 44.

INDEX OF REFERENCES

Bold italic page numbers refer to definitions and main discussions, **bold page numbers** refer to ThoughtPoints and *italic page numbers* to figures and diagrams.

C

D

Made in the USA
Middletown, DE
25 February 2015